CORRIDORS
IN
TIME

CORRIDORS
IN
TIME

A Reader in Introductory Archaeology

Edited by
BRIAN M. FAGAN
University of California, Santa Barbara

LITTLE, BROWN and COMPANY
Boston   Toronto

Library of Congress Catalog Card No. 73–21224

First Printing

Published simultaneously in Canada
by Little, Brown & Company (Canada) Limited

Printed in the United States of America

Cover Photo: Machu Picchu, the Inca fortress-city.
Photograph by George Holton from Photo Researchers, Inc.

To *Sir Mortimer Wheeler*
who has inspired so many archaeologists and who wrote:
"Dead archaeology is the driest dust that blows."

PREFACE

Corridors in Time is a sequel to an earlier anthology, *Introductory Readings in Archaeology* (Boston: Little, Brown, 1970), and began as a new edition of the original reader but evolved into a new book. Its objective is to give the newcomer to archaeology a feeling for the subject through both popular writings about prehistory and carefully selected technical articles written by professional archaeologists for their colleagues.

The emphasis lies not in recounting the results of prehistoric research, but in showing the ways in which archaeologists have approached fundamental research problems. Major emphasis is also placed on giving the non-archaeologist an insight into modern subsistence situations that are of potential use in understanding how prehistoric man made his living.

Archaeology is too new a subject to have developed much "great literature" in the sense that this term is used to refer to historical writings and English literature. Some selections in *Corridors in Time* are famous pieces of archaeology; others are hardly known outside specialist circles. The diversity aims at giving the student a sense of the incredible range and fascinating scope of twentieth-century archaeology.

To make the references available to the student in one place, they have been combined into one bibliography, which appears at the back of the book.

I am grateful to those colleagues who reviewed the outline of this anthology and made many valuable suggestions. S. Woodworth Chittick of Little, Brown suggested the project; he and his colleagues made it a pleasure to complete.

CONTENTS

PART ONE

ARCHAEOLOGICAL APPROACHES TO THE STUDY OF MAN   1

PART TWO

PART THREE

PART FOUR

CORRIDORS
IN
TIME

Part One

ARCHAEOLOGICAL APPROACHES TO THE STUDY OF MAN

"Antiquities are history defaced, or some remnants of history which have escaped the shipwreck of time."

Francis Bacon (1561–1626)

INTRODUCTION

What is archaeology? Why is it important? What do archaeologists accomplish? These are some questions that laymen ask about archaeology when they first encounter one of its many facets.

Few archaeologists have a full knowledge of their field, for it covers a time bracket of over two and a half million years, from the earliest origins of man to nineteenth- and even twentieth-century structures. Thus there are many subfields within archaeology, each with its specialists and special vocabularies. For example, scholars who study the origins of man and the earliest millennia of human prehistory work closely with geologists and natural scientists.[1] Egyptologists acquire a fluency in hieroglyphics and a knowledge of art and architecture as well as basic archaeological skills. New World archaeologists

---

[1] In this book "prehistory" or "prehistoric archaeology" is taken to refer to archaeology before written records, whence the term "prehistorian."

are considered to be anthropologists working with extinct human cultures. European prehistorians often think of themselves as culture historians, for they do not have the close contact with subsistence farmers and hunters whose direct descendants were prehistoric peoples, a contact characteristic of archaeological research in Africa, Asia, or the United States.

To most laymen, however, an archaeologist is a digger, a scholar who unearths valuable artifacts from the soil. Others think of him as a treasure hunter, like the infamous pothunter described in Part Four of this book. Archaeologists themselves have diverse opinions about their discipline. Some describe it as a battery of methods and techniques that serve as tools to discover human history before the advent of writing. In other words, the archaeologist writes history with new tools. This "culture history" approach is spurned by other authorities, who think of archaeology as part of anthropology and as a social science in its own right. Archaeology, they argue, is concerned with prehistoric human cultures, a means of enabling people to make reasoned statements about past human culture.

The aims of archaeology have been debated as well, and the arguments are well aired in the selections in Chapter 1. To a great extent, one's notion of archaeology's aims depends on his field. For example, archaeologists working on the later millennia of African prehistory, in which written records date back to a scant half century ago in many areas, tend to think of archaeology as a means to write the history of black Africa. Scholars of the American Southwest are more concerned with explaining changes in human culture over hundreds of years and, publicly at any rate, seem less concerned with historical objectives.

One eminent archaeologist has described archaeology as the "Science of Rubbish." His somewhat lighthearted view of the discipline is apt, for the archaeological record does consist of the abandoned artifacts, meals, structures, and settlements of prehistoric peoples. The archaeologist has been likened to a detective, piecing together the past from the many artifacts found in archaeological sites. Chapter 2 contains articles on strategy and reconstruction in archaeology, two by Sir Mortimer Wheeler who is one of the "greats" in archaeology. He pioneered correct methods of excavation in Europe and the Near East that have served as models for several generations of archaeologists. His essay on digging for information is a classic and provides a good background for his following description of the battle at Maiden Castle. Wheeler's story of the final resistance at Maiden Castle conveys all the fear and tension that would have prevailed during this dramatic day in the hill-fort's history. Yet the whole picture is constructed by meticulous use of archaeological sources that link together to form a narrative. This is culture history at its best.

How do excavators conjure up the sort of picture that Wheeler so ably draws? How do people interpret the artifacts they find? Adams's piece describes the wider boundaries of archaeological strategy. He points out that most archaeologists are reluctant to move far from the narrow confines of their own site or culture area to tackle what he calls "grand problems" of comparison and synthesis. Their obsession with detail makes many archaeologists suspicious of attempts to formulate general laws of cultural dynamics. Analogy is an important part of archaeological reconstruction and is in itself, as Robert Ascher shows, a tricky business.

The questions of "how" and "why" in archaeology have preoccupied scholars for over a century. Ever since the first attempts to classify the past and to subdivide stages of human prehistory, scholars have tried to account for the changes in the archaeological record. Did critical human inventions take place in one place, or were they invented independently in different parts of the world? If a dramatic invention was made in one place, how did it spread elsewhere? Did warrior bands carry it with them, imposing new technologies and economic practices on conquered peoples? Or did the new ideas diffuse slowly or rapidly to new areas? In his article on culture change Bruce Trigger summarizes some of the intense debate on cultural process in archaeology, and discusses the types of archaeological data that constitute reliable evidence for culture change.

Until comparatively recently most archaeologists were content to study sites and the artifacts in them without much concern for their ecological setting. American anthropologist Julian Steward and British archaeologist Grahame Clark were among those who began to study human culture in its ecological context. The latter excavated a hunting camp at Star Carr in northern England, where he used the technique of pollen analysis and a wealth of bone and wood fragments to make a complete reconstruction of the settlement's ecological setting. In recent years many archaeologists have moved toward an ecological approach to explain major changes in human culture. The advent of systems theory and quantitative approaches in the social sciences have been felt in archaeology, too. Systems models have been used to interpret the complex relationships between archaeological sites and their ever-changing environments. Bruce Trigger's important article on ecology gives a detailed briefing on the development of an ecological approach to the past. Trade, a topic that is peculiarly susceptible to interpretation using vast data from numerous sites in different areas and systems models, has also been invoked as a major cause of cultural change. In the concluding article in Part I, William Rathje explains how trade may have helped in the rise of Mayan civilization.

Part One includes a series of contrasting essays, each of which can form the basis for a discussion on various approaches to the prehistoric past and to the problems of reconstruction in archaeology. These selections give a flavor of the present direction of archaeology and of the problems that archaeologists meet in the field and in the laboratory.

CHAPTER ONE

What Is Archaeology?

Grahame Clark

1 THE DISCIPLINE OF PREHISTORY

The first selection, taken from Professor Grahame Clark's *Archaeology and Society*, presents an Englishman's view of prehistoric archaeology. This classic essay on prehistory, a work remarkable for its emphasis on an ecological approach to archaeology, was written in the late 1930s, a time when most Old World archaeologists tended to regard archaeology as a branch of historical study and as a discipline for studying archaeological finds in order to reconstruct the past. The role of anthropology was recognized as important, but less so than that of history. Clark's words eloquently state the European position, which is still espoused by many archaeologists, especially those who work within the confines of Europe itself rather than in Africa or in Asia where many modern societies have direct roots in the prehistoric past and have no written history.

Archaeology may be simply defined as the systematic study of antiquities as a means of reconstructing the past. For his contributions to be fruitful the archaeologist has to possess a real feeling for history, even though he may not have to face what is perhaps the keenest challenge of historical scholarship, the subtle interplay of human personality, and circumstance. Yet he is likely to be involved even more deeply in the flow of time. The prehistoric archaeologist, in particular, is confronted by historical changes

From *Archaeology and Society* by Grahame Clark, pp. 17–26, copyright © 1939 by Grahame Clark, and published by Methuen and Co. Ltd., London. Reprinted by permission of the author and publisher. Footnotes are omitted.

of altogether greater dimensions than those with which the historian of literate civilizations is concerned, and has to face demands on his historical imagination of a commensurate order; further, at a purely technical level he is likely to be met with much greater difficulties of decipherment, difficulties which can as a rule only be surmounted by calling on scientists and scholars practiced in highly specialized branches of knowledge.

Much of the fascination of archaeology indeed resides in its many-sidedness. One can safely say that there are few faculties, experiences, or fields of special knowledge that cannot contribute to or are not stimulated by its pursuit. The complete archaeologist, if such a being existed, would need to have a genius for travel, exploration, and reconnaissance; to be adept at business and administration, skilled at raising funds and obtaining all manner of permits from authorities and owners, few of whom can hope to gain from his activities, and capable of administering and directing excavations which may well turn out to be large-scale enterprises; to be a competent surveyor, draughtsman, and photographer, so that what he finds can be adequately recorded; to combine a gift for exact description and analysis with a power of synthesis and a flair for journalism; and to have the gift of tongues, or at very least an ability to digest the reports of his foreign colleagues without which his own will lack the authority that only wide reading and comparison can provide.

In addition to all these talents of the market-place, without which even the finest scholarship is likely to prove ineffective in this field, our paragon must be endowed with other qualities of a higher and a rarer order. The fruitful practice of archaeology involves to a unique degree an ability and a willingness to comprehend the aims, methods, and potentialities of fellow-workers in the most diverse branches of both humanistic and scientific study. To express the matter differently, the quality of the contributions an archaeologist is likely to be able to make depends on the degree to which he recognizes the limitations as well as the possibilities of his discipline in the elucidation of the past. The first step is to recognize that archaeology is in fact a discipline, but only one of the many disciplines needed to throw light on the more or less remote past, and the second that success is likely to depend not only on the rigor of its own proper methods, but also on the skill and sympathy with which its practitioners combine with those of cognate disciplines to solve common problems.

The discipline of archaeology imposes special requirements of its own. All archaeologists, whatever their precise field, have to depend primarily on the study of artifacts, and the classification and understanding of these call for a highly developed sense of style: the archaeologist has to rely in the first instance very largely on his appreciation of form, texture, and artistic convention if he is to distinguish correctly the products of separate cultures, discern stages of historical development, or detect the interaction of different traditions. Further, so soon as he concerns himself with attempting to reconstruct the lives of the societies responsible for the artifacts he studies, he is brought up against a new set of requirements. Even to appreciate ancient works of art it is necessary to combine with a capacity for aesthetic appreciation a wide knowledge of the techniques and history of architecture, sculpture, and painting. But the range of artifacts with the production and use of which the archaeologist has to be familiar is coextensive with the life of society. Indeed, technical processes and the artifacts shaped by them can only yield their full historical meaning in relation to the economic and social systems of which they formed an integral part. This means that archaeologists need to be aware of the work, not merely of economic and social historians, but still more, in the case of those working on preliterate societies, of the findings of social anthropology.

Again, since artifacts are made by and for people and since societies are constituted by individuals, it is vital to study the mentality and actual physical characteristics of the bearers of his cultures, and this the archaeologist can only do indirectly, since in the case of the former he is often studying people without a literature and whose language is unknown to him, and in the case of physical type and condition he is as a rule confined to skeletal traces which may often be very incomplete: for his knowledge of mentality he will have to rely mainly on what he can infer from the way in which the people he is studying have utilized their environment, behaved to each other and come to terms with nonmaterial, unseen forces, though where skulls are available he may get some help from the size and convolutions of their brains; and for physique, racial type, age, sex, medical history, nutrition, and deformation he will have to rely on anatomy and forensic medicine and, where ancient, fossil material is concerned, on human paleontology, branches of knowledge which, if he is lucky, he will find combined in the person of a physical anthropologist.

Further, the archaeologist, and more particularly the prehistoric archaeologist, must study his cultures in their geographical setting, if he is to bring them to life in all their dimensions or even understand their economic basis. It is not sufficient to study the relationship between traces of former stages of settlement and the present geographical situation: such studies may and indeed must be misleading, and the more so the older the cultures studied, since the geographical environment can no more be taken as a constant factor than can human settlement itself. What the prehistoric archaeologist has to study is the history of human settlement in relation to the history of the climate, topography, vegetation, and fauna of the territory in question. One of the greatest difficulties in such a study is to distinguish between changes in the environment brought about by purely natural processes and those produced, whether intentionally or incidentally, by the activities of human society, and this can only be resolved by intimate cooperation in the field with climatologists, geologists, pedologists, botanists, zoologists, and paleontologists in the comradeship of Quaternary research.

The archaeologist wants to know precisely what geographical conditions obtained at each stage of human settlement; the extent to which the economic activities of any particular community were limited by the external environment; and above all how far the economic activities of the people he is studying are reflected in and can be reconstructed from changes in the geographical surroundings. It is only by observing the human cultures of antiquity as elements in a changing ecological situation that it is possible to form a clear idea of even the economic basis of early settlement, see precisely how early man utilized his environment and so arrive at a fuller understanding of his intellectual, economic, and social progress.

Archaeological methods can profitably be applied to any phase or aspect of history insufficiently documented by written records, however recent in time; indeed, archaeology can not only be used to fill gaps in the documents, but also to check or corroborate them. In this respect archaeological evidence bears some analogies to the circumstantial evidence of the law courts. Human testimony, whether written or oral, has a directness of appeal that may at first sight seem to be lacking from the fragments and traces on which the detective relies for his circumstantial evidence, but the very humanity which appeals to us in literature or speech involves grave limitations. Human memories are fallible and the motives of witnesses, writers of state papers, and even historians are more mixed than they know themselves. Cross-examination in the courts and critical analysis in the study may do something to rectify or at least check the unveracities of human testimony, but they can hardly do more than reduce the area of uncertainty. Although the interpretation of scientific data by hired experts is notoriously liable to point to opposing conclusions, the value of circumstantial evidence can hardly be doubted as a check on personal testimony. In dealing with the past it is the gaps even more in many cases than the imperfections in the surviving written record that enhance the value of archaeological evidence. For instance, it has been found that more precise information about the proficiency of the men of medieval times can be obtained from a study of their scientific instruments than from their treatises alone. Similarly, excavation has recently been throwing more light on the history of medieval settlement in Denmark than could be obtained from the documents, and even in England, where the documentary record is relatively complete, there are large spheres of economic activity never or only incidentally recorded in writing.

As a general proposition it must be accepted that the value of archaeological evidence as a source of information about human history varies inversely with the extent and nature of documentary sources in the broad sense of the term. The more incomplete the historical record the heavier the reliance that must be placed on alternative kinds of evidence. Thus the value of archaeology is likely to be higher in relation at any rate to the earlier stages of the older oriental civilizations than to the classical or later European ones. Yet even in the study of the earliest literate communities archaeology is bound to play an ancillary, if not a subservient, role where any considerable bulk of inscriptions has survived, since these give an insight into the mentality and values of early societies more direct than material things can ever do. Conversely, it is in the reconstruction of prehistory, the unwritten history of all but a comparatively brief span of all humanity, that archaeology can render its greatest contribution to human understanding. . . .

No precise delimitation of the range of prehistory is likely to find wide acceptance, though it would probably be agreed by most English-speaking archaeologists that it is concerned with preliterate societies. At the lower end of the range no hard and fast line can be drawn between animal and human societies, but for practical purposes one may take the appearance of tools shaped in conformity with a recognizable tradition as a useful datum. As regards an upper limit one might accept the appearance of a more or less continuous written record as marking the end of prehistory and the beginning of what is conventionally regarded as history. Quite clearly, though, some difference of opinion is likely to exist as to precisely at what stage preliteracy gives way to literacy: attainment of literacy must in the first instance have been a slow process; and the spread of literacy was so uneven that it has taken about five thousand years for it to extend from the earliest centers over the world as a whole.

One of the results of this slow diffusion of literacy is that the prehistoric period lasted much longer in some regions than in others. Thus even in Europe marked differences can be noted as between different areas: over much of the Mediterranean coasts the prehistoric period was brought to an end by Greek and Punic colonization already by the middle of the first millennium B.C.; the extension of the Roman Empire during later centuries incorporated the rest of the Mediterranean and parts of the temperate zones within the sphere of history and, even if outlying provinces suffered a relapse into barbarism, the experience of Imperial rule was sufficiently profound to mark the end of an age; but extensive territories in the northern, central, and eastern regions of the continent remained prehistoric until gathered into the fold of Christendom in the course of the Middle Ages. Most of western and parts of southern Asia had already been drawn within the sphere of ancient oriental civilization long before Alexander's famous march, and the rise of an independent, if in part derivative, civilization in North China and its attainment of literacy soon after the middle of the second millennium B.C. had already brought prehistory to an end over extensive tracts of the Far East before direct contact was established with the West. Much of Africa on the other hand remained prehistoric until quite modern times; influences from ancient Egypt had early penetrated extensive areas of North Africa, but it was not until the establishment of Phoenician trading-stations on the coast that any part of the continent outside the Nile Valley and its immediate area passed into history; trade and commerce from the Indian Ocean must have opened up parts of the east coast comparatively early, and on the west the Portuguese extended their influence as far down as the Gold Coast before the end of the fifteenth century; but it was not until 1652 that the Dutch disturbed the prehistory of South Africa, and much of the tropical interior remained prehistoric until the middle of the nineteenth century. Australia remained for all effective purposes prehistoric until the founding of Sydney in 1788 initiated a process that was not to affect the greater part of the continent until well into the nineteenth century. When the New World was first effectively discovered by Europeans it is true that indigenous civilizations existed and that in certain of these historical records were maintained, but by far the great part of both the Americas remained prehistoric until opened up by exploration and settlement during the post-Columbian era.

It follows from this not merely that there was a broad overlap in time between the later prehistoric communities and those recording their own histories, but that simpler cultures in proximate and even in quite distant regions would even in quite early times have been liable to more or less profound influence from civilized centers. This means that the later prehistoric cultures must needs be studied in the same context as their literate contemporaries. With characteristic clarity our French colleagues have long recognized that this necessity in turn serves to differentiate the phases of prehistory anterior to the rise of the early civilizations (or at least to their impact on the prehistory of whatever area is in question) and those which betray in metallurgy or other traits the impact of ideas deriving ultimately from literate communities: it is the former alone, running from the beginning of the Old Stone Age to the Neolithic, that for them comprise *la préhistoire;* the latter they consign to *la protohistoire.* British archaeologists have generally preferred to hold to the concept of prehistory as a unitary field. Yet it is important to recognize the existence of a polarity of interest as between those concerned with the primary evolution of culture up to the discovery and spread of an elementary farming economy and those whose main interest is with the secondary devolution of culture and the transformation of primitive farming communities under impulses from civilization up to the stage at which they were capable of beginning to record their own history: for some purposes it may even be useful to speak of primary and secondary prehistory.

The general aim of prehistory is to recover as much as possible about the history of preliterate societies which by their very nature were incapable of recording it. This makes it hardly necessary to emphasize that the kind of information to be won from the prehistoric past differs profoundly from that to be gained from the history of even partially literate societies. In a sense there is justice on the side of those who have claimed that, since prehistoric peoples have and can have no history, prehistorians are attempting the impossible in trying to recover it. The distinction we have to preserve is that between history in its rigorous, academic sense, which began only when it was written down, and history in its broader evolutionary connotation, the product of the last two centuries of scientific thought, which comprehends the whole story of mankind in society. The fact that we now recognize a continuity of development, and one that can only conventionally be restricted to human societies, should not prevent us from recognizing Natural History, Prehistory, and History as separate disciplines, disciplines which differ not merely in their procedures, but still more in what they can tell us about the past.

It is the glory of history that by means of it one is enabled not merely to check general trends by reference to a multitude of particularities — one can often do this for prehistory — but actually to study the relations of individual men to one another and to the circumstances in which they found themselves, and even to discover the motives that determined or at least influenced specific choices. The prehistorian, on the other hand, lacking documentary sources, is precluded from identifying individuals; so soon as the names even of the most prominent are known we sense ourselves on the threshold of history proper and begin even in the English-speaking world to qualify our studies as protohistoric. Prehistory, as I have written elsewhere, is a social study: it deals "not with individuals or with the relations of individuals to one another and to society in general, but with societies, including their internal stratification and their local organization, and their relations to one another and to the world of nature of which in the final resort they form an integral part." Yet, though the units with which it deals are larger and though it has to work at a higher level of abstraction than history proper, prehistory is nevertheless fundamentally historical in the sense that it deals with time as a main dimension.

James Deetz

2   ARCHAEOLOGY AS A SOCIAL SCIENCE

James Deetz's essay on archaeology as a social science has been widely quoted as an eloquent statement on archaeology's role in studying human culture in the past. New World archaeologists consider archaeology to be part of anthropology, and the archaeologist to be an anthropologist who studies extinct peoples. Early archaeological research in the American Southwest by F. H. Cushing and other scholars showed that archaeology could be effectively combined with anthropology to study the ancestry of modern Indian groups who flourish in the same areas as their prehistoric forebears.

Thus archaeology added a vital time dimension to the study of early man in the New World. In recent years the divergence of approach between New World and Old World archaeologists has become less marked. Each group has become more aware of their colleagues' work in other parts of the world, which often deals with similar archaeological problems. The following selection admirably sums up the basic objectives of, and trends in, archaeology today that are amplified later in this volume.

That part of anthropology known as archaeology is concerned with culture in the past — the extinct lifeways of former peoples, how and why they changed and developed, and the significance of this to developmental process and to our understanding of culture. In short, archaeology adds a vital time dimension to the study of man. As such if it is to achieve the ends which we claim for it, archaeology must remain as closely and intimately bound up with general ethnology as possible and constantly contribute to understandings of social man.

This point needs some stress since much of archaeology in the public mind is involved with radiocarbon dating, pollen studies, glacial geology, and other areas of the biological and physical sciences. While modern archaeology could ill afford to forgo these contributions of other disciplines, they are still just contributions which make the archaeologist better able to make reasoned and valid statements concerning human culture in the past. To paraphrase Willey and Phillips, then, "archaeology is a social science or it is nothing."

Most archaeologists would agree that they are striving to achieve 3 related ends: (1) the reconstruction of culture history, often over massive segments of time; (2) the detailing of the daily lifeways of earlier cultures; and (3) the education of cultural process in a broader sense with emphasis on the dynamic aspects of culture. However, these 3 goals of archaeology are in no sense mutually independent, and it would seem in viewing their interrelationships that two of them are aspects of one larger entity.

If we were able to derive a relatively complete picture of the working of an early culture at one point in time and detail the interrelationships between that culture's various components, then the synthesis of a large number of such cultural statements would at the same time delineate process in a dynamic sense as well as provide a far more detailed historical statement. Thus, sophisticated history and cultural process are but two aspects of the same archaeological goal, differing in emphasis and perhaps in scope.

Until relatively recently, culture history as formulated by archaeologists

Reproduced by permission of the author and the American Anthropological Association from *Current Directions in Anthropology,* 1970.

has been quite coarse-grained, with great stress on the major events of prehistory such as the evolution of lithic technology over tens of thousands of years, the invention and spread of food production, the peopling of the new world, or the rise of civilization. This perspective is seen most commonly in overall syntheses, summary statements in effect (I mean here such books as Grahame Clark's *World Prehistory* as an example) of the prehistory of this or that portion of the world, or for that matter the entire world. At a more specific level in space and time, and here I'm really talking about site reports, cultural historical statements have concentrated similarly on rather general topics. The generality is much the same and only the time and space dimensions are reduced. Thus, a common and necessary portion of any site report consists of a summary of the prehistory of the region in which the site is located, and matters such as the population of the area by prehistoric culture A, B, or C, the development of subsistence techniques, or the increase in community size are the most commonly addressed.

I should make clear that I do not make light of this kind of synthesis. It is basic, important, and represents large quantities of effort expended. It is also probably possessed of a high degree of credibility if only because it is relatively general. It is when archaeology attempts to become more specific and precise, to make inferences concerning more detailed aspects of culture, that the problem of credibility becomes real. And when one moves into the realm of cultural process based on delineation of daily lifeways such precision is demanded and one must expect a credibility level comparable to that enjoyed by the more general sort of cultural historical formulation. Ideally, if it were possible to produce precise and totally reliable descriptions of the cultures of prehistoric societies l through n ... and understand their dynamics, then a far more detailed cultural historical statement would naturally follow. But it would seem that the essential first step in achieving such an end would be the development of techniques for generating reliable synchronic cultural descriptions from the past. These in turn permit insights concerning process, and as mentioned above, understanding of process leads to sound and detailed cultural history.

In this sense the three aims of archaeology are but steps in a single process. Perhaps much of archaeology in the past by not following these steps in precisely that order has produced useful but not necessarily general conclusions. If so, then the business before us as archaeologists in the late 1960s is the development of a body of method and theory which will assure such detail and precision. In fact, such a concern has been characteristic of archaeology since 1960. I should add that that is an approximate date — you could push it back or forward a few years either way you want — and that progress is now being made in a number of directions toward that end. I should like to explore some of these efforts and at the same time make some general observations regarding other possible pursuits, some of these quite tentative and speculative, but hopefully consistent with the stated purpose, and representative in a general way of current trends in modern archaeology.

The actual steps through which an archaeologist proceeds from first to last in working on his data are actually quite simple. He excavates a body of material from his site, using a set of techniques which assures control over its location and the relationship between his various components. Having done this, the next task is the careful description of the material to make it comparable to other lots from other sites. Then the body of data, having been ordered according to any one of a number of classificatory systems, is studied to determine the ways in which it reflects the behavior of the people who were responsible for leaving it behind to be discovered by the archaeologist. Recent developments in archaeology have reflected innovation in all three of these processes.

Before going further, a few words might be in order regarding the nature of archaeological data. Its most salient attributes are that it is fragmentary, and it is buried. For this reason alone much of the archaeologist's time is spent in removing this material from the earth and reassembling it into as complete a condition as possible. As we shall see later, the subterranean aspect of traditional archaeological data may have been an unrecognized impediment to obtaining the maximum understanding from it. The most important thing to realize about archaeological material, however, is that it reflects in its entirety the manner in which human behavior has made an impact upon the environment. This is true from the smallest of artifacts to the largest: a shell bead is shaped through conscious design to a certain form which reflects that design, while a Mayan temple is an aggregate of portions of the environment assembled through the same conscious process. Thus, the most fundamental relationship which the archaeologist must recognize is that between behavior and its productions. And since we agree that behavior is patterned and systematic, it follows that its reflections in its effects on the environment must be similarly patterned and it is the explication of this relationship between behavior and environment which holds the greatest promise for sharpening archaeological studies.

The imperfection and incompleteness of archaeological records has been discussed by numerous writers, all of whom have stressed its effect upon obtaining maximum information concerning its cultural authors. As Lewis Binford (1968a:5–27) has pointed out, however, this concern has at times been overstated. Yet it does pose a real problem in very many cases if one expects all portions of a whole cultural system to be represented in some way or another in the archaeological record. However, this is a totally unrealistic expectation to hold in the first place, and I hope to make some suggestions as to how this problem can be circumvented at least in part.

Looking back over the past decade, there seem to be 3 major themes which typify current trends in archaeological thinking. Other workers might perceive these somewhat differently, but I would expect at least general agreement. These include (1) an increasing concern over the integrated nature of culture and the necessity for stressing the structure of the varied content of past cultures, (2) a new stress on finer-grain techniques for the description and integration of archaeological materials, aided immensely by developing technologies in automatic data processing, and (3) an increasing concern over the proper role and use of analogy in archaeological inference. These 3 themes are closely related and when applied with care they have produced some truly impressive and important studies.

The first of these, stressing the interrelationships between various aspects of culture, was of course the dominant theme of Walter Taylor's conjunctive approach, first put forth over 20 years ago (Taylor 1948). Its reawakening in this decade is certainly due in part to Taylor's original thoughts on the subject. An example will show the difference between viewing archaeological cultures in this fashion as opposed to the more traditional perspective. If we look at changes in single categories of artifacts over time and simply describe them, we can certainly make some general statements concerning culture history while at the same time pay little or no heed to the relationship between various classes or between these classes and other nonmaterial aspects of the culture, or to the articulation of the culture as a whole with the environment.

Work in the Santa Barbara Channel region in southern California has produced a sequence of at least 3 cultures which have been subdivided in a number of ways. (I might interject here for those of you who are specialists in the Santa Barbara Channel sequence that my intention is to boil it down for the purpose of getting through this paper in something less than two hours rather than to do it violence.) In simplest terms, the earliest tradition is one characterized by heavy milling stones used in processing various wild seeds. Projectile points are relatively crude and sufficiently low in number to suggest no emphatic stress on hunting. The economy would seem to be one based on extensive exploitation of vegetable foods with some hunting supplement. Another major food source was shellfish and sites of this tradition are characteristically shell middens, in many instances of considerable depth.

Now this is followed by a second tradition which is markedly different in artifact content. Shellfish seem to have diminished dramatically and a marked increase in projectile points reflects a new heavy emphasis on hunting. These points show affinity with those from the desert areas of eastern California. Milling stones are replaced by basket-hopper mortars, small concave stones on which bottomless baskets are attached, if that's not a contradiction in terms. Someone read this and said, "Well if it doesn't have a bottom it's not a basket." But it's this little basketry cylinder, attached to the stone with asphaltum, used in conjunction with small mortars, to process vegetable materials.

The last major cultural tradition of the region sees a return to maritime orientation and, while hunting seems to be a factor, sites are now again shell middens of impressive size. Standard equipment for seed processing are massive stone bowls weighing in some cases hundreds of pounds and used with large cylindrical stone pestles.

Cultural historical formulations based on these data tend to stress certain general but valid points. There was a change in subsistence technology over time. Milling stones give way to hopper mortars which in turn give way to large stone bowls. Projectile points and their cultural correlate of hunting increase and then show a marked decline relative to other subsistence artifacts.

All of these conclusions are essentially based on considering the formal appearances of certain artifact classes. And, changes in these and the relative frequencies permit the conclusions when viewed against certain settlement data. There is, however, a rather different way to look at these same data and reach somewhat more precise understanding of some basic aspects of cultural process in southern California prehistory and at the same time make a rather more detailed cultural historical statement. This perspective, it should be emphasized, is in hypothesis form and not necessarily to be understood as a statement of fact. What is significant here is that using a viewpoint which is in accord with a conjunctive approach permits a different final statement. If we consider simply one set of artifacts, those used in processing wild seed materials, and also consider some of the ways in which they relate to other aspects of the culture in question and how those aspects in turn relate to each other, a useful processual statement can be made. Two factors appear to be involved here: portability (of the milling equipment) and the relationship of portability to the area required for seed processing; by that I mean the area on the artifact which gets involved in grinding up all these little seeds. The large early milling stones using a back-and-forth pattern of grinding with a mano must of necessity be large and heavy since an extensive grinding surface must be supported by a mass of stone. In other words, if you need to rub one rock back and forth on top of another rock in this direction it takes an overall bigger rock on the bottom to get the job done; it can't be just a half-inch thick. It is unlikely that many of these milling stones were moved from site to site frequently if at all. This, in turn, suggests relatively stable settlements with restrictive mobility, with the remote possibility that the stones were cached in some way to be used again and again on periodic return to the site. Due to the rather heavy reliance on shellfish resources and the depth of midden accumulation, the latter alternative seems less likely. I realize I just stepped right into the middle of a relatively large controversy on the early milling stones culture of Santa Barbara County, concerning whether or not they were quite mobile or permanent. But, all I can say is that I know it and I've indicated my own opinion on the subject.

In marked contrast to large heavy milling stones requiring hundreds of square inches of working surface, basket-hopper mortars are lightweight and eminently portable devices, requiring working surfaces of less than 100 square inches. The critical factor here is the shift from back-and-forth grinding to up-and-down pulverizing, requiring a minimum of abrading surfaces, with the basketry sides acting as retainers for the processed material. The new emphasis on hunting reflected by the new point types combined with more portable milling equipment may well indicate a marked increase in community mobility. Resemblances with projectile point types to the east could indicate a real movement of influence, and perhaps even people, westward. If, in addition to this, sea level elevations at the same time had an effect upon inter-tidal shellfish resources, more than sufficient factors would have been present to produce a major shift to a nomadic, hunting way of life.

Continuing from the perspective of changes in portability and the seed-processing area on the artifact, the subsequent development shows a return to a more sedentary marine-oriented life. However, seed processing continues an up-and-down pulverizing technique similar to that of the basket-hopper mortars earlier, but with the removal of those pressures which required portability. As a function of mobility, mortars were free to become larger. This would certainly be an advantage in processing large quantities of material at one time and might possibly be attuned to significant population increase and enlargement of community size.

This last tradition was that observed by the early explorers along the Pacific Coast, reaching its climax in the historic Chumash. These people were grouped in very large coastal villages with a high degree of permanence. In this context, massive heavy stone-bowl mortars make perfect sense. The pressures, cultural and environmental, which may have transformed the earlier massive milling stones to light-weight mortars are not present to reverse the trend from milling to pounding back to milling, and subsequent enlargement of seed grinding equipment seems to be in response to population growth and increased permanence of settlement.

In the example just given, it is not necessary at this point, although I suppose maybe it would be sooner or later, to demand that this is the "right" explanation. It is provided to show how change in one class of objects, as a matter of fact change in only one or two *attributes* of one specific set of objects related to one very specific activity, when considered along with the manner in which this class articulates with a larger set of cultural and ecological imperatives, suggests genuinely processual explanations. The next step in this approach would be further testing of this hypothesis to see if other items in the respective assemblages reflect in yet other ways the suggested changes in community mobility, subsistence, and population.

It might legitimately be asked whether these last conclusions are truly so different. They are, to the extent that they result from considering but one small segment of an entire assemblage. In this example, changes in a set of related attributes of milling equipment — working surface and its contingent effect on size and hence portability — can be seen perhaps to reflect a well integrated complex of changes in the culture sequence which produced them. Stress on the essential interrelatedness of cultural systems allows us to reach understandings of many aspects from a relative few. And this certainly is at least a partial answer to the problems posed by the incompleteness of the archaeological record.

This viewpoint, I must stress, is in no way original with me. For a rather similar statement of many of the same things I refer to Lewis Binford's discussion of the limitations of the archaeological record (Binford 1968a).

The second major trend in archaeological thinking in the 1960s is centered around attempts to describe artifacts in a more detailed fashion in the hope that such description might sharpen our abilities to delineate the patterns in the data which hold clues to past behavior. Traditional archaeological description has been based on the *type* concept. Thus artifacts were classified according to their formal similarities and assemblages were compared largely in terms of shared types. The artifact type is, of course, an arbitrary category based on similarities in characteristics selected by the classifier from a much larger range of characteristics. As such, it has been a useful tool to derive relatively coarse-grained groupings which, when compared, permit rather general statements of relationships between archaeological cultures in time and space. With recent emphasis on looking at artifacts in terms of variation in the attributes which, when combined, constitute types, the factors which lead to the creation of these objects can be more clearly understood. For example, a pottery type might be described as having a certain size, type of paste, decoration, a particular rim profile, and tempered with coarse sand. All pots which share in these attributes are placed in this particular type category. Of course, the artifact type is a polythetic category and, in practice, sharing the preponderance of the attributes of the ideal type is sufficient for typological placement of a single artifact. But in making such an assignment the classifier is making a number of other implicit statements. He is saying that the maker of the artifact in question executed operations A, B, and C, and so on — as many operations as there are attributes in the descriptions. And it is equally important that in doing one thing — incising a pot rim, notching an arrowhead, or grooving an axe, he did not execute any of the other alternatives known to be available to him from inspection of other type categories or other artifacts in the same assemblage. Thus, the rim might also be cord-impressed, the arrowhead left unnotched, or the axe notched rather than grooved. Two things become obvious with a little thought. The selection is in some way influenced by certain nonmaterial factors in the maker's culture, and the selection of one attribute is not influenced by the same factors as the selection of another. Thus a multi-attribute type construct will be virtually certain to be the end-product of a set of decisions and choices which represent inputs from very different sectors of the maker's culture. As such, it is a useful integrative device, but of little use to an understanding of process.

To resolve this dilemma it becomes necessary to create what is in effect a typology of attributes and consider the data in terms of the manner in which these attributes combine and recombine in response to the culture producing them. It is at the level of the discrete attribute that patterning of the type which represents specific nonmaterial aspects of the culture becomes evident. Certainly behavior shared by a relatively small number of individuals is most likely to be seen in the mode of combination of attributes on artifacts, since it is the individuals who are responsible for combining the attributes creating the artifact in the first place. Elsewhere, in my little paperback *Invitation to Archeology* (Deetz 1968), I have pointed out that there is an equation between levels of behavior and levels of attribute and artifact grouping. Thus, since individuals are responsible for combining attributes, attribute patterning reflects patterned individual behavior. Likewise the groupings of artifacts into sets which represent certain activities, knives, points, and scrapers for example, which relate to hunting and meat processing, reflect patterned behavior on the part of larger social groups within the community. Patterning in entire archaeological assemblages is indicative of behavior representative of whole communities. Thus even if it were possible to agree upon multi-attribute types which possess some cultural reality, they would not permit investigation of the most minimal level of behavior, since individual attribute patterning is the level which is relevant in this case.

There has been a series of studies in recent years which show the validity of attribute analysis in ceramics in assessing past social patterns. I refer to my Arikara study (Deetz 1965), Bill Longacre's study of Cartes Ranch Pueblo (1968), and Jim Hill's study of the Broken K Pueblo (1968) as good examples of this. All indicate in one way or another that the combination of attributes in pottery manufacture is a function of shared behavior which results from the relative solidarity of the social unit. Matrilocal potters who reside together share in certain sets of designs which are more or less distinct from those of other similar residential units. My study showed a progressively more random distribution of attributes of pottery manufacture and design accompanying the breakdown of matrilocal families from historically documented Arikara Indians. The other two studies, Longacre's and Hill's, done in a prehistoric context, tend more to show how distinctive attribute configurations are spatially segregated as were the families which produced them. So, in a way, the latter are synchronic and the former is diachronic.

The study of individual attributes in a large sample of artifacts requires a vast amount of recording and computation, and this in turn would be virtually impossible without the help of data-processing equipment. Thus developments in attribute analysis of archaeological data has in part been a function of the rapidly developing technology in the computer field. Computers were first used in archaeology in 1960 or a little earlier and by now have occupied a prominent position in the field.

The use of analogy in archaeology has been standard from the very beginning. Our view of the meaning of archaeological assemblages must be conditioned by our understandings of cultures of the present. Projectile points are identified as such, not through any inherent quality which they possess, but because similar forms are known from their use in observable contexts. Witness the significant number of unidentified artifacts from any archaeological site. They are unidentifiable in large part because no ethnographic analogue is known. There are, however, certain subtle difficulties in the use of analogy in archaeology. As Lewis Binford has pointed out in the same article I referred to earlier, there is no guarantee that all cultures of the past have analogues in the ethnographically reported present. Thus, total reliance on ethnographic and historic data runs the risk of either restricting our inferential method to an unnecessary degree or even perhaps of making mismatches between archaeological and ethnographic materials.

More fundamental to the entire problem seems to be the manner in which archaeologists implicitly seek analogies between material categories from the past and behavioral categories from the present. Thus, archaeological data, which are tangible material data, are studied to see if they could be made to reflect different aspects of social behavior. Pottery attribute patterns, for example, are said to result from, or to articulate directly with, post-nuptial residence. It would seem that implicit in such an approach is the assumption that material culture is more of a cultural by-product than some nonmaterial categories. It can be argued that an institution such as residence is every bit as much the product of behavior as is a pot or an axe. The only difference is that one can be measured and touched and the other observed and described. This is particularly true in this case because all we are doing is measuring the spatial relationships between individuals inside a hunk of the environment which we call the house. Maybe I should elaborate on this just a little more. I'm struck by the fact that there seems to be some sort of a feeling on the part of archaeologists that the categories used by the ethnographer are possessed of somewhat greater cultural truth than the categories which he imposes on his own data. There is a genuine problem here. It seems that to seek a one-to-one relationship between two different products of similar behavior runs a considerable risk of distortion. It is rather like adding apples and pears. The categories which have been devised by ethnologists to describe the cultural universe they study need not be, and in fact should not be, the categories with which the archaeologists seek correspondence in their data. If there is any logic or validity in this proposition, it follows that a largely ignored task before the archaeologist is the delineation of the nature of the relationships between behavioral and material categories as such without interposed constructs such as residence, descent, or exogamy, to name but 3 examples, all examples themselves from a more complex behavioral context. Thus, it might be argued that the most fundamental aspect of analogy in archaeology is the analogue which exists between relationships in archaeological and ethnographic data rather than between artifacts and the ethnographer's categories. I hope I've made that clear. I hate to repeat, but I'll say it one more time because it's the core statement in this whole talk: more important perhaps are those analogues which exist in archaeological and ethnographic data between material and behavior rather than between the artifacts — so many pots let's say, or so many projectile points — and the ethnographer's categories. In other words, perhaps it's time we stopped trying to find post-nuptial residence, descent, marriage patterns in our data because these in fact are classificatory rubrics which are about third or fourth order abstractions themselves which the ethnographers are responsible for and this leads us away from the central problem which I think we're involved with here.

One wonders if the development of anthropology over the last century hasn't somehow led the archaeologist into a less than suitable position with regard to the data with which he is normally charged. Material culture of living societies has traditionally been the domain of the ethnographers, and they have not been as concerned with this aspect as with other more exciting subjects. Yet the archaeologist has been restricted to data which is below the sod, and it is a matter of faith that the archaeologist is an anthropologist who digs. Yet this need not be so. And in fact, by taking into account material from above and below the ground, archaeologists are certain to gain much clearer understanding of the materials they do excavate. In other words, perhaps the traditional division of responsibilities within anthropology has unnecessarily restricted the archaeologist in achieving maximum results. A coherent and unified body of subject matter entirely appropriate to the archaeologist is the study of the material aspects of culture in their behavioral context, regardless of provenience.

I realize that in one sense I have just now abolished the field of archaeology as we know it but I sincerely think that as long as we operate in this sense somebody's got to ask these questions and someone has to get at them. We are really not doing ourselves maximum service, and I speak, I think in part at least, from experience, because about 5 years ago I suddenly discovered a whole new world which wasn't even buried at all. It was all around me. It was called houses and cemeteries and automobiles, and they're perfectly legal: you can do some pretty groovy things with hubcaps and hood ornaments just as much as you can with pre-Columbian ceramics. In this fashion, understandings of the relationship between the material and nonmaterial derived from maximum information well controlled can then be fed back into the traditional archaeological contexts for more precise inferences.

A somewhat lesser theme of archaeology in the 1960s contributes to this perspective in a number of ways. I refer here to historical archaeology — the study of historically documented material through archaeological methods. The kinds of controls available in this sort of archaeology provide a suitable context in which to examine material and nonmaterial relationships in a manner similar to that obtainable from ethnographic data. It has one extra kicker in it which makes it even nicer because it's not ethnographic and it is, to my knowledge, the only archaeological (subterranean) data which you can contend with in which you can pursue certain dimensions of control which allow you to look at it in a somewhat different way. I'll give an example in a minute.

My own work on colonial mortuary art, certainly not buried and certainly supported by historical materials, demonstrates some of the values of this approach. Recent work, as yet unpublished by archaeologists, promises to sharpen our understanding of some of the many factors which affect the frequencies of certain artifact types at different times in the past which go far beyond simple popularity. The method of seriation is based on the assumption that styles appear, increase and decrease, and finally vanish as a function of popularity. This is true, but, in aligning archaeological assemblages according to this method, it is implicitly assumed that these changes are uniformly operative on all peoples in a restricted area of time and space. Yet we know now that a simple factor such as socioeconomic status can create a marked difference in just what artifacts are present in a given household and will produce a significant skew in the proposed temporal alignments. I realize this is really operating more at the level of integrative method than it is explanation, but still it's a valid point.

One of the contributions of historical archaeology is an increased awareness that the record of the past is perhaps far more complex than we normally assume. Such a caution is a healthy thing in archaeology today, since, while we are moving toward more detailed and specific inferences about the past, it follows that a greater complexity of relationships will be perceived. And to oversimplify at this point can be quite dangerous, if not in fact disastrous.

An example will make this clear. We've been studying the faunal remains from a series of 7 seventeenth century house sites in old Plymouth Colony for the past year. From mid-century onward there is a somewhat surprising pattern in the mammalian food sources. Approximately 98 percent of the meat consumed was from domesticated animals. Hunting was an insignificant factor. Limited documentary research shows that this pattern is probably typical of the earlier portion of the century as well. A domestic-to-feral ratio of this type in the absence of controls would be interpreted as reflecting a level of efficiency of animal husbandry of sufficient height that hunting was no longer necessary. Alternately one might suggest a drastic reduction in the number of game animals. The historical facts, however, provide a very different explanation, one which it is very unlikely could be determined from archaeological analysis, again without the kind of control we've had. Legislation governing hunting rights in their native England was so restricted on the yeomanry that they endured food shortages a number of times without resorting to hunting on any significant scale. Recent research by Patrick Malone of the University of Pennsylvania, as yet unpublished, develops this and the following quite clearly. This reluctance to hunt would appear to result from a retention of attitudes toward hunting engendered prior to colonization, combined with an unfamiliarity with the use of firearms in hunting. Aiming a musket, indispensable to efficient hunting, was so totally foreign a concept that it was not even included in a 40-point manual of arms of the period. This really surprises people — at least it certainly did me. I realize this isn't a session on American history, but the fact is that the whole idea of picking out a target and selecting and shooting the target didn't come until the eighteenth century! Guns of this period were things that you held in rows of 20 or 30 people and fired broadside at the advancing company of soldiers. And if any of them fell, it was an act of God rather than your marksmanship which led to this result. So the idea of pointing it at something and letting it go was totally outside their cognitive view of what one did with a firearm.

Correlated with this was a seemingly disproportionate number of fowling pieces in household inventories of the time and a corresponding high level of waterfowl remains in the sites. (We have up to now transcribed 300 of these inventories and there will be about a thousand of them when we've finished. They are lovely things for archaeological control because they list every single artifact in an individual's house at the time of his death, often by room, and give its value. So you can control this in time over several hundred square miles and over about 70 years. And you can do all sorts of neat things with them. I think this is archaeology even though you don't use a shovel, because it is dealing with the same kind of material.) Shooting ducks requires no aiming. But the difficulty of hunting land mammals when aiming was critical to success and was sufficiently great that it contributed little to subsistence even in the face of shortages.

This paper has been but a general survey and summation of the general directions which archaeology seems to be taking at this time. Central to all of these aspects of current archaeology is its essential and vital relationship to the larger discipline which it serves. As long as this relationship is nourished and developed — I think it is nowadays — archaeology and anthropology are bound to profit in mutual fashion.

Bruce G. Trigger

3   AIMS IN PREHISTORIC ARCHAEOLOGY

The great anthropologist Alfred Kroeber once remarked that "many
scientists do not know what history is, or merely assume that it is not
science." Bruce G. Trigger, a Canadian archaeologist, has written
several essays about the broad issues of archaeology; three of them
are reprinted in this volume. In his article on aims, he points out that
archaeology has moved away from being merely a descriptive science
toward giving more attention to explaining and understanding
archaeological data. He feels that the theoretical structure of archaeology and more rigorous analytical methods and canons for
interpreting archaeological data have vital implications for the general
orientation of archaeology. Trigger discusses some new directions
in archaeology and in particular the differing approaches to the past
described in the two previous selections. The crux of Trigger's
arguments lies in his view that "archaeology best fulfils its potential
not by trying to duplicate work being done in the social sciences but
by providing detailed information about the actual course of socio-
cultural development." Trigger here excellently amplifies Kroeber's
remark quoted above.

Not long ago the theoretical literature in archaeology dealt mainly with
excavation techniques and the primary analysis of archaeological data. In
recent years, the successful realization of many of these empirical objectives, plus a rapidly increasing corpus of data, have motivated a younger
generation of archaeologists to investigate more carefully the problems that
are involved in the explanation of these data and the study of prehistory
in general. This concern has produced a spate of publications which, although they often disagree radically about particular issues, are attempting (a) to investigate the theoretical structure of prehistoric archaeology,
(b) to formulate a more rigorous canon for the interpretation of archaeological data, and (c) to pioneer new methods of analysis (Binford and
Binford, 1968; Chang, 1967 and 1968; Clarke, 1968; Trigger, 1968a).

One has to be conservative indeed to fail to appreciate the value of these
studies. However sectarian and polemical some of them are, and however
much they may bristle with an often superfluous terminology, they promise
a rich harvest in a better understanding of the significance of archaeological

From "Aims in Prehistoric Archaeology," by Bruce C. Trigger, *Antiquity*, 44 (1970),
26–37. Reprinted by permission of the author and the Editor of *Antiquity*. Footnotes are
omitted.

data. One cannot justly regard these studies as an aberration that serves only to divert professional interest from more important objectives. On the contrary, whether their authors admit it or not, most of these studies are very solidly based upon the previous achievements of prehistoric archaeology. The very fact that they are compelling archaeologists to become increasingly explicit and self-conscious about their goals, is surely evidence of the maturation of the discipline, and therefore to be welcomed.

The most vital problems that these studies pose for the profession as a whole are their implications for the general orientation of prehistoric archaeology. This is an issue of the utmost seriousness and one on which every possible point of view, including the most conservative and the most radical, deserves a careful hearing.

Until recently, it was generally taken for granted that prehistoric archaeology was an historical discipline that aimed to investigate man's past for those periods for which written records are absent or scarce. Lacking the tools of history proper, prehistorians attempted to learn about the past from the artifacts and other traces of human activity that survive in the archaeological record, much as paleontologists strive to extract information from fossils, and historical geologists search for it amongst geological strata. It is no accident that the links between these historicizing disciplines have been close, and that they share much the same conceptual basis for their methodology. Archaeology has tended to develop under the influence of history and geology as a natural history of cultural development.

It is fashionable today to say that archaeology has three aims, first to reconstruct culture history, secondly to reconstruct prehistoric patterns of culture, and thirdly to delineate cultural processes (Binford and Binford, 1968, 8–16). However, most of the "new archaeology" has tended to place considerably more emphasis on the second and third of these goals than on the first, and, in some circles, this has given rise to a divergent view of the aims of archaeology. L. R. Binford, for example, considers that archaeology should be "an objective comparative science involved in the explication and explanation of cultural differences and similarities" (Binford, L. R., 1967a, 234–235, and 1962). In a recent address to the American Anthropological Association, F. Plog has advocated a similar role for archaeology, as an "experimental social science" capable of testing hypotheses that are relevant to the theories of the social sciences and therefore contributing to the explanation of human behavior (Plog, 1968, 110). In what is undoubtedly the most rigorous and systematic single program for archaeological interpretation outlined to date, D. L. Clarke defines the primary aim of archaeology as being to explain the regularities that the archaeologist observes in the archaeological record. He argues that this will make archaeology a generalizing discipline studying material culture, structurally similar and substantively complementary to social anthropology (Clarke, 1968, 20–24).

Each of these scholars seems to view archaeology as being ideally a nomothetic or generalizing discipline having goals identical to those of ethnology and cultural anthropology. These goals, like those of the social sciences in general, are to formulate laws or regularities that will explain socio-cultural processes and associated human behavior.

It is no surprise that these same archaeologists express varying degrees of hostility toward the traditional, particularizing view of prehistory, which they stigmatize as being descriptive and lacking theoretical content. Binford denies that "reconstruction of the past" can be the ultimate aim of archaeology. If it were, archaeology would be "doomed to be a particularistic, non-generalizing field." The "reconstruction and characterization of the past" is viewed as mainly having a "role in the general education of the public" (Binford, L. R., 1967a, 235). Binford, apparently, does not believe that historical objectives have scholarly value in their own right, although here his stand is probably polemical. He has himself produced historical work of high quality (1967b) and has elsewhere expressed more moderate views on historical objectives. Plog draws a similar distinction between "processual as opposed to strictly historical analysis" and champions the use of the past "as a laboratory for testing hypotheses concerning social and cultural process" (1968, 110). Clarke appears to entertain a more modest view of archaeology's scientific goals and seems to be more sympathetic to particularizing than is either Binford or Plog (1968, 635–664). There are, however, few references to historical objectives in Clarke's *Analytical Archaeology*, and it is clear that, in this book at least, Clarke's interest in cultural process greatly exceeds his interest in history.

Most British archaeologists appear to consider such views about the aims of prehistoric archaeology to lack adequate foundations or motives. This is especially so among archaeologists whose work brings them into close contact with professional historians and who seem to share with them, consciously or unconsciously, many of the same views about the general nature and goals of their respective disciplines. It is worth noting therefore that these views have substantial roots in the American archaeological tradition. In his *A Study of Archaeology*, W. W. Taylor viewed "synthesis and content" (paleoethnology and historiography) "as middle range objectives which logically precede a study of the 'nature and working of culture.'" Of this final level he wrote "When the archaeologist collects his data, reconstructs his cultural contexts and ... proceeds to make a comparative study of the nature of culture in its formal, functional and/or developmental aspects, then he is doing cultural anthropology" (1948, 45). Likewise, in *Method and Theory in American Archaeology*, Willey and Phillips classified culture-historical integration as a descriptive operation preceding explanation, which in turn they equated with processual interpretation (1956, 9). In both these works, as in the writings of the anthropologist Leslie White (1945a), historical activities tend to be viewed as being

essentially descriptive, while the ultimate aims of archaeology are characterized as being processual, that is to say, concerned with the formulation
of general rules of cultural behavior. In addition to reflecting the prestige
of nomothetic or generalizing activities in contemporary American social
science, this insistence upon generalizing as the ultimate goal of archaeology reflects the strength of the American commitment to the idea that
prehistoric archaeology and ethnology are branches of anthropology and
therefore should share common goals.

The lip-service paid to these common goals was of little importance so
long as American archaeology was primarily interested in the recovery of
data (Taylor, 1948, 13; Willey, 1968; Schwartz, 1968). The main thrust of
the theorizing we have been discussing was clearly at the level of "culture-
historical integration." It is significant that neither Taylor nor Willey and
Phillips bothered to examine the ultimate objectives of archaeology in any
detail. A comfortable degree of ambiguity persisted between the concepts
of historical and processual explanation and the distinction between generalizing and particularizing was not seen as being of great importance.
These distinctions only became so as archaeologists grew increasingly at-
tentive to problems of explanation in archaeology, which in turn has required that the goals of explanation be considered more carefully. Archaeologists are now faced with the demands of an articulate minority that
they should use their findings, alongside ethnological data, as building
blocks in a single generalizing science of culture. I see this not as an erratic
demand, but rather as the logical culmination of one line of thought, that
has long been implicit in American archaeology. Unfortunately, the objections that have been raised against this point of view have not succeeded
so far in coming to grips with the main issues. Instead, they have revealed
that a great lack of clear thinking about major theoretical issues lies behind
the façade of much traditional archaeology.

In a recent article in this journal, Jacquetta Hawkes has reaffirmed her
faith that the final aim of archaeology is "the reconstruction of individual
events in time" (1968, 255 [reprinted in Chapter 9]), but in so doing she
has unfortunately adopted the very phraseology that exponents of the "new
archaeology" use when they wish to imply that the traditional aims of
archaeology are purely descriptive. Furthermore, as we shall see below,
her identification of history with a vaguely defined humanist approach
seriously misrepresents the nature of historical enquiry as it is understood
by most modern historians. Indeed, her view of history is not dissimilar
from the views that are held of it by the most violent antihistoricists in
archaeology. Her condemnation of natural science methods has to be interpreted as a criticism not only of current developments but of all prehistoric
archaeology since the days of Christian Thomsen.

Another paper that exemplifies the limited view of the nature of historical enquiry that has been set out by many archaeologists is Sabloff and

Willey's "Collapse of Maya Civilization in the Southern Lowlands" (1968). In this paper, the authors defend an historical approach in archaeology by attempting to show that a single event may better explain the collapse of Maya civilization than do current "processual theories" that attribute it to ecological or social factors. The event which they choose is an hypothesized invasion of the Maya lowlands from the highlands of Mesoamerica. Following the interpretative procedure already outlined by Willey and Phillips in their book *Method and Theory in American Archaeology,* they argue that "by first gaining control of the historical variables, we will then be in an excellent position to gain control of the processual ones."

This identification of history with events but not with process has provoked a well-merited response from Erasmus (1968) and L. R. Binford (1968c). Both point out that historical events cannot be understood apart from their processual contexts, and that the mere demonstration of a sequential relationship does not constitute a meaningful explanation of that relationship. Even if Maya civilization did collapse following an invasion, the reasons for its collapse must be sought in the social and economic conditions which permitted such an invasion to occur and to have such far-reaching consequences. Erasmus concludes that historical events should not be given priority over process, but has nothing to say about the implications of this conclusion for an understanding of the structure of historical explanation. Binford comes close to eliminating the dichotomy between history and process by defining a proper historical approach as one that embraces a concern with process. He claims that his main disagreement with Sabloff and Willey, and with other traditional archaeologists, is over method. According to Binford, traditional archaeologists are content to use an inductive methodology, which means they are content to formulate propositions which they believe explain the past. Binford argues that, instead, archaeologists must employ a deductive approach whereby these propositions are tested. Binford's apparent sympathy for an historical approach that embraces a concern for process is offset, however, by a tendency to characterize inductive approaches as being particularizing and deductive ones as generalizing. The deductive method is seen as leading through a knowledge of the operation of past cultural systems to the formulation of laws of cultural dynamics and cultural evolution. Rather than being explicitly rejected, the concept of history is lost sight of for reasons that are fully intelligible in terms of Binford's general theoretical framework.

We are thus presented with the unhappy spectacle of both the supporters and foes of an historical archaeology in seeming agreement that historical objectives can be satisfied at the descriptive level. This is not the first time that such a conclusion has been arrived at in American anthropology. Kroeber once accused Leslie White of having appropriated for his concept of evolution all that was significant in history while refusing to accept the rest. "It will not do," Kroeber wrote, "to gut history and leave its empty shell standing around; there might be the embarrassment of no one's claiming it" (1952, 96). The current emphasis on processual studies in archaeology seems to be threatening a sense of historical problem with a similar fate. An explicit statement by an archaeologist that the aim of history is to explain is provided by W. W. Taylor (1948, 32).

At this point in our inquiry it is necessary to pose a few hard questions. The first is this: granting that archaeology has traditionally conceived of itself as an historical discipline, is it true that archaeologists have sought only to reconstruct and describe the past? Or have they also sought to explain it? Secondly, is any attempt to justify an historical approach merely a semantic exercise, or is the concept one of vital significance for prehistoric archaeology and for understanding the relationship between it and other disciplines?

WHAT IS HISTORY?

To begin to answer these questions it is obviously necessary to clarify what is meant by historical investigation and to do this properly the archaeologist needs to look beyond his own discipline. In this and the following section I have restricted my observations to the fields of archaeology and history proper (i.e. documentary history), although similar observations could have been made with reference to historical geology, paleontology, and cosmogony. I mention these fields mainly to note that historical analysis is not limited to the study of human behavior but is also an integral part of the physical and biological sciences (Kroeber, 1952, 66–78).

It is simply not true that historical disciplines have only descriptive objectives, even in the broad sense of being interested only in determining matters of fact and discussing chronological relationships. In the last century, partly as a valid protest against the moralizing interpretations of history that were popular prior to that time, historians tended to conceive of facts as constituting the hard core of history, while interpretations were regarded as little different from personal opinion. According to the great historian, Ludwig von Ranke, the aim of history was simply "to show how it was" (*"wie es eigentlich gewesen"*). Objectivity of this sort was a congenial goal during the later nineteenth century, which E. H. Carr has described as "a great age for facts" (1962, 2–3). Unfortunately, the image that history developed of itself at this time has influenced the view that other disciplines have held of it ever since. Nevertheless, even then, it was scarcely an accurate reflection of what was going on in the discipline. Most historians were aware that interpretation played a vital role in the writing of history, even if this interpretation was based on some commonly-held view of man or society masquerading as the historian's own philosophy. Works such as Mommsen's *History of Rome* clearly derive much of their value from the manner in which their authors were able to use their personal insights into current social and political problems to explain the past (Carr, 1962, 29–38).

For a long time now, most historians have explicitly rejected the empiricist dichotomy between fact and explanation. It is generally recognized that pure description is not only a grotesque goal, but also one that is impossible of attainment. Ideally, a purely descriptive history would aim to recount in the most minute detail what happened to every person living at a particular period. Every particle of information would have to be judged as being as important as every other, and no attempt could be made to suggest the overall significance of what was happening. Such a caricature is the very antithesis of all real historical investigation, which is based upon a selection of those facts which the historian deems to be significant (Carr, 1962, 4–14). The selection of these facts is influenced by the opinions and/or the theoretical orientation of the historian. In earlier times, as we have already suggested, this orientation was preferably implicit and frequently unconscious. In an otherwise admirable discussion of explanation in archaeology, Spaulding sees the chief difference between science and history as being the latter's dependence on commonsense explanations, but this caricature clearly does injustice to the work of many modern historians (1968, 33–39).

In the 20th century the tendency has been for this sort of history to be replaced by one in which explanations are based not on personal impressions of human behavior but on solid bodies of social science theory. This development has led to the emergence of social and economic history as flourishing sub-disciplines, closely linked with sociology and economics. G. R. Elton, in his *The Practice of History* (1969, 38–56) gives a stimulating, if not always optimistic, assessment of these developments. Likewise, the findings of psychology are being used with growing effectiveness to interpret the behavior of particular historical figures under given social conditions (Erikson, 1959). While the significance of chance and determinism for history is still a subject for debate, it is increasingly being accepted that individual behavior is not random and must be viewed in terms of a social and cultural matrix which is itself subject to orderly development, that is, which can be explained, if not predicted, by general rules (Carr, 1962, 81–102).

History differs from the social sciences in that it aims to explain individual situations in all their complexity rather than to formulate general laws for indefinitely repeatable events and processes. That is what is meant by saying that history is ideographic, the social sciences nomothetic (Nagel, 1961, 547; Elton, 1969, 22–24, 41). This does not mean that historians deny the existence of general rules: rather they seek to employ them to gain an understanding of individual (i.e. unique and non-recurrent) situations. The social sciences, on the other hand, extract recurrent variables from their socio-cultural matrix so that relationships of general validity can be established between them. As Kroeber has pointed out, in history process is treated as a "nexus" among phenomena, not as a thing to be extracted from them (1952, 63).

The use of general rules to explain a concrete situation is no less an act of creative skill than is the formulation of such rules to explain repeated correlations. Because the aim is to explain a particular situation in all of its complexity, not only does the application of such rules serve as a test of theory, but, because a variety of different bodies of theory may have to be applied in conjunction with one another, historical interpretation serves as an interdisciplinary arena in which the explanatory power of different theoretical approaches may be ascertained. As Carr has said "Every historical argument revolves round the question of the priority of causes" (1962, 84).

Moreover, the fact that historians set as their goal the detailed explanation of particular historical events does not mean that they do not perceive regularities that occur repeatedly in their data or attempt to formulate general rules to explain these regularities. Such efforts are the primary motives underlying the work of historians such as Spengler and Toynbee, which, however, not all historians recognize as history (Elton, 1969, 83). For the most part, professional historians tend to regard attempts to discover "historical laws" as contributions to sociology or to one of the other social sciences, rather than to history proper (Nagel, 1961, 551). This in no way denies the right of an historian simultaneously to pursue generalizing and particularizing objectives.

Current trends in history proper thus clearly reveal the irrelevance of the traditional dichotomy between history and science. Historians use social science theories to interpret the data while social scientists, in turn, use the findings of historians as one means of formulating and testing general theories. History and the social sciences are like the two sides of a coin — complementary rather than antagonistic. Under these circumstances it is difficult to maintain that the apparent distinction between science and history is equivalent to that between the sciences and the humanities. In his *The Structure of Science*, a brilliant study of the structure of scientific explanation, Nagel has broadly defined science as those activities concerned with determining and explaining relationships between objective phenomena, as opposed to those concerned with making aesthetic or moral judgments. I feel that the term humanities is best used to refer to the latter disciplines. With a definition of science that includes both ideographic and nomothetic goals, a growing number of historians are willing to regard themselves as scientists and to make use of the findings of social sciences.

Archaeology as History

It seems to me that an instructive analogy can be drawn between developments in history and in prehistory. Prehistory has never been satisfied to be merely a descriptive discipline. Prehistorians have wanted to know not only what has existed or happened in the past but also why. The desire to discern regularities was already strong in the "evolutionary archaeology" of the last century, when much research was motivated by a desire to demonstrate progress and development in the archaeological record. This search for evidence of cultural evolution in the archaeological record was in fact the application of a deductive approach to the study of prehistory on the broadest scale possible. Even if the models of cultural processes that were used in archaeology were crude and impressionistic, and placed undue emphasis on racial factors or single mechanisms of change, such as migration, the very use of such models is evidence of a desire to explain. All too often, however, as in history, these models were unconscious reflections of the popular social philosophy of the day rather than conscious efforts to explain the archaeological record on its own terms.

Moreover, in recent times the development of prehistoric archaeology has been characterized by growing interest in using models of scientific validity borrowed from the social sciences and by insisting upon theories whose validity is subject to verification through further testing. One important breakthrough in this direction came early in the history of archaeology when Thomsen and his followers rejected the antiquarian conviction that had been current prior to that time, that the ruins of the past could be adequately "explained" by determining which historically-known tribes had produced them. In place of this, Thomsen, and later Worsaae, posed the question: from what point of view can man's past best be explained, given the nature of the archaeological record? The current demand for interpretations of prehistory that are susceptible to further testing stands squarely in the Thomsen-Worsaae tradition and should not be construed as an attack upon established principles of archaeology. Value judgments and aesthetics have a place in both history and prehistory, but to be valid they must be clearly labelled as such. In both of these disciplines the search for new methods to understand the past better and the constant endeavor to distinguish fact from fiction are not professional virtues: they are duties (Carr, 1962, 5). G. M. Trevelyan recalled Carlyle's observation that the smallest real fact about the human past is more poetical than the best of poets and more romantic than the best novel (1949, xii). I personally endorse this point of view and am in full agreement with the criticisms that have been levelled against archaeologists who seek to round out their data with unwarranted speculations in a desperate effort to produce something resembling narrative history. Whatever qualities of imagination or literary skill such works possess and however much they may appeal to the public, they no more qualify as serious works of prehistory than historical fiction qualifies as history. Long-term respect is reserved for the scholar who clearly distinguishes between his interpretations and the evidence on which they are based and thereby makes clear the limits of his knowledge.

Moreover, by using explicit models and by formulating testable hypotheses, archaeologists are helping to make archaeology an experimental, albeit ideographic, discipline. Every scrap of new data that is recovered not only permits a more detailed reconstruction of the past but also serves to test explanations that have been proposed to explain earlier data. When a particular mode of explanation is found to generate explanations that consistently fail to stand up under repeated testing of this sort, the chances are that it will be abandoned or at least used with an awareness of its limitations. The declining favor with which archaeologists view migration as an over-all explanation of change in the archaeological record is one example of this (Rouse, 1958). While personal prejudice or a scientific understanding of the nature of culture will influence an archaeologist's sense of problem and his preference for particular types of explanation, no wrong, or wrongly-applied, theory can forever survive repeated testing against new archaeological data. In this sense, W. Y. Adams is right (but looking at the data-interpretation problem from only one point of view) when he states that "only solid evidence can ultimately serve as the building blocks of history" (1968, 213).

Drawing an analogy between the development of history and prehistory, one can foresee the latter continuing to evolve as a particularizing discipline that seeks to determine and explain the course of cultural development in prehistoric times in all its detail and local colors. By its very nature, this endeavor embraces the first two goals of prehistoric archaeology that we enumerated at the beginning of this article. No historian can hope to explain events in a satisfactory manner without a detailed understanding of the socio-economic milieu in which these events took place. Rebels and great men are no longer viewed by historians as operating apart from this milieu, but rather as acquiring their noteworthy characteristics in terms of it (Carr, 1962, 47). In a similar manner, if a prehistorian wishes to provide an explanation of the development of any culture, it is necessary for him to determine, as far as possible, the nature of the social and political system at successive phases in that culture's development. Only in this manner is it possible to understand the changes that take place within such systems.

Specialized techniques are now being developed for the reconstruction of various features of prehistoric cultures. While the resulting profiles are essential for historial purposes, it is clear that they may also be of non-historical value, particularly for purposes of structural comparison in social anthropology and ethnology. Despite this, the interpretative "reconstruction" of prehistoric cultures remains as integral a part of prehistory as the reconstruction of the anatomy of a dinosaur is of paleontology.

ARCHAEOLOGY IN RELATIONSHIP TO
THE SOCIAL SCIENCES

We have been arguing that a discipline of prehistoric archaeology that is ideographic, but not merely descriptive, is not only possible but has been developing successfully during the past hundred years. Generally speaking, the goal of reconstruction has always implied explanation, and, as more evidence has accumulated and the basic cultural chronology in different parts of the world has been worked out, growing attention has been paid to it. The question we must now ask is whether prehistoric archaeology, as a discipline, must choose between concentrating on historical explanation or developing a nomothetic approach in which archaeological data are used in the same manner as ethnological data to generalize about the nature of culture. Or are both of these legitimate and profitable goals within the field of archaeology?

It is at this point, I believe, that those who support historical objectives can take the offensive. Furthermore, I am convinced that only when these objectives are recognized as being the very core of prehistory will it be possible to establish the productive working relationship between archaeology and anthropology which many archaeologists are seeking. In so far as archaeology is searching to define a productive role for itself as part of a broader science of man, the question we must consider is fundamentally a heuristic one: in what way can the study of the past best serve to advance a general understanding of human behavior?

An examination of developments in the biological sciences may help to clarify matters. In the latter discipline, evolution has long been recognized as the key unifying concept, as many argue it should be in anthropology (Harris, 1968). Yet, in biology, the success of evolution seems to lie in its being more broadly defined than in anthropology, the latter having tended to equate it with ideas about progress and increasing cultural complexity. In biology the term is used in two conceptually distinct ways to refer to differing, but clearly interrelated, approaches or fields of interest (Mayr, 1963, 9).

In the first place, evolution is used to denote all the processes that effect hereditary changes in life forms, the main ones being mutation and selection. The study of evolutionary processes is clearly nomothetic, that is, it aims to formulate general laws that explain hereditary change regardless of the particular environment, period, or life form that is involved. For obvious reasons, most of the research on such processes of change is carried out on living plants and animals. The fruit fly, for example, has been an important object of study among geneticists.

Secondly, biologists use the term evolution to refer to the actual development of life forms as distinct from the processes which explain this development. This study constitutes the discipline of paleontology, which most biologists would characterize as being ideographic and historical. Paleontology examines the nature of extinct species of animals and the lines of development that link them together by means of a detailed study of fossils and their geological context.

Charles Darwin made evolution the key concept in biology when he proposed an explanation for processes of change observed among contemporary plants and animals which, if extended to the past, was also capable of explaining more adequately than any previous theory the changes that were apparent in the fossil record. The concept that linked his two lines of argument together was that of uniformitarianism: the assumption that the products of processes that went on in the past (in this case fossils) can be interpreted in terms of processes that can be observed at work at the present time. This more general use of the term uniformitarianism does not necessarily involve Lyell's further assumption that these processes need go on at the same rate at all times. The application of the concept of uniformitarianism in the field of geology had already effected a major revolution in that discipline prior to the development of Darwin's theory. Without the mechanism that Darwin formulated to explain his observations of contemporary life, the fossil record could not have been adequately explained: on the other hand, without the fossil record significant changes wrought over long periods of time by Darwin's evolutionary mechanism — including the formation of species and higher taxa — would almost certainly not have been appreciated. Both approaches had to be interrelated to generate a full-blown theory of biological evolution and they have remained interrelated ever since.

Moreover, paleontology has not ceased to be an historical discipline since Darwin's time in spite of a growing understanding of evolutionary mechanisms. Even if detailed comparative studies of living species may be able to suggest with a considerable degree of accuracy the historical relationships between these species (Sokal, 1966), proof of such relationships has to be sought in the fossil record. Likewise, it is impossible, on the basis of present conditions and biological processes alone, to "predict" in detail the nature of species that are now extinct or the particular sequence of development that these species passed through. That this is so does not reflect any specific weakness in current biological theories of process, although there are serious gaps in understanding, particularly about mutation. Instead, the situation arises because the parameters influencing the evolution of any species are so varied and so difficult to control that any substantial "prediction" of developments in the past from present-day circumstances alone is impossible. To do this, not only would numerous biological variables have to be controlled, but the biologist would also have to have at his disposal detailed information about geological, climatic, and solar conditions in the past that exceeds anything that disciplines dealing with these phenomena are able to provide. Some day enough may be known about processes in all of these fields so that it will be possible to reconstruct the past on the basis of contemporary circumstances alone. Until that day arrives, the justification of paleontology, or of any other historical discipline, remains the same: these disciplines alone can determine and explain what has actually happened in the past. The biologist

Ernst Mayr has assessed the importance of paleontology in the following terms: "If the fossil record were not available, many evolutionary problems could not be solved: indeed, many of them would not even be apparent" (1963, 11).

The structure of biology provides a model for integrating ideographic and nomothetic objectives that the archaeologist would do well to consider, and in making this suggestion I am not being reductionist. I do not advocate that anthropologists borrow ideas about process uncritically from the biological sciences; only that they consider their overall scheme of organization. The study of process in biology may be viewed as being roughly analogous to the study of innovation and adaptation in the social sciences; processes that in a broad sense embrace all of the generalizing studies of structure and function undertaken by these disciplines. By means of the generalizations arrived at in their various branches, the social sciences are hopefully advancing toward an overall understanding of sociocultural processes, and the behavior patterns underlying them, that is valid regardless of time and place.

As in biology, it is impossible to "forecast" the past retrospectively from a knowledge of the present. Even the most general trends in cultural development have been demonstrated solely on the basis of archaeological evidence. All sorts of speculations about progress were indulged in prior to the middle of the last century, but without this evidence it would have been impossible for anthropologists to prove that the most striking tendency in human development had not been one of degeneration from a higher state or a cyclical process characterized by no overall progression. An understanding of what has happened in prehistory requires the detailed recovery and explanation of the archaeological record in every part of the world. Because such an understanding can only be obtained from the archaeological record, a serious responsibility is placed upon archaeologists not to abandon historical objectives. Pursuing the analogy with paleontology, it is possible to view the study of prehistory for its own sake as one important facet of the overall study of sociocultural evolution.

The desire to make nomothetic objectives the primary goal of archaeology is rather like a biologist attempting to use the fossilized remains of *Merychippus* to study the circulation of the blood, or the skulls of juvenile and adult australopithecines to work out general principles of bone development. Both of these problems are clearly best studied on living animals in the laboratory, although the general understanding that results, will, no doubt, be useful for interpreting fossil evidence. The logic of this has long been recognized (perhaps too dogmatically) by social anthropologists, who, wishing to generalize about the nature of society, have tended to reject all but living societies as suitable objects of study. The archaeologist who is primarily interested in formulating laws about sociocultural processes might better become a social anthropologist or an ethnologist and work with existing or historically well-documented peoples rather than with the more refractory material of archaeology.

Nothing that I have noted in recent developments in prehistoric archaeology dissuades me from this opinion. Most studies aimed at explaining archaeological data either employ a direct historical approach, in which ethnographic data are projected into the past by tracing continuities and slow changes in the archaeological record (Deetz, 1965; Binford, L. R., 1967c; Longacre, 1968), or else ethnological examples are used to formulate relationships that it is hoped can later be applied to archaeological evidence (Dethlefsen and Deetz, 1966; Clarke, 1968, *passim*). Even where the problem being tackled is wholly prehistoric, the terminology and the conceptual apparatus are derived from the study of contemporary societies (Binford and Binford, 1966b; Binford, S. R., 1968), the application of which to the past appears to be primarily a process of particularization, not one that leads to the formulation of general principles.

Nor am I impressed by another argument in favor of nomothetic goals which states that certain types of society no longer exist and our understanding of cultural variation is incomplete without them. This argument rests on the questionable assumption that all types of society that have ever existed need to be known for adequate generalizations to be made. This is clearly a confusion of nomothetic and ideographic objectives. To understand the specific conditions under which various state-organized societies evolved, archaeological data are obviously required, and the more data we have the better are our opportunities for understanding various concrete sequences of development. Yet understanding these sequences is clearly different from determining the general conditions that give rise to states. The latter requires a detailed understanding of structure and function that is best derived from the thorough study of living societies, not from an interpretation of the remains of societies as preserved in the archaeological record. If one's sole aim is to generalize about the nature of states, the information contained in E. R. Leach's *Political Systems of Highland Burma* is clearly more useful than volumes of speculation about social organization in the ancient civilizations. It is illusory to regard the study of these ancient civilizations as being primarily nomothetic: although of extreme interest and importance these studies are by their very nature fundamentally ideographic.

The acceptance that tracing and explaining the actual course of cultural development in all its complexity is the fundamental aim of archaeology does not prevent the individual prehistorian from pursuing nomothetic as well as ideographic goals. Indeed, the more interested a prehistorian is in process, the better he is likely to be able to explain the past. In biology, the comparative study of the paleontological record has led to important questions being asked about rates of development and related matters, which in turn have stimulated important lines of research in genetics and other nomothetic branches of biology. We have already noted this "feedback" between nomothetic and ideographic approaches in the study of man.

Many archaeologists are interested in learning more about the past for its own sake: others wish their work to be not only of antiquarian interest but also relevant for understanding the modern world and its problems. The idea that the latter objectives can best be attained by using archaeological data to repeat the work of the nomothetic social sciences reflects a cheaply manipulative view of the social utility of learning, a view which unhappily is all too common these days. By attempting to understand and explain the past, archaeologists are contributing to human self-awareness. Indeed, who can deny that by demonstrating that man and culture evolved from humble beginnings, the archaeologists of the last century effected as revolutionary a change in man's view of himself and of his place in nature as have Copernicus, Darwin, or Freud?

CONCLUSIONS

Given a sufficiently broad and practical definition of historical research, prehistoric archaeology has an important role to play as an historical discipline within the larger framework of the sciences of man. Such a definition includes an interest in process as well as in events and chronology. The aim of any historical discipline is not only to describe but to interpret specific events. For the present at least, archaeology best fulfils its potential not by trying to duplicate work being done in the social sciences but by providing detailed information about the actual course of sociocultural development. The particularizing nature of such a task does not imply a lack of concern with theory, but indicates that within prehistory theoretical formulations should be sought to explain events rather than as ends in themselves. It is highly unlikely that archaeologists will not make comparisons and formulate general theories about process. These theories should be recognized, however, as part of the general domain of social science rather than of prehistoric archaeology as an organized discipline.

CHAPTER TWO

Strategy and Reconstruction

Sir Mortimer Wheeler

4 THE STRATEGY OF EXCAVATION

Sir Mortimer Wheeler, the doyen of Old World field archaeologists, has done more than anyone to introduce meticulous standards of excavating. In this classic passage on the strategy of excavation, he discusses the evidence to be obtained by vertical and horizontal trenching, two basic approaches to site investigation consciously or unconsciously used by archaeologists all over the world. Most of Wheeler's sites were large ones, excavated with major facilities, but his techniques are applicable to all sizes of prehistoric settlement. The meticulous excavation of archaeological sites is central to Wheeler's philosophy of archaeology, for he constantly stresses that all excavation is destruction. No one can check the results obtained from an excavation because in digging a site one destroys much of the archives of archaeology — the layers and the contexts in which the artifacts found in a settlement are buried. And an artifact without a context is virtually useless as a source of archaeological information. Wheeler's remarks on archaeological strategy are fundamental to all excavation.

. . . From time to time the question arises: shall stress be laid (in some particular program of work) upon horizontal or upon vertical excavation? By "horizontal excavation" is meant the uncovering of the whole or a large part of a specific phase in the occupation of an ancient site, in order to

From Sir Mortimer Wheeler, *Archaeology from the Earth,* © 1954 Oxford University Press. Reprinted by permission of the author and The Clarendon Press, Oxford. Photographs courtesy of Sir Mortimer Wheeler and the Society of Antiquaries of London.

reveal fully its layout and function. By "vertical excavation" is meant the excavation of a restructed area *in depth*, with a view to ascertaining the succession of cultures or of phases and so producing a time-scale or culture-scale for the site. The two procedures are of course complementary, not antagonistic, and the excavator may be expected to attempt, if rarely to achieve, both methods of approach. But in a great majority of instances, a priority has to be determined, having regard to the state of current knowledge and the resources available.

Let us consider the nature of the evidence which the two methods may be expected to supply. Vertical excavation alone, while supplying a key to the length of an occupation, to its continuity or intermittency, and to some part of its cultural equipment, cannot be expected to reveal save in the most scrappy fashion the significant environment — economic, religious, administrative — of a human society. In other words, it leaves us in the dark as to those very factors which fit a past culture or civilization into the story of human endeavor and so make its recovery worthwhile. It is the railway time-table without a train. On the other hand, the extensive horizontal excavations which were in effect the normal practice before stratification was adequately understood generally produced an abstraction — often a very confused and misleading abstraction — unrelated with any sort of precision to the sequence of human development. They were trains without a time-table. The trains sometimes ran vigorously enough, but we knew not when they were running or where they started, or their intermediate stopping-places, or their destination.

At certain stages of research both these incomplete methods may have a substantive value; indeed, they are themselves stages in the progress of research. I am not, for example, of those who scorn the horizontal excavation (in the nineties) of the Roman town of Silchester. True it was dug like potatoes, without a shadow of the scientific nicety of the contemporary excavations in Cranborne Chase; and the resultant plan is the uncritical synthesis of a varying urban development through more than three centuries. But it gave at once, and with a rough accuracy, the general impression of a Romano-British town such as fifty years of subsequent and often more careful work have failed to equal. More exact vertical and horizontal digging on both this and other similar sites has indeed begun to reveal the sociological evolution essential to our historical perspective; but who among these later and wiser excavators has not constantly referred back with profit to the crude, primitive assemblage of Silchester?

So also elsewhere. The Glastonbury lake-village, excavated uncritically with results that are often infuriatingly baffling, has nevertheless given us the complete layout of a small Early Iron Age settlement and so enabled us to assess in broad terms the social and economic significance of such a settlement as no exacting and partial probing could have rendered possible. For that, even in moments when the evidence in detail completely fails

Figure 1   Vertical excavation — Maiden Castle, England.

us, we may be properly thankful. And let us for a moment look further
afield. One of the most dramatic and revealing of all excavated cities is
prehistoric Mohenjo-daro, beside the Indus in Pakistan. Technically the
methods adopted by a succession of excavators there became almost an
international scandal, and neither Professor Piggott nor I have been at

pains to spare the lash. But the primary marvel of the great Indus city is not that it did (or did not) develop in such-and-such a fashion between, let us say, 2500 and 1500 B.C., *but that it existed at all* in the remarkable form that extensive, if disproportionately summary, excavation has revealed to us. Its house-walls, towering accumulatively above our heads, its long straight streets, its lanes, its elaborate drainage system, its citadel — these and other things in bulk re-create a whole phase of human society even though in detail they fail to analyze it for us. Analysis — by careful vertical digging — should, of course, have accompanied all this summary horizontal clearance; but there can be no question that Mohenjo-daro takes its place as the representative of one of the great civilizations of the ancient world in some measure by virtue of the crimes of its explorers.

And since we have arrived in Pakistan, let us take again one more familiar example from that land. For a thousand years the city of Taxila stood upon successive sites in the northern Punjab, and one of these sites, of the first centuries B.C.–A.D., was extensively cleared by Sir John Marshall so that a considerable portion of a remarkable rectangular town-plan was ultimately revealed. The clearance did not conform with modern technical standards, and in fact more than one phase is represented without discrimination in the published plan. Nevertheless, the outstanding interest of Parthian Taxila is the general character of its buildings and their relation to a street-grid without known analogy in this part of Asia. Had the

Figure 2   Horizontal or grid excavation — Maiden Castle, England.

excavator concentrated on vertical digging on this deep site he would have given us valuable information for which we are still waiting; but he could scarcely have given us also the picture which we owe to him of a teeming city with its streets and temples, its palaces, and its shops. He would have given us a useful catalogue but not, as in fact he has, a vivid chapter of social history.

The four examples of horizontal digging which I have given — Silchester, Glastonbury, Mohenjo-daro, and Taxila (Sirkap) — are not very happy in that none of them was excavated with adequate skill. Technically, they all belong to the pre-Pitt-Rivers era, though Pitt-Rivers had in fact established his methods before any of them began. Needless to say, it must not be inferred that horizontal excavation is necessarily summary and unscientific! Ideally, the excavation of a town-site would begin with vertical digging, sufficient to establish the time- or culture-sequence, and would proceed to the careful horizontal digging of successive phases, one at a time. Obviously the process cannot be reversed, and at the three sites mentioned, only the careful vertical excavation of areas not yet touched can partially replace the squandered evidence. A better example of horizontal excavation on a small scale is provided by Little Woodbury near Salisbury, where Dr. Gerhard Bersu cleared the greater part of an Iron Age farmstead and was able to reconstruct both its architecture and its economy. The site was a shallow one, and the technical problem was incomparably simpler than on a deeply accumulative town-site; nevertheless, it is chastening to reflect how little of the real meaning of Little Woodbury could have been re-covered merely by vertical samples of it.

With the proviso, then, that all horizontal digging must proceed from clear and comprehensive vertical sections, the question of priority is fundamentally not in doubt. Careful horizontal digging can alone, in the long run, give us the full information that we ideally want. Vertical digging will, by itself, serve a valuable purpose in establishing the geographical distribution of a culture and its time-relationship with other cultures from place to place; but this evidence still derives its ultimate significance from a knowledge of the social environment of the cultures concerned. . . .

Sir Mortimer Wheeler

5 A PREHISTORIC BATTLE

The reconstruction of the past from archaeological data requires
imagination, insight, and sound excavation techniques combined with
sound strategy and impeccable recording. Maiden Castle is an Iron
Age hill-fort in southern England that was sacked by the Romans in
the first century A.D. Sir Mortimer Wheeler portrayed the sacking of
this settlement in great detail by using skillful inference from
archaeological data. As he documents the last hours of a long-
established fortress, his vivid description brings the siege of the
hill-fort to life. This classic example of using small finds to reconstruct the past logically applies the principles of research strategy
enumerated by Wheeler in the previous selection. His picture of the
battle of Maiden Castle is descriptive archaeology at its best. Notice
how each piece of archaeological evidence fits into a pattern to
portray the last minutes of the assault.

THE EARLY ROMAN PERIOD (c. A.D. 43–70)

And so we reach the Roman invasion of A.D. 43. That part of the army
of conquest wherewith we are concerned in Dorset had as its nucleus the
Second Augustan Legion, whose commander, at any rate in the earlier
campaigns, was the future Emperor Vespasian. Precisely how soon the
invaders reached Maiden Castle can only be guessed, but by A.D. 47 the
Roman arms had reached the Severn, and Dorset must already have been
overrun. Suetonius affirms that Vespasian reduced "two very formidable
tribes and over twenty towns (*oppida*), together with the Isle of Wight,"
and it cannot be doubted that, whether or no the Durotriges (as is likely
enough) were one of the tribes in question, the conquest of the Wessex
hill-fort system is implied in the general statement. Nor is it improbable
that, with the hints provided by the mention of the Isle of Wight and by
the archaeological evidence for the subsequent presence of the Second
Legion near Seaton in eastern Devon, a main line of advance lay through
Dorset roughly along the route subsequently followed by the Roman road
to Exeter. From that road today the traveller regards the terraced ramparts
of the western entrance of Maiden Castle; and it requires no great effort
of the imagination to conjure up the ghost of Vespasian himself, here confronted with the greatest of his "twenty towns." Indeed, something less

From *Maiden Castle* by Sir Mortimer Wheeler, Society of Antiquaries of London
(1943), pp. 61–68. Reprinted by permission of the author and the Society of Antiquaries.
Footnotes and references are omitted.

than imagination is now required to reconstruct the main sequence of events at the storming of Maiden Castle, for the excavation of the eastern entrance has yielded tangible evidence of it. With only a little amplification it may be reconstructed as follows.

Approaching from the direction of the Isle of Wight, Vespasian's legion may be supposed to have crossed the River Frome at the only easy crossing hereabouts — where Roman and modern Dorchester were subsequently to come into being. Before the advancing troops, some 2 miles away, the sevenfold ramparts of the western gates of Dunium towered above the cornfields which probably swept, like their modern successors, up to the fringe of the defenses. Whether any sort of assault was attempted upon these gates we do not at present know; their excessive strength makes it more likely that, leaving a guard upon them, Vespasian moved his main attack to the somewhat less formidable eastern end. What happened there is plain to read. First, the regiment of artillery, which normally accompanied a legion on campaign, was ordered into action, and put down a barrage of iron-shod ballista-arrows over the eastern part of the site. Following this barrage, the infantry advanced up the slope, cutting its way from rampart to rampart, tower to tower. In the innermost bay of the entrance, close outside the actual gates, a number of huts had recently been built; these were now set alight, and under the rising clouds of smoke the gates were stormed and the position carried. But resistance had been obstinate and the fury of the attackers was roused. For a space, confusion and massacre dominated the scene. Men and women, young and old, were savagely cut down, before the legionaries were called to heel and the work of systematic destruction began. That work included the uprooting of some at least of the timbers which revetted the fighting-platform on the summit of the main rampart; but above all it consisted of the demolition of the gates and the overthrow of the high stone walls which flanked the two portals. The walls were now reduced to the lowly and ruinous state in which they were discovered by the excavator nearly nineteen centuries later.

That night, when the fires of the legion shone out (we may imagine) in orderly lines across the valley, the survivors crept forth from their broken stronghold and, in the darkness, buried their dead as nearly as might be outside their tumbled gates, in that place where the ashes of their burned huts lay warm and thick upon the ground. The task was carried out anxiously and hastily and without order, but, even so, from few graves were omitted those tributes of food and drink which were the proper and traditional perquisites of the dead. At daylight on the morrow, the legion moved westward to fresh conquest, doubtless taking with it the usual levy of hostages from the vanquished.

Thereafter, salving what they could of their crops and herds, the disarmed townsfolk made shift to put their house in order. Forbidden to refortify their gates, they built new roadways across the sprawling ruins, between gateless ramparts that were already fast assuming the blunted profiles that are theirs today. And so, for some two decades, a demilitarized Maiden Castle retained its inhabitants, or at least a nucleus of them. Just so long did it take the Roman authorities to adjust the old order to the new, to prepare new towns for old. And then finally, on some day toward the close of the sixties of the century, the town was ceremoniously abandoned, its remaining walls were formally "slighted," and Maiden Castle lapsed into the landscape among the farm-lands of Roman Dorchester.

So much for the story; now for its basis. First, scattered over the eastern end of Maiden Castle, mostly in and about the eastern entrance and always at the same Romano-Belgic level, were found upward of a dozen iron arrowheads of two types: a type with a pyramidal point, and the simple flat-bladed type with turn-over socket. Arrowheads occurred at no other Iron Age level, but both types are common on Roman military sites where *ballistae* but not hand-bows are to be inferred. There, then, in the relatively small area uncovered, are the vestiges of the bombardment.

Secondly, the half-moon bay which represents the Iron Age B adaptation of the Iron Age A barbican, close outside the portals of the eastern entrance, was covered with a thick layer of ash associated with the post-holes of three or more circular or roundish huts. In and immediately below this ash were quantities of late Belgic or "Belgicizing" pottery. In the surface of the ash was similar pottery with scraps of pre-Flavian Samian. There are the burned Belgic huts, covered by the trodden vestiges of the continued post-conquest occupation for which more tangible evidence will be offered shortly.

Thirdly, into this ash a series of graves had been roughly cut, with no regularity either of outline or of orientation, and into them had been thrown, in all manner of attitudes — crouched, extended, on the back, on the side, on the face, even sitting up — thirty-eight skeletons of men and women, young and old; sometimes two persons were huddled together in the same grave. In ten cases extensive cuts were present on the skull, some on the top, some on the front, some on the back. In another case, one of the arrowheads already described was found actually embedded in the vertebra, having entered the body from the front below the heart. The victim had been finished off with a cut on the head. Yet another skull had been pierced by an implement of square section, probably a ballista-bolt. The last two and some of the sword-cuts were doubtless battle-wounds; but one skull, which had received no less than nine savage cuts, suggests the fury of massacre rather than the tumult of battle — a man does not stay to kill his enemy eight or nine times in the melee; and the neck of another skeleton had been dislocated, probably by hanging. Nevertheless, the dead had been buried by their friends, for most of them were accompanied by bowls or, in one case, a mug for the traditional food and drink. More notable, in two cases the dead held joints of lamb in their hands — joints chosen carefully as young and succulent. Many of the dead still wore their gear: armlets of iron or shale, an iron finger-ring, and in three cases bronze toe-rings, representing a custom not previously, it seems, observed in prehistoric Britain but reminiscent of the Moslem habit of wearing toe-rings as ornaments or as preventives or cures of disease. One man lay in a double grave with an iron battle-axe, a knife, and, strangely, a bronze ear-pick across his chest. The whole war cemetery as it lay exposed before us was eloquent of mingled piety and distraction; of weariness, of dread, of darkness, but yet not of complete forgetfulness. Surely no poor relic in the soil of Britain was ever more eloquent of high tragedy, more worthy of brooding comment from the presiding Spirits of Hardy's own *Dynasts*.

The date of the cemetery was indicated by a variety of evidence. Most obvious is the Roman arrowhead embedded in the vertebra, but other associated relics point to the same conclusion. The seventeen pots put into the graves at the time of burial are all of that Wessex "Romano-Belgic overlap" class which has long been recognized at Jordan Hill, Weymouth, and elsewhere. The gear with one of the skeletons included, as has been remarked above, a Roman "ear-scoop," the use of which may or may not have been understood more clearly by its Belgic possessor than by the modern antiquary; at least it implies Roman contacts which, in Wessex, appear not long to have anticipated the Roman Conquest. One grave, moreover, contained a late British coin, and though it was impossible to say safely whether the coin was inserted at the interment or was incorporated in the loose ash into which the grave was cut, at least it was dropped within a very short time of the event. And finally, the materials included in the strata which "bracket" the cemetery are themselves, as noted above, sufficient to indicate a date at the end of the pre-Conquest period.

There, then, is the climax of the more human side of the story of conquest. But on the structural side the evidence for that event and for its sequel is no less vivid. On the topmost Belgic road-metal, in both portals of the eastern entrance but particularly in the southern, excavation revealed the tumbled stones from the massive walls that had formerly flanked the entrances. Here and there the fallen stones lay overlapping, like a collapsed pack of cards, in the sequence in which they had formerly stood as a vertical wall. With them was no cascade of rampart-earth such as might have implied a fall through subsidence, even could one presuppose the coincidence of the simultaneous fall of every part of the structure; the walls had been deliberately pulled down and no attempt had been made to replace them. But that was not all. Over the debris in each portal a new road had been built, metalled like the Belgic roads now buried beneath them. The new roads partially covered the surviving bases of the flanking walls, showing that the condition of these today is identical with their condition at the time of the road-building and confirming the permanence of the structural ruin. No provision of any kind was made in the new scheme for a gate; not a single post-hole was associated with the new road, and indeed the mutilated rampart-ends would have provided a poor setting for a fixed barrier. The implications of all this are evident. The entrance had been systematically "slighted" and its military value reduced permanently to a minimum; but traffic through it did not cease, no interval occurred in the continuity of the occupation.

That this dramatic episode should be ascribed to the Roman invader is proved by a liberal supply of associated evidence. The road-surface underlying the tumbled sidewalls in each portal is the last of a series of three or more which are all interleaved with British coins of the late "south-western" type, and with the coins were Belgic or cross-bred "BC" sherds, and fragments of Roman amphorae. Samian pottery was not found in these levels. On the other hand, in and on and beside the new road-surface which was laid down *over* the fallen walls, Samian sherds began to occur with some freedom. Where identifiable, these sherds are mainly of pre-Flavian type or fabric, and, in the whole of the eastern entrance, only *two* Samian sherds (both of them from the surface-soil) are later than the Flavian period. A detailed analysis, by Dr. T. Davies Pryce and Mr. J. A. Stanfield, ... may here be summarized ... :

Samian sherds from the eastern entrance
Datable fragments are assignable as follows:

To the pre-Flavian period	45
To the Nero-Vespasian period	9
To the Flavian period	4
To the Antonine period	2

Many small fragments, which do not admit of approximate dating, appear to be pre-Flavian.

Dr. Pryce concludes that the Samian from the entrance "indicates a definite occupation in the pre-Flavian period. The evidence for its continuation into the Flavian period is slight." It should be emphasized that seventeen of these Samian sherds, all ascribed by Dr. Pryce to the time of Claudius and Nero, were found embedded either in the road-metal of the new road in the southern portal (where the structural evidence was clearest) or in the layer of trodden mud upon its surface. On the other hand, the two Antonine sherds were both, as already remarked, in mixed topsoil.

Two conclusions emerge from this structural and ceramic evidence. First, the destruction of the sidewalls of the entrance occurs exactly between the Belgic and the Claudian occupation of the site: i.e., at the moment of the Roman invasion. Secondly, the occupation of the site continued, in spite of this interruption, to the beginning of the Flavian period, i.e., to

c. A.D. 70, whereafter a break supervened. Other evidence amplifies this result.

A test-section cut through the rampart between the portals of the entrance revealed one of the large post-holes of the Belgic palisade or revetment. The post, like its equivalents on site E, had been about a foot in diameter, and its socket was 4 ft. deep. At a depth of 2 ft. in the filling of the socket (and 4 ft. from the present surface) occurred a Samian sherd of distinctively early fabric, and in the same filling were two bronze scales of a Roman cuirass. These objects indicate that the socket was empty in early Roman times, and the complete uniformity of the filling indicates rather the uprooting of the post than its gradual decay. There is at least a strong probability that the slighting of the entrance was accompanied by a removal of the stockade along the rampart.

... The sherds ... from the main occupation may be considered in summary here.... On this site, the thick layer of Belgic occupation passed, without structural division, into the early Roman, and its topmost portion contained Samian pottery. This has been examined by Dr. Pryce, who reports that every sherd is Flavian or pre-Flavian, with a strong predominance of the latter: the evidence for occupation actually within the Flavian period is "very meagre." In other words, the evidence here — and, it may be added, elsewhere in Maiden Castle — tallies exactly with that of the eastern entrance.

The picture is now complete in outline. Disarmed at the Roman Conquest, Maiden Castle remained in use for about a quarter of a century after the invasion, a pre-Roman city still in all essentials, partaking only a little of the cultural equipment of its conquerors. The picture is a reasonable and convincing one. The first generation of Roman rule was preoccupied with the subjugation of the difficult hill-countries of the north and west, with the development of mining areas, the planning of arterial roads, the founding or development of those few towns which had an immediate military or commercial function. Dorset offered, it is true, iron ore on a modest scale; but between Sussex and the Mendips there was little mineral wealth to attract the Roman prospector in the first flush of conquest. Wessex could wait. There was no urgent need to upset the traditional economic basis of the urbanized peasantry which crowded the downlands. To do so would have been to court added political difficulties at a time when difficulties were already manifold. It was better that, under surveillance, the Wessex farmers should for a time (and doubtless in return for the periodical payment of just or unjust dues) be allowed to maintain themselves in the fashion which they knew. The removal or, alternatively, the ennoblement of their rulers would rob them of independent leadership. A few police-patrols would do the rest.

Here, too, the evidence fits comfortably into place. The famous little Roman fort set in a corner of the Iron Age town on Hod Hill near Blandford — some 20 miles from Maiden Castle — has not been scientifically excavated, but pottery and other objects have been recovered at various times from it or its immediate vicinity. This material includes many Roman weapons and some Samian pottery dating from the time of Claudius and Nero. The occupation, in other words, was something more than transitory, and would appear to have lasted approximately from the time of the Roman invasion to c. A.D. 60 or a little later. With this supposition the comparatively elaborate plan of the Roman earthwork agrees: it is not that of a mere "marching camp," but rather that of a "semi-permanent" work possessing some of the attributes of a permanent fort. At its strategic point above the valley of the Stour, this little Roman hill-fort was a fitting center for the policing of a part of the native hill-town region during the interval between conquest and romanization.

The period of guarded *status quo* came to an end, it seems, in the reign of the actual conqueror of Maiden Castle. Under Vespasian and Domitian, notably in the governorship of Agricola, the systematic development of the civil life of Roman Britain was at last undertaken throughout the lowland region. Hitherto such development had been in a large measure opportunist; it now became an avowed part of the official policy for the final and complete subjugation of the provincials. Towns were rebuilt in the comfortable Roman fashion or were newly founded; and among the new foundations — if the available evidence is representative — would appear to have been Dorchester, Durnonovaria or Durnovaria of the Itinerary. Of seventy-five Samian sherds from Dorchester, examined by Dr. Pryce in the Dorchester Museum, four or less are likely to be earlier than Vespasian. The proportions of early and late sherds, on a comparison of the groups from Dorchester with those from the main occupation of Maiden Castle, are thus approximately reversed; and, on the evidence, it may be affirmed provisionally that the occupation of the two sites is complementary. Dorchester begins where Maiden Castle ceases, i.e., c. A.D. 70. The sequence is doubtless significant. In Gaul under Augustus the process of romanization had entailed the removal of the more inaccessible hill-populations to new Roman cities founded under official auspices in the valleys. In Britain it is reasonable to suppose that, in the equivalent regime of the Flavians, a similar procedure was followed: that Flavian Caerwent, for example, became the Roman focus for the little native towns of Llanmelin and Sudbrook, that Uriconium was (then if not earlier) the heir of the *oppidum* on the Wrekin, and similarly that Roman Dorchester inherited something of the population and prestige of Maiden Castle. Certain it is, at least, that after the beginning of the Flavian period the eastern entrance of Maiden Castle fell into disuse. A layer of humus 7–9 in. deep was found to overlie the early Roman road-surfaces, implying that the site was, at the end of the first century A.D., as overgrown as in modern times.

When we come to examine the final phase of Maiden Castle, it will be seen that this layer of barren mold intervenes between the first- and the fourth-century levels, so that its context is not open to doubt. In the second and third centuries A.D. Maiden Castle had reverted to downland or to tillage.

Of the actual moment of the official abandonment of the site, a vestige may indeed be recognized with some probability at the fruitful eastern entrance. Reference has been made in a preceding section to the stone-faced platform or bastion on the western flank of the southern causeway cut through the original barbican in phase IV (c. end of first century B.C. or beginning of first century A.D.). As excavated in 1936, this revetment was preserved to a maximum height of five courses; but the remainder of the wall still lay piled up alongside, upon the metalling of the roadway. The evidence compelled certain inferences:

(i) The wall had been *deliberately* pulled away from the bank which it revetted, for the bank itself stood firm and had not fallen forward with the masonry, as would have been the case if the latter had been thrust outward by pressure from the bank.

(ii) The wall had not been demolished for the reuse of its stonework, since the fallen stones lay untouched where they had fallen.

(iii) The fallen stones lay on, and in contact with, the actual metalling of the road: i.e., they had fallen when the road was still in use and unencumbered with the covering of wind-blown earth which (as experience shows) accumulates within a month on exposed surfaces at Maiden Castle.

(iv) Both the road and the adjacent city went out of use immediately after the fall, since the debris blocked a good half of the roadway and — an important point on a stoneless site where stone is proportionately valuable — had not been appreciably plundered for its useful building-material.

It is fair to infer that this important and striking structural feature of the entrance had been "slighted" deliberately at the precise moment when the population was finally moved down from the ancient city to the new Roman town which must now have been prepared in the valley below. It is not difficult to imagine something of the pomp and circumstance with which this revolutionary incident in the history of the region was carried out — the solemn procession of civic and religious authorities, perhaps with some rather anxiously important emissary of the provincial government in attendance; and the ultimate ceremonial defacement of a work which had already, a generation previously, received its first and more drastic disarming at the moment of conquest — the earlier slighting carried out, perhaps, at the actual order of Vespasian, commander of the Second Legion, and the later slighting under the remote eye of Vespasian, now emperor of Rome.

Robert McC. Adams

6 ARCHAEOLOGICAL RESEARCH STRATEGIES

Robert McC. Adams has for many years worked in Near Eastern archaeology, principally on the origins of urban life. The article that follows is a statement about research strategies in general, which carries on where Wheeler stops. Adams looks at the relationship between archaeology and the natural sciences and describes some ways in which archaeologists have moved toward a greater reliance on scientific methods and strategies. His view of strategy is wider than Wheeler's; he argues that archaeologists have been reluctant to tackle what he calls "grand problems of comparison, generalization, and synthesis." Most archaeological work in the field remains descriptive and little concerned with the causes of events in prehistory. Cultural process and the necessity for rigorous sampling of archaeological sites are forgotten in the urge to exacavate an arbitrarily chosen site that may or may not answer the questions about a particular area or a research problem carefully formulated in the laboratory.

Archaeology, in the minds of most laymen, probably has two aspects. One involves explorations in exotic lands — sun and sand, the menace of wild tribesmen, the lure of treasures from the East. The other involves the painstaking excavation, restoration, and display of individual antiquities that are thought to be the primary focus of study — a kind of philately of art styles or material objects abstracted from their cultural surroundings and handsomely illustrated on quarto volume plates or placed in museum cases.

At first glance, neither of these images of archaeology has much to do with prevailing concepts of scientific research as they are usually formulated with especial reference to the natural sciences. Instead, both seem to stress a subjective quality of scholarship — beginning with the inexplicable act of discovery beneath the sand and then proceeding almost mystically from physical description to intuitive reconstruction of forgotten historical events. Any attempt to wrest meaning from broken, unrecognizable artifacts seems, after all, to partake more of imagination than of plausibility. In fact, this is almost the direct antithesis of laboratory-generated procedures involving the inductive fashioning of explanatory hypotheses and then rigorous empirical testing.

Reprinted from Robert McC. Adams, "Archaeological Research Strategies: Past and Present," *Science* 160 (June 14, 1968): 1187–1192. Copyright 1968 by the American Association for the Advancement of Science. References are omitted.

Now that science is in the ascendancy, and the expansion of research frontiers into interstellar space and subatomic structure are proclaimed virtually as national goals, archaeology nonetheless thrives as never before. Paperback books, popular articles, and news media communicate even quite specialized or rather doubtful findings of archaeological research to an ever larger public; the number of recognized practitioners of the subject climbs at every professional meeting; and the scale and diversity of archaeological undertakings mounts steadily. In a recent article the director of the University Museum in Philadelphia (one of the outstanding institutions in the field) speaks of "the archeology explosion." Why is this? Is the growth of the field a mere epiphenomenon of the powerful forward surge of research in the natural sciences? Is it a consequence of international attempts to solve balance of payments problems by attracting growing numbers of tourists to newly opened archaeological monuments and museums? Worse still, is it possible that man's increasing interest in the unearthing of his past is an outgrowth of increasing uncertainties over his future — that archaeology has prospered because it panders to a prevailing mood of escapism?

To some degree, all of these possibilities may be true. But the deeper truth is that the scientific dimensions of archaeology have grown most rapidly. Although the process is disorderly and controversial at many points, profound changes can be discerned not only in immediate research strategies but also in underlying structures of thought. This is less an explosion than a revolution in the sense that it is a broad shift from one paradigm to another not unlike the shifts which Thomas S. Kuhn has metaphorically outlined for the history of physics. In any case, the major current changes offer parallels with many disciplines in the natural sciences. In choosing to discuss them, I am perhaps throwing another slender bridge across the void between the hard and soft sciences, or even between the sciences and the humanities. We all deplore this void; I attempt to span it because frequently we may overestimate its breadth and importance.

A brief description of the earlier stages in the maturation of archaeology as a discipline may help to clarify the issues in dispute at the present turning point. As the field emerged, one concern was the confirmation of its basic stratigraphic assumptions. Exploration in its own right was equally important, at least until the maps of empty continents began to fill with archaeological discoveries. Some geographical voids still remain, but the once commanding appeal of exploration has cumulatively been reduced to a secondary level. The last lost civilization was brought to light in the Indus Valley during the 1920's. It can reasonably be said that no unsuspected discovery of like magnitude awaits the spade of any future digger.

In addition to purely exploratory and methodological concerns, several other themes dominated early work. Viewed retrospectively, the most repugnant was an often highly competitive interest on the part of the major museums in excavating or otherwise acquiring beautiful objects with a minimum of supervision or record keeping. Such activities are now prevented by law in most countries — the United States is not one of them — but the two generations or so that have elapsed since the end of that era of pillaging have not erased its memory in much of the underdeveloped world.

Another major concern was the verification and amplification of written records that play a central role in our cultural heritage. Schliemann's work at Troy falls into this category; so also does the heavy concentration on biblical sites in Palestine. This objective persists, although tempered by increasing cautiousness in interpretation and much reduced in relative importance. So also, more regrettably, does a preoccupation with seeking origins. The quest for origins has contributed very little of scholarly importance, but continues to be encouraged by the distorted values that the news media attach to what is first.

This heterogeneous assortment of initial objectives reflects the diversity in modes of thought among those who, in the latter part of the 19th century, called themselves archaeologists. Recent work in the history of ideas is making us increasingly aware of the degree to which the intellectual paternity we proclaim for ourselves today often has more in common with the origin myths of primitive peoples recorded by anthropologists than with the actual roots which nourished our contemporary academic disciplines. Nevertheless, two partially distinct paths of development may be traced well into the past. The first to take shape involved the rediscovery of the classical world as a complex, viable, and aesthetically pleasing civilization that yet was culturally distinct, pagan, and temporally remote. This brought together almost from the beginning the private collector, the historian of art, and the philologist. The acquisition of monuments through excavations stimulated the formation of an objective, external view of entities like style and culture.

The other intellectual taproot of archaeology led largely through the terrain of the natural sciences. It probably began in the 18th century, with the uniformitarian assertions that the earth's surface should be regarded as a system of matter in motion over immensely long time periods. Later this was linked with speculations on natural selection and evolution in the biological world, and ultimately with Darwin's classic synthesis. Of course, the separation we draw retrospectively between these two sources of ideas may be somewhat artificial. Only as scholarship became a specialized, university-based activity, in the later 19th century, did the outward form of archaeological reports in both categories cease to be that of a description of travels that could appeal to a wide audience.

With the shift in focus of activity from private travelers and collectors, to public museums, and finally to university departments, began the bifurcation of the field that continues today. At least in the United States, all of prehistory and all of the aboriginal New World fell within the province of anthropology, a discipline in the generalizing, comparative tradition of the social sciences. Each of the literate civilizations of the Old World, in distinction, became the province of a more specialized, humanistic tradition of study in which archaeological interests generally have been secondary to those of documentary historians and philologists. Even though a few individuals manage to keep an uneasy foot in each camp, the division is nonetheless deep and genuine. This makes the task of speaking of the field as a whole considerably more difficult. Since most of the visible ferment has at least originated in the domain of the anthropologists, one is justified in placing major emphasis there.

The next broad stage in the growth of archaeology involved a virtual preoccupation with systematics. The guiding assumption was that styles uniformly followed a curve of normal distribution, changing gradually in both time and space, so that a plotting of the distribution of formal similarities in time and space would provide a reliable index of cultural and historical relationships. Consciously conducted, empirical tests of this assumption have been conspicuous by their absence; it supplied the seemingly self-evident paradigm of normal science by which alone a pattern of order and significance could be imposed on increasing masses of descriptive data. The main objectives of new research became the extension and progressive refinement of chronological charts showing the succession and distribution of clusters of formal similarities in artifacts that were called "cultures." Except in the hands of a few vigorous theorists of the time like V. Gordon Childe, interpretation was generally confined to descriptions of changing architectural and artifact inventories at individual sites, and to assessments of trade, migration, and culture contact that could be deduced from formal similarities linking different sites.

With due allowance for obvious regional variability, this was roughly the state of affairs at the time of the long hiatus that the second world war induced in fieldwork. In spite of the small number of institutions actively involved, there had been some impressive accomplishments. Leaving aside substantive discoveries, a number of classic monographs had been published by meticulous excavators, or soon would be finished on the basis of materials already in hand. Imposing standards of excavation technique and descriptive analysis had been erected, in other words, against which archaeological undertakings everywhere were increasingly subject to critical comparison. A systematic framework of temporal and spatial distributions had been at least roughed out for most areas and in some had been highly refined. Without such a framework, the more analytic, causally oriented approaches of more recent decades never could have been initiated. Nevertheless, we can best describe and evaluate present trends in the field not as they have built continuously upon this underlying body of methods and assumptions but as they have radically enlarged it and even departed from it.

Of the greatest importance has been the elaboration of an emphasis on an ecological approach. Descriptive statements on climate and environment already were included in some traditional site reports, but now the questions asked and the methods followed bear little resemblance to this prototype. What is seen as crucially important for study is no longer some uniform, predetermined set of obvious environmental features but the points of articulation between the subsistence activities of a particular human group and the wider natural and social setting within which it operated. The focus of concern, then, is the shifting, complex set of adaptive responses which must characterize any community, ancient or modern, and which in turn can help to explain the changes it undergoes through time. Average annual rainfall, for example, is an obvious and once frequently cited statistic which now is seldom regarded as important. What counts more is the reliability of its onset and periodicity during the growing season, the frequency with which it fails to meet the minimum needs of cultivation, or the destructive intensity of the storms in which it falls. Factors like these are critical in explaining changing subsistence productivities and hence also many related sociocultural changing features including patterns of settlement. As often as not, a perceptive assessment of the setting of an archaeological site along such lines goes far beyond even the best contemporary data gathered for other purposes, and requires the gathering of additional data as a part of the archaeological project itself.

Rainfall is only one among a very large number of features which might be used as an example. The trend has been toward reliance on greater and greater numbers of converging lines of evidence for both ancient and modern environments — soils, bones, pollen, geomorphology — in order to discover unsuspected cultural variables, to reduce ambiguities in interpretation, and to deal with the interlocking effects of the widest possible range of adaptive relationships. This in turn requires other reorientations, principally in the training of students and in the increased funding of projects. In some of the most important and productive undertakings of recent years, such as those concerned with the locally differentiated processes by which plants and animals were independently domesticated in the Old and New worlds soon after the end of the Pleistocene, the greater part of the effort and expense has been directed at the analysis of ecological variables rather than at all of the traditional classes of archaeological findings taken together.

The immense broadening of effort that an ecological approach requires has altered the social milieu of the research itself. The organizational model increasingly being followed is not dissimilar in some ways to that of the physical sciences. Groups of collaborators form, whether on one faculty or several, and institutionalize their relations in a variety of ways. Unlike the very large research groups currently active in physics, however, such groups in archaeology still remain characteristically fluid in internal structure and egalitarian in outlook; a serious deficiency is that these groups do not have long-term support from technicians. The groups are not tied to particular laboratories or to expensive equipment like particle accelerators, but they are constrained by equally effective geographical limits. Long experience in an area is almost a necessity in fashioning a valid ecological approach, and in the case of work overseas one must add to this the need for linguistic competence and for a wide knowledge of administrative procedures and political realities within a host country. Moreover, these groups also generally tend to work within the bounds of a particular focal problem, probably in large part because of close operating relationships with natural scientists whose contributions are most appropriate for those problems. Natural scientists, in fact, form a major component of such groups. However, since the core problems remain those of understanding changes in human culture, the responsibilities for direction, coordination, synthesis, and fund raising generally remain with the archaeologist.

The increasing emphasis on an ecological approach also is related to a growing dissatisfaction with narration or description for its own sake. This has brought in its wake a correspondingly heightened interest in seeking causal explanations of a deterministic character, and such explanations usually have stressed ecological factors. At the extreme, it has been suggested that environmental differences are virtually the only explanation of cultural differences, aside from periodic quantum jumps in the availability of nonhuman energy resulting from the growth of technology. More persuasive, although less sweeping, is the position taken on this question by a coherent, highly innovative group of "new" or "process-oriented" archaeologists, one of whose number recently formulated it as follows.

> ... [T]he process school would like to move crucial decisions ... farther from the individual by arguing that systems, once set in motion, are self-regulating to the point where they do not even necessarily allow rejection or acceptance of new traits by a culture. Once a system has moved in a certain direction, it automatically sets up the limited range of possible moves it can make at the next critical turning point. This view is not original with the process-school archeologists — it is borrowed from Ludwig von Bertalanffy's framework for the developing embryo, where systems trigger behavior at critical junctures and, once they have done so, cannot return to their original pattern. The process school argues that there are systems so basic in nature that they can be seen operating in virtually every field — prehistory not excepted. Culture is about as powerless to divert these systems as the individual is to change his culture [Binford, 1968a:14].

There are several points worthy of notice here. For one, this is by no means to be equated with the naive assertions of geographical determinism that were in wide circulation a generation or two ago. Cultural and environmental features are seen as closely interacting, rather than the former being either the helpless pawn of the latter or else free to improvise within well-defined limits imposed by the environment. At the same time, the stimulus and model are quite explicitly of biological rather than historical origin. It is fair to say that all schools of historical thought today, including the Marxists, have moved well away from rigorously deterministic modes of interpretation which tend to limit and distort all but the grossest, most self-evident kinds of social and cultural change. By taking its lead from ontogenetic analogies rather than from the broad trend of historical studies of human groups, this school of archaeologists lays itself open to the serious charge of reductionism.

That the dominant regularities of cultural behavior should be imposed by sustaining or unstabilizing ecological interactions is surely only a hypothesis. The extent of validity of that hypothesis is a matter for empirical determination rather than prejudgment, and hardly can be determined convincingly so long as attention is confined to systems that fit biological patterns alone. There is, to be sure, a heuristic defense for pursuing this strategy, at least where documentary evidence is not available.

> Obviously, individuals *do* make decisions but evidence of these individual decisions cannot be recovered by archeologists. Accordingly it is more useful for the archeologist to study and understand the system, whose behavior is detectable over and over again. Obviously, this approach is too deterministic for some purposes, but for others it is of great theoretical value [Flannery, 1967:119].

Included in the program of this small but growing group of process-oriented archaeologists are a number of other features which serve to differentiate their approach from the traditional one. To begin with, they place heavy emphasis on formal procedures for critically testing deductively drawn hypotheses against independent sets of data. Hence very little tolerance is shown for intuitive interpretations or analogies, on the grounds that judgments about the correctness of the latter must depend to a large extent on a subjective sense of internal consistency and fit that cannot be replicated.

In addition, their attitude toward the limits of interpretation attainable from archaeological findings is characteristically an expansive, optimistic one. The traditional starting point for archaeology has been that differing degrees of preservation and later disturbance usually limit the evidence directly recoverable from the ground to only a fragment of that laid down originally. Moreover, even before they were diminished by the effects of time, archaeological data were only the material vestiges of much more complex behavioral patterns of which no direct trace survives. But rather than limiting their concerns to questions of subsistence, technology, and economy that can be most directly and unambiguously answered from the archaeological record, the process-oriented archaeologists observe that social organization and even ideology must have influenced and been influenced by these other realms of organized behavior at innumerable points. On this basis, a leading spokesman states flatly that "data relavant to most, if not all, the components of past socio-cultural systems *are* preserved in the archaeological record. Our task, then, is to devise means for extracting this information from our data." Clearly, this group has moved away from sifting and synthesizing what is known of an extinct way of life as a whole through its archaeological vestiges, and has centered its interests instead on the formulation of more sharply focused, but also more adequately testable, hypotheses.

I do not mean to imply that process-oriented archaeology will or should replace the traditional reliance on induction. Its protagonists have called attention to defects in prevailing strategies of study, and have fashioned an approach within which ecology becomes not merely a fashionable slogan but an organizing concept. Nevertheless, relatively few propositions have been advanced and fully documented by members of the process school as to systemic interrelationships involving material, ecological, and sociological components. The bane of subjective interpretations and categories still affects much of the primary data on which they depend, albeit somewhat disguised by increasingly sophisticated quantitative manipulations. Although of great methodological interest, most such propositions to date remain merely plausible; validation, or even the evaluation of probability, has proved again to be a difficult goal to pursue through the complexities that surround man and his works.

Moreover, it seems hard to deny that the central creative activity in archaeology, like in all scholarship, lies in induction, in outstripping the narrow base of available facts to suggest new and essentially speculative unities. Formal analytical procedures are surely a useful adjunct to qualities of reflective judgment in assessing the consistency, utility, and fit to these hypothetical unities or explanations, but they are hardly likely to become a full-scale substitute. Both will surely remain, their complementarity enhancing archaeology's claims to work within the framework of a genuinely scientific methodology when the current agitation subsides. What the ferment does indicate, however, is that issues at the core of any philosophy of science now have become critical for a discipline many would unhesitatingly assign to the humanities.

Another major trend of thought in archaeology involves the increasing tendency to study cultural change as evolutionary change, recognizing the unique properties that culture imparts to the human record but nonetheless employing biological models for certain of its most significant or widely recurrent features. Most emphatically, this does not imply a return to crude popular notions of cultural Darwinism, such as the direct competition of inherently unequal and antagonistic groups for survival. I refer instead to some of the underlying conceptions of contemporary evolutionary biology: variable populations, rather than individuals or types, as the units upon which alone the action of selective pressures can be understood; the delicate, many-vectored mechanisms of the process of natural selection itself; adaptive radiations, through which populations rapidly evolve to fill new ecological niches; and, finally, the conceptualization of the results of evolution as a progression of irregular but irreversible transformations.

How are these conceptions reflected in current archaeological research? Partly in the increasing attention being given to ecology that has already been mentioned. But equally important, greater emphasis is being given to the critical processes of transformation that have led from one general level of organizational complexity in human society to another. Unlike the earlier use of stages as little more than typological constructs, the problem of the basic structural features of these successive quantum levels, and of the detailed sequence of steps by which they emerged in parallel instances, now are becoming uppermost. Transitional processes rather than static conditions are the focus of an unprecedented, if still loosely coordinated, attack by a considerable number of individuals at different institutions here and abroad, providing clusterings of greatly heightened activity within what previously had been a diffuse scattering of projects and problems. Among such developmental processes are, for example, the independent origins of agriculture, urban centers, and primary technological complexes like metallurgy or, more generally, pyrotechnics. And in the same way that key processes of change have been identified, key regions of change are receiving correspondingly increased attention. Central Mexico apparently was such a region within the much broader area where aboriginal civilization once flourished in Middle America, and the intensified surveys and excavations there in recent years are a good illustration of the point.

Having alluded to variable populations as the crucial unit of evolutionary analysis, I must return to this theme to describe an important additional trend in thought. Variability is always present in the inventory of artifacts that the archaeologist recovers, but from former acceptance of curves of normal distribution in space and time as a priori assumptions, archaeologists have moved to empirical studies of geographic variability and tempos of change. Processes of innovation, stylistic drift, and diffusion all are brought under scrutiny wherever circumstances permit adequate control over differences in time. Similarly, patterns of spatial variation that do not approximate the normal ones now are being regarded as significant clues to the kinship and other social groups of which the makers of the artifacts were members. A variety of new models and methods are required in the search for correspondences of this type, most of them originally developed by locational geographers; among them are linear regression and multivariant-factor analyses in order to detect nonrandom clusterings of variables dependent upon one another. From a holistic conception of extinct cultures as bodies of shared norms, changing only in response to the slow movement of stylistic variables except where subjected involuntarily to external influences, we have come to expect sharp accelerations and retardations of change and wide differences in the range of variability. By relating such differences to their cultural and natural setting, a new and powerful tool has been fashioned not merely for documenting the fact of change more accurately and interestingly than heretofore, but also for supplying convincing explanations of it.

And what of advances stemming from the physical sciences? It may have struck some as odd that I have yet to mention the dating and detection devices whose impact on archaeology is perhaps the most widely publicized aspect of my subject. The delay to the end is deliberate, for while their contribution is certainly very great it does not alter the whole structure of thought to the same degree as the other new features with which I have dealt.

Radiocarbon dating is the best and most important example. In one sense, as a recent overview states, it has "revolutionized archaeological ideas concerning the chronology of human events during the last 40,000 years." The worldwide synchronism of late glacial and postglacial climatic phases, the timing of agricultural origins and dispersals, the succession of cultural periods in many areas where long stratigraphic sequences do not exist to provide them securely, and the correlation of the Maya and Christian calendars are mong the many important issues to which radiocarbon determinations have contributed decisively. One can argue also that the use of radiocarbon led indirectly to a considerable improvement in prevailing standards of fieldwork, requiring greater sophistication in sampling, in the detection of disturbances and contaminants, and in the evaluation of context if the resultant dates were to withstand critical comparison with others. Moreover, the slowly advancing precision of the system, both with regard to individual determinations and more especially to the cumulative series of them, has opened up the prospect of more carefully controlled studies of change in the future than any heretofore possible.

Errors and misinterpretations on the part of archaeologists have not been uncommon, but the principal deterrents to the realization of this potential are inherent in the radiocarbon process itself. The expression of standard deviations from the mean determination at times has been taken to imply absolute limits within which the age of the specimen must fall, and at other times has been ignored altogether by archaeologists. But even in the absence of these two linked forms of confusion the existence of a still fairly large plus or minus range for each dated specimen limits any fine-grained analysis of change. There has been considerable progress in recognizing sources of contamination, but this also implies that the reliability of determinations is to some degree dependent on when, how, and by whom they were made. Most important, the recognition of a number of factors which have exercised an irregularly distorting influence on the production of the carbon-14 isotope in the upper atmosphere for a time threatened to increase our interpretive uncertainties almost beyond tolerable limits. Recent empirical determinations based on bristlecone pine tree-ring sequences of known age are helping to correct these very considerable sources of error from the late sixth millennium B.C. onward, but determinations of greater age still remain disturbingly uncertain. None of this is intended to minimize the major contribution that radiocarbon dating has made. In the aggregate, it has supplied a system of absolute chronology that was essentially lacking previously. But numerous examples could be cited indicating that it remains unwise to rely very heavily on individual dates or even groups of dates. And unless ways can be found to obtain a further increase in optimum accuracy by an order of magnitude, studies of the dynamics of change based on the archaeological record will continue to be noteworthy more for their promise than for their performance.

In some ways, the availability of a whole series of supplements and alternatives to radiocarbon provides the greatest hopes for archaeology. Even within the age range for which radiocarbon is now the preeminent method, determinations based on the thermoluminescence of pottery offer certain potential advantages. Principal among these is that pottery is itself a human artifact, while occasionally there has been a considerable interval between the lifespan of some organic material dated by radiocarbon and its employment as an artifact. Thus far, however, the margin of error in the thermoluminescent method is still much larger than with the radiocarbon method. Of greater current importance are measurements of the thickness of a hydration layer that forms continuously on chipped artifacts of obsidian. Since the rate of hydration varies with temperature, the method at first sight is not very promising for absolute chronology. However, it can very sharply distinguish components of different relative age within a particular site or area where the temperature is essentially a constant, and its low cost permits multiple determinations. Finally, for sites too old to be subjected to radiocarbon analysis, thorium-uranium, protactinium-uranium, and potassium-argon dating also are in use. The remote geochronological horizons to which they are applicable make them of particular importance for advances in the understanding of the biological evolution of the human species.

Space permits only the briefest mention of the promising beginnings made with a variety of detecting and locating systems. Magnetometers of rapidly increasing sensitivity have been shown to be effective in mapping ruined settlements beneath as much as 5 meters of overburden. Grids of soil resistivity measurements have been employed for the same purpose at shallower depths. Aerial photography is becoming an increasingly commonplace adjunct of both surveys and excavations, and there is considerable experimentation with the use of high resolution, multi-band and photogrammetric techniques. Underwater archaeology, only the romantic province of the untrained skin diver a few years ago, is now an elaborately equipped, highly specialized field of its own. Without any doubt at all, the use of these and similar approaches will become a regular, even dominant, feature of archaeology in the decades immediately ahead. But again, their present importance is more in the realm of promise than of published performance. And the changes in the basic tenets of archaeological thought that I have emphasized are largely anterior to and independent of them.

Some of my colleagues will object that the emphasis I have given to these new trends of thought also is more of a hope or a promise than a balanced estimate of accomplishments to date. Probably they are at least partly correct. My personal bias has always been to look less at what the world is — or was at a given time — than at what it is — or was then in the process of — becoming. I would insist that the new paradigm I have tried to describe is taking hold, particularly among the younger members of the profession. On balance, however, there is little doubt that most of the work in the field is still descriptively, rather than causally, oriented.

In relatively few studies is the central problem of explaining change directly considered in terms of either the relevant data sought or the conceptual apparatus used. In spite of the widespread acceptance in theory of regional-ecological models that should depend on rigorous statistical sampling, the predominant focus of research for most investigators remains the arbitrarily chosen slice of a particular ancient site that is excavated. Specialists in the natural environment are still too often employed as technicians "expected to provide ready answers to poorly formulated questions," rather than engaged in a genuinely collaborative study. Problems and objectives too often are formulated only as armchair generalizations, rather than as sharply focused hypotheses to which definitive answers must be sought in regional or local sequences. Meanwhile, separated by a wide gulf from the former, the conduct of much research at the local level remains practically innocent of relevance to any theoretical problem whatever.

Holistic presuppositions about societies in general also have not been sufficiently clarified and tested. As a result, there may well be an excessive emphasis in archaeological interpretation on stability rather than instability as the salient human condition. To phrase this differently, an oddly antiquated, almost Victorian emphasis continues on institutions and behavior that performed integrative functions — art styles, rituals, elites — at the expense of conflict, marginality, and dissonance as sources of creativity and change. Possibly for the same reason, most reconstructions of archaeological sequences still consist of a succession of qualitatively distinct, smoothly functioning phases or stages rather than of the continuous interplay of forces marked at intervals by new transformational forms. Finally, most of us remain excessively timid, reluctant to tackle the grand problems of comparison, generalization, and synthesis, even though the certainty of being found in frequent error if we did so ought to be heavily outweighed by the opportunity to deepen, sharpen, and ultimately justify our inquiries. But, before I allow these criticisms of the present state of archaeology to seem overwhelming, perhaps I should ask whether at least some of them do not have analogs in the natural sciences as well.

Robert Ascher

7 ANALOGY IN ARCHAEOLOGY

The basis of all archaeological interpretation is analogy, that is, the assumption that nonobserved behavior can be discovered through the study of relevant, observed behavior. Much interpretation of artifacts in archaeology proceeds by comparing the tools of living peoples with implements made by prehistoric man to try to discover the use of archaeological finds. This approach, together with other aspects of analogy, is thwart with dangers and limitations. In the article that follows, Robert Ascher describes the history and the potential of analogy in archaeology. Modern researchers, realizing the limitations of analogy, restrict its use to comparisons between peoples with similar material cultures and environments. For a detailed account of the application of analogy to New World archaeology, read Lewis R. Binford's well-known article "Smudge Pits and Hide Smoking: The Use of Analogy in Archaeological Reasoning" (1967c: 1–12). Binford's article is a sequel to Ascher's piece, itself an admirable starting point for the study of analogy in archaeology.

The work of the archaeologist can be divided into four tasks. First there is the formulation and refinement of concepts; second, data gathering and processing; third, the interpretation of the data; and finally, synthesis. The four tasks are obviously related in a hierarchical scheme: concepts enable meaningful synthesis, synthesis depends on interpretation, and interpretation is ultimately founded on archaeological data.

Substantial progress has been made in approaches to the first, second, and fourth tasks in recent years. Productive work on concepts is illustrated by the successful *Seminars in Archaeology* of the Society for American Archaeology. The appearance of the new journal *Archaeometry* under the auspices of The Research Laboratory at Oxford, with its concentration on the application to archaeology of instruments developed in other disciplines, indicates how vigorous the attack on the second task has been. The ambitious work *World Prehistory* by Grahame Clark, if not wholly successful, demonstrates that a synthesis of human prehistory on a global scale is now feasible. What can be demonstrated for concept formulation, data gathering, and synthesis, cannot be easily shown for archaeological

From "Analogy in Archaeological Interpretation" by Robert Ascher, *Southwestern Journal of Anthropology*, 17, no. 4 (1961), 317–325. Reprinted by permission of the author and the Editors of the *Journal of Anthropological Research* (formerly *Southwestern Journal of Anthropology*).

interpretation. If it is granted that acceptance of synthesis must vary with confidence in interpretation, it becomes apparent that interpretation warrants attention.

The most widely used of the tools of archaeological interpretation is analogy. In its most general sense interpreting by analogy is assaying any belief about non-observed behavior by referral to observed behavior which is thought to be relevant. The purpose of this paper is to examine this single interpretative tool. Concentration is on analogies where no historical records are available as aids. Evidence which suggests that there is cause for concern with the present status of analogy as an interpretative tool is presented and some suggestions are sketched.

The introduction of analogy into archaeology can be traced to the era of the classical evolutionary ideology. Analogy in this period was elementary: if it were true that certain living peoples represented early phases of human history, then the interpretation of the remains of extinct peoples could be accomplished by direct reference to their living counterparts. A monument to this logic is Sollas' *Ancient Hunters*. In this work the Tasmanians, Australian Aborigines, Bushmen, and Eskimos were enlisted as modern representatives of four successive paleolithic complexes. The question of the use of any class of paleolithic tools could be satisfied by direct referral to one of the four groups. For example:

> Anthropologists are generally agreed that the Palaeolithic "coup de poing" was not provided with a haft, but was held directly in the hand; and that it was not used simply as a "chopper": it is extremely gratifying therefore to find that the Tasmanians had no notion of hafting their homologue, or rather analogue, of the "coup de poing," and that it served a variety of purposes, among others as an aid in climbing trees.[1]

Interpretation in this mode, however, was not without its anachronisms. It was noted that living representatives of early periods occasionally enjoyed the use of classes of objects which were thought to be distinctive of later periods. In discussing the Australian Aborigines, for example, Sollas noted that polished stone axes ". . . are supposed to be the exclusive characteristic of the Neolithic period; but as the Australians are still in a Paleolithic stage of culture, they present us in this case with an exception for which various explanations may be found." In resolving this problem Sollas calculated that they might have invented it themselves or borrowed it from neighbors, but he eventually concluded with the suggestion that the Australian Aborigines learned to polish stone via an extensive network which at one time stretched from Australia to Europe.[2]

[1] Sollas 1911: 74.
[2] *Idem*, pp. 179, 207–209.

The critical reaction to the evolutionary assumptions, coupled with both the unexplained residues resulting from this early approach and the recovery of new data, forced reconsideration. As a result analogy was partitioned, and now at least two broad categories of analogy are recognized.[3]

The first category encompasses the classical evolutionary usage with appropriate shrinkages in the length and breadth of the time and space dimensions. In those areas of the world where history grades into archaeology, or where, in the absence of written documents, analysis of current or recent practices and archaeological data indicate continuity, archaeological data is interpreted by analogy to historical or living groups. In parts of the Near East, for example, archaeological evidence for the process of beer brewing can be interpreted by referral to both ancient texts and contemporary practices. The folk-cultures of Europe exhibit farming tools and practices, structures such as houses and granaries, and devices for transportation, which can be linked directly with the prehistoric past.

What is called the "folk-culture approach" by students of Old World archaeology is paralleled in the New World by the "direct historical approach." Both approaches admit the initiation of study from either end of the time scale. It is legitimate, presumably, to study the historically known prior to close examination of the archaeological unknown, or, reversing the order, to proceed from the archaeologically known to the historically unknown. If there is any subtle difference between the Old and New World approaches it is only that the longer time span in the Old World encourages the conception of smooth continuous passage from archaeology into history whereas in the New World the line between the two is more severely drawn.[4]

The withdrawal of the application of analogy from archaeological data where living representatives were assumed, to data where living or documented representatives could be demonstrated, left uncovered a vast temporal and spatial tract for which archaeological data existed. In order to cover this tract, consisting of over ninety-five percent of human history and a large proportion of the globe, a second category of analogy came into use. This second category is here called the new analogy to distinguish it from analogy where historical continuity was assumed, as in the past, or is demonstrated, as in the present.

Anxious to avoid the mistakes of the early evolutionary school, and in the absence of any universal and unique model to guide in the recasting

---

[3] A third category has sometimes been distinguished. This third category includes analogies to properties common to all men such as the need for capturing energy and the possession of a language. For purposes of interpretation this third category is meaningless. One does not need to undertake archaeological investigation to know that the individuals in a particular culture engaged in these activities. The question which the archaeologist seeks to answer is what were the particular patterns of a prehistoric people in carrying out these and similar activities.

[4] Compare Steward 1942 with Hawkes 1954.

of interpretative tools, the new analogy has been set in a restrained format. In effect, the new analogy consists of boundary conditions for the choice of suitable analogs. A consideration of the canon for the selection of analogs, the qualifications placed on the power of the tool, and an example may characterize the theoretical posture of the new analogy.

According to Clark the archaeologist should "... restrict the field of analogy to societies at a common level of subsistence," and should "... attach greater significance to analogies drawn from societies existing under ecological conditions which approximate those reconstructed for the prehistoric culture under investigation than those adapted to markedly different environments." [5] Willey would select cultures on "... the same general level of technological development, perhaps existing under similar environmental situations." [6] V. Gordon Childe advised that an analog "... drawn from the same region or ecological province is likely to give the most reliable hints. ..." [7] In summary, then, the canon is: seek analogies in cultures which manipulate similar environments in similar ways.

The qualifications on the new analogy are weighty. The mass of archaeological data yields subsistence or subsistence-connected information; hence, relevant analogies are to be initially restricted to this domain. The archaeologist is cautioned that the new analogy can provide only "... useful clues to general conditions, it can be a dangerous guide to the particular manifestations of culture ... ," [8] or may "... in fact afford only clues in what direction to look for an explanation in the archaeological record itself." [9] The connection between the living culture or cultures and the archaeological culture in question is purely formal; there is no implication of direct generic relationship nor are any dimensions of space and time implied.

The following citation, from the interpretation of the mesolithic site of Star Carr, is an excellent example of the new analogy:

> The character of the finds suggests that we have to deal at Star Carr with a community rather than with the activities of a specialized group. The masculine element is sufficiently emphasized by the importance of hunting and by the evidence of great activity in the manufacture of tools and weapons. On the other hand, to judge from analogy with the hunting peoples of North America and Greenland, the importance of skin-working at Star Carr argues for the presence of women. Among the Eskimos generally women are mainly responsible for flaying the kill and preparing the skins for use. Men certainly play their part, especially in the hard task of thin-scraping caribou skins or when

[5] Clark 1953: 355.
[6] Tax, *et al.*, 1953: 229.
[7] Childe 1956: 51.
[8] Clark 1953: 355.
[9] Childe 1956: 49. See also Clark 1951.

for some magical reason, as in preparing drum-skins among the Caribou Eskimos, it is considered wrong for women to undertake some
particular task. Generally, though, it is agreed that the task is predominantly feminine and in fact constitutes the main part of women's
labor.[10]

It would be misleading to imply that the restraint advocated in some
quarters is practiced wherever archaeological data is interpreted by analogy.
In fact, it would not be difficult to site numerous cases in which less caution in the choice and use of analogs is clear. Consider, for example, the
following attempt to interpret the *absence* of the caudal vertebrae of the
otherwise well represented bovids in the important Australopithecine sites
in the Makapansgat valley.

To "tail" anything still signifies to "track it down." The leaders of
Bushmen hunting parties, when tracking down their prey, signal to
one another silently with the bushes or tails of the Cape fox. Tails
spontaneously form flexible whips or flagella for beating thickets and
grass-lands after game. The flagellum was one of the badges of the
Pharaoh! The brush of a fox is the trophy of the chase. The warriors
of Predynastic Egypt all wore bushy tails, that look suspiciously like
fox-tails, and Pharaohs are delineated on Egyptian monuments retreating from the presence of gods looking back and trailing the bushy tails
of an animal behind them. Horse-tails used to be emblems of rank
formerly in Turkey, the rank depending on. the number of tails (e.g.,
a pasha of three tails). Every South African witch-doctor carries an
animal's brush preferably that of a wildebeste as every European witch
carried a broom. It seems likely from the significance attached to tails
universally by mankind in myth and history that their disappearance
from the Makapansgat breccia is significant; they were all probably in
great demand as signals and whips in organized group-hunting outside
the cavern.[11]

In the engaging, less extreme example below an attempt is made to
interpret the persistence of certain ceramic motifs in northern Georgia,
U.S.A. Unlike the previous example, an awareness of boundaries is shown,
if not rigorously adhered to.

I am not quite sure to what extent we can measure ethnic continuity
in terms of ceramic continuity. Modern women of our civilization seem
much bolder than men in quickly adopting new fashions which seem
to display no continuing evolutionary or gradual developmental stages,
although these fashions definitely run in cycles. Modern women's
status and functions, however, are of course quite different from those

10 Clark 1954: 10.
11 Dart 1957: 167–168.

of the average southern squaw. Perhaps in the aboriginal Southeast, important new cultural traits that appeared suddenly and are the criteria for many of our major archaeological period designations were exclusively male interests: new weapons, pyramidal mounds, cult paraphernalia, things adopted by conquered or converted men; while the ladies stayed at home and made pottery that changed only gradually as the generations passed. Or perhaps we might better look at our own china dishware to see an expression of conservatism in spite of almost annual changes in foreign policy, Kinsey attitudes, hemlines, and hairdos. Even the atomic age will probably not change our chinaware, except maybe to break more of it.[12]

If the caution of the new analogy did not curb many, it did inhibit others to the point of not undertaking interpretation at all. In 1948 Taylor's *A Study of Archaeology* confronted New World archaeologists with their hesitancy to venture contextual interpretations. What Taylor did not realize was that to some conscientious archaeologists the strictures on interpretation, at least interpretation by analogy, may have in practice appeared formidable. More importantly, one student has argued that the new analogy is ineffectual in important areas, a second that interpretation by analogy is untenable; a third has abandoned hope of making any impartial judgment of the reasonableness of an archaeological interpretation. It will be instructive to consider these three points of view.

Hawkes perceives several kinds of cognition in archaeology. The distinction between them is marked by the degree to which history can be used in the interpretation of archaeological data. The kind of cognition for which the new analogy must be employed is ". . . a world wholly anterior to textual-historical evidence." In this world, Hawkes contends, interpretation cannot penetrate much beyond technology and subsistence. It is in these very aspects that man, according to Hawkes, is most similar to other animals. Where man is most unlike other animals, for example, in the possession of social, political, and in particular, religious institutions and systems, interpretative tools are near powerless.[13] An extreme position is taken by Smith: "It used to be thought," Smith writes, "that studies of surviving primitive peoples would provide the necessary analogies for interpreting prehistoric societies; but in the event the extension of ethnological studies has only served to show what an incredible variety of codes of behavior in fact actuate human conduct." Given this diversity, to ask for interpretation which utilizes living groups, is to demand "logical alchemy." Statements resulting from interpretations by analogy are assertions, not arguments, according to Smith. Imagine a situation in which at a given site one house structure is larger than all other house structures.

[12] Wauchope 1949: 23.
[13] Hawkes 1954: 161–162.

If the larger structure is called an X, and not a Y or a Z, where X, Y, and Z refer to uses of a single large structure in living groups, then "You can't really say that you *know* that it is [an X], and if someone criticizes your assertion, it is impossible to produce sufficient evidence to convince him you are necessarily right." Smith finds interpretation by analogy indefensible and argues for its abandonment.[14] A third position is taken by Thompson. He grants primacy to the role of analogy in interpretation but contends that an evaluation of its use in any particular instance can be made only by assessing the competence of the user. Thompson dismally maintains that there is no way to improve this situation other than hoping for "... improvements in the methods of measuring the amount of faith we place in an individual's work." [15]

From the foregoing discussion it is apparent that there is no general agreement on the new analogy, either in theory or practice. Certainly a call to abandonment is sufficient cause for discomfort. If it were not for the fact that analogy in archaeological interpretation has suffered chronic ambiguity since the nadir of classical evolutionary simplicity, an impasse could be said to exist. The following suggestions are sketched to aid in placing analogy on a firmer foundation.

1. For any given archaeological situation there usually exists more than a single analogy which can be used in the interpretation of the data. The real problem is to select from this finite range of possible analogs the one which offers the *best solution*. Selection of the best solution is most efficient when the least satisfying solutions are eliminated in a systematic way. Thus, a first elimination may be made on the basis of the economies, a second on the basis of the distances from the archaeological situation to the possible analogs as measured in terms of space, time, and form, and a third elimination may be based on the closeness of fit of the relationships between forms in the archaeological situation with relationships between forms in the hypothesized analogous situations. It may be that archaeologists in seeking analogs work in a systematic manner; but if they do it is seldom evident in the final solutions offered. Consider the following example:

> In this new soil, which was sticky and grey compared to the loose brown material in which the painted pottery had been deposited, we found polished-stone axes, polished-stone chisels, and flint sickle blades shiny from grain gloss. There was a brief alert when we thought we had come upon a burial, but it was a false alarm. Lying side by side in the soil were two large human thighbones, brown and shiny, polished from much handling. As they were completely alone, they were

14 Smith 1955: 4–6.
15 R. H. Thompson 1956: 331–332.

not part of a burial at all. All I could think of to explain their presence was that the ancient inhabitants of the Canary Islands, who were Neolithic people, had consecrated their kings by holding just such a pair of bones over their heads, and that pairs of thighbones were also used in the rituals of some of the Nilotic tribes of the Sudan. Perhaps the kings of Hotu had been similarly initiated into office. Who knows?[16]

If a systematic approach were used (it is not clear whether or not it was used in the above example), and the alternative solutions for a particular situation stated instead of the usual statement of a single solution (as above), there would be no need to examine credentials (which, in the above case, are extraordinary), but only the argument and the result. There is no touch of alchemy in the procedure outlined. Solutions to any problem are at best approximations arrived at by the elimination of those least likely. Simply, what is being suggested is the introduction of a clear systematic approach and considered statements of results in terms of degrees of likelihood.

2. It has been argued that the existing ethnological literature is inadequate for the purposes of archaeological interpretation because it contains either ideal descriptions of technologies, detailed descriptions without behavioral correlates, or no descriptions of technologies. On this basis it has been proposed that the archaeologist turn to the living community to compile his own inventories.[17] There is no question as to the merit of this suggestion.[18] If the argument which leads to the suggestion is valid, however, then the procedure outlined in section 1 above might be acceptable in theory but not possible in practice. Is the argument valid?

There does exist, as has been emphasized by Kidder and Forde, a rich and suitable literature which is neglected by the archaeologist.[19] The store of information on pottery manufacture and its associated behavior, for example, is copious. A codification of this literature and other similar information banks would be useful. There are, further, at least some quantitative models based on ethnographic data which are available and qualitative models can be designed to fit the needs of the archaeologist.[20] Behavioral interpretation, in terms of degrees of likelihood, beyond subsistence-connected activity, is only apparently remote.

3. The past and the present, it is often claimed, serve each other; archaeology depends on ethnographic data for interpretation; ethnology can make use of temporal depth that studies of the past may provide. This dogma,

---

[16] Coon 1957: 186.

[17] Kleindienst and Watson 1956: 76–77.

[18] This idea is of course not novel. For an excellent example see D. F. Thompson 1939. Unfortunately most of the studies of this type have been directed at demonstrating that many aspects of a culture are not preserved in archaeological data.

[19] Tax, *et al.* 1953: 231–232.

[20] For examples of the use of both types of models see Ascher 1959 and 1961.

useful as it may be for certain purposes, has contributed to drawing a fast distinction between the ongoing and the extinct, the living and the dead. It is my contention that no clear distinction exists with regard to the material evidence of culture. The point is not trivial, for the generally assumed polarity between the ongoing and the extinct has resulted in the total neglect of striking relevant data.

Every living community is in the process of continuous change with respect to the materials which it utilizes. At any point in its existence some proportion of materials are falling into disuse and decomposing, while new materials are being added as replacements. In a certain sense a part of every community is becoming, but is not yet, archaeological data. The community becomes archaeological data when replacement ceases. What the archaeologist disturbs is not the remains of a once living community, stopped as it were, at a point in time;[21] what he does interrupt is the process of decomposition. The observational fields of ethnology and archaeology overlap on that proportion of a living community which is in the process of transformation. It is the study of this very special corpus of data within the living community which holds the most fruitful promise for analogy in archaeological interpretation.

[21] This erroneous notion, often implicit in archaeological literature, might be called the Pompeii Premise.

CHAPTER THREE

Theoretical Approaches

Bruce G. Trigger

8 CULTURE CHANGE IN ARCHAEOLOGY

Bruce G. Trigger's essay on culture change is an admirable
exposition on the basic principles of invention, diffusion, and
migration as applied to archaeological data. Explanations of man's
prehistoric past have been fashionable for many centuries. But only
in the last one hundred and fifty years have archaeologists thought
consciously about the mechanisms that have caused human cultures
to change. Were such innovations as food production, the bow and
arrow, or the wheel invented in one place and then spread all over
the world by bold mariners or warrior bands? Or did they come into
being in different places quite independently? If so, what were the
causes of independent invention? The search for explanations in
archaeology and the study of cultural process are ultimately bound
up with questions of this nature, for archaeologists today are much
more concerned with "why" and "how" than with "what." Trigger's
article is a chronicle of some varying cultural processes and the ways
in which they can be identified in the archaeological record. The
numerous examples are admirable case studies of archaeologists at
work and should be consulted as such.

Among prehistorians, the study of culture change is primarily an examination of invention, diffusion, and migration (Kroeber 1948:344–571). It is
generally believed that these three concepts, judiciously applied, can be

used to explain all of the changes observed in the archaeological record. A large literature has grown up around each of them and an even larger one around the controversies concerning the relative importance of each as a factor in culture change.

INVENTION

By the term invention or innovation is meant the creation of any new idea, that is, the conceiving of something not previously known to the inventor. An invention is a "mutation" that comes about through the modification of an idea in the light of experience or the combining of several old ideas to produce a new one (Kroeber 1948:352–374; R. B. Dixon 1928:33–58). The concept definitely excludes the acquisition of new ideas from a source external to the individual. Most innovations, like the majority of biological mutations, are minor ones and are unimportant, either because they remain idiosyncratic or because they replicate something that is already known to others. The solving of a crossword puzzle is an innovation of the latter sort.

The term innovation is, therefore, most often reserved for a socially significant innovation, whether it be a new machine or technical process, an institutional change — such as the development of representative government — or a scientific or philosophical discovery. Innovations may be the result of either planned research or accidental discovery. Many important changes, particularly in the social sphere, do not come about as the result of a single discovery but rather are the cumulative product of many small innovations, often made simultaneously by different people.

DIFFUSION AND MIGRATION

Diffusion is the name given to the process by which an invention gains social acceptance. It refers to the spread of new ideas or new units of culture from one person or group to another. If a parallel can be drawn between innovation and mutation, diffusion may be described as the process of selection by which a trait either is added to those that are already part of a culture or else manages to replace an existing trait. The successful diffusion of a trait is the result of a process of evaluation in which individuals and groups come to appreciate and accept it. This evaluation is made in terms of the needs and belief systems of the culture involved and the choices made by one culture may not be the choices made by another (Erasmus 1961:17–97). Particularly in the area of technology, the acceptance of new traits depends on whether or not they are perceived as promoting a culture's more effective exploitation of its environment.

Some anthropologists distinguish between primary diffusion, which takes place within the culture in which a trait was invented, and secondary diffusion, which is the diffusion of a trait beyond it (R. B. Dixon 1928:

59, 106). It is argued that the chances of a trait diffusing within its culture of invention are greater than the chances of it being accepted by other cultures, where needs and values may be different. Traits may spread independently of one another or in clusters. When an entire foreign culture is accepted by a group, the process is called assimilation (Kroeber 1948: 415–428). A cluster of traits which spread together may or may not be functionally interrelated. The former are usually called a "logical trait-complex." One example is the horse-complex, which seems to have evolved in Central Asia, and comprises, in addition to the horse itself, the bridle and bit, saddle, quirt (whip), harness, cart, and the use of mare's milk for food (R. B. Dixon 1928:158). This collection of traits spread throughout much of Northern Asia and, with the exception of the use of mare's milk, throughout Europe. Other clusters of traits may not be functionally related but merely travel together since various contacts exist between groups which permit them to do so. Accidental trait-complexes tend to be more ephemeral than logical ones and are subject to more drastic changes and substitutions.

Diffusion involves the spread of ideas and, as such, must be distinguished from the spread of goods as a result of trade or warfare. The Eskimos, for example, trade with the Europeans for iron goods and these goods have become an important part of their culture. In spite of this, they have never learned to make these tools for themselves. In other words, while the idea of using iron tools has spread to the Eskimos, the ideas of iron production have not. From a cultural point of view, the statement that iron tools have diffused to the Eskimos is incorrect. What we mean is that the Eskimos obtain iron tools from the Europeans. The fact that they do so, means that Eskimo culture is no longer self-sufficient, but has become dependent on European technology. This illustrates another characteristic of diffusion.

As a trait moves from one culture to another, it is rare if all of its attributes move with it. The idea of adding an outrigger to a canoe may diffuse from one culture to another, yet in the second culture the boat will probably be built according to local traditions of carpentry, which may be very different from what they were in the original culture. The basic idea of the chemical composition of gunpowder spread from China to Europe, but because the technology and political structure of Europe were different from those of China, gunpowder was developed differently and came to play a very different role in Europe from what it did in China. An extreme example of limited diffusion is the spread of writing from the Americans to the Cherokee in 1821 (Kroeber 1948:369–370). A half-breed Indian by the name of Sequoya did not learn how to read English, but by observing his American neighbors he grasped the basic idea that it was possible to represent sounds with written symbols. Working on his own, he invented a syllabary of 86 characters (many borrowed from the English alphabet, but in no case used to represent their original sound values), which he then used to write his own language. In this example, only the *idea* of writing, not that of the alphabet, let alone the original sound values of the letters, spread from one culture to another. Such extreme examples are sometimes called stimulus diffusion or stimulus invention (Kroeber 1940; 1948:368–370), meaning that only general principles, rather than all of the details associated with a complex invention are diffused, and that these general principles stimulate what is in most respects a new invention. In one sense, almost all examples of diffusion between cultures are examples of stimulus diffusion, since a trait rarely manages, or is required, to carry all of its technological, let alone, conceptual attributes with it from one group to another. In order for a nation, such as China, to build its own atomic bomb, it is not necessary for its scientists to learn how Americans produce a nut or bolt.

It is also important to note that, while diffusion frequently results in the spread of a trait over vast distances, it does so because an idea is transmitted from one person to another. The expansion of a people who carry their culture with them may likewise result in the geographical spread of a trait, but the spread is not diffusion, since no new individuals or groups share the trait after the movement has taken place. By contrast, the learning of the English language and American patterns of behavior by an immigrant to the United States *is* an example of cultural diffusion, although it is one that in no way involves the geographical spread of a trait or trait complex. Diffusion refers to the spread of traits socially from individual to individual, and ultimately from group to group, rather than to their geographical movement.

Because of this, we must thus distinguish between the spread of ideas and the movement of peoples. The latter is usually called *migration*. Often these two concepts are not clearly separated since, it is argued, the spread of ideas always comes about through people meeting and interacting. Frequently, migration is classified as a subset of diffusion and distinctions are drawn between the diffusion of culture that is accomplished through large-scale movements of people and that which is accomplished without it (MacWhite 1956:17). In fact, the situation is more complex and definitions of this kind merely blur the distinction between the spread of ideas and the movement of people. The spread of a people can, for example, lead to the geographical expansion of a culture, without the spread of elements of this culture to new groups (such as was the case with the Viking settlements in the New World); on the other hand, movements of population can be an important agent of cultural diffusion (as in the Spanish conquest and settlement in Mexico). In still other cases, cultures can diffuse without people moving (such as the spread of Latin culture throughout the western Roman Empire) or people can move without the diffusion of culture taking place (the total assimilation of immigrants).

The various combinations that are observed of these suggest that the migration of people and the diffusion of ideas are independent concepts that are better kept conceptually separate when we interpret historical phenomena.

DISTINGUISHING INDEPENDENT INVENTION, DIFFUSION, AND MIGRATION

The prehistorian is interested in formulating rules that will allow him to distinguish changes in culture resulting from diffusion, migration, and independent development. The data he uses come either from archaeological excavations or from distributional studies. By and large, the prehistorian is not interested in investigating these processes on an interpersonal level, but rather in distinguishing how they are involved in the interaction between cultures or large societal units. On this level independent development normally means that the trait was invented inside the culture being investigated, and diffusion means diffusion between cultures.

Evidence of the act of invention is rare in the archaeological record. Where it occurs, it most often takes the form of idiosyncratic creations that are distinguishable because of their uniqueness, but which, because they did not gain acceptance in any culture, are historically inconsequential (Rouse 1960:313). It is more frequently claimed that an invention occurred in a particular culture because likely prototypes for some new trait can be found in an earlier related culture. Mud-covered baskets, for example, are often argued to be the forerunners of pottery (Arkell 1957). In the majority of cases, however, such proposals remain at the level of speculation.

Similarly, clear-cut evidence of diffusion or migration is frequently lacking in the archaeological record. Where substantial changes take place in a short period of time, the prehistorian seeks to discover if these result from the arrival of a new people with an exotic culture, or if the new traits appear as a result of local invention or trait diffusion from somewhere else.

Much of the theoretical literature that discusses how to distinguish between diffusion and independent development has grown out of attempts to provide historical explanations for trait distributions in the absence of archaeological evidence. There is general agreement that if a trait has a continuous distribution over a wide area, it probably had a single origin, followed by diffusion. If evidence of the trait is not found outside its present area of diffusion, there is also a tendency to assume that it originated somewhere within that area. Where archaeological evidence is lacking, culture historians have tended to assume (much as linguists do about the origin of language families) that, all other factors being equal, a trait probably originated somewhere near the center of its present distribution or else in the area where it presently has the greatest elaboration and complexity. Principles such as these were first enunciated by Edward Sapir (1916) in his paper on "Time Perspective in Aboriginal American Culture" and have since been used by Nelson (1919), Kroeber (1925), Wissler (1926), and many other anthropologists. The principle that older traits generally have wider distributions than more recent ones is now generally recognized as having too many exceptions to be useful (R. B. Dixon 1928:69–72). Likewise, the once popular theory that trait-complexes develop and spread from a common center has been criticized because it ignores the fact that new traits can be added to a complex anywhere throughout its distribution (R. B. Dixon 1928:167–181). In spite of this, there is general agreement that, when used with caution, distributional analyses can produce results of historical value, particularly when traits are analyzed one at a time.

Serious disagreements occur when ethnologists attempt to deal with discontinuous trait distributions, and it is in this area that various techniques have been developed which it is claimed can distinguish between diffusion and parallel development. These theories, none of which has ever proved quantifiable, are based for the most part on general and unproved assumptions about the nature of culture and human psychology. Those who believe that different human beings can easily arrive at similar conclusions tend to assume that parallel inventions are common in human history; while those who believe that man is uninventive and that any sort of complex invention is unlikely to be arrived at twice, stress diffusion as the main process underlying culture change. Attempts to evaluate these positions from a psychological point of view have been, and for the most part remain, highly impressionistic.

The first anthropologist to expound the theory of parallel development was Adolf Bastian (Daniel 1963:107; Lowie 1937:30–38). Bastian, who had travelled widely, believed all minds were much alike and concluded that under similar circumstances human beings would arrive at similar solutions for the same problem. As a result, cultural development in different parts of the world tends to follow similar lines, whether or not there is any communication between these regions. De Mortillet had this sort of idea in mind when he proposed his "law of similar development," on the basis of which he argued that the paleolithic sequence found in France would prove to be a universal sequence of cultural development. The same concept of human nature underlies all unilineal theories of cultural evolution with the exception of that of the Vienna school, which postulates a single line of development producing cultures which then diffused throughout the world (Graebner 1911; Schmidt 1939).

Bastian's view of human nature has been objected to, not because anthropologists disagree with his assumption that human beings are much alike, but because environmental conditions vary from one region to another and the range of alternative cultural solutions for most problems is usually quite broad. Hence, different cultures evolve alternative solutions to the same problem and thereby undergo divergent development.

The more extreme diffusionists have based their work on the assumption that human beings are totally lacking in inventiveness. Innovations are believed to be so rare that even very general traits such as pottery, domestic plants, or mummification can have had only one origin. This concept underlies the work of the Vienna school and that of the "extreme diffusionists" in England during the early part of this century. The latter constructed schemes of culture history which saw all civilization derived from ancient Egypt (G. E. Smith 1915; Perry 1923) or Mesopotamia (Raglan 1939), and believed that all supposedly "advanced traits" (such as mummification, no matter what form it took) could be traced back to a place of origin in one of the ancient civilizations of the Old World (R. B. Dixon 1928:244–264; Daniel 1963:104–127). Vestiges of this sort of thinking can still be found in A. J. Arkell's (1957) claim that pottery was invented only once, or in Munro Edmonson's (1961) attempt to compute a diffusion rate for culture during the neolithic period by plotting the distance between the points at which traits such as pottery and metal tools are known to appear first in different parts of the world.

One anthropologist who attempted to study human inventiveness was A. L. Kroeber (1948:341–343; 364–367). He observed that many things were not only invented more than once, but that in the scientific field the same discovery was often made within the same year by scientists who had no knowledge of each other's work. This obviously happens because scholars throughout the world are conscious of similar problems and have a common pool of ideas to draw from. Generalizing from this, Kroeber postulated that the more two cultures are alike, and the more their needs are the same, the more likely they are to come up with similar solutions to the same problems. The initial similarities, however, can arise from different sources. Two cultures can be alike because they spring from a common source, and, under these conditions, similar inventions merely help to offset the differences that inevitably must arise as a result of separate development. On the other hand, similarities can develop in historically unrelated cultures that have a similar general adaptation to their environment. Formal similarities can thus result from historical interconnections, functional similarities, and finally from similar cultures (for either of the two reasons given above) generating further similar inventions. In order to distinguish which of these factors is at work in a given situation it is necessary to have either detailed historical information or a highly sophisticated understanding of the nature of culture change. In most situations where historical reconstructions are attempted, the information in neither category is adequate to produce fully satisfactory results. All too often in the past, anthropologists have tried to supplement a lack of historical information with theories of culture that would allow them to reconstruct the past from present-day distributional evidence alone. In the next section I will discuss why most of these efforts have proved futile.

The Weakness of the "Culture Historical" Approach

Many debates about historical connections have centered on the nature of the evidence that is needed to prove that similar traits in two cultures are historically related. Graebner argued that the probability of traits found in different areas being historically related varies according to the resemblances in form and function that they exhibit (which are not simply in the nature of the phenomenon) and also according to the number of such traits that the regions involved can be found to have in common. He called these his criteria of "quality" and "quantity." While few ethnologists would deny the general validity of these principles, there is much disagreement as to the way they can be applied. It is sometimes argued, for example, that a large number of similar traits, although not proven to be of common origin, create as great a probability of historical connections between two cultures as do close resemblances in a small number of items.

Ethnologists usually begin by trying to discover whether or not similar traits in two or more cultures are genetically related (that is, derived from a common source), rather than by trying to prove independent invention. One basic assumption, contained in Graebner's criteria of quality, is that the more complex an item of culture is, the greater is the chance of being able to prove common origin. The literature is full of comments to the effect that a particular sort of object is too complicated to have been invented twice. These statements, however, almost invariably turn out to be personal judgments, with little in the way of scientific theory or a reliable estimate of probability to support them. The result is that objects that one anthropologist believes are related, are considered by another not to be. At present, clear-cut decisions are possible only in a limited number of cases, and these are determined largely by the nature of the evidence being considered.

Some objects found in two or more cultures may be shown not only to be "genetically" related but to be products of the same culture. In the recipient cultures these objects are usually called "trade goods," regardless of the means by which they passed from one culture to another. Such objects can usually be distinguished from indigenous material through differences in form and manufacture and also by the fact that they lack historical antecedents in the local culture. No one doubts, for example, that the Roman coins or Central Asian Buddhas that are found in archaeological sites in Scandinavia are trade goods (Stenberger [1969]:124–130). Such objects are similar in every way to other examples known to be of foreign origin and there are no stylistic or technological antecedents in Swedish culture that could account for such a perfect parallelism in design and workmanship. The presence of the same kind of trade goods in two cultures

demonstrates contact (however indirect) between them, and this strengthens the chances that ideas could have been exchanged as well as objects.
Trade goods thus provide evidence of the existence of channels of communication that can be used to argue the possibility of cultural diffusion.

Zoologists, likewise, may show that domestic plants or animals are not
indigenous to certain areas, since the wild species that gave rise to them
do not, and probably never did, occur there (McCall 1964:91–101). The
genetic constitution of plants and animals frequently constitutes an effective means of distinguishing varieties that share a common origin from
those that are the result of parallel development. Moreover, the genetic
relationship between tame plants and animals and their wild ancestors
provides evidence of their place of origin. The absence of both native wild
goats and ancestral forms of wheat or barley in North Africa in post-
Pleistocene times indicates, for example, that these items must have been
brought into this area, probably in domestic form, from Southwest Asia
(Reed 1960:130–134). Plant and animal studies, like trade goods, produce
irrefutable evidence of contacts between different regions and, thus, are
useful for demonstrating the possibility that traits could have diffused
along the same routes. Care is needed, however, not to generalize indiscriminately on the basis of such evidence.

In order to demonstrate historical connections, one must first eliminate
the possibility that the similarities in the items being compared are in fact
products of convergent development. For many years, diffusionists argued
that all pyramidal structures had their origins in ancient Egypt. The fact
that the Egyptian pyramids were tombs covering the graves of kings,
while the Mesopotamian ziggurats were platforms supporting the temples
of important deities did not deter such speculation. It was assumed that
whatever differences, in form and function, were found among pyramidal structures in different parts of the world, were the result of divergent
development and that all these structures could be traced back to a common prototype. Since that time, archaeologists have shown that the Egyptian
pyramid developed from the mounds of sand that were originally used to
cover individual graves. These developed into an elaborate sun symbol,
which in functional — although perhaps no longer in conceptual — terms
served the same purpose. The ziggurat, on the other hand, appears to have
been an elaboration of the low platforms used (and still used) in southern
Iraq to raise houses and public buildings above the level of the river.
Far from being the result of divergence from a common prototype, any
similarities between the Egyptian pyramid and the Mesopotamian ziggurat
appear to be the result of historically unrelated convergent development
from totally different origins.

Once upon a time it was believed that similarities in social organization
were indications of widespread historical connections. Morgan (1871:387),
for example, argued that since many North American Indian tribes have

the same general system of kinship as have the Tamils in southern India, both groups were historically related. It is clear, however, that since social organization is limited in its variations and is highly correlated with economic organization, it is often convergent in its evolution. No one would argue that since the Nyoro of Central Africa have an Omaha kinship system, they are historically related to the Winnebago of the United States, or would even suggest that the idea of the state had a single origin. Mere typological similarities in social or political organization are no proof of an historical relationship among different groups.

Languages provide an even more instructive example of the lack of historical significance that can be attributed to structural similarities. In the last century it was often argued that typological or structural similarities between languages were indications of historical relationship. Today, it is clear that tone languages have evolved independently in Africa and the Far East and that sex gender is no proof that the Khoisan (Bushman) and Indo-European languages are historically related. Demonstrably related languages, such as those of the Indo-European family, display a wide variety of structural variation, from Latin, which is essentially a synthetic language, to English, which is essentially analytic.

Such structural principles are poor evidence of historical relationships among languages, because types are limited in number and therefore the possibility of convergence is high. Much more reliable proofs of historical relationships can be found in those features of language in which chances of arbitrary association play a significantly greater role. Each word or morpheme (except perhaps for the words "mother" and "father") (Murdock 1959b) is a completely arbitrary association of sound and meaning. In any two vocabularies a linguist expects that no more than four percent of the words will share the same association of form and meaning because of coincidence. Any greater degree of similarity indicates either that words have been borrowed between these two languages or that they share a common origin. According to Greenberg (1957:39–40), an examination of the core vocabulary of the languages involved, and a comparison of the degree to which linguistic similarities between two languages are shared with others that are equally related, will allow the linguist to distinguish the latter kind of relationship from the former. Proof of either sort of historical relationship between languages thus depends not on structural similarities but on a significant number of arbitrary associations between form and meaning.

Unfortunately, in the nonlinguistic domains of culture it is frequently impossible to estimate how arbitrary a trait is and what is the likelihood that the same form could have evolved independently several times. We frequently do not have enough understanding about the behavior of culture to apply Graebner's criteria of quality and quantity intelligently. It is even far from clear, in many cases, to what degree these criteria are distinct.

The margin of doubt concerning whether similarities are due to convergence or diffusion is therefore frequently very great.

Applying the criterion of quality, one expects that the more resemblances there are between traits from different cultures, the greater is the chance that they are derived from a common historical source. It has become apparent that general categories, such as pottery or mummification, are meaningless units of comparison, since they cover broad areas of culture and often share few similarities in content. They are, therefore, extremely susceptible to multiple invention. Comparisons must consider specific traits or a complex of closely related traits.

The first task is to determine whether traits that look alike, really are. Just as in linguistics, meaningful lexical comparisons are based on words similar in sound and meaning, so with culture: the categories being compared should be alike both in form and function (Steward and Setzler 1938). Form and function are possibly less arbitrary, yet vary with respect to each other more in the field of culture than they do in linguistics. Hence, the possibility of disparate origins and "false convergence" should be investigated, when any category is found whose members lack a one-to-one correlation in these two (Steward 1929). For example, through a careful analysis of the wear patterns on 300 so-called "celts," J. Sonnenfeld (1962) found that these objects had been put to very different uses in different cultures. Moreover, in this instance, he found no evidence of a significant correlation between form and function. The analysis of the function of a trait, in the sense of both its technological use and its role in the culture as a whole, should be carried out, wherever possible, independently of form so that these two categories of information can later be compared.

It is also obvious that, to constitute satisfactory evidence of a historical relationship, the traits being compared should be nonfunctional. Arrowheads are manufactured out of only a few materials and have a limited number of shapes; hence, it is not inconceivable that various combinations of these attributes have been reinvented many times. Some functions, particularly technological ones, can be determined fairly easily; others are more subtle and it would be folly to pretend that the present state of anthropology can take account of all of them. For example, little is understood about such relationships as those between art styles and social structure, which require a more sophisticated understanding of psychological mediations than is possible at present. For this reason, it is not always possible to distinguish functional and nonfunctional criteria.

Various studies indicate that the possibility of convergent development of elaborate trait-complexes, is greater than common sense would lead one to believe. Therefore, complex similarities in related traits do not necessarily indicate a historical relationship between two cultures.

In 1913, Alexander Goldenweiser enunciated his "principle of limited possibilities" which proposed that parallel and convergent developments are likely to occur for two reasons. The first reason was the usual psychological one, namely, that the range of human reactions to similar problems is frequently limited; hence the chances of the same trait being invented more than once are quite high. The second reason was modelled after the biological concept of selection. It proposed that since the range of traits that any one culture may be able to integrate successfully is limited, features that are different to begin with, often end up being channelled along similar lines. Just as natural selection causes animals having very different origins (such as bats and birds) but occupying similar ecological niches to develop along similar lines, so cultural traits that are different in origin may grow alike if they find themselves in a similar cultural environment. Since anthropologists, unlike biologists, usually are unable to distinguish similarities resulting from convergent development from ones that indicate common origin, they are often unable, from analysis of form and function alone, to determine which of these two factors has been at work.

The principle of limited possibilities is the basis of Rands and Riley's (Riley 1952; Rands 1961) concept of pattern elaboration. These men argue that most innovations are extensions of previously existing patterns, rather than creations along completely new lines. Hence the choices among various alternatives that have been made at any one period will tend to restrict the range of choices that are possible later. Once the nucleus of a complex has been established through a set of primary choices, later traits will tend to develop sequentially from it. Rands and Riley (1958) have illustrated this concept with a comparison of the methods of torture employed by the Iroquois, Aztecs, and Tupinamba (the latter a Brazilian tribe). This complex is analyzed by breaking it into component traits on varying levels of generality. The authors conclude that many of the detailed similarities in ritual and technique found in the methods of torture employed by these three groups may be convergent elaborations of a limited number of more general traits that may or may not be historically related. Hence, limitations of choice, as well as functional necessity, may be a factor promoting convergence and thus helping to increase the difficulty of determining whether or not similar traits are historically related.

In a paper discussing two similar games of chance, the first an Aztec, the second a Hindu one, Charles Erasmus (1950) has argued that it is impossible to use probability theory to estimate the likelihood of diffusion as opposed to independent development. In particular, this argument is directed against Tylor's (1879) suggestion that the probability of the recurrent invention of an item of culture varies inversely with the number of common elements that are involved in the complex. In order to apply Tylor's formula one would have to know (1) the exact number of possible alternative combinations that each element in these two games has, (2) all of the opportunities for their combination, and (3) that each of these elements is independent of the others, in the sense that the occurrence of one does not bias the probability of the occurrence of any of the others. The growing understanding of limited possibilities and of pattern elaboration emphasizes how difficult it would be to satisfy the last of these requirements.

Graebner's second criterion, that of quantity, proposes that the greater is the number of qualitative resemblances between two areas, the greater is the chance of there being an historical connection between them. The traits being compared ideally should be independent of each other, if each is to constitute a separate piece of evidence. It is frequently difficult, however, to determine if traits are, in fact, independent. Royal brother-sister marriages, retainer burials, the restriction of gold for the use of the upper classes, and the employment of dwarfs as household servants may be considered as individual traits or as part of a pattern related to a highly stratified society. Since it is difficult to determine whether the elements being compared are truly independent, the same problems that beset the statistical use of quantitative evidence burden the use of qualitative evidence. In fact, it becomes impossible to separate these two categories of data.

In addition to accepting interrelated traits as independent evidence of a historical relationship, there is also frequently a tendency to ignore the relative significance and validity of the individual relationships being proposed and to concentrate mainly on the number. The basic assumption seems to be that if enough similarities are discovered, a few mistaken ones will not greatly bias the evidence. This of course is fallacious. The significance of no item that is used in a quantitative argument is any greater than its individual qualitative value as established in terms of the criteria stated above.

Moreover, when culture areas are being compared, there is all too frequently a tendency to compare traits collected from different cultures within the area and even from different periods. It is argued that proof of historical connections need not depend on detailed comparisons between individual cultures, since traits probably diffused between the two areas gradually and over different routes. Statistically, however, by increasing the number of cultures that traits are selected from, one naturally increases the probability of finding cultural parallels and the value of the evidence is thereby diminished. Rowe (1966) has recently compiled a list of 60 traits common to the Andean and ancient Mediterranean civilizations in order to illustrate the danger of assuming that even a large number of casual similarities between two remote regions is proof of a historical connection between them. Taken individually, and subjected to careful scrutiny in terms of the criteria we have discussed, scarcely any of these traits would escape elimination. They are either too general, too obviously functional, or too interdependent. Considering the vast array of cultures involved and the nature of the traits, any that are not eliminated using these criteria could easily be attributed to chance. Evidence that one plant of Peruvian origin, such as the potato, was known in Europe prior to 1492 would constitute infinitely better evidence of a historical connection between these two areas than do 60 doubtful traits.

A final criterion, often employed in distinguishing between diffusion and independent development, is the ease of communication between the regions involved. Graebner called this the criterion of continuity. While distance and the nature of the terrain undoubtedly affect communication, it is not easy to estimate the effect that these factors have on diffusion, since many cultural variables intervene. Estimates of the ability or desire of ancient peoples to travel frequently vary. An illustration of this is the recent dispute between Sharp (1957) and Suggs (1960) concerning the ability of the Polynesians to use astronomical sightings to chart courses across long stretches of the Pacific Ocean. The notion of routes also causes difficulties. R. B. Dixon (1928:231) argued that it would be unlikely for various traits to have diffused from Southeast Asia to the tropical regions of the New World, since they would have been forgotten during their bearers' long sojourn in the intervening Arctic and temperate regions. However, if recent suggestions of trans-Pacific connections prior to 1492 (Ekholm 1964) are ever confirmed, the significance of this argument would be greatly diminished.

It is clear, then, that even close formal similarities in traits or trait-complexes do not necessarily indicate a common origin. The limitation of possibilities, through various functional constraints, and the similar needs and nature of man, all conspire to make repeated invention, parallel development, and convergence not only possible, but fairly common. When two cultures share many specific, seemingly nonfunctional traits, it seems logical to postulate some sort of historical relationship between them, just as when two languages contain many words with similar sounds and meanings, it is possible to infer some sort of historical relationship between them, either genetic or diffusionary. When dealing with material culture, we must be more cautious, however, since the make-up of few items of culture is not functionally determined, or at least influenced, in some way. Sometimes, historical relationships can be demonstrated by discovering artifacts in one culture which can be demonstrated to be local imitations of objects originally manufactured in another. An example is the crude, but detailed, imitations of Greek coins found in the La Tene culture of western Europe (Powell 1958:100–102). Even so, without the perspective that only archaeology can provide, it is often impossible to tell whether close similarities, even between nearby cultures, are the result of their divergence from a common ancestor, the convergence of two originally different cultures, or a combination of both. We have already seen in our discussion of pyramids that, in the absence of archaeological evidence, very wrong conclusions may be reached, but once such evidence becomes available, the answers to most problems concerning the types of artifacts that are preserved in the archaeological record are quickly forthcoming. These, in turn, provide the basis for a reasonable discussion of the history of those items of culture that have not been preserved.

It was suggested not long ago that proof of diffusion or independent development does not rest on archaeological evidence but rather on "a set of theoretical principles that must be objectively applied to each case" (Meggers 1964:522). Linguistics has almost reached the point where this is possible. When dealing with other areas of culture and with artifacts, however, present theories are clearly insufficient to allow us to reconstruct the past using ethnological evidence alone. Solid inferences must be based on archaeological evidence, which, if it is sufficient, may allow us to distinguish between the alternative hypotheses that the study of trait distributions raises. Moreover, the further we move into the past the more completely we must rely on purely archaeological evidence.

What are the criteria that can be used to determine whether similar objects in noncontiguous cultures are historically related?

(1) It must be demonstrated that the objects or traits in question are genuinely similar in form and function and have enough nonfunctional criteria in common to at least suggest that the similarities between them are likely to result from a common origin. Occasionally, a particular trait or trait-complex is sufficiently unique that its very nature demonstrates a historical relationship. No one doubts that maize or tobacco came from the New World or that the English spoken by the inhabitants of Bombay is of British origin. Most traits, however, are not clear-cut.

(2) Where proof of diffusion seems likely, it must be shown next that the objects that appear to share a common origin are not the products of convergent evolution. To answer this question, detailed archaeological data are required concerning the historical antecedents of the objects in question in the various cultures in which they are found. We have already noted how archaeological evidence shows that the Egyptian and Mesopotamian "pyramids" developed from entirely different, and historically unrelated, antecedents. Historical analysis also shows that certain highly stylized Mayan motifs, which G. Elliot Smith (1924) claimed were the heads of elephants (and hence were evidence of Hindu influence in Mayan culture), were in fact curvilinear stylizations of the head and bill of a native parrot. Archaeological evidence, by allowing prehistorians to trace the local antecedents of various traits, makes a valuable contribution toward distinguishing traits that are genetically related from those that result from convergence.

(3) It is fair to presume that whenever a trait capable of surviving in the archaeological record diffused from one area to another over land, it

left traces of its passing along the way. Hence, even if a trait now has a discontinuous distribution, it should be possible to prove archaeologically that at some period its distribution was not discontinuous. This evidence should take the form of a series of archaeological sites, which either marks the route along which the trait moved or else shows its former distribution to have embraced the gaps between the regions of its present occurrence (Rouse 1958). The sites within this area should be dated so that one can discover where the trait originated and how it spread. If, for example, a trait turns out to be older at two ends of its total distribution than it is in the middle, the archaeological evidence would favor multiple origins with an overlapping distribution rather than a single origin. The same test might profitably be applied to traits with presently continuous distribution, a few of which may turn out to have had more than one origin. It is obvious that it is impossible to find any archaeological evidence for many traits, and for others the evidence will be very scanty. In these cases, proof of historical connections cannot be ascertained. Nevertheless, if archaeological evidence of historical connections between two areas is forthcoming, then the possibility is enhanced that various other traits, of which no archaeological evidence remains, may have had the same history. It is also clear that, even when we are dealing with ethnographic traits that undoubtedly share a common origin, only archaeological evidence can demonstrate at what period and by what route they diffused.

(4) When intervening areas are not susceptible to archaeological investigation (as is the case in Polynesia where islands are separated by vast stretches of ocean) the argument that similar traits are genetically related must rest largely on the proof of the historical relatedness of traits, such as languages and crops, whose nature is such as to permit no doubt of their common origin. The fact that a Malayo-Polynesian language is spoken on Easter Island, and that typical Polynesian crops are grown there, is infinitely better proof of the close historical relations between that island and the rest of Polynesia than Heyerdahl's reed boats and stonework are proof of a historical connection with South America. The genetic relationship of the former traits is assured but the genetic relationship of the ones listed by Heyerdahl is only a matter of conjecture.

DISTINGUISHING DIFFUSION AND MIGRATION

Various criteria have been established to help to distinguish pure trait diffusions from cultural changes brought about by movements of people. Most of these criteria are designed to pinpoint major discontinuities resulting from the total replacement of one population by another. This kind of treatment, as we have noted before, ignores the fact that movements of people and traits at times take place quite independently of each other, and consequently disregards the variety of situations in which movements of population and of cultural traits can and do occur. In 1939, W. M.

Flinders Petrie listed nine types of culture change (excluding independent invention) all but one of which involved migrations of people. Although this list reflects a rather melodramatic view of culture change, it has the merit of recognizing the wide variety of circumstances under which culture change can come about. Its categories include: (1) general substitution of population, (2) killing the men and scattering the women, (3) killing the men and capturing the women, (4) enslaving the men and taking the women, (5) victors ruling over slaves, (6) victors ruling over stable populations, (7) mixture of diverse peoples, (8) assimilation of immigrants, and (9) merely the adoption of foreign ideas. Another list, anthropologically more sophisticated, was drawn up by Eoin MacWhite in 1956. It distinguished between various types of organized invasions, casual immigration, and the different ways trait diffusion (acculturation) can come about through raiders, foreign visitors, or local groups being in contact with neighboring cultures. These lists differ from the one below in that they treat the entire problem from the point of view of culture change and fail to include instances where changes in population took place with little or no corresponding change in material culture. From the point of view of human history, population movements of the latter sort are as significant as the ones that bring about major cultural changes. The particular categories we discuss are obviously points on a continuum, and not a set of rigidly defined situations.

I. The first kind of change is the total replacement of one population and their culture by another. Normally, a change of this sort involves one group driving out another and occupying its former homeland. This probably happens most frequently between adjacent and culturally similar groups and under these conditions "culture change" (as opposed to population change) is minimal. When the invaders are culturally different from their predecessors, the break is usually quite apparent in the archaeological record and where distinct populations are involved there may even be a noticeable discontinuity in physical type. While total changeovers of this sort are relatively rare, one would think they could be detected easily in the archaeological record. Such, however, is not always the case.

To begin with, one must be certain that the sharp break in the cultural continuity of the archaeological record is real and not merely apparent. Evidence from one site or from only a small area may not adequately reflect what has happened elsewhere. Thus, the first task of the archaeologist is to determine that the discontinuity he has noted holds true in terms of the whole culture. Secondly, he must determine that the total sequence has been recovered and that no period has been overlooked. It is possible that for ecological reasons, or perhaps because of unstable political conditions, a region was abandoned for a time before a new population moved in or the old one returned. The failure to note this temporal gap could result in a misunderstanding of the relationship between the cultures occupying the region before and afterward and might even result in interpreting the same local tradition at two stages in its development as being two unrelated cultures. Such problems can be reduced to a minimum by extensive excavations and a careful study of the stratigraphic and chronological evidence. Finally, the archaeologist must examine the content of the cultures he is studying as thoroughly as possible. . . .

Secondly, whenever it is possible to do so, it must be demonstrated that there was a genuine change in population. This requires evidence that the previous population was abruptly replaced by a new one. Where racial differences are noted between the skeletons associated with the two cultures, it must be shown that the change in physical type took place abruptly and at the same time the change in culture came about. Evidence of only a gradual change in physical type would, of course, weaken the argument that a total (or almost total) replacement of population took place.

Thirdly, something must be found out about the nature of the replacement. Often, the clues will consist of evidence of widespread destruction, followed by the settlement of people with a different culture. This evidence must be more convincing than the small collection of apparently unburied bodies that Mortimer Wheeler has suggested indicates that the Indus Valley city of Mohenjodaro was sacked (Dales 1964). The documentation of how replacement took place requires extensive and carefully controlled excavations, and it appears that the archaeological record for few cultures is equal to this task.

As further proof of the intrusive nature of the new culture, the archaeologist not only must demonstrate that it suddenly replaced an older one, but, must also show where and from what antecedents the intrusive culture developed. In short, the new culture must be shown to be native to another region. This requirement rules out attempts to attribute the origins of "new" cultures to unknown regions. This is particularly important in Northeast Africa where little archaeological work has been done outside the Nile Valley, and where many a hypothetical antecedent of some Nile Valley culture is said to exist in some region that is archaeologically unknown. While no prehistorian must be denied the right to controlled speculation, the tendency of some scholars to pile one unsubstantiated hypothesis on another, often to the point where they ignore meaningful evidence close at hand, has incited a rather positivistic reaction among their less romantic colleagues.

Finally, Rouse (1958) is correct in suggesting that the route of any migration should be worked out and the distribution of all the sites checked to see if the resulting pattern makes sense historically. Furthermore, the archaeologist should attempt to find out if environmental and cultural conditions would have permitted a migration to take place. Such environmental factors are especially important in ecologically marginal regions, such as North Africa, where there have been considerable variations in climate.

The difficulties that replacement hypotheses can run into when there is a lack of detailed archaeological data are demonstrated by the recent questions raised concerning the validity of the "Neanderthal hypothesis" (Brace 1964; Coon 1965:52, 53). For a long time, many physical anthropologists believed that the Classic Neanderthal men of western Europe differed radically from *Homo sapiens*, perhaps even constituting a separate species of hominid. Although relatively few skeletons had been found, and few sites were excavated that belonged to the transitional period, it was widely accepted that Neanderthal man, along with his Mousterian culture, had been swept aside between 30,000 and 40,000 years ago by modern *Homo sapiens*. It was assumed that these latter types, coming from the east, brought with them the earliest Upper Paleolithic [blade] cultures found in Europe. Even those who did not consider the Classic Neanderthals to be a separate species, saw them as being brushed aside, much as the North American Indians were by the Europeans, with only a few of their racial traits managing to survive in a very diluted form in remote regions.

Today this theory is being widely challenged. It has been suggested not only that the Classic Neanderthals of western Europe may have evolved into *Homo sapiens* in that area (aided perhaps by genetic drift from other regions), but also that the Mousterian culture evolved of its own accord into the Upper Paleolithic Perigordian I culture of western Europe. Once the theoretical issue is framed in this way, the current lack of archaeological data becomes evident, since it renders virtually impossible any final solution of this problem at this time.

II. The second type of culture change is that resulting from the movement of an organized group of people into a new area. Such groups settle down alongside the native population, as conquerors and rulers — as the Tussi were in Ruanda (Murdock 1959a:350; Willey 1953a); as subjects of the native population — as Bedouin groups from Palestine and Arabia often were in ancient Egypt; or else they interact with the local population on a basis of equality. Under these conditions, the incoming group may preserve its sense of ethnic identity and much of its own culture for a long time. Eventually, however, the old and the new cultures blend and may produce a single culture made up of various traits from each of the ancestral ones. In general, the relative importance of the contribution made by the two cultures will depend on the size and importance of the groups involved as well as the degree to which the incoming culture is adapted to its new environment. Various factors, such as the desire of the dominant minority group to preserve their sense of identity vis-à-vis their subjects, may impede the total blending of the two cultures. Special situations may also produce highly distorted forms of cultural blending. If, for example, large numbers of men from a particular tribe are killed in war and the women of the tribe marry outsiders, various traits from the old culture that are associated with women will be more likely to survive than those associated with men. An example of this is reported in the Lesser Antilles, where the Caribs are said to have killed off the Arawak men, but married the women (Rouse 1964:502). While the Caribs adopted the Arawak language, their arrival appears to have terminated the relatively elaborate, priestly religion of earlier times which centered on the worship of deities known as *zemis*. In this instance, cultural merging could be expected to take place quite rapidly.

In these situations the problem of proof is even more difficult than it is with total replacements. At one time there was a tendency to attribute almost every change in culture to the intrusion of some new groups or "master race" (Daniel 1963:104–127, 139–153). Unfortunately, using this model of culture change uncritically, almost any new trait can be attributed to the intrusion of a new group, while cultural continuities in the same culture can be ascribed to the survival of the native population. Thus, this sort of explanation can be read into almost every example of cultural change that is found in the archaeological record. To avoid unbridled speculation, strict rules are needed to govern such interpretations. The purpose of these rules — which are simply a modification of the ones required to prove total replacement — is to help the prehistorian to distinguish culture change that really does result from the arrival of new populations from changes that come about as a result of internal developments or trait diffusion.

In order to demonstrate that the innovations observed in the archaeological record were brought in by an organized migration, sites belonging to the intrusive culture associated with this group must be found and dated to the period when, or just before, the new traits became general in the local culture. These sites must be shown to belong not only to a culture that is different from contemporary cultures in the area, but also one for which a homeland and place of origin can be located elsewhere. In addition, the route of the migration must be found, its direction traced, and conditions shown to be such as to permit a migration over the route proposed (Rouse 1958). Finally, it must be shown that the culture is genuinely intrusive, in the sense of permanently occupying the region. In the seventeenth century, hunting bands from Northern Ontario frequently spent the winter living in encampments outside Huron villages, where they traded dried meat and skins for corn meal. This interaction between the Huron and Algonkians may have introduced various items of Algonkian culture to their hosts, but their settlement in Huronia was merely part of their annual cycle and did not result in any permanent Algonkian settlement in this region. Proof of population movement requires a demonstration that the incoming groups actually settled in the region (which may be done in part by showing that their settlements were permanent ones) and that they and their culture gradually mingled with the indigenous one. This in turn, requires archaeological evidence of the gradual mingling of cultural traits over time and (assuming that the intrusive groups were different to begin with) physical anthropological evidence showing genetic mingling.

Clearly, it is sufficiently difficult to satisfy these criteria so that certain instances of major culture change resulting from the blending of two groups (especially when this went on quickly and, therefore, is hard to detect in the archaeological record) are likely to be ruled out for lack of evidence. The validity of this hypothesis can be considerably reduced, however, if, as more archaeological data accumulate, it can be demonstrated that the individual traits that were assumed to be brought in by the intrusive culture (and hence all at one time) actually appear in the archaeological record at different times. This is often the case. It is felt by many prehistorians that it is better to have criteria that are sufficiently strict so that certain (apparently) good cases are ruled out for lack of evidence, rather than to have rules so loose that any instance of culture change can be interpreted as being of this type. The logic behind this is that situations where proof of membership in this category is not forthcoming fall into a recognizable residual category. Later, when more evidence is available, they may be restudied and assigned to this one. Confusion reigns when none of the categories being used is clearly recognizable as a residual one.

III. A third type of change involves the organized migration of large numbers of people, but is characterized by little cultural change in the region they enter (at least of a sort that is detected in the archaeological record). In these instances the intrusive population accepts the material culture of the area it moves into. This can occur either because the group moves rapidly and carries little of its own culture along with it, or because the area into which it moves is ecologically different from the one it left and its old culture is unsuited to the new conditions. It can also happen where the culture of the new area is considered by the migrants to have greater prestige than their own. When nomads, such as the Hebrews, settled in Palestine, they quickly adopted the material culture of the farming and urban groups who already lived in the area. Likewise, the Philistines, who settled in the Canaanite cities along the coast, after what appears to have been a rapid flight from their original homeland, adopted the native culture of the region so completely that only a new style of tomb and a few artistic motifs can presently be used to distinguish them from the original population (Kenyon 1960:221–239). To the archaeologist who has no knowledge of historical records, the archaeological evidence, consisting mostly of towns pillaged by the invaders and later rebuilt in much the same style as before, would probably be insufficient to suggest that important ethnic and linguistic changes had taken place. Similarly, the Germanic invasions of much of the western Roman Empire led to such a swift adoption of Latin culture by them that the period of invasion might easily appear in the archaeological record as merely one of political instability and cultural decline, rather than as a period that also saw considerable movements of population.

Clues that suggest the intrusion of organized groups are signs of war, cultural decline, and fairly rapid cultural change, the latter being induced, in part by the decline in culture and in part by social and cultural innovations introduced by the intruders. This sort of evidence is rarely sufficient, by itself, to prove that new groups settled in the region. Evidence of rapid changes in physical type may increase the probability of migration, but here again caution must be exercised against unwarranted speculation based on inadequate data. Archaeological evidence of intrusion may be found in the form of the temporary camps and settlements of the invaders prior to acculturation. These sites are probably scarce and difficult to identify. It seems more difficult to find evidence of this sort of change than to find evidence of types I and II. The evidence is also often more ambiguous and difficult to interpret, since it is hard to tell the difference between the sites of an intrusive mobile population and those of groups of raiders who merely passed through a region.

In some cases, the intrusive population may adopt the local material culture, yet impose its own language on the region. In such instances, lexicostatistical data may reveal when a particular speech community underwent expansion and thus may provide clues concerning population movements. Such evidence, along with historical accounts, suggests that the Nubian-speaking peoples arrived in the Nile Valley from the southwest sometime during the Ballana period, although there are few indications of cultural discontinuity at this time. Apparently, they adopted the culture of the region and yet arrived in sufficient numbers to replace the earlier local language, Meroitic (Trigger 1966). A similar situation seems to hold with the arrival of the Greeks in Crete, an event that appears to have preceded rather than brought about the collapse of Minoan culture. Commenting on this situation, Fritz Schachermeyr has observed:

> It is a great mistake to assume that historical events are always reflected in the archaeological record of stylistic phrases. Many historical upheavals occurred without leaving any such traces behind them (Palmer 1965:180–181).

The absence of linguistic evidence does not, of course, prove that population movements never occurred, since the intrusive people may have adopted the language as well as the material culture of the region into which they moved.

IV. A fourth type of culture change is that resulting from an influx of outsiders who do not enter a culture as an organized group, but rather as individuals or families who find a place for themselves within the existing social order. These people may come as settlers, refugees, missionaries, slaves, or as the foreign husbands or wives of members of the indigenous group. Some may acculturate very quickly, others, for religious or other social or cultural reasons, may seek to preserve certain aspects of their old culture within a new social setting. Such people, especially those who possess special skills, can be important agents of diffusion. In Tudor times, the English government offered substantial incentives to foreign craftsmen to induce them to settle in England and teach their skills to English workers (Hodgen 1952:174–176). This is an example of the deliberate encouragement of migration in an effort to effect culture change. When such migrations continue from a single source over a long period of time, they can result in a considerable amount of cultural convergence. The conversion of the northern part of Lower Nubia from Christianity to Islam appears to have come about as more and more Egyptian Moslems bought land in that region and began to settle down and convert their neighbors (Trigger 1965:149). The main characteristic of this sort of change is that all the various traits being introduced do not appear at the same time, as they do when introduced by population replacements and organized migrations. Moreover, it does not interrupt the essential continuity of the indigenous culture. For this reason, it is extremely difficult for the archaeologist to distinguish between this sort of culture change and the results of simple trait diffusion.

Since the newcomers of unorganized migrations are usually absorbed directly into the fabric of the existing society, intrusive sites are not associated with them. Only rarely is it possible to find ghettos made up of numbers of such immigrants, who lived together in order to retain certain aspects of their old way of life. Such situations are hard to distinguish from the results of organized migration and in many ways they represent, socially as well as archaeologically, an intermediate type. Even if foreign households can be discovered within communities, it may be difficult to tell whether they belonged to itinerant groups visiting the community or to immigrants who came to live there. Where the native people and the migrants are physically different, the discovery of significant numbers of new skeletal types, and of the gradual mingling of new physical characteristics with those of the local population, may shed light on this problem. While the effect of this sort of migration on the genetic constitution of the population may be significant, the cultural effects are probably little different from those of trait diffusion. Hence, the difficulties of distinguishing the two do not create a serious problem. Moreover, the more massive the migration is, the greater is the chance the prehistorian will be able to detect it. Thus, the chance of noting this kind of change tends to vary more or less directly in proportion to its historical importance.

V. Unorganized migrations take place that have no marked effect on the recipient culture. Under these circumstances, the immigrant accepts the general culture of the society into which he is moving. This normally happens if he believes the latter culture to be more desirable than the one he has left. Unskilled prisoners, slaves, or migrant laborers are unlikely to possess any special skills that they can transmit to such a culture. At most, they may retain some of their old beliefs and personal habits and perhaps pass some of these on to their children. This is especially likely to happen if they are alienated from the new society by a sense of inferiority or are refugees forced to flee their native land but still sentimentally attached to it.

While movement from society to society, both forced and voluntary, is characteristic of complex societies, it is not unknown in primitive ones. Occasionally, it can take place on a large scale and yet leave little imprint on the recipient culture. Among the Iroquois, for example, large numbers of prisoners frequently were incorporated into the society of their captors, often so completely that they would refuse repatriation even when the opportunity for it was freely offered to them. From a cultural viewpoint such movements are often of minor importance, but in terms of understanding population dynamics and social organization they are of considerable interest. Unfortunately, it is very difficult to find evidence of such movements, although some work may be done in this direction, either through physical anthropology or through studies of shifts in the overall distribution of population.

VI. Our sixth category is trait diffusion. All culture diffuses as a result of contact between people, but trait diffusion involves no permanent shifts in population. Trait diffusion comes about either as a result of prolonged casual contacts between neighboring groups, or as a result of contacts between specialists such as traders or artisans. The itinerant craftsman, the wandering pilgrim, and the ambassador to a foreign country, all potential instruments of diffusion, do not represent any permanent exchange of population between two groups. Occasionally, the archaeologist may discover clear-cut evidence of mechanisms of diffusion, such as ... Assyrian trading posts in Anatolia. ... Evidence of contact more often takes the form of trade goods or similar innovations appearing in nearby cultures at approximately the same time. Where traits have continuous distributions, and the possibility of diffusion from a single point of origin is high, it is necessary only to correlate each trait in time and in space in order to show where it originated and in which direction it moved. If the earliest point of occurrence coincides with a region where the trait has obvious cultural prototypes, the chances of it having evolved there are high. Where proof of continuous distribution is not forthcoming, individual traits must be judged according to the criteria set forth above, and some personal decision arrived at regarding the probability of independent development as opposed to common origin. Whenever possible, evidence should be sought concerning the nature of the contacts involved in trait diffusion. Unless they consciously avoid or reject foreign traits, adjacent cultures probably exert a wide range of influences over each other as a result of fairly continuous general contacts. The diffusion of some ideas over long distances may require considerably more specialized mechanisms.

Since all cases of diffusion, for which actual population movements have not been proven, form part of this category, it is in effect a final residual one. Within it, it is frequently impossible to distinguish between trait diffusion that definitely was unaccompanied by population movements of any type and those cases where migration may be involved, but is not proved to be.

VII. The final cause of culture change that must always be considered is independent invention. The problems of distinguishing traits that appear as a result of independent invention from those that appear as a result of diffusion have been discussed above. No further treatment is required here.

CONCLUSION

We have been examining the various cultural processes associated with movements of people and with the invention and dispersal of cultural traits. Although we have not examined in any great detail the idea of a culture as a functionally integrated system, we have stressed the importance for any sort of historical reconstruction of knowing the role that the various artifacts being studied have played within any particular culture. While the existing cultural system may affect the innovation and acceptance of new traits, this does not prevent us from studying the history of individual traits in their own right. The examination of these traits, both individually and in their cultural setting, provides a basis for making inferences about the processes of cultural change, such as we described in the last section.

We have also seen that even when the prehistorian makes full use of all the archaeological, physical anthropological, and linguistic data at his disposal, he is still often unable to discern all of the historical factors that have shaped cultural change. The reliability of deductive explanations, based on general theories of the nature of culture, is very low. Reliable explanations are only possible if we have detailed archaeological (both cultural and physical) and linguistic data. The solution to most problems requires increasingly refined local chronologies and the detailed investigation of the culture history of adjacent regions. The archaeological recovery and analysis of cultural and skeletal data is slow, painstaking work, but it is the basis on which most of the progress in prehistoric studies is built. The interpretation of this evidence is enhanced by a growing understanding of the nature of culture change, by the prehistorian's awareness of theoretical developments in the fields of ethnology and social anthropology, and by the creative application of these findings to the interpretation of the archaeological record. These problems of interpretation constitute the true theoretical domain of prehistory and represent a range of skills different from, but at least as extensive, as those that must be possessed by the field archaeologist.

Bruce G. Trigger

9 ARCHAEOLOGY AND ECOLOGY

An ecological approach to archaeology has become an increasingly significant trend in recent years. Its importance was recognized in Europe before the Second World War and was highlighted by Grahame Clark's excavations at the Star Carr hunting camp in northern England in 1947. Since the publication of *Star Carr*, ecological archaeology has become an important aspect of field research in the Old World. Julian Steward, an anthropologist in the New World, pioneered in ecological studies of the past. In the following important paper Bruce Trigger describes how ecological approaches developed and relates them to other theoretical developments. He discusses two approaches to ecology, the one deterministic, the other an open system approach. Trigger attempts to assess the potential impact of ecological approaches on archaeology, and argues that the future shows great promise. This paper should be read as a logical continuation of Trigger's preceding article.

HISTORICAL SURVEY

Prehistoric archaeology began to develop in the first half of the last century with the realization that a coherent study of the past could be based on archaeological data alone. Since that time, archaeologists have engaged in a continuing search for theories and techniques that will permit them to wrest as complete an understanding of human behavior as possible from their data. Yet, in spite of these ambitions, archaeologists habitually have been apologetic about the nature of their data, which, they have generally agreed, are more limited in scope and more difficult to interpret than are those used by historians and ethnologists. It is not surprising that much of the theorizing in archaeology has been concerned with

From "Archaeology and Ecology," by Bruce G. Trigger, *World Archaeology*, 2, 3 (1971), 321–336. Reprinted with permission of the author.

stratagems which, it was hoped, would maximize the output of archaeological data and permit archaeology to compete on a more equal footing with the other social sciences. These stratagems sometimes have led archaeology astray and to some extent continue to do so.

The earliest of these stratagems reflects the important role played by the concept of *unilineal evolution* in the last century. At that time, it was widely maintained that all societies evolved in a fixed sequence; the only variable and apparently unpredictable feature being the rate of development, which differed among cultures. Less advanced societies that survived to the present were viewed as examples of stages which the more advanced societies had outgrown. All present-day cultures were arranged in a single continuum from simplest to most complex, and this continuum was assumed to represent all but possibly the very primitive stages through which the most advanced cultures had developed. The strictly archaeological aspect of interpreting archaeological data was thus limited to determining the level of sociocultural development particular artefact assemblages had reached; the rest was no more than an exercise in applied ethnography (Clark 1957:170–172; Daniel 1968a; 1968b:57–63).

With declining interest in unilineal evolution, the concept of cultural *diffusion* quickly gained in importance. Although the early diffusionists frequently were rigorous in their methodology and paid much more attention to the formal properties of artefacts than their predecessors had done, they were no more interested in studying artefacts as parts of a cultural system than the latter had been. Instead, they concentrated on tracing the origin and spread of specific types of artefacts (Montelius 1899; Childe 1925). Yet long before matters were carried to an untenable extreme in the hyperdiffusionary theorizings of ethnologists such as G. Elliot Smith and W. J. Perry, most archaeologists were at least vaguely aware that the concept had limited explanatory potential. Above all, it was realized that in order to be able to explain why diffusion had occurred, the archaeologist needed to understand the nature of the recipient culture (Trigger 1968b:528–529). Attempts to acquire such knowledge led British archaeologists to develop two approaches, both of which were concerned with adaptive features of individual cultures and therefore were, at least implicitly, ecological. This encouraged the development of a functional and systemic view of culture in place of the early diffusionist "bits-and-pieces" interpretation.

The first and more rudimentary approach was a geographical one, which became popular in Britain through the cartographic work of O. G. S. Crawford (1921) and H. J. Fleure's and W. E. Whitehouse's (1916) studies of prehistoric distributions of population in Wales. While often criticized for being overly deterministic, Cyril Fox's work (1923, 1932) established beyond doubt the value of a geographical approach to prehistory.

The second, and more important, result of a growing interest in adaptation was the development of what Grahame Clark (1953b) has called the "economic approach" to the study of prehistory. This approach led to a complete restructuring of the goals and general orientation of British archaeology and has provided the foundations for modern archaeological interpretation. While concepts borrowed from ecology played an important role in the development of this approach, their main effect was to increase the interest of archaeologists in the empirical study and comparison of individual archaeological cultures. The result was the formulation of an implicitly functional approach to the study of prehistoric cultures, within which interest was to remain largely focused on the economic sector. Site reports such as *Star Carr* (Clark 1954) and synthetic studies such as *Prehistoric Europe: The Economic Basis* (Clark 1952) illustrate the success of this approach.

Growing interest in adaptation encouraged archaeologists to collect data that permitted a far more detailed reconstruction and interpretation of the economic basis of individual prehistoric cultures than had been attempted hitherto. From the 1920s on, increasing attention was paid to plant and animal remains in archaeological sites with a view to reconstructing patterns of subsistence. Artefacts took on new significance as elements within systems of production and distribution. Archaeologists had to forge closer links with palaeoecology and to develop, or adopt, an imposing array of techniques for eliciting new information from their data (Biek 1963; Brothwell and Higgs 1963; Cornwall 1958; Dimbleby 1967; Hodges 1964; Rosenfeld 1965; Semenov 1964). More specialized techniques for recovering data also had to be developed and this encouraged even greater attention to detail in excavation of sites.

As a result of these developments, archaeologists gained confidence in their ability to use archaeological data to reconstruct and interpret the economic patterns of individual prehistoric cultures. On the other hand, they grew generally less optimistic about how much could be inferred about the social, intellectual, and spiritual life of prehistoric cultures (Childe 1951:55). Christopher Hawkes (1954:161–162) was expressing a widely-held view when he argued that the techniques which produce artefacts were easy to infer to, subsistence-economics fairly easy, social/political institutions considerably harder, and religious institutions and spiritual life the hardest inferences of all.

Nevertheless, a theoretical justification for this approach was evolved, which served to minimize the significance of the seeming weakness of archaeological data for reconstructing social customs and beliefs. It was argued that economic institutions played a leading role in any culture and determined, at least in a general way, the social structure and value systems that were associated with it. The materialist view that was implicit in this corresponded in a general way with much of the thinking of the time and, in particular, with Marxist theory, which Childe (1936; 1942;

1946) proclaimed was the basis of several of his own highly influential interpretations of archaeological data. Progress had been made, however, in two directions. First, instead of the whole culture being treated in this way, only its non-economic aspects were. Secondly, archaeologists generally regarded reconstructions of this sort as being far more tentative and speculative than their predecessors had done. On the whole, the idea was rejected that broad general theories could be used to predict in detail the nature of specific cultures.

THE AMERICAN SYSTEMIC APPROACH

It was to be expected that as the interpretation of prehistoric economic patterns grew increasingly routine, enterprising archaeologists would seek to devise methods to study the apparently less tractable aspects of prehistoric cultures. It is perhaps no accident that the first explicit demand to move in this direction was made in the United States, where archaeological methods lagged behind those in Britain and where the close academic ties that had bound archaeology and ethnology together during the period when unilineal evolutionary theory was in the ascendant had never been dissolved. A concern to justify and strengthen this association appears to account, at least in part, for the unprecedented outpouring of programmatic statements there during the past decade (Binford and Binford 1968; Chang 1967; 1968; Deetz 1967; Willey and Phillips 1958).

The initial step in this direction was the publication of Walter W. Taylor's (1948) *A Study of Archaeology*. This book was a much-deserved reaction against the prolonged survival in American archaeology of an interest in identifying culture units, working out local chronologies, and tracing external cultural connections, much in the spirit of the early diffusionists. Taylor attacked the neglect of non-material aspects of culture and the failure of archaeologists to consider artefacts in a functional context. Yet, instead of advocating that Americans adopt the British approach, Taylor argued that they should view their artefacts as products of total cultural systems and attempt to reconstruct these systems, at least in general outline. The functionalism that Taylor was advocating differed from that of the British by being much more explicit and seeking to embrace as much of culture as possible. Taylor was attempting, in effect, to introduce into archaeology a view of culture broadly similar to that which Malinowski had advocated for studying contemporary peoples.

Taylor argued that archaeologists should strive to create conditions in which archaeological and ethnographic information could be used for the same purpose; to generalize about the nature and working of culture. The very different nature of the two kinds of data was not seen as an obstacle to archaeology and ethnology sharing common goals and constituting homologous branches of a single discipline. Taylor's point of view was adopted by Willey and Phillips (1958), who paraphrased Maitland's famous dictum with the statement that "American archaeology is anthropology or it is nothing" (p. 2). Later, L. R. Binford (1962) challenged the assumption that most of the information to be derived from archaeological data concerns technological and economic matters. He argued that artefacts must be viewed as products of total cultural systems, which, in turn, are made up of functionally interrelated subsystems. Especially when viewed in its archaeological context, every artefact may provide information, not only about the economy, but also about the social structure, aesthetic concepts, and religious beliefs of its makers (and/or users). Binford suggested that the unequal amount of information that archaeological data shed on various aspects of culture may result not so much from the nature of the data, as from the failure of archaeologists to develop adequate interpretational skills. This is perhaps a somewhat polemical position, but is undeniably an antidote against naïve complacency!

On a programmatic level, Taylor's approach has had far-reaching impact. There is widespread agreement that artefacts must be studied as products, and therefore as reflections, of cultural systems. There is also growing interest in developing techniques to elicit new kinds of information from archaeological data; particularly concerning social (and to a lesser degree political) structures. Much more attention is now being paid to the micro-distribution of artefacts within individual sites in the hope that these distributions will shed light on the social behavior of the people who made or used these artefacts (Hill 1966; 1968; Longacre 1968). Related to this is an increasing concern with settlement patterns, which are viewed as the fossilized stage on which social action has taken place (Chang 1958; 1962; 1968; Trigger 1965:2). Multivariant analysis of stylistic variation, along lines pioneered by James Deetz (1965), has helped to shed valuable light on prehistoric residence patterns, although archaeologists have tended to draw unwarranted inferences about other features of social organization from such data (Aberle 1968). Archaeologists have also been making forays into the ethnographic literature to search out detailed correlations between aspects of material and non-material culture that can be used to interpret archaeological data (Chang 1958; 1962; Cook and Heizer 1968). Many of these studies require manipulating vast quantities of data and have been practicable only with the assistance of computers.

In spite of early attempts to view burials as fossilized rituals (Fox 1959; Sears 1961), there have been few, if any, comparable advances in the study of belief systems or aesthetics, although inconclusive efforts have been made to discover regularities between art styles and certain aspects of social organization (Fischer 1961). The most successful studies remain those which are text-aided or grounded in the direct historic approach. In several highly successful attempts to deal with more general problems of interpreting art and burial customs, Peter J. Ucko (1968; 1969; Ucko and Rosenfeld 1967) has reaffirmed that the best use that can be made of ethnographic analogy in these areas is to broaden the archaeologist's awareness of unsuspected alternatives in the possible significance of his data. Yet, even if recent efforts to interpret the non-economic aspects of prehistoric cultures have had their greatest success in dealing with socio-political organization, they nevertheless mark the beginning of an attempt to extend the empirical reconstruction and explanation of prehistoric culture into new areas and to upgrade field methods to provide new kinds of data.

These practical developments have helped to stimulate interest in a thorough reappraisal of the theory and assumptions of prehistoric archaeology. The ultimate purpose of these discussions is to define the future aims of prehistoric archaeology and to establish an effective relationship between this discipline and the other social sciences. In the course of these discussions, almost every concept that has ever been considered by archaeologists has come under scrutiny (Bayard 1969; Binford, L. R., 1962; 1965; 1967c; Binford and Binford 1968; Chang 1967; 1968; Clarke 1968; Deetz 1965; Trigger 1968b). Some of these concepts have been made more explicit, but in many cases clarification has resulted in hitherto unforeseen points of disagreement being recognized. It is indicative of the continuing importance of the British economic approach that much of the debate about cultural theory (as distinguished from general methodology) concerns problems that can be grouped under the general heading of ecology. Here two opposing views can be distinguished: one tending toward a narrower and more deterministic conceptualization of ecology than has prevailed among archaeologists hitherto; the other toward a broader and more empirical approach. Many individual positions fall somewhere between these two extremes and therefore a discussion of these tendencies as ideal types may do injustice to the subtlety of certain positions. Nevertheless, I believe that such a discussion is justified in terms of the light it sheds on the general issues that are involved. It will also demonstrate the extent to which current controversies are embedded in the past history of archaeological theory.

DETERMINISTIC ECOLOGY

Deterministic ecology has been influenced heavily by the cultural materialist approach in American anthropology, the growth of which is closely linked to that of cultural ecology and neo-evolutionary theory generally (Harris 1968). Yet, in spite of its largely American origins, the deterministic approach in archaeology is based on many of the key concepts of the British economic approach. Total cultures are studied as adaptive systems, as Grahame Clark advocated they should be. Both approaches share a materialist bias, but in place of the tentatively expressed British assumption that loosely-defined economic institutions play a leading role in the development of other features of culture, deterministic archaeologists have tended to adopt Leslie White's (1949) more rigorous premise that total cultures are the product of their technology interacting with the natural environment. In a recent study, for example, we are informed that "the settlement pattern... is an essential corollary of subsistence" and that "Variations between cultures are responses to differing adaptive requirements of specific environments; accordingly, varying ecological potentialities are linked to different exploitative economies and the latter, in turn, to differing integrative requirements met by differing forms of social structure" (Struever 1968a:134–135, 133); in another study, on the advice of David Aberle, Struever (1968b:311) has expressed a more open approach to ecology.

While White (1945:346) has warned that his general theories cannot be used as a basis for making inferences about the specific features of individual cultures, not all archaeologists have chosen to take this admonition seriously. They assume that if White's deterministic hypotheses are correct, any archaeologist who is able to reconstruct the technology and environment for an individual prehistoric culture should be able to predict what the rest of this culture, or at least its key features, was like (Meggers 1960). Shortcomings in such reconstructions are considered as the result of inadequacies in general anthropological theory, not in archaeological data or the archaeologist's ability to interpret these data. Archaeological studies which concentrate on subsistence patterns and assign to them a leading role in the evolution of other aspects of culture have considerable support for the investigation of both simple (Struever 1968b) and complex (Sanders 1968; Sanders and Price 1968) societies.

The materialist approach and the idea that culture can be reconstructed by broad analogy provide much scope for the application of neo-evolutionary theory in archaeology. Evolutionary theory in anthropology has always been preoccupied with problems of cultural typology and has operated on the assumption that the degree of variation in the total morphological pattern of individual cultures is strictly limited (Rouse 1964). Moreover, the search for causal relations has been conceived of as an effort to explain the similarities, rather than the "unique, exotic and non-recurrent particulars" (Steward 1955:209), observed in these patterns. At present, this is equally true of the unilineal evolutionism of Leslie White (1959) or V. Gordon Childe (1942, 1951) or the multi-lineal evolution of Julian Steward (1955), even though the latter attempts to account for patterns of variation resulting from adaptations to a variety of different kinds of environments. The cultural theory that underlies both approaches is, in fact, very similar (Sahlins and Service 1960). Cultures are viewed as made up of "core" features, which are basic to their general structure, and other features which are not. The core features are mainly technological and social structural and are posited to develop in response to the adaptive needs of a culture. They occur, therefore, in a limited number of total patterns, which represent responses to specific classes of environments by peoples at various levels of technological development. Thus, by determining which total cultural pattern corresponds most closely to his data, the archaeologist is assumed to acquire knowledge of the key features of his culture. In this manner, cultural evolution becomes a "practical research tool" for archaeologists (Meggers 1960).

It is ironic that just as new techniques are being devised to elicit independent information about social structure from archaeological data, arguments should be advanced that resemble so closely those advocated by earlier schools of archaeological interpretation to justify not basing their interpretations on a detailed exegesis of such data. Technology and environment have replaced index fossils and the economy as a datum line, but the faith remains that cultural patterns are limited enough in variety that the major outlines of any culture can be inferred from knowledge of only one part of it.

Another important feature that the deterministic approach has in common with neo-evolutionary theory is its anti-diffusionist bias. An interest in diffusion is interpreted as being antithetical, or irrelevant, to the study of cultures as adaptive systems. It is argued that diffusion occurs less frequently than uncritical archaeologists have claimed and that it is usually trivial in its consequences, at least as far as adaptation is concerned. It is also maintained that if conditions are right for a trait to be adopted in a recipient culture, a homologous trait, or one that has similar socio-economic significance, would ultimately evolve even if that culture were to remain totally isolated (Binford 1963; Sanders and Price 1968:58–73; Renfrew 1969). Such a position is the mirror-image of the early diffusionists' lack of concern with the manner in which traits became integrated into recipient cultures.

On the whole, the deterministic approach tends to be more narrowly focused and more dogmatic than its economic predecessor. None of its major concepts is new and, taken individually, each of them has been criticized in various ways. The deterministic approach has been unduly protected by the theoretical prestige which has accrued to it through its close ties with cultural materialism and neo-evolution. Yet, to point out the shortcomings of the deterministic approach does not necessarily imply a totally, or even partially, negative evaluation of these more general hypotheses. What the archaeologist must be concerned with is the degree to which these concepts are of practical value for interpreting his data.

In this respect, it must be observed that cultural materialism and its allied approaches, whatever their ultimate value, are, as yet, neither sufficiently sophisticated nor comprehensive to be able to explain the cultural variability noted in the ethnographic record, even if interest is confined to "core" items. Most ecological explanations of ethnographic data are *ad hoc,* in the sense that they adduce plausible reasons to account for what is observed, but are unable to demonstrate that, given the same set of conditions, alternative solutions would be either impossible or highly unlikely.

Widely differing explanations are offered concerning how particular features of culture are adaptive, and anthropologists are far from agreed that all behavior can best be interpreted in this manner (Harris 1966).

Because of the complexity of cultural phenomena and the inadequacy of our present understanding of culture process, all deterministic, and indeed all functional, approaches remain essentially non-predictive, except at very general or mundane levels. An analogy with the biological sciences is perhaps instructive. Although the understanding of biological processes far exceeds that of socio-cultural ones, the biologist is unable to predict the specific changes that any particular species will undergo through time. This is largely because he is unable to control, to a sufficiently accurate degree, for a large number of external variables, including geological, climatic, and solar conditions, as well as for the other plants and animals that are part of the eco-system. Thus, the complexity of the parameters that must be controlled for, even more so than the problems of understanding process, rules out the possibility of detailed and far-reaching predictions, either forward or backward in time. The current inability of social scientists to control for the even greater number of variables that affect cultural processes rules out the possibility of cultural theory being used by archaeologists as an "effective research tool" for reconstructing individual prehistoric cultures (Trigger 1970:33–35).

A sharp distinction must be drawn between the manner in which non-archaeological evolutionists seek to reconstruct the past using only their understanding of cultural theory and of present conditions and the archaeologist's efforts to understand the past as it is reflected in the archaeological record. The scenarios of cultural evolution that non-archaeological anthropologists have produced to date are largely descriptive generalizations, often highly impressionistic ones, rather than adequate explanations of the processes that have shaped the evolution of culture. For the archaeologist, the latter must be synonymous with the actual record of human development as revealed by culture historical research. The general schemes of cultural evolutionists can neither aid the archaeologist to interpret individual prehistoric cultures, nor, being themselves the product of cultural theory, can they contribute information that will permit archaeologists to understand cultural processes better.

There is a tendency, as Paul Tolstoy (1969:558) has pointed out, for determinists to consider worthy of attention only those traits with which their theories appear equipped to deal. These studies are generally restricted to dealing with structural features that are cross-culturally recurrent; the implication being that fundamental causal relationships (that is, those which concern adaptation to the environment) can be discovered only through the examination of such features. Although no criteria have ever been established that can discriminate objectively between the core and non-core characteristics of a culture, it is generally agreed that the former are those which play an active role in adapting the culture to its environment. Other features, such as art styles or symbols of rank, are treated as "outward symbols," functionally related to the core, but of only peripheral structural significance. While concentration upon structural features can be extremely useful, as I have argued at length elsewhere (1968b: 533–537), at best it offers a partial view of culture which must be complemented by an examination of less obviously recurrent or adaptive features. Archaeologists must never lose sight of one of anthropology's basic assumptions: that culture as a whole (and not merely those aspects which are causally related with the environment) is orderly. They must strive therefore to explain the total range of variation in their data and not be content merely to deal with gross structural similarities.

Another major shortcoming of deterministic ecology is its tendency to study individual cultures as closed systems; a procedure reminiscent of the organic fallacy in social anthropology. This bias is clearly related to the desire to study environmentally adaptive features of culture, but when applied dogmatically it is unrealistic for understanding both structure and process. Few cultures, if any, have existed in total isolation from all others. Many have been in such close contact with their neighbors that they lack the clear-cut boundaries which anthropologists find so convenient (Trigger 1967:151). Networks of social, political, and economic relations tend to proliferate across cultural boundaries and link cultural systems together. Viewed in structural terms, the impact that different cultures have had upon one another is far from insignificant. No one would deny, for example, that the spread of industrial technology, and of an associated international economic system, has had an enormous impact outside the area of western Europe where the Industrial Revolution was initiated. Because of variations in local culture, as well as in natural resources and the circumstances under which industrial technology was introduced, the impact of this technology has been different in each of these areas, and from what it was originally in western Europe. Some determinists postulate that eventually all industrial societies will tend to evolve a very similar set of social, economic, and political institutions which are ideally suited to an industrial technology, much as Childe (1951) postulated that divergence followed by convergence is the normal process in the evolution of societies from one level of technological adaptation to another. Yet to dismiss the experience of the Third World as being of little evolutionary interest, as White's unilineal approach would lead us to do, is clearly inadequate both from an historical and a processual point of view. While it is legitimate, and highly desirable, to study the history of particular peoples in terms of the continuing evolution of their social systems, this does not provide a theoretical justification for ignoring either diffusion or the impact that interacting societies have had upon one another's socio-political institutions. Cultures clearly must be treated as important components in each other's environment.

Finally, we must reject the last-ditch defense that a deterministic ecological approach is better suited to the interpretation of simple societies than it is to more complex ones. Such an argument is based on the assumption that structurally primitive societies are more directly dependent on their environment and, therefore, strictly limited in terms of the adaptive responses that are open to them. Such an argument is based on an unduly simplistic view of simple societies (Lee and DeVore 1968) and is reinforced by the relatively small amount of archaeological data that is available concerning any single primitive culture. Complex societies, such as those of ancient Egypt or of the Maya, simply leave behind too wide a range of archaeological evidence not to give rise to doubts about such formulations. This has helped to expose overenthusiastic attempts to distort such societies and fit them into unsuitable preconceived patterns. There is neither archaeological nor ethnological evidence to support the assumption that primitive cultures are necessarily any more lacking in adaptive variation than are complex ones.

Deterministic ecology thus appears to combine many of the weaknesses of the older evolutionary and economic approaches and fails to take advantage of recent significant advances in the interpretation of archaeological data. Its attempt to reconstruct prehistoric cultures on the basis of an assumedly limited variation in total morphological pattern seems to be theoretically unjustified and unproductive of new insights such as are derived from attempts to explain in detail the archaeological evidence for particular cultures.

Open-System Ecology

What I have called open-system ecology consists of a body of assumptions shared by various archaeologists who nevertheless have never thought of themselves as members of a particular school of archaeological interpretation. Because of this, there is less programmatic literature associated with this approach than there is with deterministic ecology, although the number of substantive studies is probably greater. Most of the assumptions of the open-system approach are in accord with recent developments in cultural ecology generally and they reflect growing confidence among archaeologists in their capacity to interpret basic data. For these reasons, the open-system approach appears to be a more progressive, and ultimately a more productive, development than deterministic ecology.

The open-system approach is based on the assumption that cultural ecology is concerned with the total manner in which human groups adapt to and transform their environments. Cultures are conceived of as being at least partially open systems, some of whose institutions may be tied in with those of other cultures. Because of this, simplistic efforts to treat cultures as self-contained units may impede the interpretation of archaeological data. Cultural systems are seen as having to adapt to a total environment made up both of natural elements and of other cultures.

Open-system ecology assumes that there is a considerable degree of individual variation among both ethnological and archaeological cultures. While cultural phenomena are assumed to be orderly and hence subject to scientific enquiry, the open-system approach insists that any explanation of culture must prove its worth by being able to cope with patterns of variation observed in real cultures, rather than with the variations hypothesized to exist among a limited number of ideal types, such as the neo-evolutionists postulate. Order must be sought, not in neat cultural typologies, but rather through understanding those processes by which cultural similarities and differences are generated. Only in this manner can sufficient allowances be made for the wide variety of contingent factors that influence the development of any one culture. The open-system approach also argues that, because of the complexity of these external factors and the archaeologist's inability to control for them adequately, it is not possible to reconstruct the whole of a cultural system from knowledge of only part of it. Instead, it insists that every facet of a prehistoric culture that can be reconstructed must be done so through the interpretation of data relevant to that part. For the same reason, it is doubted that the core features of any one culture can be distinguished on an *a priori* basis from non-economic, non-adaptive features.

Open-system ecology remains interested in subsistence patterns and economics, but assumes that developments affecting any one aspect of culture can ultimately produce further adjustments throughout the system and affect the system's relationship with its natural environment. Hence, open-system archaeologists are equally interested in studying trade, communications, political organization, warfare, population movements, religious ideas, disease patterns, and other features of, or influences by, culture, as far as this can be done from the archaeological record, in order to construct as complete a picture as possible of factors which influence the adaptation of a society to its total environment, both natural and cultural (Trigger 1972). Moreover, while interest remains high in studying whole cultures, there is also a growing interest in examining in detail the functional relationship between restricted segments of prehistoric cultures, such as irrigation systems and political organization. Such studies are important from an ecological point of view because they contribute to the better understanding of the adaptive features of a culture.

The open-system approach has been one of several factors promoting a growing interest in the study of archaeological settlement patterns (Trigger 1965; 1968b). It is assumed that the quantity, type, and distribution of the material remains of human activities (including settlements, houses, fields, and artefacts) constitute reliable evidence concerning the manner in which former inhabitants adjusted to their environment and that all of the factors that influenced this adjustment are reflected, either directly or indirectly, in the settlement pattern. Attempts to explain settlement patterns therefore should result in a more comprehensive understanding of this adaptation than a study that concentrates on subsistence patterns or the economy and which tries to explain the settlement patterns only, at best, in terms of these factors (Struever 1968a:134–135). It is recognized, of course, that a settlement pattern is the product of a variety of factors, some of which reinforce certain trends, others of which are opposed to one another. The pattern therefore is often a compromise among a number of conflicting tendencies. A simple example is the contradiction in some agricultural societies between the desire for dispersed homesteads in order to be near fields and for nucleated settlements for protection against enemies. It is not always possible to untangle the forces that have been at work, given the sort of archaeological data that are normally available. It is suggested, however, that the attempt to explain an archaeological settlement pattern constitutes a dynamic approach to the study of the cultural ecology of prehistoric societies.

The first substantial effort to study settlement patterns in this manner was Gordon Willey's report on the Virú Valley in Peru (1953b). In this study, Willey treated settlement patterns as a reflection of "the natural environment, the level of technology on which the builders operated, and various institutions of social interaction and control which the culture maintained" (p. 1). He demonstrated that not only the development of subsistence patterns, but also political and economic competition between valleys and changes in the relationship between the sacred and secular areas of cultures had played important roles in shaping the development of settlement patterns in the Virú Valley. Moreover, the development of subsistence patterns only became intelligible once these other factors had been taken sufficiently into account.

In *Land behind Baghdad*, R. McC. Adams (1965) carried the approach further by using archaeological and historical evidence to demonstrate that political and economic factors had played a more important role than had technological ones in shaping the development of irrigation systems in a part of Iraq over a 6,000-year period. Similarly, studies of Nubian culture history have shown that the size and distribution of population in this region, from at least 3000 B.C. to the present, have been determined not only by subsistence patterns but also by trade, warfare, political organization, religious beliefs, and disease patterns and especially by Nubia's relationships with Egypt and the Sudan (Trigger 1965; 1972). The vast array of factors that has been shown to influence settlement patterns in these regions clearly demonstrates the theoretical limitations of deterministic ecology. Moreover, in none of these studies is it claimed that the full range of factors has been deduced or their relationship to one another completely worked out. In each study at least some of the factors are known from historical rather than archaeological data.

Within an open ecological framework, studies of subsistence patterns take on new significance. Michael D. Coe (1969) has pointed out that hitherto most theorizing about ancient ecosystems has been limited to the "supposed permissive or limiting effects of major biomes, such as desert, steppe, or tropical forest" upon cultural development. He cites, as examples of such theories, Wittfogel's (1957) thesis that despotic states arise to provide the controls needed to administer large-scale irrigation systems or Meggers's (1954) related theory that tropical forest environments preclude the independent rise of complex societies and eventually destroy such of them as are introduced from outside. Coe and Flannery (1964) argue that such general theories do not take account of the variations within major biomes and for this reason frequently are not in accord with the facts. This is essentially the same kind of objection that has already been levelled in this paper against the neo-evolutionist approach to the study of culture. In their work on lowland Mesoamerica, Coe and Flannery suggest that the explanation of cultural development requires a detailed knowledge of the micro-environments to which individual people actually adapt. It is through an understanding of such micro-environments and of the kinds of adjustments that the members of any one culture have made to those available to them that a picture of subsistence patterns and of their carrying capacity may be built up. More recently, in a discussion of his work on Oaxaca, Flannery (1968) has pointed out that some groups do not adapt to micro-environments as much as to a small number of plants and animals that may cross-cut several such environments. He has suggested that cybernetic-type models may help to provide useful explanations of stability and change in such adaptations (for a discussion of this suggestion see Doran 1970). Coe (1969) has followed the recent lead of geographers and economists in arguing that agricultural systems must not be viewed as independent variables in the study of culture but rather as parts of a much broader cultural system and therefore as responsive to changes initiated in various other parts of the system. He stresses that social, cultural, ceremonial, and religious factors may influence subsistence patterns, particularly in so far as they effect changes in population. He also stresses the potential value of analytic concepts borrowed from geography, such as central-place theory, nearest neighbor analysis, and von Thunen's "isolated state" theory for the analysis of archaeological data and the generation of new explanatory models. The tendency to view population, not as an automatic response to food production, but rather as related to the total cultural pattern and hence influenced by many different kinds of factors is clearly an integral part of the open-system approach. Such ideas serve to tie some of the most recent thinking in archaeology in with modern ecology in general.

CONCLUSIONS

Archaeologists must learn to live with the realization that their desire to study whole cultural systems cannot be realized. This, however, is not meant to be an unconstructive comment. On the contrary, the real weakness of much modern archaeology can be attributed to the tendency of many archaeologists to treat their discipline as being merely the "past tense of ethnology" or a kind of "paleoanthropology," rather than defining its goals in terms of the potentialities of its data. Archaeologists must learn to ask the kinds of questions with which their data are equipped to deal (Clarke 1968:12–24).

The relationship between archaeology and ecology is bound to be affected by such questions. As long as ecology was conceived of in a deterministic fashion, it appeared to be an approach totally adapted to take advantage of the strong points of archaeological data and to circumvent their weak points. Now, however, it is apparent that because archaeology is unable to reconstruct whole cultural systems, an ecological approach can at best be partially applied and that the lessons drawn from it will tend to be limited to the relationships between certain adaptive features of culture. From a theoretical point of view, the main contributions that prehistoric archaeology is likely to make in the near future will concern the manner in which specific economic, social, and demographic variables interact with one another in specified environmental settings over long periods of time. Subject to these limitations, prehistoric archaeology has a unique contribution to make to an understanding of the manner in which culture evolved down to the beginnings of recorded history.

William L. Rathje

10   THE ORIGIN AND DEVELOPMENT OF LOWLAND CLASSIC MAYAN CIVILIZATION

Trade was a major factor in cultural and technological changes in prehistoric times. Although many hunting and gathering societies were able to remain largely self-sufficient in terms of food supplies and raw materials, farmers and city dwellers had to rely on others for many products. Salt, metal objects, grain, skins, building materials, and ornaments are but a few commodities exchanged between different societies before the advent of cash economies. Archaeologists have long been concerned with trade and its role in the formation of states. A sizable literature has grown around obsidian trading, saltworking, and the long-distance trading of exotic ornaments in amber, jade, and glass — to say nothing of metals and fabrics. William L. Rathje, in a somewhat technical article, describes how trade contributed to the formation of Mayan civilization in the lowlands of Mesoamerica. The southern Mayan lowlands do not

possess the resources essential to the households engaged in
subsistence agriculture; yet this was the area where the basic
elements of classic Maya civilization first came together. Rathje
reconstructs a provocative model of the procurement and distribution
systems needed to redistribute resources for efficient agriculture.
This approach has important theoretical implications for other areas.
This article should also be read in conjunction with Chapter 7.

A major archaeological problem today seems to be — why did the lowland Maya civilization evolve in its ecological setting? This paper will develop a hypothesis to explain the evolution of lowland Classic Maya civilization.

Since I subscribe to cultural ecology, the environmental configuration of
the Petén rain forest is an obvious beginning. This expansive ecological
zone has been characterized as lacking developmental potential because:
(1) the environment is redundant in access to resources; (2) transportation of goods is difficult; and (3) slash-and-burn agriculture is the main
subsistence technique. As a result, it is thought that there was little stimulus
toward trade and redistribution; nucleated centers were rarely maintained
and a scattered light settlement was typical; and there were no obvious
changes in the subsistence system through time which would have required
community efforts and caused increasing ceremonialism (Meggers 1954;
Palerm and Wolf 1957; M. Coe 1961; Sanders 1964; Webb 1964).

Sanders (1964:236) concludes that there were few integrative factors
operating in ancient Maya society and many disruptive ones. Accepting
this characterization of the rain forest environment, how can the inception
of lowland Maya civilization be explained?

The stress of Meggers (1954:817), Sanders (1964:238), and Sanders
and Price (1968:142–145) upon a diffusion of civilization into the lowland
rain forest raises a major issue. Since acceptance usually occurs only where
the diffusing complex is useful, what was the function of that complex?
By Sanders' own admission, there would have been little advantage to
sustain a well integrated organization in the Maya lowlands.

Most other hypotheses propose that the Maya cult developed, not out
of economic need, but merely to glorify itself (Webb 1964:420–422). I find
this an ineffective hypothesis. Therefore, the function of socio-political integration in lowland rain forest environments is a crucial question.

In solving this problem, an understanding of the conjunction of environment and technology is significant. Every household (the minimum
production-consumption unit, i.e., extended family, nuclear family, etc.)
needs basic resources to efficiently exploit a given eco-zone. I define basic

Reproduced by permission of the author and the Society for American Archaeology
from *American Antiquity* 36 (3), 1971.

resources as those which are present archaeologically, ethnohistorically, and ethnographically, in every household participating in a specific subsistence configuration, in this case the maize agriculture complex. I will discuss three resources here: igneous or hard stone metates, razor-sharp obsidian tools, and salt.

The metate is found in every household in Mexico. Because stones wear and leave grit in ground corn, the harder the stone the more efficient the metate. Data on excavated metates in the Maya area indicate that subcrystalline limestone metates are rarely found, as natural limestone is too soft to be efficient. Limestone metates occur abundantly only in areas close to major sources of semi-crystalline limestone, such as on the upper Usumacinta and near the Sierra de Yucatán. In areas where both igneous rocks and limestone were readily available, metates were almost exclusively made from the igneous stone. In areas where major deposits of semi-crystalline limestone and igneous rock were lacking, specifically in the northeast Petén, domestic metates were made of imported stone.

Over 2,000 metates have been excavated at Tikal. Only 15% were of native limestone. Eighty-five percent were made of imported stone: quartzite, granite, travertine, etc. (Culbert 1970). In addition, Fry, in his excavations for the Tikal sustaining area survey, found that metates were made of igneous materials as far from the site center as 3.5 km and as early as the Preclassic (Fry 1969:86, personal communication). For the central Petén, the nearest source of igneous stone is the Maya Mountains of Belize. The distance from Tikal to this source is at least 90 km. Whether or not the Tikal population could have survived without imported metates is a moot point: the data indicate massive importation of igneous metates from distant sources by at least the Preclassic.

Obsidian blades with razor-sharp cutting edges are another basic resource. Although obsidian sources are only found in the highlands, flake-blades of obsidian are abundant everywhere in the lowlands. Housemound excavation data from the Maya lowlands indicate that: there is no area where flint served alone in the production of cutting tools; obsidian was utilized everywhere, in some places exclusively; the amount of obsidian in the tool complex was a direct function of the distance from obsidian sources. Therefore, obsidian seems to have been needed, at the very least, to supplement flint tool complexes and was imported everywhere in quantity.

Salt is as essential as water and for precisely the same reason. The chemical requirements of the human body demand that the salt concentration in the blood be kept constant. In areas depending primarily on a vegetarian subsistence diet, a human being needs a minimum of 2–5 g of mineral salt per day (Bloch 1963).

Salt was one of the most important items of trade in precolumbian Mexico (McBryde 1945:46, 72, 60). After the conquest, traffic in feathers and gold ceased, but the salt trade continued (Thompson 1964:20). The Petén is completely without a local mineral salt source. During the sixteenth century, salt for the northwest Petén had to be imported from northern Yucatán (Scholes and Roys 1968:59). Salt for the Usumacinta drainage and Belize was obtained from northern Yucatán and from beds on the upper Chixoy in the Guatemalan highlands (Thompson 1964:20–22).

The point of these data is, given that certain household tools and condiments were considered crucial enough through time to be imported everywhere in the lowlands in quantity and over vast distances, they must have been highly desired by the local populace and must be considered basic resources essential to the efficiency of the practiced subsistence economy.

Most areas of highland Mesoamerica are not far away from one or more sources of these essentials. In the lowlands, however, these resources are few and far between. Because of this highland/lowland dichotomy of resource distribution, there is also a highland/lowland dichotomy in the way in which these goods are mined, worked, collected, and redistributed (Wolf 1967; Nash 1967).

Today, in the highlands where different resource zones are closely spaced, a network of local markets provides for distribution of essential goods. In this system, the unit of production, consumption, and market interaction is the household (Tax and Hinshaw 1969:84; Nash 1967; Wolf 1967). In the lowlands, many resources are not within local reach. The highland household's market function is replaced in the lowlands by supra-household organizations. Instead of a market interaction network, there are hacienda supply stores, local shops, emporiums, and traveling merchants, all depending heavily upon long-distance freight transport provided by postconquest means — mules, trucks, motorboats, and airplanes. Ultimately, as Redfield put it, today the city and its complex organization make trade accessible to small store owners and itinerant merchants by bringing large quantities of goods within their reach (Redfield 1941:156; Wolf 1967).

This present-day highland-household/lowland-supra-household dichotomy in methods of resource distribution seems to have been equally valid before the conquest. Thompson concludes that this is because lowland long-distance travel calls for larger and more organized bodies than does highland travel over shorter routes (Thompson 1964:2). Lowland trade was not merely an extension of face-to-face exchanges common in the highland market system (Chapman 1957:115). The prerequisites of long-distance trade were capital accumulation of available produce and complex organization for security and leadership far above that which a single household could muster.

In pre-mule days, the upper limit a single cargador could carry was 100 lbs, or 2 metates and 6 manos (McBryde 1945:73). The utter impossibility of door-to-door selling of highland resources into an area stretching several thousand square miles is apparent. Trade as an extension of the lowland environment required an elaborate system of redistribution. Obviously, evenly distributed bases where goods could be concentrated as sources of supply for individual households would be advantageous in the rain forest environment. The lowland ceremonial center provided the supra-household capital, organizational potential, integration of scattered population, as well as bases of distribution and supply for preconquest trade; the ceremonial center was the minimal unit of autonomous economics (Leone 1968:127–128).

The need within every household for basic resources therefore created a bridge between ecology and socio-political organization (Sahlins 1958, 1963; Fried 1967). Such organization functioned to insure procurement and distribution of needed resources. Households are quite capable of autonomous direction of their own production. Therefore, one measure of the integrative potential of socio-political organization is decided in how much autonomy the household must give up to secure basic resources.

Independently, a lowland household would have a difficult time obtaining the items necessary to its economic success. For trade in basic resources to reach every household consistently, goods and authority, extracted at the expense of every household, had to be concentrated into a very few hands. This situation selected for lowland developments in socio-political interaction and organization. The advantage of a consistent supply of basic resources and therefore of complex organization, major capital expenditure, and distributional centers provided a way to invest resources and administrative ability in a fashion that brought political, economic, and social integration and control. Those people who could key into long-distance trade successfully would have restricted access to basic resources that could increase efficiency of every household unit and thus they would become integrative nuclei to scattered household populations.

We have considered the lowlands as a whole; now sectors within the lowlands deserve attention. Large lowland areas can be divided into two parts: (1) an outer buffer zone which borders the highlands or major transportation systems; and (2) an inner core or central area, landlocked and secluded from resources by the buffer zone. The division is between areas near to, and areas removed from, highland resources; however, there are no major differential distributions of resources within the lowlands which create this division. Thus, although the core area is more remote from strategic resources, it can only offer the same environmental produce as the closer buffer zone in exchange for them.

An important aspect of the differences in highland and lowland internal trade is the fact that the highland regional diversity and resulting market system provides a network through which scarce goods can easily move. A metate maker can exchange his product for salt, obsidian, pottery, and wood products, thus distributing metates to areas with salt, obsidian, clay, and wood resources. In the lowlands, the number of interactions are severely limited by the lack of differentially distributed resources. There is little economic motivation for the buffer zone to pass on scarce highland resources to the core area in exchange for the products which the buffer zone already has in quantity (see Figure 1). Since neither the core environment nor technology can increase the dependability of supply, the rudiments of human interaction become crucial in consistently obtaining needed resources.

The core environment and geographic position selects for the development of complex organization that can maximize its potential to compete with the buffer zone in highland trade — including the ability to mount large trading expeditions, support factories in resource areas, maintain trade routes, and schedule its efforts in terms of dealing with numerous areas. If complex organization is necessary to obtain resources, then community ceremonial interaction and luxury paraphernalia are equally necessary to maintain stratification and organization (Flannery 1968:100; Fried 1967:32; Rappaport 1967:105–109; Binford 1962; Sabloff and Tourtellot 1969). The environment and geographic position of the core, thus, also select for the elaboration of services and products that reinforce community integration. Such services and commodities are the only scarce resources the core area can tap; its exports will therefore be the by-products of community stratification — a specific ceremonial configuration producing access to the supernatural in terms of temples, altars, ritual and astronomical knowledge, polychrome pottery, ceremonial paraphernalia, and other items of status reinforcement (see Figures 1 and 2).

Several factors are obvious: There is a limit on socio-political development in rain forest environments; the only scarce resources that lowland core areas have to market for strategic goods are the by-products of superior socio-political organization. Therefore, if the buffer zone is socio-politically developed, the best a core area can do is compete on an equal organizational base. Because of spatial proximity the buffer zone will obviously maintain control over strategic resources. Thus, the core area's advantage cannot develop if, at the time of settlement, competing and resource areas are already developed to or beyond the potential of the rain forest.

I hypothesize that given the preconditions of environment, subsistence base, technology, and the existence of basic resources not located in the lowlands, complex socio-political organization in the rain forests of Mesoamerica developed originally in response to the need for consistent procurement, importation, and distribution of non-local basic resources useful to every household. This is a specific formulation of a more general explanatory statement previously proposed by Sahlins (1958), Fried (1967), [James] Hill (personal communication), and others: complex socio-political organization rises in response to the need for procurement and allocation of critical resources or services.

This hypothesis must be tested with available archaeological data. The data utilized in this paper are from the Maya area, although data from the Olmec area provide an equally valid test (Rathje [1972]). Using the hypothesis, I predict the earliest evidence of complex socio-political or-

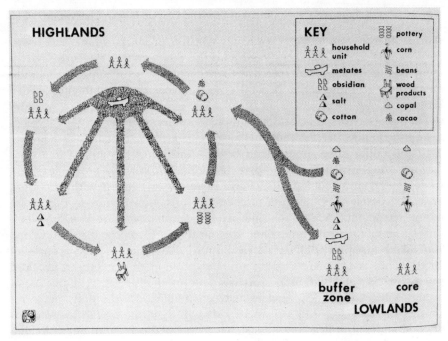

Figure 1   A model of the exchange potential of natural resources between high-land, buffer zone, and core areas.

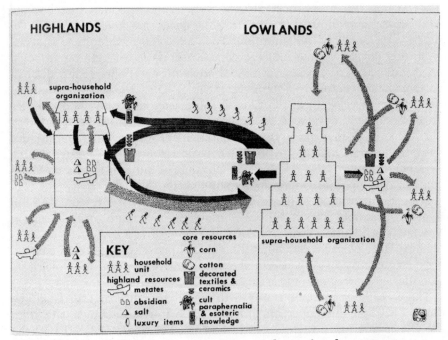

Figure 2   A model of the exchange functions of the core's cult organization.

ganization will occur in the resource deficient core area of the Maya lowlands. No sites of equal complexity will be found in the buffer zone.

Here is a good opportunity to compare hypotheses. Sanders and Price
(1968) predict socio-political development where zones of differing production are closely spaced, especially in alluviated floodplains. Thus, the first
cult developments should, according to Sanders and Price (especially as
interpreted by Adams 1969), occur in the buffer zone.

Granted, the first known heavily populated settlements of the Maya
lowlands are located along rivers, but Sanders and Price (especially as
interpreted by Adams 1969) are not predicting the location of settlements
however early. They are predicting the location of the first development
of the Maya cult, for which I do not feel Xe or any other buffer zone Early
Preclassic settlements qualify. In fact, most of the buffer zone did not
develop complex organization until the late Classic. These data do not deny
the importance of economic symbiosis in stimulating socio-political development, especially in the highlands; they do show that additional factors have
effected lowland cultural development.

If the chiefdoms and cult of the lowland Maya did not develop in the
buffer zone, did they develop in the core as I predict? First, the core area
of least resource exchange potential must be defined. Because of the ethno-
historic record, it is possible to plot postconquest Yucatán population distributions (Figure 3). The only area that can be confirmed as largely
vacant by the records is the center of the northeast Petén (Thompson 1951:
390; 1966:29; Scholes and Roys 1968:463–464; MacNutt 1908:2–29; Means
1917:124–129). This pattern is supported archaeologically (Bullard 1960;
1970). The northeast Petén is one of the areas most distant from salt, obsidian, and igneous stone resources. Obviously, it was not an area with any
special tradeable environmental resource not found abundantly in the rest
of the Maya lowlands (Sanders and Price 1968:169). This then I define
as the lowland core area, the area hardest to reach, with the least economic potential; the one area that was too much trouble to settle and
supply with basic resources in the sixteenth century (Figure 4).

Most Mayanists today believe that the Maya cult complex, in a recognizable constellation, crystallized first within the lowland core area, the
northeast Petén (Willey 1966:117; Thompson 1967:35; W. Coe 1965). The
2 largest sites of the Maya cult, Mirador (Figures 3, 4, site 28) and Tikal
(Figures 3, 4, site 6), are within this core area. One confirmation of the
prediction is provided by stela inscriptions, the earliest of which occur within
the core area (Morley 1937–1938; I. Graham, personal communication).

A second prediction is that: (1) core area influence will spread into
areas vital to the procurement of basic resources — into buffer zones, along
trade routes, and into resource areas; and (2) this influence will take the
form of wholesale importation of the by-products of complex socio-political
organization — cult ideology, cult technology, and manufactured cult commodities from the core area.

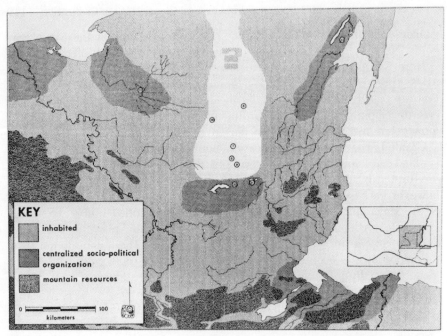

Figure 3   Sixteenth-century population distributions in central Yucatán (after Scholes and Roys 1968; Thompson 1967). The numbered sites are: Tikal, 6; Uaxactun, 7; Balakbal, 8; Uolantun, 9; Mirador, 28; Tapoxte, 31; Itzamkanac, 32; Chetumal, 33; El Zapote, 35.

After the original appearance of the cult in the northeast Petén, it spread into the buffer zone (see Figure 5). The Usumacinta-Pasión drainage, which was a major sixteenth-century trade route, produced Piedras Negras (Figure 5, site 13), Yaxchilan (Figure 5, site 12), and Altar de Sacrificios (Figure 5, site 11) as cult members. Altar's river junction location stands in a special relationship to the Guatemalan highlands. The only salt sources near the lowlands are located up the Chixoy River from Altar. During the Early Classic, strong influences from the Petén spread over the highlands. Most interesting is the fact that later, when much of the highlands became isolated from core area influences, the salt producing Chixoy area remained within the Petén diffusion sphere and in the Chama district (Figure 5, no. 30) one of the great polychrome styles of Mesoamerica emerged (Rands and Smith 1965:131, 144). All of these influences from the Petén passed through strategically located Altar into important highland resource areas. Altar was the only one of the major tested Usumacinta-Pasción sites with an Early Classic cult development of consequence.

Another important buffer zone cult center developed at Copán (Figure 5, site 10), an area geographically in the highland resource zone near obsidian sources and on a Postclassic trade route. During the Copán ar-

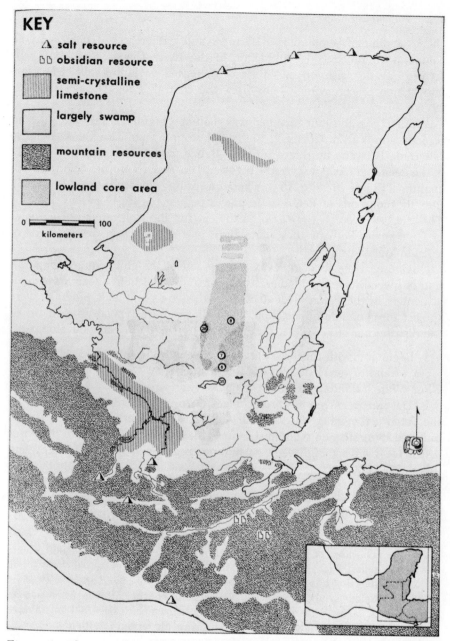

Figure 4 *The central Yucatán core area and surrounding resource zones (after Thompson 1964; Dirrección General de Cartografía 1964; Blom 1932; Graham 1967). The numbered sites are: Tikal, 6; Uaxactun, 7; Balakbal, 8; Mirador, 28; El Zapote, 35.*

chaic, a minimal population of farmers and gatherers had only sporadic contact with the outside. Suddenly, in the Early Classic, the Maya cult arrived. Trade with outside regions increased including the wholesale importation of ceremonial items from the central Petén (Longyear 1952: 32, 68, 70).

Another possible cult member was Tulum (Figure 5, site 14), located directly across from Cozumel, the island stopping point in the Postclassic salt trade between northern Yucatán, Belize, and Honduras. Also of note is the seemingly one-way trade between the Petén core area and Dzibil-chaltun (Figure 5, site 15), where according to Andrews (1965:305) literally thousands of Petén trade pieces pepper the Early period deposits. The Yucatec were enthusiastic customers for the decorated polychromes of Guatemala. Perhaps these data form part of the early development of a Petén-Yucatán salt trade.

Obviously, from its complexity, the spread of the cult required importation of specialists and skilled craftsmen or training of buffer zone individuals at centers in the Petén. Socio-technic and ideo-technic cult products were subject to wholesale importation. The following are typical assessments of the distribution of core area ceramics during the cult's early development:

1. Beginning with the Protoclassic and continuing into the Early Classic ... is a trend toward massive production and extensive distribution of Petén Gloss Ware (Rands and Smith 1965:533).

2. Decorated and monochrome black ware types from the environs of the Petén ceremonial centers reached Barton Ramie in abundance or were imitated by craftsmen who must either have been schooled in the Petén or instructed by persons directly emanating from Petén sources (Willey and others 1965:350).

The ideology and technology of temple architecture, glyphic writing, astronomical knowledge, stela erection, carved eccentrics, and jades diffused similarly. Morley and Brainard conclude:

> The area of Classic Maya culture constituted nearly 100,000 square miles, a major segment of Mesoamerica. Over this region there is evidence of a rapid spread of calendric innovations and an identity of religious symbolism as well as a series of concurrent changes in pottery. ... This remarkably wide-spread homogeneity occurred in an area notable nowadays for its nearly impassible terrain [1946:46].

Thus, the disadvantages of dispersed settlement, great distance from resources, poor transportation, and central location in an area whose redundancy mitigated against local exchange all worked toward integrating communities; and complex socio-political organization in the lowland Maya rain forest developed originally in response to the need for consistent procurement, importation, and distribution of basic resources useful to every household.

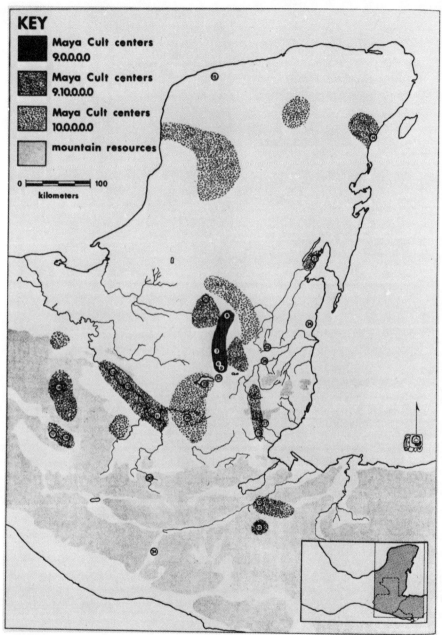

Figure 5 The spread of the Maya cult as represented by the spread of the stela cult (after Morley 1937–1938). The numbered sites are: Tikal, 6; Uaxactun, 7; Balakbal, 8; Uolantun, 9; Copán, 10; Altar de Sacrificios, 11; Yaxchilan, 12; Piedras Negras, 13; Tulum, 14; Dzibilchaltun, 15; Tonina, 16; Comitan, 17; Chinkultic, 18; Pusilha, 19; Calakmul, 20; Ichpaatun, 21; Quirigua, 22; Tayasal, 23; Altun Ha, 24; San Jose, 25; Barton Ramie, 26; Lubaantun, 27; Seibal, 29; Chama Valley, 30; Kaminaljuyu, 34; El Zapote, 35.

Part Two

MAN BEFORE HISTORY

*"Time, which antiquates antiquities, and hath
an art to make dust of all things, hath yet
spared these minor monuments."*

Sir Thomas Browne (1605–1682)

INTRODUCTION

Hunting and gathering have been the basis of human subsistence for all but a few millennia of human existence. Indeed,
only within the past fifteen thousand years have agriculture,
stock breeding, and, later, urban life, been viable ways of
life. Much archaeological research is concerned, then, with the
remains of hunting camps, the sites of specialized gatherers or
fishermen, and farming settlements ranging in size from a small
cluster of huts to a village covering several acres.

The next three chapters present some selected writings
about hunters and farmers in prehistory. These selections
do not include merely descriptive accounts of the results
of excavations, but essays about general aspects of
human development, case studies from prehistoric or modern times that are examples of the types of evidence that
archaeologists are looking for, and detailed reconstructions
conjured up from a collection of archaeological finds.

Hunters form the topic in Chapter 4, where S. L. Washburn
and C. S. Lancaster look at the evolution of hunting and John
Pfeiffer discusses the development of hunting methods in

prehistory. Joe Ben Wheat's account of a Paleo-Indian bison
kill in Colorado provides a vivid picture of an exciting game
drive that occurred many thousands of years ago.

Charlton Ogburn examines some theories relating to the
earliest human settlement of the New World. When this
anthology was compiled, we debated including the latest reports
on discoveries of early human fossils in East Africa and
elsewhere. But we decided against this, for new finds are
constantly in the news, and any papers included would soon be
dated. The essays selected stem from our desire to synthesize
a huge body of data from many disciplines. Prehistorians have
realized that archaeological evidence from Stone Age living
floors alone will never give a complete picture of the earliest
human cultures.

Therefore, anthropologists have studied the behavior of
nonhuman primates such as the baboon and chimpanzee to
try to understand the social and cultural behavior of early man.
Many readers are undoubtedly familiar with the work of Jane
van Lawick-Goodall (1965, and reported in National Geographic)
on the chimpanzees of Gombe stream in Tanzania. Another
approach has been to study living hunters and gatherers such
as the Bushmen of the Kalahari Desert or the Australian
aborigines. Scholars like Richard Lee and Richard Gould have
spent many months in the field studying the life of hunting
bands. John Yellen and others have plotted the remains of
abandoned hunting camps, carrying out a form of "living
archaeology" to establish what survives from an abandoned
hunting camp; their objective is to provide a basis for reconstruction and interpretation of early living sites.

A major emphasis has been placed on behavioral studies, in
radical contrast to the situation twenty years ago when few
archaeologists looked farther afield than the stone tools or the
bones of the rare fossil humans they discovered. Washburn and
Lancaster's article results from the synthesis of an enormous
accumulation of behavioral research on apes and modern
hunter-gatherers. They and other authors have shown that
hunters do not starve for most of the year, eking out a pre-
carious existence off game and vegetable foods. This traditional,
Victorian view of the starving hunter has been abandoned
because of recent research. These studies indicate that hunters,
even in harsh desertic environments, enjoy much leisure, often
more than many farmers of more recent times. "The Evolution
of Hunting" is in many respects a controversial essay,
containing many statements that are not widely accepted. But

the vigorous debates revolving around the origins of man are evident from this contribution.

John Pfeiffer's essay, like those of Joe Ben Wheat and Charlton Ogburn, is more descriptive, although he dwells on the development of big-game hunting and the origins of fire as important factors in the evolution of hunting. Wheat's article shows the essential continuity of hunting methods from pre-historic times into the past few centuries, for American Indians were still using somewhat similar techniques to hunt large game animals on the plains at the time of the first white settlement. Ogburn describes some theories about the earliest settlement of North America in an article that complements that by Lionel Casson in Chapter 7.

By some ten to fifteen thousand years ago, many bands of hunters were enjoying increasingly specialized ways of getting their food. Chapter Five includes some examples which draw heavily on accounts of modern gatherers to amplify the archaeological record. Fishing has long been an important economic strategy at seaside and lakeside localities. Sites like Galatea Bay in New Zealand were probably occupied for considerable periods, often on a seasonal basis for shellfish and other foods. Fishermen and shell collectors leave large shell middens behind them, huge accumulations of abandoned fish bones and shells which should have meticulous excavation. And, as Wilfred Shawcross shows, the amount of information that can be recovered from a shell midden excavation is astonishing.

The gathering of vegetable foods is usually less well attested in the archaeological record, for plant remains are less tangible and easily destroyed, despite development of new recovery techniques in recent years. From the earliest times man undoubtedly relied on vegetable foods for much of his livelihood, exploiting fruit trees in season and sometimes harvesting wild grasses where they grew in extensive stands. The deliberate harvesting of wild grasses and the gathering of vegetable foods are still practiced by many subsistence farmers, who rely on such foods in famine years or in times of stress. From intensive collecting, it may have been a short step to the cultivation of cereal and root crops for food. As the great anthropologist Edward Tylor observed many years ago, most hunters and gatherers are well aware of the germinating properties of seeds or roots. The questions remain: why and when did agriculture first start?

The origins of agriculture and of animal domestication have provoked almost more discussion in archaeology than other topics. An enormous and often polemical literature surrounds the various theories of agricultural origins, which are mainly centered around an origin for food production in the Near East. The dramatic discovery of early farming villages in this area caused V. Gordon Childe to propose his famous hypothesis of a "Neolithic Revolution" to explain the sudden appearance of agriculture and domestic animals in the Near East. Childe's hypothesis has been widely accepted in both archaeological and lay circles, for the concept of major revolutions in human history is popular. Childe said that a climatic change occurring some ten thousand years ago in the Near East was a major factor in forcing man into closer association with plants and animals and from that into exploiting both for his own survival.

More recent investigations have focused on an ecological approach to the problem of origins. Several alternative theories have been proposed, of which Kent V. Flannery's is probably one of the most widely accepted. He feels that climatic change was not responsible for the development of agriculture, but that an important shift in hunting and gathering practices took place some millennia before the origins of cultivation. Near Eastern hunters began to exploit a broader range of vegetable and game resources and were soon using a wide range of resources on a seasonal basis. Then cultivation developed as a deliberate attempt to duplicate wild stands of cereal grasses on margins of the best zones, as population densities rose in the optimum habitats for the wild cereals. Space limitations prevent including more articles on the origins of agriculture, but Childe's and Flannery's hypotheses give some idea of the debate's range.

What was early farming like? Was the farmer's life one of ease, or one of lesser leisure than that of the hunter? How can archaeologists reconstruct prehistoric agriculture? Chapter 6 includes an example of prehistoric agriculture from the Illinois Valley and an instance of modern subsistence farming that outlines the potentials of archaeological research into subsistence agriculture.

CHAPTER FOUR

Hunters

S. L. Washburn
C. S. Lancaster

11 THE EVOLUTION OF HUNTING

In 1966, the Wenner-Gren Foundation for Anthropological Research, which has probably influenced the future development of anthropology more than any other research organization, supported a major conference on "Man the Hunter." The results of this conference, which brought together some 75 scholars who were involved in research on hunters and gatherers, were published in a remarkable volume of essays (Lee and De Vore, 1968). A major article on the evolution of hunting from this book follows. Anthropologists S. L. Washburn and C. S. Lancaster discuss the general characteristics of man that can be attributed to the hunting way of life. Much of their paper is highly controversial and parts of it are not widely accepted by other scholars. But Washburn and Lancaster make the fundamental point that to understand man the hunter, one must examine the biology, psychology, and customs that separate man from the apes. Their article admirably states some issues being faced by archaeologists and others concerned with the early evolution of man.

It is significant that the title of this symposium is Man the Hunter for, in contrast to carnivores, human hunting, if done by males, is based on a division of labor and is a social and technical adaptation quite different

Reprinted from Richard B. Lee and Irven De Vore, editors, *Man the Hunter* (Chicago: Aldine Publishing Company, 1968); copyright © 1968 by Wenner-Gren Foundation for from that of other mammals. Human hunting is made possible by tools, but it is far more than a technique or even a variety of techniques. It is a way of life, and the success of this adaptation (in its total social, technical, and psychological dimensions) has dominated the course of human evolution for hundreds of thousands of years. In a very real sense our intellect, interests, emotions, and basic social life — all are evolutionary products of the success of the hunting adaptation. When anthropologists speak of the unity of mankind, they are stating that the selection pressures of the hunting and gathering way of life were so similar and the result so successful that populations of *Homo sapiens* are still fundamentally the same everywhere. In this essay we are concerned with the general characteristics of man that we believe can be attributed to the hunting way of life.

Perhaps the importance of the hunting way of life in producing man is best shown by the length of time hunting has dominated human history. The genus *Homo* has existed for some 600,000 years, and agriculture has been important only during the last few thousand years. Even 6,000 years ago large parts of the world's population were nonagricultural, and the entire evolution of man from the earliest populations of *Homo erectus* to the existing races took place during the period in which man was a hunter. The common factors that dominated human evolution and produced *Homo sapiens* were preagricultural. Agricultural ways of life have dominated less than 1 per cent of human history, and there is no evidence of major biological changes during that period of time. The kind of minor biological changes that occurred and which are used to characterize modern races were not common to *Homo sapiens*. The origin of all common characteristics must be sought in preagricultural times. Probably all experts would agree that hunting was a part of the social adaptation of all populations of the genus *Homo,* and many would regard *Australopithecus* as a still earlier hominid who was already a hunter, although possibly much less efficient than the later forms. If this is true and if the Pleistocene period had a duration of three million years, then pre-*Homo erectus* human tool using and hunting lasted for at least four times as long as the duration of the genus *Homo.* No matter how the earlier times may ultimately be interpreted, the observation of more hunting among apes than was previously suspected (van Lawick-Goodall, 1965) and increasing evidence for hunting by *Australopithecus* strengthens the position that less than 1 per

Anthropological Research, Inc. Reprinted by permission of S. L. Washburn, the editors, and Aldine Publishing Company. Footnotes are omitted.

Note: This chapter does not deal specifically with the culture history of hunter-gatherers but with some basic thinking behind man's long history as a hunter and with some attempts to reconstruct hunting and gathering from the fragmentary finds from archaeological sites. Readers interested in the culture history of hunter-gatherers should consult: Chester S. Chard, *Man in Prehistory* (New York: McGraw-Hill, 1968); Grahame Clark, *World Prehistory: A New Outline* (Cambridge and New York: University Press, 1969); and Brian M. Fagan, *Men of the Earth* (Boston: Little, Brown, 1974). — Ed.

cent of human history has been dominated by agriculture. It is for this reason that the consideration of hunting is so important for the understanding of human evolution.

When hunting and the way of life of successive populations of the genus *Homo* are considered, it is important to remember that there must have been both technical and biological progress during this vast period of time. Although the locomotor system appears to have changed very little in the last 500,000 years, the brain did increase in size and the form of the face changed. But for present purposes it is particularly necessary to direct attention to the cultural changes that occurred in the last ten or fifteen thousand years before agriculture. There is no convenient term for this period of time, traditionally spoken of as the end of the Upper Paleolithic and the Mesolithic, but Binford and Binford (1966a) have rightly emphasized its importance.

During most of human history, water must have been a major physical and psychological barrier and the inability to cope with water is shown in the archaeological record by the absence of remains of fish, shellfish, or any object that required going deeply into water or using boats. There is no evidence that the resources of river and sea were utilized until this late preagricultural period, and since the consumption of shellfish in particular leaves huge middens, the negative evidence is impressive. It is likely that the basic problem in utilization of resources from sea or river was that man cannot swim naturally but to do so must learn a difficult skill. In monkeys the normal quadrupedal running motions serve to keep them afloat and moving quite rapidly. A macaque, for example, does not have to learn any new motor habit in order to swim. But the locomotor patterns of gibbons and apes will not keep them above the water surface, and even a narrow, shallow stream is a barrier for the gorilla (Schaller, 1963). For early man, water was a barrier and a danger, not a resource. (Obviously water was important for drinking, for richer vegetation along rivers and lakeshores, and for concentrating animal life. Here we are referring to water as a barrier prior to swimming and boats, and we stress that, judging from the behavior of contemporary apes, even a small stream may be a major barrier.)

In addition to the conquest of water, there seems to have been great technical progress in this late preagricultural period. Along with a much wider variety of stone tools of earlier kinds, the archaeological record shows bows and arrows, grinding stones, boats, houses of much more advanced types and even villages, sledges drawn by animals and used for transport, and the domestic dog. These facts have two special kinds of significance for this symposium. First, the technology of *all* the living hunters belongs to this late Mesolithic era at the earliest, and many have elements borrowed from agricultural and metal-using peoples. Second, the occasional high densities of hunters mentioned as problems and exceptions at the symposium are based on this very late and modified extension of the hunting and gathering way of life. For example, the way of life of the tribes of the Northwest Coast, with polished stone axes for woodworking, boats, and extensive reliance on products of the river and sea, should be seen as a very late adaptation. Goldschmidt's distinction (1959, pp. 185–193) between nomadic and sedentary hunting and gathering societies makes this point in a slightly different way. He shows the social elaboration which comes with the settled groups with larger populations.

The presence of the dog (Zeuner, 1963) is a good index of the late pre-agricultural period, and domestic dogs were used by hunters in Africa, Australia, and the Americas. Among the Eskimo, dogs were used in hunting, for transportation, as food in time of famine, and as watchdogs. With dogs, sleds, boats, metal, and complex technology, Eskimos may be a better example of the extremes to which human adaptation can go than an example of primitive hunting ways. Although hardly mentioned at the symposium, dogs were of great importance in hunting, for locating, tracking, bringing to bay, and even killing. Lee (1965, p. 131) reports that one Bushman with a trained pack of hunting dogs brought in 75 per cent of the meat of a camp. Six other resident hunters lacked hunting packs and accounted for only 25 per cent of the meat. Dogs may be important in hunting even very large animals; in the Amboseli Game Reserve in Kenya one of us saw two small dogs bring a rhinoceros to bay and dodge repeated charges.

With the acquisition of dogs, bows, and boats it is certain that hunting became much more complex in the last few thousand years before agriculture. The antiquity of traps, snares, and poisons is unknown, but it appears that for thousands of years man was able to kill large game close in with spear or axe. As Brues (1959) has shown, this limits the size of the hunters, and there are no very large or very small fossil men. Pygmoid hunters of large game are probably possible only if hunting is with bows, traps, and poison. It is remarkable that nearly all the estimated statures for fossil men fall between 5 feet 2 inches and 5 feet 10 inches. This suggests that strong selection pressures kept human stature within narrow limits for hundreds of thousands of years and that these pressures relaxed a few thousand years ago, allowing the evolution of a much wider range of statures.

Gathering and the preparation of food also seem to have become more complex during the last few thousand years before agriculture. Obviously gathering by nonhuman primates is limited to things that can be eaten immediately. In contrast, man gathers a wide range of items that he cannot digest without soaking, boiling, grinding, or other special preparation. Seeds may have been a particularly important addition to the human diet because they are abundant and can be stored easily. Since grinding stones appear before agriculture, grinding and boiling may have been the necessary preconditions to the discovery of agriculture. One can easily imagine that people who were grinding seeds would see repeated examples of seeds sprouting or being planted by accident. Grinding and boiling were certainly known to the preagricultural peoples, and this knowledge could spread along an Arctic route, setting the stage for a nearly simultaneous discovery of agriculture in both the New and Old Worlds. It was not necessary for agriculture itself to spread through the Arctic but only the seed-using technology, which could then lead to the discovery of seed planting. If this analysis is at all correct, then the hunting-gathering adaptation of the Indians of California, for example, should be seen as representing the possibilities of this late preagricultural gathering, making possible much higher population densities than would have been the case in a pregrinding and preboiling economy.

Whatever the fate of these speculations, we think that the main conclusion, based on the archaeological record, ecological considerations, and the ethnology of the surviving hunter-gatherers, will be sustained. In the last few thousand years before agriculture, both hunting and gathering became much more complex. This final adaptation, including the use of products of river and sea and the grinding and cooking of otherwise inedible seeds and nuts, was worldwide, laid the basis for the discovery of agriculture, and was much more effective and diversified than the previously existing hunting and gathering adaptations.

Hunting by members of the genus *Homo* throughout the 600,000 years that the genus has persisted has included the killing of large numbers of big animals. This implies the efficient use of tools. . . . The adaptive value of hunting large animals has been shown by Boulière (1963), who demonstrated that 75 per cent of the meat available to human hunters in the eastern Congo was in elephant, buffalo, and hippopotamus. It is some measure of the success of human hunting that when these large species are protected in game reserves (as in the Murchison Falls or Queen Elizabeth Parks in Uganda), they multiply rapidly and destroy the vegetation. Elephants alone can destroy trees more rapidly than they are replaced naturally, as they do in the Masai Amboseli Reserve in Kenya. Since the predators are also protected in reserves, it appears that human hunters have been killing enough large game to maintain the balance of nature for many thousands of years. It is tempting to think that man replaced the saber-toothed tiger as the major predator of large game, both controlling the numbers of the game and causing the extinction of Old World saber-tooths. We think that hunting and butchering large animals put a maximum premium on cooperation among males, a behavior that is at an absolute minimum among the nonhuman primates. It is difficult to imagine the killing of creatures such as cave bears, mastodons, mammoths — or *Dinotherium* at a much earlier time — without highly coordinated, cooperative action among males. It may be that the origin of male-male associations lies in the necessities of cooperation in hunting, butchering, and war. Certainly butchering sites, such as described by F. Clark Howell in Spain, imply that the organization of the community for hunting large animals goes back for many, many thousands of years. From the biological point of view, the development of such organizations would have been paralleled by selection for an ability to plan and cooperate (or reduction of rage). Because females and juveniles may be involved in hunting small creatures, the social organization of big-game hunting would also lead to an intensification of a sexual division of labor.

It is important to stress, as noted before, that human hunting is a set of ways of life. It involves divisions of labor between male and female, sharing according to custom, cooperation among males, planning, knowledge of many species and large areas, and technical skill. Goldschmidt (1966, pp. 87 ff.) has stressed the uniqueness and importance of human sharing, both in the family and in the wider society, and Lee (personal communication) emphasizes orderly sharing as fundamental to human hunting society. The importance of seeing human hunting as a whole social pattern is well illustrated by the old idea, recently revived, that the way of life of our ancestors was similar to that of wolves rather than that of apes or monkeys. But this completely misses the special nature of the human adaptation. Human females do not go out and hunt and then regurgitate to their young when they return. Human young do not stay in dens but are carried by mothers. Male wolves do not kill with tools, butcher, and share with females who have been gathering. In an evolutionary sense the whole human pattern is new, and it is the success of this particularly human way that dominated human evolution and determined the relation of biology and culture for thousands of years. Judging from the archaeological record, it is probably that the major features of this human way, possibly even including the beginnings of language, had evolved by the time of *Homo erectus*.

THE WORLD VIEW OF THE HUNTER

Lévi-Strauss urged that we study the world view of hunters, and, perhaps surprisingly, some of the major aspects of world view can be traced from the archaeological record. We have already mentioned that boats and the entire complex of fishing, hunting sea mammals, and using shellfish was late. With this new orientation, wide rivers and seas changed from barriers to pathways and sources of food, and the human attitude toward water must have changed completely. But many hundreds of thousands of years earlier, perhaps with *Australopithecus*, the relation of the hunters to the land must also have changed from an earlier relationship which may be inferred from studies of contemporary monkeys and apes. Social groups of nonhuman primates occupy exceedingly small areas, and the vast majority of animals probably spend their entire lives within less than four or five square miles. Even though they have excellent vision and can see for many miles, especially from tops of trees, they make no effort to explore more than a tiny fraction of the area they see. Even for gorillas the range is only about fifteen square miles (Schaller, 1963), and it is of the same order of magnitude for savanna baboons (DeVore and Hall, 1965). When Hall tried to drive a troop of baboons beyond the end of their range, they refused to be driven and doubled back into familiar territory, although they were easy to drive within the range. The known area is a psychological reality, clear in the minds of the animals. Only a small part of even this limited range is used, and exploration is confined to the canopy, lower branches, and bushes, or ground, depending on the biology of the particular species. Napier (1962) has discussed this highly differential use of a single area by several species. In marked contrast, human hunters are familiar with very large areas. In the area studied by Lee (1965), eleven waterholes and 600 square miles supported 248 Bushmen, a figure less than the number of baboons supported by a single waterhole and a few square miles in the Amboseli Reserve in Kenya. The most minor hunting expedition covers an area larger than most nonhuman primates would cover in a lifetime. Interest in a large area is human. The small ranges of monkeys and apes restrict the opportunities for gathering, hunting, and meeting conspecifics, and limit the kind of predation and the number of diseases. In the wide area, hunters and gatherers can take advantage of seasonal foods, and only man among the primates can migrate long distances seasonally. In the small area, the population must be carried throughout the year on local resources, and natural selection favors biology and behavior that efficiently utilize these limited opportunities. But in the wide area, natural selection favors the knowledge that enables a group to utilize seasonal and occasional food sources. Gathering over a wide and diversified area implies a greater knowledge of flora and fauna, knowledge of the annual cycle, and a different attitude toward group movements. Clearly one of the great advantages of slow maturation is that learning covers a series of years, and the meaning of events in these years becomes a part of the individual's knowledge. With rapid maturation and no language, the chances that any member of the group will know the appropriate behavior for rare events is greatly reduced.

Moving over long distances creates problems of carrying food and water. Lee (1965, p. 124) has pointed out that the sharing of food even in one locality implies that food is carried, and there is no use in gathering quantities of fruit or nuts unless they can be moved. If women are to gather while men hunt, the results of the labor of both sexes must be carried back to some agreed upon location. Meat can be carried away easily, but the development of some sort of receptacles for carrying vegetable products may have been one of the most fundamental advances in human evolution. Without a means of carrying, the advantages of a large area are greatly reduced, and sharing implies that a person carries much more than one can use. However that may be, the whole human pattern of gathering and hunting to share — indeed, the whole complex of economic reciprocity that dominates so much of human life — is unique to man. In its small range, a monkey gathers only what it itself needs to eat at that moment. Wherever archaeological evidence can suggest the beginnings of movement over large ranges, cooperation, and sharing, it is dating the origin of some of the most fundamental aspects of human behavior — the human world view. We believe that hunting large animals may demand all these aspects of human behavior which separate man so sharply from the other primates. If this is so, then the human way appears to be as old as *Homo erectus.*

The price that man pays for his high mobility is well illustrated by the problems of living in the African savanna. Man is not adapted to this environment in the same sense that baboons or vervet monkeys are. Man needs much more water, and without preparation and cooking he can only eat a limited number of the foods on which the local primates thrive. Unless there have been major physiological changes, the diet of our ancestors must have been far more like that of chimpanzees than like that of a savanna-adapted species. Further, man cannot survive the diseases of the African savanna without lying down and being cared for. Even when sick, the locally adapted animals are usually able to keep moving with their troop; and the importance to their survival of a home base has been stressed elsewhere (DeVore and Washburn, 1963). Also man becomes liable to new diseases and parasites by eating meat, and it is of interest that the products of the sea, which we believe were the last class of foods added to human diet, are widely regarded as indigestible and carry diseases to which man is particularly susceptible. Although many humans die of disease and injury, those who do not, almost without exception, owe their lives to others who cared for them when they were unable to hunt or gather, and this uniquely human caring is one of the patterns that builds social bonds in the group and permits the species to occupy almost every environment in the world.

A large territory not only provides a much wider range of possible foods but also a greater variety of potentially useful materials. With tool use this variety takes on meaning, and even the earliest pebble tools show selection in size, form, and material. When wood ceases to be just something to climb on, hardness, texture, and form become important. Availability of materials is critical to the tool user, and early men must have had a very different interest in their environment from that of monkeys or apes. Thus, the presence of tools in the archaeological record is not only an indication of technical progress but also an index of interest in inanimate objects and in a much larger part of the environment than is the case with non-human primates.

The tools of the hunters include the earliest beautiful manmade objects, the symmetrical bifaces, especially those of the Acheulian tradition. Just how they were used is still a matter of debate, but, as contemporary attempts to copy them show, their manufacture is technically difficult, taking much time and practice and a high degree of skill. The symmetry of these tools may indicate that they were swung with great speed and force, presumably attached to some sort of handle. A tool that is moved slowly does not have to be symmetrical, but balance becomes important when an object is swung rapidly or thrown with speed. Irregularities will lead to deviations in the course of the blow or the trajectory of flight. An axe or spear to be used with speed and power is subject to very different technical limitations from those of scrapers or digging sticks, and it may well be that it was the attempt to produce efficient high-speed weapons that first produced beautiful, symmetrical objects.

When the selective advantage of a finely worked point over an irregular one is considered, it must be remembered that a small difference might give a very large advantage. A population in which hunters hit the game 5 per cent more frequently, more accurately, or at greater distance would bring back much more meat. There must have been strong selection for greater skill in manufacture and use, and it is no accident that the bones of small-brained men (*Australopithecus*) are never found with beautiful, symmetrical tools. If the brains of contemporary apes and men are compared, the areas associated with manual skills (both in cerebellum and cortex) are at least three times as large in man. Clearly, the success of tools has exerted a great influence on the evolution of the brain, and has created the skills that make art possible. The evolution of the capacity to appreciate the product must evolve along with the skills of manufacture and use, and the biological capacities that the individual inherits must be developed in play and practiced in games. In this way, the beautiful, symmetrical tool becomes a symbol of a level of human intellectual achievement, representing far more than just the tool itself.

In a small group like the hunting band, which is devoted to one or two major cooperative activities, the necessity for long practice in developing skills to a very high level restricts the number of useful arts, and social organization is relatively simple. Where there is little division of labor, all men learn the same activities, such as skill in the hunt or in war. In sports (like the decathlon) we take it for granted that no one individual can achieve record levels of performance in more than a limited set of skills. This kind of limitation is partially biological but it is also a matter of culture. In warfare, for example, a wide variety of weapons is useful only if there are enough men to permit a division of labor so that different groups can practice different skills. Handedness, a feature that separates man from ape, is a part of this biology of skill. To be ambidextrous might seem to be ideal, but in fact the highest level of skill is attained by concentrating both biological ability and practice primarily on one hand. The evolution of handedness reflects the importance of skill, rather than mere use.

Hunting changed man's relations to other animals and his view of what is natural. The human notion that it is normal for animals to flee, the whole concept of animals being wild, is the result of man's habit of hunting. In game reserves many different kinds of animals soon learn not to fear man, and they no longer flee. James Woodburn took a Hadza into the Nairobi Park, and the Hadza was amazed and excited, because although he had hunted all his life, he had never seen such a quantity and variety of animals close at hand. His previous view of animals was the result of his having been their enemy, and they had reacted to him as the most destructive carnivore. In the park the Hadza hunter saw for the first time the peace of the herbivorous world. Prior to hunting, the relations of our ancestors to other animals must have been very much like those of the other non-carnivores. They could have moved close among the other species, fed beside them, and shared the same waterholes. But with the origin of human hunting, the peaceful relationship was destroyed, and for at least half a million years man has been the enemy of even the largest mammals. In this way the whole human view of what is normal and natural in the relation of man to animals is a product of hunting, and the world of flight and fear is the result of the efficiency of the hunters.

Behind this human view that the flight of animals from man is natural lie some aspects of human psychology. Men enjoy hunting and killing, and these activities are continued as sports even when they are no longer economically necessary. If a behavior is important to the survival of a species (as hunting was for man throughout most of human history), then it must be both easily learned and pleasurable (Hamburg, 1963). Part of the motivation for hunting is the immediate pleasure it gives the hunter, and the human killer can no more afford to be sorry for the game than a cat can for its intended victim. Evolution builds a relation between biology, psychology, and behavior, and, therefore, the evolutionary success of hunting exerted a profound effect on human psychology. Perhaps, this is most easily shown by the extent of the efforts devoted to maintain killing as a sport. In former times royalty and nobility maintained parks where they could enjoy the sport of killing, and today the United States government spends many millions of dollars to supply game for hunters. Many people dislike the notion that man is naturally aggressive and that he naturally enjoys the destruction of other creatures. Yet we all know people who use the lightest fishing tackle to prolong the fish's futile struggle, in order to maximize the personal sense of mastery and skill. And until recently war was viewed in much the same way as hunting. Other human beings were simply the most dangerous game. War has been far too important in human history for it to be other than pleasurable for the males involved. It is only recently, with the entire change in the nature and conditions of war, that this institution has been challenged, that the wisdom of war as a normal part of national policy or as an approved road to personal social glory has been questioned.

Human killing differs from killing by carnivorous mammals in that the victims are frequently of the same species as the killer. In carnivores there are submission gestures or sounds that normally stop a fatal attack (Lorenz, 1966). But in man there are no effective submission gestures. It was the Roman emperor who might raise his thumb; the victim could make no sound or gesture that might restrain the victor or move the crowd to pity. The lack of biological controls over killing conspecifics is a character of human killing that separates this behavior sharply from that of other carnivorous mammals. This difference may be interpreted in a variety of ways. It may be that human hunting is so recent from an evolutionary point of view that there was not enough time for controls to evolve. Or it may be that killing other humans was a part of the adaptation from the beginning, and our sharp separation of war from hunting is due to the recent development of these institutions. Or it may be simply that in most human behavior stimulus and response are not tightly bound. Whatever the origin of this behavior, it has had profound effects on human evolution, and almost every human society has regarded killing members of certain other human societies as desirable (Freeman, 1964). Certainly this has been a major factor in man's view of the world, and every folklore contains tales of culture heroes whose fame is based on the human enemies they destroyed.

The extent to which the biological bases for killing have been incorporated into human psychology may be measured by the ease with which boys can be interested in hunting, fishing, fighting, and games of war. It is not that these behaviors are inevitable, but they are easily learned, satisfying, and have been socially rewarded in most cultures. The skills for killing and the pleasures of killing are normally developed in play, and the patterns of play prepare the children for their adult roles. At the conference [James] Woodburn's excellent motion pictures showed Hadza boys killing small mammals, and [William] Laughlin described how Aleuts train boys from early childhood so that they would be able to throw harpoons with accuracy and power while seated in kayaks. The whole youth of the hunter is dominated by practice and appreciation of the skills of the adult males, and the pleasure of the games motivates the practice that is necessary to develop the skills of weaponry. Even in monkeys, rougher play and play fighting are largely the activities of the males, and the young females explore less and show a greater interest in infants at an early age. These basic biological differences are reinforced in man by a division of labor which makes adult sex roles differ far more in humans than they do in nonhuman primates. Again, hunting must be seen as a whole pattern of activities, a wide variety of ways of life, the psychobiological roots of which are reinforced by play and by a clear identification with adult roles. Hunting is more than a part of the economic system, and the animal bones in Choukoutien are evidence of the patterns of play and pleasure of our ancestors.

THE SOCIAL ORGANIZATION OF HUMAN HUNTING

The success of the human hunting and gathering way of life lay in its adaptability. It permitted a single species to occupy most of the earth with a minimum of biological adaptation to local conditions. The occupation of Australia and the New World was probably late, but even so there is no evidence that any other primate species occupied more than a fraction of the area of *Homo erectus.* Obviously, this adaptability makes any detailed reconstruction impossible, and we are not looking for stages in the traditional evolutionary sense. However, using both the knowledge of the contemporary primates and the archaeological record, certain important general conditions of our evolution may be reconstructed. For example, the extent of the distribution of the species noted above is remarkable and gives the strongest sort of indirect evidence for the adaptability of the way of life, even half a million years ago. Likewise all evidence suggests that the local group was small. Twenty to fifty individuals is suggested by Goldschmidt (1959, p. 187). Such a group size is common in nonhuman primates and so we can say with some assurance that the number did not increase greatly until after agriculture. This means that the number of adult males who might cooperate in hunting or war was very limited, and this sets limits to the kinds of social organizations that were possible. Probably one of the great adaptive advantages of language was that it permits the planning of cooperation between local groups, temporary division of groups, and the transmission of information over a much wider area than that occupied by any one group.

Within the group of the nonhuman primates, the mother and her young may form a subgroup that continues even after the young are fully grown (Sade, 1965, 1966; Yamada, 1963). This grouping affects dominance, grooming, and resting patterns, and, along with dominance, is one of the factors giving order to the social relations in the group. The group is not a horde in the nineteenth-century sense, but it is ordered by positive affectionate habits and by the strength of personal dominance. Both these principles continue into human society, and dominance based on personal achievement must have been particularly powerful in small groups living physically dangerous lives. The mother-young group certainly continued and the bonds must have been intensified by the prolongation of infancy. But in human society, economic reciprocity is added, and this created a wholly new set of interpersonal bonds.

When males hunt and females gather, the results are shared and given to the young, and the habitual sharing between a male, a female, and their offspring becomes the basis for the human family. According to this view, the human family is the result of the reciprocity of hunting, the addition of a male to the mother-plus-young social group of the monkeys and apes.

A clue to the adaptive advantage and evolutionary origin of our psycho-

logical taboo on incest is provided by this view of the family. Incest prohibitions are reported universally among humans and these always operate
to limit sexual activity involving subadults within the nuclear family. Taking
the nuclear family as the unit of account, incest prohibitions tend to keep
the birth rate in line with economic productivity. If in creating what we call
the family the addition of a male is important in economic terms, then the
male who is added must be able to fulfill the role of a socially responsible
provider. In the case of the hunter, this necessitates a degree of skill in
hunting and a social maturity that is attained some years after puberty. As
a young man grows up, this necessary delay in his assumption of the role of
provider for a female and her young is paralleled by a taboo which prevents him from prematurely adding unsupported members to the family.
Brother-sister mating could result in an infant while the brother was still
years away from effective social maturity. Father-daughter incest could also
produce a baby without adding a productive male to the family. This
would be quite different from the taking of a second wife which, if permitted, occurs only when the male has shown he is already able to provide
for and maintain more than one female.

To see how radically hunting changed the economic situation, it is necessary to remember that in monkeys and apes an individual simply eats
what it needs. After an infant is weaned, it is on its own economically and
is not dependent on adults. This means that adult males never have economic responsibility for any other animal, and adult females do only when
they are nursing. In such a system, there is no economic gain in delaying
any kind of social relationship. But when hunting makes females and young
dependent on the success of male skills, there is a great gain to the family
members in establishing behaviors which prevent the addition of infants,
unless these can be supported.

These considerations in no way alter the importance of the incest taboo
as a deterrent to role conflict in the family and as the necessary precondi-
tion to all other rules of exogamy. A set of behaviors is more likely to persist
and be widespread, if it serves many uses, and the rule of parsimony is
completely wrong when applied to the explanation of social situations.
However, these considerations do alter the emphasis and the conditions of
the discussion of incest. In the first place, a mother-son sexual avoidance
may be present in some species of monkeys (Sade, 1966) and this extremely
strong taboo among humans requires a different explanation than the one
we have offered for brother-sister and father-daughter incest prohibitions.
In this case, the role conflict argument may be paramount. Second, the
central consideration is that incest produces pregnancies, and the most
fundamental adaptive value of the taboo is the provision of situations in
which infants are more likely to survive. In the reviews of the incest taboo
by Aberle and others (1963) and Mair (1965), the biological advantages
of the taboo in controlling the production of infants are not adequately

considered, and we find the treatment by Service (1962) closest to our own. In a society in which the majority of males die young, but a few live on past forty, the probability of incest is increased. By stressing the average length of life rather than the age of the surviving few, Slater (1959) underestimated the probability of mating between close relatives. Vallois (1961, p. 222) has summarized the evidence on length of life in early man and shows that "few individuals passed forty years, and it is only quite exceptionally that any passed fifty."

That family organization may be attributed to the hunting way of life is supported by ethnography. Since the same economic and social problems as those under hunting continue under agriculture, the institution continued. The data on the behavior of contemporary monkeys and apes also show why this institution was not necessary in a society in which each individual gets its own food. Obviously the origin of the custom cannot be dated, and we cannot prove *Homo erectus* had a family organized in the human way. But it can be shown that the conditions that make the family adaptive existed at the time of *Homo erectus*. The evidence of hunting is clear in the archaeological record. A further suggestion that the human kind of family is old comes from physiology; the loss of estrus is essential to the human family organization, and it is unlikely that this physiology, which is universal in contemporary mankind, evolved recently.

If the local group is looked upon as a source of male-female pairs (an experienced hunter-provider and a female who gathers and who cares for the young), then it is apparent that a small group cannot produce pairs regularly, since chance determines whether a particular child is a male or female. If the number maturing in a given year or two is small, then there may be too many males or females (either males with no mates or females with no providers). The problem of excess females may not seem serious today or in agricultural societies, but among hunters it was recognized and was regarded as so severe that female infanticide was often practiced. How grave the problem of imbalance can become is shown by the following hypothetical example. In a society of approximately forty individuals there might be nine couples. With infants born at the rate of about one in three years, this would give three infants per year, but only approximately one of these three would survive to become fully adult. The net production in the example would be one child per year in a population of forty. And because the sex of the child is randomly determined, the odds that all the children would be male for a three-year period are 1 in 8. Likewise the odds for all surviving children being female for a three-year period are 1 in 8. In this example the chances of all surviving children being of one sex are 1 in 4, and smaller departures from a 50/50 sex ratio would be very common.

In monkeys, because the economic unit is the individual (not a pair), a surplus of females causes no problem. Surplus males may increase fighting in the group or males may migrate to other groups.

For humans, the problem of imbalance in sex ratios may be met by exogamy, which permits mates to be obtained from a much wider social field. The orderly pairing of hunter males with females requires a much larger group that can be supported locally by hunting and gathering, and this problem is solved by reciprocal relations among several local groups. It takes something on the order of 100 pairs to produce enough children so that the sex ratio is near enough to 50/50 for social life to proceed smoothly, and this requires a population of approximately 500 people. With smaller numbers there will be constant random fluctuations in the sex ratio large enough to cause social problems. This argument shows the importance of a sizable linguistic community, one large enough to cover an area in which many people may find suitable mates and make alliances of many kinds. It does not mean either that the large community or that exogamy does not have many other functions, as outlined by Mair (1965). As indicated earlier, the more factors that favor a custom, the more likely it is to be geographically widespread and long lasting. What the argument does stress is that the finding of mates and the production of babies under the particular conditions of human hunting and gathering favor both incest taboo and exogamy for basic demographic reasons.

Assumptions behind this argument are that social customs are adaptive, as Tax (1937) has argued, and that nothing is more crucial for evolutionary success than the orderly production of the number of infants that can be supported. This argument also presumes that, at least under extreme conditions, these necessities and reasons are obvious to the people involved, as infanticide attests. The impossibility of finding suitable mates must have been a common experience for hunters trying to exist in very small groups, and the initial advantages of exogamy, kinship, and alliance with other such groups may at first have amounted to no more than, as Whiting said at the conference, a mother suggesting to her son that he might find a suitable mate in the group where her brother was located.

If customs are adaptive and if humans are necessarily opportunistic, it might be expected that social rules would be particularly labile under the conditions of small hunting and gathering societies. At the conference, Murdock [in Lee and DeVore, 1968, chapter 1] pointed out the high frequency of bilateral kinship systems among hunters, and the experts on Australia all seemed to believe that the Australian systems had been described in much too static terms. Under hunting conditions, systems that allow for exceptions and local adaptation make sense and surely political dominance and status must have been largely achieved.

CONCLUSION

While stressing the success of the hunting and gathering way of life with its great diversity of local forms and while emphasizing the way it influenced human evolution, we must also take into account its limitations. There is no indication that this way of life could support large communities of more than a few million people in the whole world. To call the hunters "affluent" (Lee and DeVore, 1968, chapter 9b) is to give a very special definition to the word. During much of the year, many monkeys can obtain enough food in only three or four hours of gathering each day, and under normal conditions baboons have plenty of time to build the Taj Mahal. The restriction on population, however, is the lean season or the atypical year, and, as Sahlins recognized, building by the hunters and the accumulation of gains was limited by motivation and technical knowledge, not by time. Where monkeys are fed, population rises, and Koford (1966) estimates the rate of increase on an island at 16 per cent per year.

After agriculture, human populations increased dramatically in spite of disease, war, and slowly changing customs. Even with fully human (*Homo sapiens*) biology, language, technical sophistication, cooperation, art, the support of kinship, the control of custom and political power, and the solace or religion — in spite of this whole web of culture and biology — the local group in the Mesolithic was no larger than that of baboons. Regardless of statements made at the symposium on the ease with which hunters obtain food some of the time, it is still true that food was the primary factor in limiting early human populations, as is shown by the events subsequent to agriculture.

The agricultural revolution, continuing into the industrial and scientific revolutions, is now freeing man from the conditions and restraints of 99 per cent of his history, but the biology of our species was created in that long gathering and hunting period. To assert the biological unity of mankind is to affirm the importance of the hunting way of life. It is to claim that, however much conditions and customs may have varied locally, the main selection pressures that forged the species were the same. The biology, psychology, and customs that separate us from the apes — all these we owe to the hunters of time past. And, although the record is incomplete and speculation looms larger than fact, for those who would understand the origin and nature of human behavior there is no choice but to try to understand "Man the Hunter."

John Pfeiffer

12   MAN THE HUNTER

Scientific writer John Pfeiffer has published a remarkable account of early man, *The Emergence of Man* (New York: Harper & Row, 1970). It is essential reading for all students of prehistory. Pfeiffer has also written shorter accounts of early hunters, of which the following is

an excellent sample. The article continues on Washburn and
Lancaster's subject of the evolution of hunting, but also ranges
widely over such topics as the origins of firemaking, the evolutionary
impact of big-game hunting, and the effects of corporate hunting.
Pfeiffer points out that the past is alive in man, for man's behavior
includes hangover responses from the times of hunter-gatherers.
Mankind has been civilized for only a few thousand years — small
wonder that some behavior is inappropriate. The thought-provoking
"Man the Hunter" provides background for further study of the
Stone Age and for the remaining essays in this chapter.

Whatever one happens to think about the future of man, and the pessimists seem more vocal than the optimists nowadays, we have certainly
enjoyed a spectacular past. Indeed, viewed in broad biological perspective,
the past has been a success story without precedent. The first "hominid,"
the first member of the family of man, started out as nobody in particular,
as a face in the crowd. He was one species among a wide variety of primates, and not a particularly distinguished species at that. Most of his
fellow primates had been around a long time before he arrived on the
scene and were more fully adapted to life in the trees.

That was some fifteen to twenty million years ago, only yesterday in
evolutionary terms, and a great deal has happened since then. A near ape
confined to narrow stretches in and around tropical forests has developed
into the most widespread of all primates. We live practically anywhere
— in treeless polar regions, in bare and bone-dry desert places, in the thin
atmosphere of mountain slopes more than three miles high — and our eyes
are currently on the stars, on the possibility of settling elsewhere in the
solar system or beyond. We, the descendants of a minor breed, have become dominant with a vengeance, the only species with the power to re-
make or ruin a planet.

There can be no simple explanation for the phenomenon of man. But
considerable evidence supports the notion that one of the major forces in
prehistory, in the process that led to human beings, was the rise of hunting.
Hunting represented a significant break with deep-rooted primate traditions. All primates but man live predominantly on plant foods, and if our
ancestors had followed established feeding patterns and remained vegetarians, the odds are that we would still be more apish than human, still
be wild animals foraging in the wilderness.

Hunting was no exception to the general rule that far-reaching changes
in human evolution — in the evolution of all species, for that matter — come
at a slow pace rather than in melodramatic bursts. In the beginning it was

From John Pfeiffer, "Man the Hunter," © 1971 American Heritage Publishing Co.,
Inc. Reprinted by permission of the author and the publisher from *Horizon*, Spring 1971.
Illustrations are omitted.

simply a case of stopgap measures calculated to obtain a somewhat larger supply of food than could be provided by plants alone, an activity that apparently could be pursued without radical changes in living habits. But there were changes as hunting became more and more prevalent, until it resulted in the reshaping of hominids both biologically and socially, and to such an extent that important aspects of our behavior today reflect the persisting influence of events that took place during the distant prehistoric past.

According to continuing research, much of it not yet published, this development included the three following stages:

Individual hunting. A stage during which hominids went chiefly after small game and probably did some scavenging; starting perhaps 5,000,000 or more years ago.

Group hunting. This stage was marked by an increasing emphasis on big game, sharing, and sexual division of labor, and began about 1,500,000 years ago.

Corporate hunting. The final stage probably featured the exploitation of great migratory herds on a large-scale, systematic basis, with long-range planning and food storage, and started some 40,000 to 50,000 years ago.

For a glimpse of the earliest hunting hominids, imagine that you are a spectator transported by a time machine to a world long since vanished, an African savanna world that still belongs to zebras and giraffes and vast antelope herds and their predators. Some strange and yet half-familiar animals are squatting not far from a rocky ledge, feeding on grass and roots. They look rather like small chimpanzees, except that when one of them hears a rustling sound, he stands upright like a man and listens intently, with a surprisingly human expression on his face.

Suddenly he sees what made the noise, a hare moving near a low thorn-bush, and is off after it. The chase ends quickly. The hare darts away in a swift zigzag path, easily outdistancing its pursuer for fifty yards or so, and seems well on its way toward a successful escape. But then it leaps over a log and freezes in its tracks on the other side, crouching against the ground as though being stone-still would make it invisible. The hominid comes running up to the log, reaches over to grab the hare, and kills it with one neck-wringing motion. Picking up a sharp rock, he proceeds to dismember his victim and eat it raw on the spot.

This brief and hypothetical encounter is based partly on studies of fossil remains found in Africa during the past forty-five years and partly on observations of the behavior of living primates in the wild. The first hunters weighed fifty pounds or so on the average, stood about four feet tall, and belonged to a breed known as "australopithecines," or "southern apes," although the name does not do them justice. They were rather less than humans, to be sure, but considerably more than apes.

The australopithecines were a product of ten million years of evolution. The predecessors had begun shifting from fruits and other forest foods to such open-savanna fare as grasses and roots and grains, perhaps because of population pressure in the trees, and not long before, the australopithecines had lived on a similar diet. Now they were vegetarians in the process of being corrupted. Not that meat eating is remarkable for primates. Contemporary savanna-dwelling baboons will eat vervet monkeys, hares, and fauns that happen to lie in their paths, but only occasionally, and more than 99 per cent of their food is plant food.

But baboons eat larger quantities of meat during droughts, and the australopithecines may have had to do the same. For them, however, it was not a matter of occasional dry-season emergencies. Dry conditions were spreading over wide continental areas, producing a permanent "emergency," which is probably the chief factor that brought about meat eating on a regular basis. The practice started at least two or three million years ago, the age of the oldest known stone tools (bashing and cutting tools found during the past year near Lake Rudolf in Kenya), and may well have started two to three million years before that.

We can make some educated guesses about the hunting techniques of remote prehistory. For example, like the aborigines of the Australian Western Desert, our ancestors may have erected blinds near water holes, piles of rocks behind which they could hide until their prey came within striking distance. They were probably capable of building such simple structures. Excavating in the Olduvai Gorge — one of the world's richest sites for hominid remains — Louis Leakey, director of the Center for Prehistory and Paleontology in Nairobi, has found traces of a stone wall or windbreak in deposits nearly two million years old.

Then as now, survival required an intimate knowledge of the ways of other animals, particularly an ability to take advantage of their instincts, their built-in escape tactics. The sight of a potential meal moving away at top speed can be a highly discouraging experience for a relatively sluggish predator, and it takes a special kind of wisdom to keep up the chase, confident that sooner or later the prey will go into a freeze-and-crouch pattern. Hares do this, as do certain birds, including a type of partridge whose bones have been found at some of the oldest Olduvai campsites.

Stalking is another ancient and effective technique. But as Leakey has learned from years of practice, it demands a measure of patience rarely found among hunters who are not playing for keeps, whose lives do not depend on hunting. Once, near a lake outside Nairobi, he camouflaged himself with leafy branches stuck in his belt and started stalking a gazelle about 250 yards away. He advanced slowly as long as the gazelle had its head down to graze. But whenever it stopped grazing and raised its head to look around, he stopped too. He was always one move ahead of the animal. For example, he anticipated the instant of head-raising: "Just before the gazelle looks up, it seems to raise one shoulder a bit higher than the other. That's my signal to stop moving."

Leakey kept on the alert, observing the positions of other gazelles and nearby birds that might call out in alarm at a sudden movement and give him away. He noted possible sources of food in case his prey should escape, such things as a large snail, birds' nests, and an anthill. At last, after two long hours of stalking, he found himself poised only six feet from the gazelle. The hunt ended when he brought it down with a flying tackle, perfected during his university rugby days.

Hunting resulted in a breakdown, or rather, a partial breakdown, of rugged individualism. As far as getting food is concerned, each member of a troop of nonhuman primates is strictly on its own. That even includes infants after their first year: if a mother is feeding and her infant reaches for some of her food, she will push the child away. But hunting involves sharing, apparently from the very beginning. The existence of australopithecine base camps suggests that they established places where they could await the return of hunters with meat for the troop.

Inevitably, as the hunters became more ambitious, there was more to share. Small game predominated at the oldest Olduvai living sites — hares, tortoises, rats, lizards, and migratory birds, as well as the young of various antelopes. But excavations at later sites in Africa and Europe indicate a gradually increasing preference for a diet that included a higher proportion of big game, a change dictated largely by economics. It may take many hours of intensive small-game hunting to yield the amount of food represented by the killing of a single large antelope. Two or three men hunting together for big game in abundant savanna lands can obtain far more than two or three times as much meat as a lone man in search of small game.

Such tactics were important not only as a way of obtaining meat in large packages. From the standpoint of survival, they were not strictly necessary. Our prehistoric ancestors could, and often did, get along quite adequately, if less efficiently, on a diet consisting solely of small game and various kinds of plants. The shift to the hunting of big game is noteworthy mainly for its social impact. In fact, it helped trigger the most significant chain of developments in the evolution of hominids since they came down from the trees and took up meat eating in the first place.

This trend probably began gathering momentum between 2,000,000 and 1,000,000 B.C., and was certainly well established by about 300,000 years ago. The oldest known prehistoric site outside Africa, the Vallonet cave located on a Mediterranean cliff in France, contains a few chopping tools that were used nearly a million years ago and a museumful of large-animal fossils, including those of rhinoceros, hippopotamus, brown bear, wild boar, and deer. A somewhat more recent site near the village of Torralba in north-central Spain, excavated by Leslie Freeman and Clark Howell of the University of Chicago, has yielded, among other things, the remains of some forty horses and as many elephants, most of which seem to have been deliberately driven into a swamp.

The fossil record hints at the full evolutionary impact of this sort of activity. The period that saw the rise of big-game hunting also saw a notable expansion, and probably a basic reorganization, of the hominid brain and the coming of creatures who had definitely crossed the borderline region between pre-man and man. The most advanced australopithecines had brains with a volume of some 600 cubic centimeters, about the size of a small grapefruit. Estimates based on a study by David Pilbeam of Yale University suggest that within a million years their descendants had brains averaging more than half again as large — and in some cases twice as large, which is almost comparable to the brains of people today.

Pilbeam and other investigators point to a direct relationship between big-game hunting, the development of more complex brains, and the appearance of the first men, members of the species Homo erectus. Natural selection went to work on the hunters. Bands that happened to include individuals with larger-than-average brains tended to outhunt and outlive bands made up of smaller-brained individuals. The inference is that the former were better able to think things through beforehand — preparing ambushes and pitfalls, arranging schedules and signals, using and improving whatever crude form of language they had at the time, and making better tools, a development that seems somehow to have been closely connected with the development of language.

Another advance contributing to the hunting way of life was the use of fire, the earliest known traces of which have been found in a cave not far from Vallonet. The lights went on about 750,000 years ago. Little spots of fire appeared in valleys that had always been dark at night. Fire, originally brought into caves for warmth, acquired another function, that of keeping animals away; and later it was used as an offensive weapon to stampede animals. Signs of burned grass indicate that fire may have been used at Torralba to drive big game into bogs.

Fire also brought a longer day. Hominids, like most forest and savanna animals, had always lived sunrise-to-sunset lives. Now they had extra time to gather at firesides when the hunt was done and review the day's successes and the day's failures, the big ones that got away. The hearth became the first family circle. We have no archaeological proof of ritual activities during this period, but it is quite possible that legends and hunting ceremonies, accompanied by dancing and rhythmical noisemaking, originated around early hearths. Flame and the crackling of burning wood and the moving shadows on cave walls aroused a variety of emotions, and may have served as a kind of stimulant.

Life was becoming more and more complicated, even in those days. The expansion of the brain itself, the most human thing about human beings, introduced a host of difficulties and confronted nature with a bio-engineering problem that has never been solved to everyone's satisfaction. The birth of bigger-brained babies called for an enlarged female pelvic opening and wider hips. But there are limits in that direction, one of them being the fact that wider hips result in an undesirable decrease in running speed and general mobility. So evolution achieved a compromise: hips became a little wider, while babies were born with brains designed to do most of their growing after birth.

The compromise was in line with an established trend in primate evolution; the repercussions have been enormous. The brain of a newborn rhesus monkey has already attained 75 per cent of its final adult size, and the infant is ready to forage for itself at the age of one. But Homo erectus infants came into the world with brains only about a fourth of adult size; the infants were helpless for four or five years, and more completely helpless than the offspring of any other primate. Incapable of either following or clinging to their mothers, they evolved special ways of actively attracting and summoning grownups, notably with the smile and an entire repertory of cries.

Bigger brains affected the habits of mothers as well as those of infants. Prolonged infant dependency meant prolonged maternal dependency. Just as infants needed a mother's care longer, so mothers relied more than ever before on males for defense, help in obtaining food and firewood, and more active participation in the rearing of offspring. The psychoanalyst Erik Erikson of Harvard speaks of the fear of being abandoned as "the most basic feminine fear, extending over the whole of a woman's existence," and that fear may have developed during Homo erectus times, along with new ways of attracting and holding males.

The typical pattern for female primates, for all female mammals, is to be sexually receptive during a brief period of the month only. They come into estrus, or sexual heat, at or immediately following ovulation, tending to be indifferent and unreceptive during the rest of the month. The human female is the only female in which estrus has disappeared, and according to one theory, the evolutionary advantage of the disappearance was that she could become sexually receptive throughout the month and thus improve her chances of tying the male, and eventually a particular male, more securely to her and her offspring.

Developments like these marked the beginnings of monogamy, and an early phase in the prehistory of the human sort of love. They also marked changes in males, changes emphasized in an important study by Lionel Tiger of Rutgers University. Male-male ties were becoming stronger, along with male-female ties. Hunting gave a new meaning to the feelings of man for man. Relationships became closer, more emotionally charged, in the excitement of the chase and the kill, the satisfaction of working as a team, and the sharing of intense experiences and nights at remote camps.

Larger brains, prolonged infant and maternal dependency, changes in sexual behavior — these were some of the consequences of the new kind of primate co-operation that came when a few men began making a regular practice of going out together to kill meat on the hoof. But the story of hunting has another, a final, chapter. The shaping of modern man may have been related to further advances in the technology of killing big game and may have involved events following the appearance of Neanderthal man about 100,000 years ago.

Neanderthal man was a full-fledged member of our species, Homo sapiens, which had appeared more than 150 millenniums earlier with the passing of Homo erectus. His forehead was lower and more sloping than ours, and he had heavier limbs and heavy bone ridges over his eyes. Contrary to popular opinion, however, he was neither brute nor savage; he stood fully erect and is known to have been a highly accomplished hunter. Investigators who have spent time among the Eskimos still do not understand how he managed to live through the long and bitter glacial winters of western Europe.

His fate was determined not by climate but by the evolution of a superior breed. Neanderthal man represented a special kind of Homo sapiens, a subspecies that never made it, but came very close. He lived always on the verge of becoming fully human, or at least as human as we are. For example, judging by a few recent finds of shapes scratched on bone, he was groping to express something and had a vague feeling for pattern and design.

One region of special interest in the study of Neanderthal man lies at the eastern end of the Mediterranean, along the slopes of mountain ranges running roughly parallel to the coastline of Israel, Syria, and Lebanon. This region includes three sites on which traces of a transitional people have been found, people who were definitely Neanderthals, but not like those typical of western Europe. In a cave and nearby rock shelter on the slopes of Mount Carmel, for example, investigators have excavated the remains of individuals with less massive brow ridges, somewhat more rounded skulls, more prominent chins, and smaller faces. The remains date back 40,000 to 50,000 years.

Sally Binford of the University of New Mexico, an archaeologist who has excavated in the Near East, has a theory about why the change occurred in that region and at that time. For one thing, the climate was becoming slightly drier, producing a pattern of seasonal rainfall and affecting the behavior of wild cattle and other herd animals. During the summer the animals grazed on the relatively damp coastal plains, and during the fall, when grasses became scarce, they moved up along green wooded valleys into the foothills, where highland meadows were watered by late fall rains.

Up to this point in human evolution most hunters probably killed one animal at a time, the idea being to stalk a herd and go after a particular individual, often an individual weakened by advanced age or injury. Lions, wild dogs, and other carnivores use similar tactics, which are well suited for groups of three or four hunters. But conditions were ripe for a change along the slopes of the Near Eastern mountains, and according to Miss Binford, late Neanderthal people had the wits to take advantage of their opportunities.

This was the beginning of corporate hunting, with its emphasis, as it were, on "mass production" methods. Large groups of hunters, perhaps as many as twenty to thirty, gathered to wait, not at places where the game was, but at places where their prey could be expected to come in the near future — at narrow passes and natural blinds along the traditional routes of migratory herds. Certain sites in the area are located at such points and include what may be interpreted as further evidence for the Binford theory, a sharp increase in the proportion of wild-cattle bones. Incidentally, the animals did not behave like the docile, mild-eyed creatures of contemporary pastures; the bulls measured more than six feet at the shoulder and were probably fierce, fast on their feet, and well built for fighting back.

Corporate hunting, the most advanced stage of prehistoric food gathering, may have provided the main stimulus for the coming of the most advanced of the hominids. New tactics presumably brought a new need for the ability to look ahead and devise increasingly sophisticated plans. Great quantities of tools would have to be manufactured beforehand, and individuals assigned to special tasks in preparing ambushes and killing, in large-scale butchering, and finally in sharing the meat. These and other organized activities would have favored the development of the brain, not so much in its over-all size, since Neanderthal man had a brain as large as ours, but in certain areas — especially those areas located at the front and sides of the brain and concerned with language and long-range planning.

The record is clear on one basic point. About 35,000 to 40,000 years ago the heavy-browed Neanderthal man of western Europe was replaced by Cro-Magnon man, and prehistory's golden age had begun, an age that culminated in the magnificent cave art of southern France and Spain. The general opinion is that the newcomers originated in the Near East and adjacent areas, and that they were people essentially like us. Or, to put it another way, we have a great deal in common with them psychologically and socially, which is perhaps the most important reason for the current interest in human evolution among scientists and laymen alike.

The past is not something over and done with. It is alive in man, in the sense that some of the things he does most easily, the things that come most naturally, are hang-over responses considerably less useful and relevant today than they once were. We have been wild animals roaming the wilderness for more than 15,000,000 years, hunters for perhaps 5,000,000 years, and civilized — or rather, partially and intermittently civilized — for the last few millenniums only. So it is hardly surprising that upon occasion we behave inappropriately.

According to one estimate, the world's total hominid population two or three millions years ago was about 125,000 individuals, all of them in Africa. Man has been a minority species so long that he reacts to "ghost" circumstances, circumstances that no longer exist, like the punch-drunk ex-prize fighter who the instant he hears a bell is up and on his feet in fighting stance. The sight of a stranger in a small town may arouse the precise feelings of hostility and distrust that the sight of a stranger aroused long, long ago, when hominids spent their entire lives as members of small hunting bands and anything new was a shock and a threat.

Being frightened by novelty is only part of man's instinctive small-band psychology, only one sign that he lives partly in a vanished world. His capacity to care for others tends to be limited. Generally speaking, a person feels deep love for a few close relatives only, and perhaps for a few close friends. Beyond that, there is a rather rapid falling off of concern; he is not really moved by the problems and frustrations of people across the street or across the hall. This is fundamentally a hunter's behavior, the psychology of one who lives his life among a few of his fellows, rarely seeing anyone else.

Man's instinct is to take, and to take right now while the taking is good. After ages of living on his own among more numerous species, hunting and being hunted, learning to get his share of food and shelter, he has become a master exploiter. Now he has made a world that no longer has a place for exploiters, and yet his relationship to the land and to other animals continues to be primarily one of exploitation. He continues to behave as though the world were still a place of savannas and virgin forests that covered continents.

The existence of such instincts does not mean that man is doomed, that he is innately a killer and must sooner or later wipe himself out. Of all species Homo sapiens is by far the most adaptable. But change is never easy, and it demands a real effort — an act of creation — to control and modify behavior rooted in the past. The problem is to design environments as appropriate for modern man as the wilderness was for prehistoric man.

Studies of contemporary hunters, like the Bushmen of Africa's Kalahari Desert, indicate that man has lost certain important things in the process of becoming civilized. In most hunting societies men and women live on equal terms with one another, and murder and warfare are extremely rare. Class distinctions and mass killing come with the passing of the hunt. Furthermore, hunters generally have an easy life. Travelers from affluent societies are responsible for the myth that primitive peoples are, and have always been, engaged in a bitter struggle for survival. Richard Lee of Rutgers reports that the Bushmen require no more than two or three days to obtain a week's supply of food, even in a semi-desert environment. They spend the rest of the time talking, playing games, and visiting friends and relatives. Man has never known true leisure since the end of his hunting days.

These facts do not call for a return to the hunt, a "return to nature." But they provide insights into current efforts to recover the desirable features of a past way of life, equality and nonviolence and leisure, as well as to modify the undesirable features, such as the distrust of strangers and novelty in general. Man today is what he has always been, a creature in transition — and, despite the pessimists, a creature with a future.

Joe Ben Wheat

13   A PALEO-INDIAN BISON KILL

> How did prehistoric man hunt? What methods did he use to kill the large game animals whose broken bones abound on his abandoned camp sites? Economic evidence from archaeological sites based on animal bones and other organic remains is usually incomplete. Occasionally, however, the archaeologist can make an astonishingly complete reconstruction of life in the past, for example, from a site where many animals were stampeded into a narrow defile, killed, and then butchered, as is described by Colorado archaeologist Joe Ben Wheat in the following selection. In this vivid reconstruction of the bison kill at the Olsen-Chubbuck site in Colorado, the excavators of the bison bones were even able to hypothesize about the wind's direction on the day of the hunt. Wheat studied a big-game hunt of a type that used methods perfected by millions of hunters, from the early millennia of the Stone Age up to recent times. Big-game drives were commonplace in Africa half a century ago and occurred in North America in the nineteenth century. Human hunting methods have changed little during the past thirty thousand years, and many techniques have a far longer ancestry.

BISON KILL — A RECONSTRUCTION
OF THE OLSEN-CHUBBUCK SITE

Down in the valley the little stream flowed gently southward. Pleasant groves of trees were heavy with their new burden of early summer leaves. Here and there small herds of bison were drinking. In the lush prairie

From Joe Ben Wheat, "The Olsen-Chubbuck Site: A Paleo-Indian Bison Kill" (as edited by Ernestine Green). Reproduced by permission of the author and the Society for American Archaeology from *Memoirs of the Society for American Archaeology* 26, 1972. Photograph by Joe Ben Wheat; courtesy University of Colorado Museum. References are omitted.

bottoms, paralleling the stream and occasionally crossing it, were the main bison trails. Those currently in use were narrow grooves cut into the sod. Older abandoned trails were visible; some had become small rivulets emptying runoff water into the stream, but others had become filled with earth and grass, and were visible as narrow, bright green ribbons against the paler green of the less well fertilized prairie. For countless years, the bison each spring had moved gradually northward and eastward, along similar trails, up the smaller tributaries such as this one, into their summer grazing ranges. To the east, the prairie sloped gently upward to the level High Plains country, and narrow, undulating, bison trails led to the grassland there. Out of the valley bottom, other trails led westward to grazing grounds in the uplands near a low divide. On the approach to this western divide, the slope at first steepened sharply, then flattened out into a small basin before rising gradually again to a low pass into the valley beyond. At one time, this narrow basin had been drained by a small stream which carried runoff waters to the southeast. However, an abandoned bison trail had gradually diverted the flow of this stream, and in the process had become a gully, or arroyo, some 2 or 3 m (6–10 ft) wide and about 2 m (6.5 ft) deep. Seeps and small pools lined the sides and bottom of this arroyo. To the north, a small herd of 200 to 300 long-horned bison — cows, bulls, yearlings, and young calves — were grazing in the small valley. A gentle breeze was blowing from the south.

As the bison grazed, a party of hunters approached from the north. Quietly, under cover of the low divide to the west and the steep slope to the east, the hunters began to surround the grazing herd. Moving slowly and cautiously, keeping the breeze in their faces so as not to disturb the keen-nosed animals, they closed in on the herd from the east, north, and west. Escape to the south was blocked by the arroyo. Now the trap was set.

Suddenly the pastoral scene was shattered. At a signal, the hunters rose from their concealment, shouting and yelling, and waving robes to frighten the herd. Spears began to fall among the animals, and at once the bison began a wild stampede toward the south. Too late, the old cows leading the herd saw the arroyo and tried to turn back, but it was impossible. Animal after animal pressed from behind, spurred on by the shower of spears and the shouts of the Indians now in full pursuit. The bison, impeded by the calves, tried to jump the gully, but many fell short and landed in the bottom of it. Others fell kicking, twisting, and turning on top of them, pressing those below ever tighter into the confines of the arroyo. In a matter of seconds, the arroyo was filled to overflowing with a writhing, bellowing mass of bison, forming a living bridge over which a few animals escaped. Now the hunters moved in and began to give the coup de grace to those animals on top, while underneath, the first trapped animals kept up the bellows and groans and their struggle to free themselves, until finally the heavy burden of slain bison above crushed out their lives. In minutes the kill was over.

One hundred ninety bison lay dead in and around the arroyo. Tons of meat awaited the knives of the hunters — meat enough for feasting, and plenty to dry for the months ahead — more meat, in fact, than they could use. Immediately, the hunters began to butcher their kill. From the top of the heap, they dragged the carcasses back and rolled them onto their bellies, flexed the forelegs alongside and extended the hind legs behind the body, to help support the great bulk. They slit the skin the length of the back, and, peeling the skin down, began to strip the meat away from the hump and ribs. A foreleg cut from another animal was used as an adze to break the ribs near their juncture with the backbone, to give access to the interior where the vital organs were delicacies awaiting them. The shoulders were removed, then the backbone was severed just behind the rib cage. The neck was cut just in front of the ribs. Jaws were cut away from the skull and broken apart at the joint to free the tongue, or else the throat was slit and the tongue pulled through and cut off. The hind quarters were disjointed and stripped of their meat. As it was cut off, some of the flesh was eaten raw, but most of the meat was laid on the skin to keep it clean. Animal after animal was butchered. As the days passed, amid the feasting on internal organs and fresh meat, the drying of meat went on, assuring a supply to last until the next kill. While the meat was drying, skins were prepared for use as robes, and containers were made from the horns, which had been removed by breaking off the core from the skull. Many of the leg bones were broken and the marrow removed. Some carcasses were wedged well down into the arroyo, and these were too heavy for the hunters to move. The beautifully flaked spear points which had killed these animals went unretrieved. Wherever a leg jutted up, it was cut off, and other accessible parts were butchered; but much remained which could not be cut up. No attempt was made to salvage the bison trapped in the very bottom of the arroyo.

For many days, the butchering, feasting, preparation of hides, and meat-drying went on. In time, however, the meat remaining on the carcasses became too "high" for use, and the hunters had dried as much meat as they could carry; so finally they moved on, leaving the gully filled with bones and rotting flesh. As the summer wore on, rain water drained into the arroyo, carrying sediment with it, but the carcasses blocked free flow of the water and caused the stream to dump its load of silt and sand, covering the mass of rotting flesh and bones. Within a few years, the upper part of the arroyo was filled, although there continued to be a shallow wash to the eastward.

Several thousand years passed before this last remnant of the arroyo was filled, and the climate became drier and hotter. During this time, another group of hunters and gatherers moved into the area and camped for a time on the hill to the west and on the ridge to the north. Their campsites were marked by the remains of pit ovens and by a few of their characteristic indented-base, stemmed dart points, as well as some scrapers and other crude tools. One or 2 of their tools were lost in the, by now, nearly filled wash.

Still later, other groups camped and hunted near the old bison kill, but by this time no evidence of the old arroyo was left on the surface.

By 1880, there were no bison left, and the last Indians began to be replaced by White cattlemen. In 1947, the sod was broken for planting; shortly thereafter, the combination of drought and fierce winds that marked the early 1950's began to erode away the upper deposits that had covered the gully and the terrace through which it had been cut. By 1957, the bones that filled the one-time arroyo were once again exposed on the surface [Figure 1].

The foregoing is a reconstruction and interpretation of events which transpired over a period of some 10,000 years. In over a quarter of a century of practicing archaeology, I have, from time to time, discovered evidence which made real and immediate the people whose remains and relics were being uncovered. For the most part, these instances have been minute fragments of a continuum whose whole was too diffuse, whose time span too long, and whose practitioners too alien, to call to mind a picture of events which could be sustained from more than moments.

However, at the Olsen-Chubbuck site there was unfolded a picture so complete within itself, whose action was so brief and self-contained, that, except for minor details, one could almost visualize the dust and tumult of the hunt, the joy of feasting, the satisfaction born of a surplus of food, and finally, almost smell the stench of the rotting corpses of the slain bison as the Indians left the scene of the kill to seek other game in other places. Time seemed, indeed, to be stilled for an interval, and a microcosm of the hunters' life preserved. This is what I have tried to convey. The evidence from which I have drawn, in perhaps too firm lines, a picture of the kill, constitutes the body of this study. . . .

LAYOUT OF EXCAVATION

Before the University of Colorado Museum took over excavation of the Olsen-Chubbuck site, a furrow had been plowed lengthwise through the outcropping of bones. This had damaged the upper bones to a certain extent, but it had shown the deposit to be linear, and had defined the orientation of the bone bed. This furrow, in addition to the pits excavated by Olsen and Chubbuck, enabled us to estimate closely the course of the ancient gully which contained the bone bed.

A base line, oriented 80° magnetic (June 19, 1960) was established along the south side of the bone bed and generally parallel to it [Figure 2]. This base line was divided into 2 m (6.56 ft) sections numbered consecutively beginning with Section 1, well beyond what we believed to be the eastern end of the bone deposit, and continuing westward beyond the

Figure 1   River of bones.

known extent of the site [Figure 2]. These sections were then staked out at right angles to the base line. The width of each section was determined by the width of the arroyo and its contained bone deposit. Each section took its number from the stake at its southeastern corner.

The pits dug by Chubbuck and Olsen lay between the east end of Section 16 and the west end of Section 10, thus encompassing all or part of Sections 10, 11, 12, 13, 14, 15, and 16. The eastern extremity of this pit was not dug in a vertical face but, rather, sloped from the surface, beginning some 30 cm (1 ft) east of the line dividing Sections 10 and 11, and sloping some 50 cm (1.6 ft) westward into Section 11.

Eastward, beyond the Olsen and Chubbuck pit, the bone bed did not outcrop on the surface but sloped down as the bottom of the arroyo sloped. Thus, from Section 10 eastward, there was an ever-increasing overburden of fill above the bone bed.

RECORDING

A contour map of the site was made, including the surrounding area [Figure 2]. A hand level mounted on a tripod, and a surveying rod were used for this purpose. A plane table and alidade were used during the 1960 season to plot in additional excavations and features.

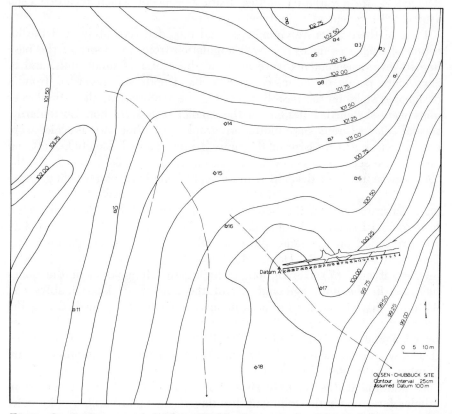

Figure 2   Contour map of Olsen-Chubbuck site with additional data compiled from Department of Agriculture aerial photographs.

When we began excavation of the site, we had the impression, gathered from the surface outcrop and the exposed faces of the Olsen-Chubbuck pit, that the bone bed consisted almost entirely of disarticulated bones which the Indians, in an excess of tidiness, had tossed into the arroyo following the butchering. Hence, we planned to excavate the site by arbitrary 30 cm (1 ft) levels within each section, and to record the bones merely by section and level. However, it very quickly became apparent that, while there was a quantity of disarticulated bones, there were also many articulated segments of skeletons. These segments consisted of varying numbers of bones — 2 or 3 articulated vertebrae, a whole foot, and so on, including, as we later discovered in the lower deposits, whole animals. It seemed clear that these segments represented portions of the bison which were cut off during the butchering process. We reasoned that, if we could recover enough of these segments, we should have considerable first-hand data as to the butchering techniques of the Indians. Thus, it became necessary to devise some sort of recording system which would enable us to secure the maximum amount of data regarding the bones. We ultimately decided to use a variation of the "feature" concept which regarded each articulated segment as a "butchering unit."

Each of these units was numbered and recorded separately, and the location of each was measured by triangulation from 2 or more of the base line stakes. Measurements were made to the center of small units, and to 2 or more points on large, complex units. Depth was recorded from a designated stake on the base line. During the 1958 season, all of the larger units were sketched, but some of the smaller ones were not. Customarily, several adjacent units were plotted on graph paper, but various scales were used according to the size of the units being recorded. Isolated, scattered bones were recorded, somewhat haphazardly, in the field books. By the 1960 season, we had developed more refined methods of recording, especially with regard to the isolated bones. Each unit was recorded and drawn on a separate page in the notebook or on larger sheets of graph paper, to a standard scale of 20 cm (0.65 in) to 1 in (2.54 cm). Standard data were recorded on the same sheet, as follows: (1) Site designation; (2) Unit field number; (3) Date; (4) Excavator; (5) Recorder; (6) Photo number, if any; (7) Description, including the designation of the bones included in the unit, age and sex of the animal, if determinable; (8) Attitude, that is, the lay of the unit in relation to the bone bed and the boundaries of the arroyo; (9) Relationship to other units; (10) Location, by triangulation; (11) Depth; (12) Remarks, if any; (13) Disposition, that is, what parts saved or discarded; (14) University of Colorado Museum number, if the unit was saved.

In addition to the separate sheet for each unit, each was recorded in tabular form under the following headings: (1) Field number; (2) Brief description; (3) Notebook page or separate graph sheet number; (4) Photo number; (5) Disposition.

Isolated bones from each section were also recorded in tabular form, with the following data for each: (1) Field number; (2) Name of bone; (3) Description of bone, that is, complete, proximal fragment or distal fragment; (4) Age of animal, that is, adult, immature, or juvenile; (5) Disposition, that is, saved or discarded. If the bone was saved, the Museum catalog number assigned was entered. If the bone, upon further clearing of the adjacent bone bed, was discovered to be part of an articulated unit, the unit to which the bone was assigned was entered under "Disposition."

Field numbers were used to facilitate the taking of notes, even though permanent catalog numbers were assigned to all, and entered on many, of the bones in the field. Field numbers for articulated units consisted of the section number followed by a letter, for example, 6-H. Isolated bones were designated by the section number followed by a serial number, for example, 6-184. Permanent unit numbers were assigned later in the laboratory, for example, Unit 231.

Because of the complexity of the mass of bones, we experimented with photo-mapping. A frame 1 × 2 m (3.28 × 6.56 ft) was strung with cord, lengthwise and crosswise at 20 cm (0.65 ft) intervals, to produce a 20 cm grid. After the uppermost level of bones had been exposed, each unit and each isolated bone was numbered with a Marks-a-lot ink marker (black proved to be permanent, red impermanent), so that the number was visible from a camera position directly above the bone bed. The grid frame was then placed over the bones, leveled, and oriented. Half of each section could be photographed at each exposure. A ladder-tripod 3.65 m (12 ft) high was erected and centered over the frame, and, with leveled, vertically oriented camera, an exposure was made. In this manner, a complete photo-map was made of the entire upper level of the bone deposit. Lower levels were not completely photo-mapped, as the decreasing complexity of the deposit made it feasible to map them by more normal means.

Photographic coverage included oblique photos of each section at each level, and of many of the units. Each artifact was photographed in place, whether isolated or included in a bone unit. Cross-sections were photographed, light filters being used to bring out the texture and stratification of the natural deposits. "Progress" and "general" photographs were made from time to time as seemed indicated by the conditions.

Below the uppermost level, a number was marked on isolated bones as they were lifted only if they were to be saved. Those discarded were assigned a number and recorded in the tables as previously indicated, but were not actually numbered. Units continued to be numbered in the ground. . . .

HUNTING PATTERN AT THE OLSEN-CHUBBUCK SITE

The Olsen-Chubbuck site preserved a classic example of the mass slaughter of a herd of bison by stampeding them across a natural obstacle, in this case an arroyo. Whether or not the arroyo was formed by the erosion and deepening of an abandoned bison trail, as appears likely, the part it played in the kill is clear: it constituted the trap into and across which the bison were stampeded by the Indians.

The evidence for the role the stampede, itself, played in the kill lies in the orientation of the skeletons and in the massed, violently twisted and contorted positions in which they were found; approximately the position where they met death by suffocation, by being trampled to death, or by injury suffered from the spears of the hunters, perhaps terminated with the coup de grace. In Hind's description of the destruction of a bison herd in a pound, it is clear that, to a certain extent, some animals were able to mill around until they were killed by the Indians. Hence, some of the bodily positions were the result, not of the stampede into the pound, but of the frenzied milling of the bison in the pound. In a natural trap such as an arroyo, the confines of the trap itself would at least partly determine the position of the animals, for there was no chance of milling about. The relative narrowness and linearity of the Olsen-Chubbuck arroyo would, of necessity, force some of the trapped bison into an orientation parallel to that of the arroyo. Nevertheless, there should be evidence of violent death in the positions of the bodies of the bison trapped as a result of being stampeded into the arroyo.

While the majority of the bison in the upper half of the Olsen-Chubbuck arroyo had been butchered, and thus are not pertinent to this problem, the lower half of the arroyo, particularly from Section 20 eastward, contained the skeletons of 40 whole or nearly whole animals, or animals which, because of their position in the arroyo, had been only partly butchered, in addition to those that may have been in the section dug by Olsen and Chubbuck.

Almost without exception, every whole or nearly whole skeleton overlies or is overlain by skeletons of other whole or nearly whole animals, often by 2 or 3 others. This would suggest that those first into the arroyo had no chance to get out and were covered by those following so rapidly and so violently that they were simply wedged into the position they landed in, only to be pushed, twisted, and torn by the impact of those following.

Of the 40 bodies still approximately in the position in which they met death, 15 had been violently twisted on or around the axis formed by the vertebral column. In many of these, the back appeared to have been broken just behind the rib cage and the forepart of the animal rotated up to 45°. In a few cases the neck appeared to have been broken and twisted forward of the rib cage. Eleven other bodies had been forced into a violent curve. Of this number 3 were completely doubled up into a "U" shape, with the rear end wedged against the north side of the arroyo and the fore-quarters and head wedged against the south side, the vertebral column making a continuous arc across the width of the arroyo. In still other units, it was not possible to determine whether or not the bodies had been twisted because the forepart of the body had been removed, presumably for butchering.

Eighteen of the bodies had their rear legs in an abnormal position. In some, it would seem that the animal had simply squatted to get into position to leap out of the arroyo but was foiled because, before it could jump, it was pinned down by another animal. In a few cases the animal hit or slid into position with the rear legs extended and was not able to return them to a normal flexed position. In still others, the twisting of the forepart of the animal had resulted in extension of the rear legs to one side while the forelegs extended to the other. Eleven bodies had forelegs in an abnormal position, in some cases extended to the front or side of the body, and in others extended to the rear, parallel to the body, as if they had hit on the chest or head and had not been able to pull the legs back into a flexed position before they were buried by the avalanche which followed them.

When the bison jumped, the positions in which they landed depended in part on the positions of the bodies they landed on, or on the shape of the arroyo at that particular point. About half of the bodies either landed in a horizontal position, or we lack data in our records on the point. However, 10 animals landed front downward and were held in that position, head down and rear end up. Another 10 landed with the rear end down and the head and forepart up. Two bodies lay on the back, 1 in the very bottom of the arroyo. The other had evidently been spun around in mid-air and had hit the south bank of the arroyo, then had slid clear to the bottom with one rear leg jackknifed up the north side of the arroyo, the other extended at right angles to the body along the arroyo bottom. Altogether, 3 animals were found in a vertical position, being held upright by the surrounding press of other bodies. One of these was a calf only a few days old, head down, that was pressed against the north side of the arroyo. Another was a large mature bull which had landed against the south wall of the arroyo with the rear legs and pelvis oriented east and the front legs and shoulder girdle oriented west. This animal had collapsed into a vertical heap of bones after the meat had decayed.

There can be no doubt that the stampede ran from north to south, or, perhaps more accurately from northwest to southeast. Of the 39 whole or nearly whole bodies for which orientation data were recorded, not a single animal was oriented to the northern half of the compass. Nine animals were oriented to the southeast, and 9 to the south, including 3 whose bodies lodged in a "U" shape across the arroyo. Three bodies were oriented to the southwest. Twelve animals were oriented to the east, including most of those from Section 10 eastward, and 6 were oriented to the west. It is important to note, in connection with those oriented to the east or west, that they were all in the narrow inner channel of the arroyo, and that they were forced to assume an easterly or westerly orientation by having been wedged into the channel. Thus, without exception, those animals, the orientation of whose bodies was without constraint from the physical limitations of the arroyo, were oriented southeast, south, or rarely, southwest.

There is, of course, very little direct evidence of the surround or partial surround which normally would have accompanied and precipitated the stampede across the arroyo. We discovered no physical evidence for the construction of wings of "deadmen" to direct the stampeding herd into and across the arroyo. Nevertheless, there is some evidence which suggests that hunters were stationed along the sides of the moving herd as well as to the rear of it.

This evidence consists of the fact that projectile points were found associated with bodies in the lowest part of the arroyo as well as those in the middle and upper parts. Point 10,972 lay inside the rib cage of Unit 272, a nearly complete animal which lay on the very bottom of the arroyo. Point 10,486 had apparently lodged in Unit 148, which also lay in the lowest part of the arroyo. Unit 131 had been penetrated from the side by Point 10,485 which ultimately had lodged inside the pelvic girdle. This animal lay somewhat above the lowest level but was clearly not one of the last into the arroyo. Olsen and Chubbuck found their Points F-6, F-9, and F-12 at depths near 1.3 m (4.26 ft), and their Points F-10 and F-7 among bones at a depth of almost a meter (3.28 ft), which would have placed the animals with which they were associated near the bottom of the deposit.

Given the size and speed of the stampeding herd, it would appear highly unlikely that these points could have lodged where they struck their quarry had they been shot from the rear of the herd. On the other hand, spears shot from the flanks of the moving herd would normally have struck some of the lead animals, coercing the herd into a narrower path and across the arroyo. These animals would have been the first into the arroyo, where they were found. That the shooting continued until the arroyo was completely filled is evidenced by the finding of points embedded in one animal in the sternum of Unit 152 and near the bones of other units near the top of the bone bed, and representing, therefore, some of the last animals to be trapped.

These data can only be suggestive, but coupled with the knowledge that the conditions only suggested by the distribution of the projectile points in the bone bed would have been the normal, rather than exceptional, hunting technique employed in a kill such as the Olsen-Chubbuck, they lend weight to the idea that a partial surround preceded the actual stampede which eventuated in the kill itself.

Reference to [Figure 2] will show that the catchment basin to the north and northwest was the only place where general concealment of the hunters could have been effected until they were ready to start the stampede. The ridge to the west, the low divide to the northwest, and the ridge to the northeast and east afforded a physical cover for most of the area north of the arroyo, behind which the hunters could work their way into position. If there was, in addition, plant cover, and if the breeze was blowing from the south or southeast, as would be normal for late spring and early summer, then the classic conditions would be met for the Olsen-Chubbuck kill. . . .

THE OLSEN-CHUBBUCK BISON HERD

The composition of bison herds and the time of calving both have a bearing on the time of year that the Olsen-Chubbuck bison kill occurred. The skeletons in the bone bed were from nearly 200 animals of both sexes and of all ages. Sex was determined on a total of 58 units, of which 42 were adult and 16 immature. Sex was not determined on any of the juvenile skeletons. Of these 58 units, 25 (43.10%) were male and 33 (56.90%) were female. Age was determined for 269 units. It will be noted that this figure includes some cases where determinations were made on what must have been different elements of the same animal. Of the 269 age determinations, 153 (56.88%) were adult, 100 (37.17%) were immature, and 16 (5.95%) were juvenile. Of the latter, 1 or 2 appeared to be not more than a few days old, while most appeared, from the stage of growth, to be a month or possibly 2 months old. No fetal calves were found.

From evidence based on the sex and age ratios in the bone bed, it appears that the kill could have occurred as early as April or as late as August, with most data suggesting a time fairly late in the calving season but before the onset of the rutting season. The ages of the calves found point to late May or early June. The absence of fetal calves may be due to accident of either preservation or excavation, since we do not have detailed information on the skeletons excavated by Chubbuck and Olsen. In passing, it should also be noted that fetal calves were considered to be a great delicacy by some of the historic Plains tribes, and the absence of them in the bone bed could be due, in part, to their having been taken as food. In any case, their absence suggests a time toward the end of the calving season.

Finally, there is no way to establish the total size of the herd which was stampeded across the Olsen-Chubbuck arroyo (since you can't count the ones that got away), but the number of animals trapped was near the optimum size of the small grazing herds expectable prior to the rutting season. While this does not preclude the possibility of the trapping of a small segment of the huge aggregations of animals normal during the rutting season, it does not support it.

In summary, it would appear that a date of late May or early June best accommodates the known biological evidence as to the time of year that the Olsen-Chubbuck bison kill occurred.

Ethnographic sources concerning seasonal variation in the utilization of bulls and cows also point to a time prior to the rutting season. According to most observers, . . . bulls were normally consumed only during May and June, since they were then in prime condition. During the calving season, the cows tended to be poor in flesh, but by the end of the season, that is, late May or early June, they, too, were once again becoming good to eat. Since there is ample evidence in the Olsen-Chubbuck site that both bulls and cows were butchered, a date of late May or, more probably, early June is suggested. . . .

BUTCHERING TECHNIQUES AT THE
OLSEN-CHUBBUCK BISON KILL

The analysis of the bone bed at the Olsen-Chubbuck site has produced a considerable amount of evidence of the process of butchering followed there. It will be recalled that at the beginning of excavations, the assumption was made that most of the articulated skeletal segments which we found, in fact represented those parts of the animals that were cut off during the butchering, and that the essential uniformity of such segments reflected a standardized pattern of butchering.

Eight categories of articulated units were ultimately denominated, of which 6 can be termed "butchering units." Complete skeletons and partly-butchered carcasses represent special cases with regard to the utilization of the Olsen-Chubbuck kill. The 6 groups termed "butchering units" are: pelvic-girdle units, rear-leg units, front-leg units, foot units, vertebral-column units, and skull units.

In the Olsen-Chubbuck bone bed, the sequence in which the various kinds of units and non-articulated bones were deposited, and the fact that they formed distinct bone piles, gives a reasonably accurate picture of the manner in which the butchering operations were carried out at the kill site. It may be well at this point to recapitulate, briefly, the general sequence observed in the deposition of the bone bed before passing on to an interpretation of the evidence with regard to the butchering process.

Except for the shallow west end of the arroyo, the lowest level of bones consisted mainly of whole animals or animals which, because of their relatively inaccessible position in the arroyo, were only minimally butchered. In general, the elements or units which were cut off of these partly-butchered animals reflected not a general pattern of butchering, but only what the hunters were able to reach. Hence, except for having contributed a number of odd units and non-articulated bones to the bone piles, they are not of particular importance here.

In the upper part of the bone bed, whenever the order of deposition was clear, groups of front-leg units were the first elements to have been emplaced. Such groups consisted of 2 or 3 to as many as 15 units. Sometimes both the right and left legs of the same animal were found together. The units which composed a group were nearly always fairly close together, with considerable distance separating them from the nearest similar group.

Following the deposition of the front-leg units, groups of pelvic-girdle units, consisting of 2 or 3 to 8 individual units, were emplaced. More than half of these retained some lumbar vertebrae. Sometimes the rear legs were still attached, but often 1 or both legs had been removed prior to the disposition of the pelvic girdle.

Overlying the pelvic-girdle unit groups were the groups of rear-leg units. Each group contained from 2 to 6 units and, as in the case of front-leg units, both right and left legs of the same animal were sometimes found together.

Leaving foot units aside for the moment, the next units to be emplaced were the vertebral-column units. As few as 2 and as many as 35 vertebral-column units were found in a single group. Ribs had been removed or broken from many of the thoracic vertebrae units, but others still retained some or all of the ribs.

Generally, the last units or groups of units to be emplaced were the skull units. Two to 27 skulls were included in each group. Slightly more than half of the skulls had the mandibles removed. A number of the skulls still retained some or all of the cervical vertebrae, and in a few cases, these vertebrae were pulled forward over the top of the skull. The hyoids were missing from some of the skulls that retained the mandibles.

Foot units had an irregular distribution in the bone bed. A few isolated foot units were found deep in the deposit and possibly are the result of disintegration rather than of butchering. Generally speaking, those foot units and groups of foot units suitable for use as hammers were found near the center of the vertebral-column groups, but fairly deep in relation to them. . . .

When the kill was finished, the area in and around the arroyo must have been strewn with dead bison of all ages and sexes. Access for butchering those on the flats on either side of the arroyo presented few problems, but the contorted mass of animals actually caught in the arroyo had to be pulled, shoved, rolled, or otherwise moved so that the cutting-up could proceed. In part, this may have been done by some preliminary butchering before the major part of the carcass was moved, a technique mentioned in some of the historical literature. In any event, a point was reached in the removal or clearance process when the hunters were unable or unwilling to move the carcasses from their constricted positions in the arroyo. It would be difficult, if not impossible, to say whether this point was reached because the manpower available made it impossible to lift more of the huge animals up and out of the arroyo, or whether there were more animals killed than could be utilized. In either case, when this point was reached, it left a number of whole animals along the bottom of the arroyo which were not butchered at all. However, those parts which could be reached without moving the whole animal were cut off, resulting in what we have termed partly-butchered units. The variety of the parts butchered out, in relation to the position of the partly-butchered units in the bone bed, makes this rather clear.

There is some minor evidence of the impromptu feasting on tidbits, probably in part uncooked, which was a standard part of historic bison kills. The fact that almost 40% of the disarticulated hyoids were found in the lowest level, and another 30% in the middle level, suggests that before the heavy butchering got under way, the tongue was removed in the classic Plains method of slitting the throat, pulling the tongue through, and cutting it off. This was often eaten raw in historic times, as were the liver, spiced with gall, the lips, the udder, and some of the organs and glands, none of which would leave evidence in the archaeological record. However, since some 40% of the disarticulated scapulae were found in the lower levels, it suggests that the carcass was opened early in some animals, perhaps to give access to the internal organs. The distribution of disarticulated ribs, almost half of which were found in the lower levels, supports this interpretation, as well as suggesting that scapulae and humps, which had to be removed before the ribs could be taken, were among the first items to be cut off of individual animals, as they were in historic times. Ribs and humps were normally cooked, although we found no evidence of fire at the Olsen-Chubbuck site. The fact that we did not find such evidence is not conclusive, however, because it will be remembered that wind deflation had removed some of the top layers of the soil.

It appears that when the heavy butchering began, a number of bison were butchered simultaneously rather than that single animals were butchered in succession. When these were finished, another group would be butchered. The evidence for this is that the segments which were cut off and stripped of their meat were discarded in groups of like units rather than individually, helter-skelter. The occurrence in groups also suggests that the butchers were working fairly close together, but whether this implies a family group working together, a larger kin group, or simply a number of individuals, I can discern no sure way of determining. Likewise, while it is possible to demonstrate that Bone Pile B accumulated before Bone Piles A and C, the temporal relationship to the bone piles in the central and western portions of the arroyo is unknown. Thus, there could have been 2 or 3 cooperating groups working simultaneously, or there could have been only 1 group which butchered one group of bison after another.

In butchering an individual bison, the first step seems to have been to roll the animal onto its belly with the legs positioned to serve as props to maintain the carcass in an upright position. Then, the skin was cut along the back and stripped off the sides. As among the historic bison hunters, the skin was probably cut into halves along the belly and used as a "table" to receive the meat as it was cut away from the bones. The "blanket of flesh" which immediately underlies the skin was probably removed next, to expose the front leg. The front leg was then removed, the meat stripped off by laying open the muscles, as described by James in 1820, the bones removed and, minus any bones saved for particular purposes, discarded, still articulated, in a heap.

The evidence for this sequence of events is that wherever the order of deposition in the bone piles was clear, the first bone units to be emplaced were front-leg units, showing that they were the first skeletal elements to be cut off and processed. In order that the front leg could be removed, it was first necessary to remove the "blanket of flesh" and the skin which covered it. Many of the front-leg units found together in the groups appear to be pairs, suggesting that both front legs were removed at nearly the same time, a feat only to be accomplished by having the animal propped up on the belly. In this position, the skin was usually cut down the back. The fact that this procedure was the most widely used Plains Indian technique also tends to give weight to this interpretation.

The various cuts of meat over the ribs and along the vertebral column were next removed. At this point, the ribs were frequently broken away near their point of articulation to the vertebral column. A number of instances of ribs being broken near the head and, conversely, of rib-heads still articulated to the vertebral column, are evidence of this procedure. The distribution of foot units, centering near the vertebral-column units, suggests that feet were cut off and used as hatchets in this process, as in historic times. The removal of the meat along the vertebral column exposed the backbone behind the rib cage, and it appears that the backbone was severed somewhere between the rib cage and the pelvis, and the rear end separated.

The flesh was then cut away from the pelvis and the head of the femur was exposed. Once the rear legs were cut off, the pelvic girdle was discarded onto the growing bone pile, where it fell on top of or among the previously discarded front-leg units. The meat was then cut away from the bones, and the rear legs, again minus those bones saved for particular uses, were discarded, still articulated, on the bone pile overlying the pelvic-girdle units.

Here it may be well to point out the reason for believing that the meat on both front and rear legs was cut off by laying open, or dissecting into their component parts, the muscles, and removing the leg bones, as observed by James. Such a method left relatively few scars on the bones, and remarkably few of the bones from the Olsen-Chubbuck bone bed showed much evidence of heavy cutting on the bone itself.

It appears that when the rear part of the animal had been butchered, the head and neck were separated from the vertebral column, usually just in front of the rib cage. Probably at this point the sinews that lined the backbone were removed and the vertebral-column units discarded. At about the same time, the head was being processed and the neck meat stripped off the cervical vertebrae. Evidence that the neck meat was taken is that in several cases the cervical vertebrae were pulled forward and lay over the frontal portion of the skull, something possible only if all the meat had been removed from the neck. Furthermore, the fact that less than half of the skulls still retained any cervical vertebrae suggests that, in the process of removing the neck meat, the neck was often severed from the skull.

The tongue was then removed, if it had not been taken previously. While some may have been removed by the throat-slitting process, most, at this point in the butchering process, seem to have been removed in different fashion. The lower jaw was cut away from the skull, entirely or on one side, and the mandibles broken at the symphysis, thus permitting the tongue to be removed entire. That this was the common method is evidenced in the fact that more than half of the skulls had both mandibles removed, and 4 others had only 1 mandible still articulated.

Horns appear to have been broken off occasionally and the cores removed and thrown onto the bone pile. On the other hand, there is virtually no evidence that the brain case was deliberately broken open to get at the brains. The 2 or 3 instances in which the skull was broken open may have been the result of accident rather than intention.

When the skull was stripped of all desirable parts, it, too, was discarded on the bone pile, among and on top of the vertebral-column units.

It appears that during the butchering process, a number of individual bones were, for various reasons, cut apart from their related units and retained, while most of the unit, still articulated, was discarded. Once processed, these bones were discarded on the bone piles. Frequently, groups of the same elements, such as scapulae, femora, or cannon bones, occurred together, suggesting that the elements of a group of animals were processed together. The horizontal distribution pattern suggests that a sort of disassembly line was in operation. Thus, when a high percentage of 1 element was found in 1 section, a peak occurrence of its distal continuation would be found in an adjacent section rather than in the same one.

In summary, it will be noted that the butchering techniques evidenced at the Olsen-Chubbuck site, with few exceptions, adumbrate the pattern observed and recorded by the early explorers and by the ethnographers. One difference is in one of the methods of removing the tongue, since mandible breakage is not recorded for the historic Indians. The apparent lack of use of the brains, either as food or for tanning at the Olsen-Chubbuck site, also differs from the usual pattern. Perhaps the most striking apparent difference, however, is degree of organization noted in the butchering at the Olsen-Chubbuck site, in contrast to the general individual approach to butchering by the later Indians. It is possible that such organized butchering was practiced in historic times, but if so, it does not appear strongly in the literature. . . .

AMOUNT, CONSUMPTION, AND PROCESSING OF MEAT

The ethnographical and historical literature demonstrates that the amount of edible meat on a bison carcass should never be taken as an indication that the amount available was, in fact, always utilized. There were many factors involved in the amount of meat actually taken. In a mass slaughter obtained by the various forms of surrounding and impounding, frequently there were simply more bison killed than could be utilized. Individual and tribal preferences must often have dictated those parts of each animal to be taken, or even whether a particular animal would be butchered at all. Spoilage caused by weather elements such as rain, temperature, and humidity, and time itself, would certainly have rendered a portion of the kill unfit for use. Even the earliest historic records, Hennepin, for example, indicate that frequently only the tongue and choice parts were taken, especially if there was no current shortage of meat. Therefore, it is impossible to say, as a generalization, that each buffalo killed provided a definite quantity of meat produce. Conversely, the quantity of bison bone found in a habitation site should never be taken as indicative of the quantity of meat consumed there, since most of the meat would have been transported as boneless fresh or preserved meat unless the kill had been very near the camp. . . .

UTILIZATION OF THE OLSEN-CHUBBUCK KILL

In an interpretation of a bison kill, a number of factors must be considered. These include the length of time necessary to process the kill, as well as the length of time that the meat remained edible for fresh consumption; the amount of meat consumed daily under "feasting" conditions and the number of people to feast; the weight of the preserved produce, the weight a person would carry under aboriginal conditions, and the number of persons to carry that weight. If dogs were present, they would both shorten the time necessary to consume the fresh meat, and enable the transport of larger quantities of produce, as well as the camp gear of the hunting group. Data bearing on these factors at the Olsen-Chubbuck site have been brought together in Table [1].

When a kill was "heavy" butchered, as was the Olsen-Chubbuck kill, it was primarily for the purpose of laying in a supply of preserved meat and skins. At such times, the hunting party, which usually included the whole camp, band, or even several bands together, men, women, and children, would normally remain in residence at or near the kill site until the major part was consumed and processed, when the entire group would move in search of other game. Times ranging from a few days to more than a month for the processing of a single kill have been recorded in historic times. Apart from butchering, there are few data on the length of time necessary to process an animal, but many activities such as drying meat, making pemmican, and preparing skins were carried on simultaneously by various members of the camp, and a period of a month or even less would appear adequate for the processing of the Olsen-Chubbuck kill. Historical data on the amount of meat consumed under "feasting" conditions

Table 1 *Reconstructed parameters for the utilization of the Olsen-Chubbuck kill.*

	50% of Kill Preserved				33% of Kill Preserved			
	Lbs.	Kgs.	Days	Dogs	Lbs.	Kgs.	Days	Dogs
Quantity of Meat Butchered or Available:								
"Useable" meat butchered at kill	59,647	27,071			59,647	27,071		
Tallow available at kill	4,460	2,025			4,460	2,025		
Marrow available at kill	965	438			965	438		
"Variety" meat available at kill	4,025	1,825			4,025	1,825		
Total meat butchered or available	69,100	31,323			69,100	31,323		
Amount of Meat Used Fresh or Wasted:								
"Useable" meat	29,825	13,535			39,963	18,138		
Tallow	2,230	1,012			2,974	1,350		
Marrow	483	216			643	292		
"Variety" meat	4,025	1,825			4,025	1,825		
Total	36,563	16,588			47,605	21,634		
Number of Days required at 10 pounds per person per day to consume fresh:								
200 persons			18*				24*	
150 persons			24*				32*	
100 persons			37*				48	
50 persons			73				95	
100 persons plus 100 dogs			22*				29*	
50 persons plus 100 dogs			32*				41	
Weight of Meat Preserved – Total Use:								
"Useable" meat, dried	5,965	2,707			3,996	1,814		
Tallow in bags or pemmican	2,230	1,012			1,486	675		
Marrow, in bags or pemmican	483	216			322	146		
Total weight of preserved meat	8,678	3,935			5,804	2,615		
Weight of 50 half robes	350	159			350	159		
Total weight to be transported	9,028	4,094			6,154	2,774		
Average weight to be transported by:								
200 persons	45*	20.4*			31*	13.9*		
150 persons	60*	27.3*			41*	18.6*		
100 persons	90	41			61*	27.8*		
50 persons	180	82			122	55.6		
Number of dogs to transport total weight				180				122
Weight of Meat Preserved – Back-Fat Only:								
"Useable" meat	5,965	2,707			3,996	1,814		
Back-fat only, in bags or pemmican	850	386			566	257		
Marrow, in bags or pemmican	483	216			322	146		
Total weight of preserved meat	7,298	3,309			4,884	2,217		
Weight of 50 half robes	350	159			350	159		
Total weight to be transported	7,648	3,468			5,234	2,376		
Average weight to be transported by:								
200 persons	38.2*	17.4*			26*	11.9*		
150 persons	51*	23.2*			35*	15.9*		
100 persons	76.5	34.8			52*	23.8*		
50 persons	153	69.6			104	47.5		
Number of dogs to transport total weight				153				104
* Feasible values								

such as apparently prevailed at the Olsen-Chubbuck kill, record amounts ranging from about 10 lb (4.5 kg) per person per day to more than 30 lb (13.6 kg). Considering the probable variation in the amounts consumed by women and children, and the fact that some waste must have occurred, I have used 10 lb (4.5 kg) as the basis for computing fresh meat consumption at the Olsen-Chubbuck kill. A train dog's ration of fresh meat was 8 lb (3.6 kg) per day. With the exception of Lewis H. Morgan, who provides a ratio of 1 lb (0.45 kg) of dried meat for every 12 lb (5.4 kg) of fresh meat, every observer records a ratio of 1:5, or 20 lb (9.07 kg) of dried meat to 100 lb (45.5 kg) of fresh meat, which is the figure I have used. Data on tallow are unsatisfactory. I have used the Belcourt and Ross figures for one set of computations, but because the "depuyer" or "back fat" is consistently mentioned as having been taken by the Indians of historic times, I have computed for this also, using a value of 10 lb (4.5 kg) per animal, for both the "heavy" and "light" butchered animals in the Olsen-Chubbuck site. Marrow seems to have been consistently taken, so, on the basis of historical pattern, as well as the evidence of broken and missing marrow bones in the Olsen-Chubbuck site, I have assumed that it was taken there, and have used the figure 3.3 kg (7.5 lb) per animal butchered. Although the average dressed buffalo robe weighed about 10 lb (4.5 kg), because of the larger *B. occidentalis* hide, I have computed half-robes at 7 lb (3.28 kg) each for this reconstruction. Among the early historic Buffalo Indians, the woman and the dog were the usual burden bearers, a woman's normal load being about 100 lb (45.5 kg). Men usually carried only their weapons for hunting and ready protection along the way, although they might carry some burden when moving camp or at other times, as might also the children. Loads of from 30 lb (13.6 kg) to 100 lb (45.5 kg) have been recorded for dogs, but the average figure is about 50 lb (22.7 kg), and that is the figure I have used.. . .

Because of the complete and systematic butchering at the Olsen-Chubbuck site, and because of the taking of some meat usable only in dried-meat or pemmican form, there is every reason to assume that the maximum possible use was made of the kill there, both with regard to the consumption of fresh meat and the preservation of meat. Obviously, it is impossible to control all of the variables, but of all the possibilities cited, some appear inherently more plausible than others because they fall within the known limits of time, amount of meat consumed, and the amount of produce which, together with the camp gear, could be transported. Conversely, some of the groups posited may be eliminated because they could not reasonably have carried out the evident exploitation of the kill. Thus, a group of 50 persons alone could neither have consumed half or two-thirds of the meat butchered while the meat remained edible, nor have been able to transport the preserved produce of the remaining half or third. A hundred persons could have consumed half of the meat fresh, but transport of the remaining half would have been at the very limit of possibility; while they could, with some difficulty, transport the produce from one-third of the kill, they could have consumed the remaining two-thirds only with great difficulty. One hundred fifty, or 200, persons could have consumed half or two-thirds of the kill easily, and could have as easily transported the remaining half or third in the form of preserved meat. If, therefore, the hunters who made the Olsen-Chubbuck kill were without dogs to help in the transport of the produce and the camp equipment, I believe a group of not less than 150 to 200 persons were involved, for fewer than that could hardly have carried out the observed utilization of the kill. On the other hand, if the hunters had 100 or so dogs, a band of no more than 50 persons could have accomplished the observed results, although a somewhat larger group of 75 to 100 would fit better in terms of the probable time span involved. That the butchering operation was organized there can be little doubt. Because of the season of the kill, and the pattern of utilization, it would appear reasonable that the hunt was an organized, cooperative spring kill, of the sort commonly observed on the Plains in early historic times, but it may have been only the highly organized utilization of a random kill.

In my attempt to analyze and interpret the utilization of the Olsen-Chubbuck kill, it has been necessary to make a number of assumptions and to indulge in a certain amount of speculation. However, these have been guided and controlled by the evidence within the site itself, and by the pattern of utilization of such a kill by the Indian bison-hunters of historic times. Furthermore, despite the obvious difficulties of such an interpretation, I believe that it is inherently valuable, because only by bringing together the data from specific sites and viewing them within the framework of an established pattern can we penetrate beyond the relatively safe and easy establishment of chronology and morphological form to move toward an understanding of prehistoric cultures as functioning entities. Finally, if archaeology gains nothing more from this kind of approach than the ability to pose more meaningful questions and to define the sort of evidence and analysis needed to answer them, the discipline will have gained. It is within this framework and for these reasons that the foregoing attempt has been made.

Charlton Ogburn, Jr.

14 THE FIRST DISCOVERY OF AMERICA

The archaeological literature on the first Americans is so enormous and so highly technical that a suitable introduction to the subject is hard to find. The following short article by Charlton Ogburn, Jr., includes some important academic issues involved: the Bering Land Bridge, the extinction of Pleistocene faunas, and the material culture and the economy of the earliest settlers. Unfortunately, archaeological remains of the earliest periods of human settlement in the New World are far from common; only a few sites earlier than 15,000 B.C. have come to light, most of the finds consisting of a scatter of crudely flaked stone tools. Not until about 8000 B.C. do sites contain in any numbers the remains of animals hunted by early Americans. Because of the article's brevity, Ogburn glosses over many details and points of controversy. The interested reader is referred to Thomas C. Patterson's *America's Past: A New World Archaeology* (Glenview, Ill.: Scott, Foresman, 1973), for more detailed information and a bibliography.

Few such momentous events in human history can have taken place with so little to indicate their importance. The setting was near the top of the world, in a time of brutal cold, and probably about as bleak as any imaginable. A low, rolling plain stretched out to the horizon — treeless and largely without even shrubs, in part probably steppelike, in part covered with a matted assemblage of lichens, sedges, and depressed flowering plants. Swept by merciless winds through the long winter, it was a place of boggy lowlands in the brief summer; for while little snow or rain fell on it, there was scant drainage. The ground was perpetually frozen, except when the summer thaw reached a few inches down. The ice was probably extruded here and there into mounds as high as a hundred feet. Similar landscapes may be found in parts of western and northern Alaska and in the Barren Lands of Canada, with the difference that the latter bear marks of the ice sheet's visitation: innumerable lakes and ponds, boulders, and hillocks of rubble and gravel. "A monotonous, snow-covered waste," the explorer Warburton Pike wrote of the tundra seventy years ago, where "a deathly still-

From Charlton Ogburn, Jr., "The First Discovery of America," © 1970 American Heritage Publishing Co., Inc. Reprinted by permission from *Horizon*, Winter 1970. Illustrations are omitted.

ness hangs over all, and the oppressive loneliness weighs upon the spectator until he is glad to shout aloud to break the awful spell of solitude."

The actors in the drama that was to unfold with so little of the dramatic were seemingly as unpromising as the country that swallowed them up. Unless they were hardier than the toughest Eskimos they must have worn furs, with coverings for their hands and feet, and lived in tents. However, these garments and shelters can only have been crudely pieced together. They undoubtedly had fire, but the only fuel their grim surroundings could have offered would have been animal fats, dried animal droppings, and perhaps a scanty brush. As for food, they probably scavenged for carrion, and when that failed, hunted down the living, their fellow dwellers of steppe and tundra — musk-oxen, caribou, and mammoths. To bring down such formidable quarry, and defend their kill and themselves from the packs of giant Arctic wolves, they had weapons fitted with flaked stones. For shafts, they must have had to return periodically to the southern coast for driftwood. The stone points, probably made of flint or obsidian, were similar to those used at the peak of Neanderthal culture, in the period that archaeologists call Mousterian, after the cave of Le Moustier in southwestern France.

At best, one might have thought these inhabitants capable of merely clinging to the edge of survival from one generation to the next. Yet if one could have looked into their eyes and read the potentialities there, one might have seen brilliant pioneer agriculturalists; the creators of splendid and complex civilizations; masters of such abstract knowledge as positional mathematics, astronomy, and calendric calculation; metallurgists and metalworkers with few, if any, superiors; engineers of networks of roads and of suspension bridges; priests of elaborate religions; builders of pyramids and of magnificently carved temples filled with superb statuary; lovers of fine cloth, gold ornaments, color, and pomp; some of the world's most accomplished practitioners of cavalry warfare; the possessors, in actuality or legend, of that nobility ascribed to the proud and stoic red man. For, if current archaeological reasoning is correct, the progenitors of the widespread and varied tribes of the American Indian were these mid-Paleolithic proto-Mongoloids of "Beringia."

Speaking of that time, Professor William S. Laughlin of the University of Wisconsin says: "The Bering Strait area is still commonly visualized as a narrow path or trail over which people hustled, in one direction, on their way to take up positions in which they would presently be discovered. . . . In fact, the Bering Land Bridge was an enormous continental area extending nearly 1,500 kilometers from its southern extremity, now the eastern Aleutians, to its northern margin in the Arctic Ocean" — as far as from Boston to Savannah — and it "endured for a longer time than that documented for the entire period of human occupancy in America." For a large part of that time it was probably inhabited by bands of Stone Age men, trekking this way and that as the movements of game dictated, with no notion of migration in their heads.

Perhaps no other major highway of history has fewer human visitors today. The Alaskan and Siberian shores of the Bering and Chukchi seas are just about the remotest parts of the United States and the U.S.S.R. respectively. An American who journeys to Cape Prince of Wales, at the tip of the Seward Peninsula, or a Russian who journeys to the end of Chukotka Peninsula, will find himself within fifty-six miles of the other's country, which he is likely to have thought of as being on the other side of the world. That is the width of Bering Strait, which the Russian-employed Danish explorer Vitus Bering sailed through in August, 1728, demonstrating that the Old World and the New were physically separated. In Bering Strait the waters of the Bering Sea, the northernmost part of the Pacific, meet those of the Chukchi, an extension of the Arctic Ocean, which also communicates with the North Atlantic. It is a place of haze and fog, of frozen wastes, ice-free for only a few months of the year. As inhospitable and distant as the remains of Beringia are, they have recently attracted considerable scientific attention. At the end of August, 1965, a symposium on the land bridge was held at Boulder, Colorado, as part of a congress on the Pleistocene Age. The papers delivered there have since been published under the title *The Bering Land Bridge*. Edited by David M. Hopkins of the U.S. Geological Survey, a leading student of this austere region, it appears to tell all that is currently known of its subject.

In the long perspective of the "Recent-Life," or Cenozoic, era — also called the Age of Mammals — which goes back sixty million years, the connection between Siberia and Alaska is normal. That they were connected during most of this vast stretch of time is clearly shown by the similarities between the faunas on either side of the bridge and by the evidence of an interchange of mammals between the continents.

If the faunas of two areas are alike, it is a fair conclusion that the areas are, or were until very recently, connected. Every living thing is under unremitting pressure to achieve a more profitable adaptation to its environment — improve or disappear is the choice perpetually facing most species in this ruthlessly competitive world. When a barrier impedes the movement of living things, the plants and animals on either side, responding to differences in soils and climates, will change in different directions. However slight the first divergences may be, they will increase with the passage of time.

According to the fossil evidence, there was a period forty-five million years or so ago and one some thirty million years ago when movement between Eurasia and North America was temporarily impeded. But the first known submergence of the land bridge took place only about ten or twelve million years ago. The event is marked by the appearance in the Atlantic

Ocean of fossils of marine creatures from the Pacific and of Atlantic fossils in the Pacific — for one creature's land bridge is another's land barrier, just as one creature's water barrier is another's water avenue. In this case the water avenue led over the top of the world. Among the migrants were the early walrus — a Pacific form — which turned up on the east coast of North America, and the first true seal — an Atlantic form — which made it to California. Why the land bridge went under, and why, not very long afterward comparatively speaking, it re-emerged, is not known. In any case, the exchange of land animals was resumed. The ancestor of the American mastodon crossed eastward, and long after the reopening of the bridge, *Plesippus,* the "almost-horse," which was the first to have the stalwart proportions of modern varieties, crossed to Asia, to give rise to the early Old World equines (though not to the domestic horse, which derived from a later migrant from North America).

When *Plesippus* crossed it, the bridge had had an unbroken existence of perhaps six million years, but *Plesippus* may have got over just in time; for late in the Pliocene period, which preceded the Pleistocene (the period of the ice ages), the seas once more closed over the land, and Bering Strait reopened. Again, as millions of years before, marine fauna were exchanged between the Atlantic and Pacific oceans. This took place three and a half or four million years ago. Ever since that time the separation of Siberia and Alaska has been normal, and their reunion exceptional.

Speculation that a northern land bridge had permitted man to reach the New World began many years ago. David Hopkins has traced the hypothesis back as far as Fray José de Acosta, a Spanish missionary who in 1590 wrote a history of the Indians. The Bering Strait area was a natural choice for the probable site, both because the Old World and the New stand closest there and because of the obviously Asian origin of the American Indian. Not until 1934, however, did it dawn on the scientific community that what had brought the land bridge into being was the lowering of sea level caused by the extraction of water from the oceans to form the snow that turned into the great ice sheets of the glacial epochs. To expose the Bering land bridge, the oceans would have to drop 150 feet from today's level, which is probably 250 feet below where the level actually would be were it not for the water now held in the Greenland and Antarctic ice sheets. To lower the oceans by the requisite amount, four million cubic miles of water would have to be removed from them — which would take a lot of snowflakes. And at the time of the ice sheets' greatest extent, the oceans stood not 150 feet but probably more than 300 feet below their present level. That gives some conception of how monstrous the ice sheets were.

There were four ice ages during Pleistocene times. Each was set apart by long eras of climates that were probably a good deal milder than those of today. The oceans then stood higher than they do now, and forests grew well up into what is now arctic tundra. The interval between the second and third ice ages lasted probably hundreds of thousands of years, and that between the third and fourth, probably scores of thousands. A mere fifteen thousand years have passed since the fourth ice sheet began its conclusive (we may hope) retreat. In each ice age there were fluctuations in the extent of the sheet and hence in sea level. Geologists believe that the Bering land bridge came and went at least six times — one estimate is as high as ten — beginning with its first reemergence in the Pleistocene, which is said to have taken place more than two million years ago.

We are not to imagine, however, that throughout these periods the land animals of one continent enjoyed easy access to the other. The situation was not so simple. To begin with, forest animals could no longer make the crossing at àll, but the land bridge in Pleistocene times was too cold for trees.

In addition, we must not forget at least one very formidable complication. The growth of the ice sheet naturally kept pace with the lowering of the seas; the more water that was evaporated from the oceans and converted into snow, the greater the extent of the ice sheet on which it fell. Even before the withdrawal of water reached its maximum, the sheet expanding westward across Canada would have met the alpine glaciers that flowed down from the high elevations of the Rocky Mountains and buried all but the taller summits of the range. Gates of ice thousands of feet thick would thus have closed, barring any further dispersal of land mammals southward. All mainland Canada would have been covered, like Antarctica today, by ice as much as two miles deep, and Alaska, largely ice-free above its southern regions, would in effect have been part of Siberia.

Thus for the past several million years two barriers have had to be removed to permit movement by land between Asia and North America proper, and for the larger part of the time that the water barrier has been withdrawn, the ice barrier has been in place. Not only was the dispersal of animals from one continent to the other impeded but it was influenced in another way by the sequence of openings and closings. In the early phase of an ice age the route between the continents would be open all the way, giving the mammals of one an equal chance with those of the other to make the crossing. As ice accumulated and Beringia was further exposed, Asian animals would have found it even easier to cross to Alaska. There, coming up against a solid wall of ice — for the glacial gates would by then have closed — they would have had to remain; but thousands of years later, at the end of the ice age, they could have passed southward down the widening corridor, if they had survived. Many surely did. However, a yak-like species of *Bos* and the steppe antelope, or *Saiga*, became extinct before the way south opened up.

The odds were more heavily against animal migration from the New World to the Old. By the time the ice sheet had retreated and opened the way north to Alaska for American animals, the land bridge would probably have been almost, or already, submerged. Moreover, as they pushed northward on the heels of the retreating ice, the original North American fauna would have encountered an immigrant fauna moving southward that was more inured to the harsh conditions left in the wake of the ice. Finally, the new fauna would have come from the much larger and more varied continent of Eurasia and would thus have been more efficient because of stiffer competition; an insular fauna is generally no match for a more cosmopolitan one. Only two mammals from the New World succeeded in establishing themselves in the Old during later Pleistocene times, when the tide was running particularly heavily in the opposite direction, and they were of Eurasian descent. These were the musk-ox and the caribou, which became the reindeer of Europe. Two mammals of more truly American origin had successfully breasted the tide earlier in the Pleistocene. While two is not many, these were, long afterward, to give history a direction and momentum it could otherwise hardly have had. The ancestors of the horse and camel had come from the Old World originally, way back at the dawn of the Cenozoic, but then they had been diminutive — perhaps the size of a fox terrier. North America had built them up to their present proportions before sending them back home again.

The New World's Pleistocene accessions from the Old World account for nearly all the characteristic mammals of northern North America, many of which have established themselves in the southern regions of the continent as well. The earlier comers, which were pushed south by the ice sheet, gave rise in the course of thousands of years to the plains bison, the black and grizzly bears, the coyote, the kit fox, the American badger, skunks, the Rocky Mountain goat, and the bighorn — all fairly well Americanized forms. Descendants of the later arrivals are still similar to, or even indistinguishable from, their Eurasian relatives. These include the moose (which can hardly be told from the Scandinavian elk), the American "elk," or wapiti (which resembles the European red deer, or even more closely, an Asiatic stag), Alaskan brown bear, gray wolf, red and arctic foxes, wolverine, weasel, ermine, otter, and forest bison. The last is akin to the once widespread European bison, or wisent.

But what about man? What do we know about the crossing of our own species? The date of this event is one of the big questions of archaeology; estimates span almost the whole period of the last ice age. The carbon-14 dating of charcoal from campfires indicates that ten thousand years ago there were hunters in northern Colorado; Folsom man is the name given to them. The Toldense culture in southern South America seems to have been contemporaneous. Earlier, between eleven and thirteen thousand years ago, there were Indians living on the plains of Texas and Mexico. At about the same time, according to the carbon dating of mussel shells associated with human bones found in 1966 near the juncture of the Snake and Palouse rivers, there were Indians in Washington state — "Marmes Man" they were called, in an announcement of July, 1968, that claimed their bones were the oldest human remains ever found in the New World. The next month a very fine bone needle less than one inch long and only one-thirty-second of an inch in diameter was found at the site and ascribed to Marmes Man. Yet, according to Hansjürgen Müller-Beck of the University of Freiburg, only the postulation of human migration to North America at a far earlier date, perhaps twice as long ago, can resolve the problems of assigning a date to that migration.

What these problems come down to is this. First, if man had not come across the land bridge until twelve or thirteen thousand years ago, he would have brought a different technology from the one he evidently did bring. Secondly, if he came as early as his tools would indicate, he must, because of the condition of the land bridge, have come even earlier — much earlier — than his tools alone would warrant our believing. A flat, bullet-shaped projectile-point imbedded in a bison vertebra from a Folsom site, and now on display in the Smithsonian Institution's Museum of Natural History, is a beautiful piece of work, perhaps hardly to be improved on. Yet the technique of its manufacture would appear to be "Mousteroid," derived from the Neanderthal technique of thirty-five thousand years ago. This would seem to be true, too, of the tools found with Folsom man's predecessors. Even such a technically advanced implement as the needle found in association with Marmes Man could, Dr. Müller-Beck believes, have been produced with typical paleo-Indian gravers. Yet fifteen thousand years ago, at the latest, more advanced techniques had replaced the "Mousteroid industries" not only throughout Europe but even across Siberia. These were the "Aurignacoid industries," named for the cave district of Aurignac in southwestern France, only about a hundred miles south of the cave of Le Moustier. Instead of producing an edged implement by flaking away most of a nodule of flint, as their early Old Stone Age predecessors did, the men of the later Old Stone Age were able to strike blade after blade for various purposes from a single core of flint, thus greatly economizing in the use of a material that probably was becoming scarce, and certainly was heavy to carry on long excursions. They had also learned to make flint chisels of a kind called burins, with which bones, antlers, and ivory could be handily worked. If the first immigrants to America were content with the old Mousteroid techniques, it could only have been because they had not been introduced to the new, the Aurignacoid.

But if the new techniques reached eastern Siberia fifteen thousand years ago, why is it not fair to deduce that men first crossed the land bridge then? The answer is that if they had waited until so recent a time as that, they would have run into the ice barrier.

Well, suppose they had. Might they not have stuck it out in Alaska until the glaciers parted between fourteen and eleven thousand years ago, and then pressed southward? To begin with, there is a very great question whether, given the length of time needed for vegetation to recloak the ice-stripped land and render it habitable, they could have made it in time to be living on the Texas plains thirteen thousand years ago. Beyond that, Dr. Müller-Beck argues that to have survived the increasingly severe climatic conditions in Beringia and Alaska, they would almost surely have had to possess the "well-developed bone technology" of the Aurignacoid industries. And presumably, from being in contact with their fellows in Siberia, they *would* have possessed it. Yet the first human immigrants to North America evidently did not.

To set the limits of the time of their probable arrival requires a look at the chronology of the fourth ice age. The latest major reign of the cold most likely began early enough to drain Bering Strait by forty thousand years ago. Since by that time man apparently had learned to wrest a living from the tundra, he may conceivably have crossed to the New World then, though the kind of tools he would have brought with him have never been found in the Americas. At any rate, a period of moderate temperatures that divided the fourth ice age into two parts saw the land bridge flooded again sometime after thirty-five thousand years ago. Then the cold returned, and between twenty-eight and twenty-five thousand years ago the land bridge re-emerged. By that time Mousteroid toolmaking techniques that would have enabled their practitioners to hunt down the largest game — musk-oxen, caribou, bison, and mammoths — had spread across Siberia. The proto-Mongoloid huntsmen of eastern Siberia could well have moved by stages across the widening land bridge into Alaska without any consciousness of a departure from the routine of their people.

That is what Dr. Müller-Beck believes they did twenty-eight thousand years ago. With game animals keeping pace with the grass and tundra growth as it reclaimed the land evacuated by the sea, the huntsmen who depended on them would probably not have been far behind. Those who reached Alaska and ventured southward would have been driven into the present forty-eight states when the continental ice sheet reached the ice-bound Rocky Mountains, about twenty or even twenty-three thousand years ago.

What would one not give to be able to see our continent through the eyes of those first comers! Today only Africa can give us a conception of what the Pleistocene fauna of North America was like, and tomorrow very likely nothing will. The plains and prairies thundered to the hoofs of bison — not only the kind familiar to us but giants of their species with horns having a six-foot spread. There were ten species of horses, ranging in size from that of a Shetland pony to hulking creatures as big as the largest Shire stallion bred by man. There were camels of many species, including giant llamas and the great *Camelops,* which stood taller than the largest camel of today; Folsom man hunted it, as he did the giant bison, and as his forerunners must have also.

We think of elephants as tropical, but the first Americans shared the continent with four species of them — Pleistocene immigrants like themselves. The shaggy Siberian, or woolly, mammoth with its humped back and high-domed head, its huge tusks incurved, was at home south of the ice sheet around the world, reaching southern New England. The more southerly mammoths were quite possibly hairless. One of these, the imperial mammoth of the Great Plains, stood over thirteen feet high at the shoulder, several feet taller than large African elephants of today. Mastodons the size of Indian elephants browsed in the coniferous forests across the country; more than a hundred skeletons have been found in New York State alone.

As bulky as elephants were the long-clawed giant ground sloths, which lumbered about on the sides of their feet and, rearing up, could feed on foliage twenty feet high. The ground sloths had come up from South America, as had the glyptodonts — armadillos superficially resembling long-tailed tortoises and up to twelve feet long. There were beavers the size of bears and bears before which a grizzly would have quailed. Among the beasts of prey were great dire wolves, an American lion larger than any today, and several species of saber-toothed cats, which reached their peak of size and power in the Western hemisphere.

Along the margins of the ice sheet, as far south as Pennsylvania, southern Illinois, and Iowa, was tundra, and grazing on the tundra were musk-oxen and caribou. Below the tundra stretched a northern forest of fir and spruce. The arid West would scarcely have been recognizable to us today, for ice ages (and this is part of their mystery) are times of unusually heavy precipitation. Great Salt Lake was ten times its present size. Another lake, almost as big, occupied the lowlands of western Nevada. Death Valley, the driest — and hottest — spot in North America today was itself at the bottom of a lake. The grasses of the Great Plains must have been as lush as those that amazed the first white invaders of the prairies, whose horses disappeared in the eight-foot-high bluestem.

As the climate warmed and the ice receded, a momentous occurrence took place. It is recorded in a deposit of some ten thousand years ago in a rock shelter in Texas. The object is a burin, and it marks the appearance of Aurignacoid industries in North America. The logical inference is that they had come through contact between the first comers, the paleo-Indians spreading north in the wake of the shrinking ice sheet, and inhabitants of Beringia who had spread east and south in its wake.

The element of drama lacking to begin with when the proto-Mongoloids wandered unwittingly into the New World must have been present at the meeting with the strangers from the north. For more than ten thousand years — longer than the entire span of human civilization — the paleo-Indians had been cut off from the rest of the world by the oceans and the wall of ice stretching across the continent south of Canada. And then suddenly there were men from beyond that bleak landscape the ice had left — men with better tools than theirs and probably with better made and more protective clothing, perhaps with a cast of countenance unlike any seen before, and certainly speaking a totally incomprehensible tongue.

Where had these men come from? They may have been in Alaska all the while and have received the new techniques from Siberia long before, or they may have come fairly recently from Siberia. While the land bridge would have gone under before the ice barrier was removed, a period of renewed cold may have set in between thirteen and eleven thousand years ago, and the land bridge may have reemerged while the way was also clear to the south.

In any event, the bringers of the new techniques were not Aleuts or Eskimos. Those true Mongoloids apparently did not appear in Alaska until about 8,500 years ago, when the only means of getting there was by boat.

The meeting between the paleo-Indians and the newcomers from Alaska (who may very well have been Athabaskan Indians) marked the end of the Pleistocene period and the beginning of the Recent. The end of the Pleistocene fauna was at hand, too. The disappearance of the super-mammals everywhere but in Africa has long confronted science with a mystery. What makes it mysterious is that the vacated ecological "niches" were not taken over by new and better adapted forms. The rapidity with which the horse reoccupied its ancestral lands when the Spanish reintroduced it to the New World in the sixteenth century demonstrates that the niche had remained unoccupied. In North America, as Paul S. Martin of the University of Arizona has observed, over a hundred Pleistocene species were wiped out, including about 70 per cent of those with an individual weight in adulthood of more than a hundred pounds.

Dr. Martin dismisses the conventional theory that climatic changes accompanied by changes in vegetation were more than the megafauna could adjust to. The agency of destruction, he argues persuasively, was man — man the Stone Age killer, employing the tactics of range-firing and game-driving that would send herds over cliffs and doom hundreds of animals for the sake of a few carcasses. Then perhaps he hunted down the scattered remnants for the prestige that attaches to the slaughter of an imposing beast, "even today within our own society." The poignancy of this zoological impoverishment of the world is sharpened by the evidence of how recently it was concluded. In his *History of Land Mammals in the Western Hemisphere* William B. Scott points out that most American mastodon skeletons that have been found long postdate the ice sheet; several have been discovered in bogs covered by only a few inches of peat and with much of their hair and stomach contents preserved. He cites also the case of the skeleton of a ground sloth discovered in a cave in New Mexico with the ligaments and some of the skin still adhering to it.

One might well wonder how many people must have crossed the land bridge to have wrought all the changes that stemmed from that migration.

W. S. Laughlin suggests that the movement of only a few groups of fifty to one hundred members each across the land bridge could have accounted for the number of human beings in the New World when Columbus discovered it, and would be consistent with the bitterly inhospitable character of the terrain and with the extent of observed diversity among the Indians today — who, given the variety of the areas they have inhabited and the time they have inhabited them, are a people of notable physical uniformity. And very likely that is all there were, a few hundred hungry, shivering tribesmen, thanks to whom the mightiest of Pleistocene mammalry were to vanish from the hemisphere, the empires of the Incas, Mayas, Toltecs, and Aztecs were to rise, and our forefathers in the next influx from the Old World were to be compelled to run a bloody gamut of Iroquois and Cherokee, Shawnee and Choctaw, Sioux, Blackfoot, Comanche, Cheyenne, Paiute, and Navaho.

CHAPTER FIVE

Intensive Collectors and the Transition to Food Production

Wilfred Shawcross

15 FISHING AND PREHISTORIC DIET IN NEW ZEALAND

The reconstruction of prehistoric diet is a comparatively new field of research, one that requires an extremely critical assessment of archaeological data. Fishing has long been an important human subsistence activity, but one peculiarly difficult to reconstruct from archaeological data. About twenty thousand years ago, more and more coastal and lakeside populations began to specialize in fishing, sometimes to the exclusion of virtually all other activities. By six thousand years ago, specialized fishing and shell-collecting bands were flourishing in both the New World and the Old World, accumulating in many instances vast shell middens, heaps of discarded shells and fish bones. The excavation of such settlements has become a complex and painstaking field of research, one exemplified by the somewhat technical article by Wilfred Shawcross that follows. Galatea Bay lies on an offshore island of the North Island of New Zealand. The site examined dates to within the last five hundred years. In terms of world prehistory, the settlement is hardly of major significance. But Shawcross's methods enabled him to make a graphic reconstruction of the inhabitants' diet and to highlight some of the possible ways to study prehistoric fishermen in New Zealand and elsewhere.

It has not been possible to obtain any clear evidence for the age of the site, owing to the absence of a suitable assemblage, or, for that matter, any corresponding sequence to which it might be related. However, the presence of cannibalism and the absence of European goods indicates that it is likely to be no later than Proto-historic, which is itself in New Zealand terms a rather variable quantity. Theoretically, no early limit need necessarily be put on its age, though the absence of Moa,* relative absence of rocky shore shellfish, and the specialized nature of the site may be quoted as negative evidence against an early age. The one fishhook may well be a late form, and the relatively thin soil which has accumulated on top of the midden suggests a recent age. Lastly, in an important and as yet unpublished study of the fishhooks of Murihiku, Mr. Jan Hjarnø observed the scarcity of later, prehistoric fishhooks in that area prior to a final line-fishing efflorescence. A distinct possibility exists that this decrease of line-fishing may correspond to a high development of net fishing. The early European explorers, notably Captain Cook, commented on the remarkable development of nets in New Zealand, Cook describing such a net as five fathoms deep and 400 long. Augustus Hamilton (1908) and Elsdon Best (1929) illustrate a wide and highly-developed range of nets from more recent times. It may thus be that the virtual absence of hooks from the site can be explained by the use of net-fishing. The estimated sizes of the sub-fossil snapper were examined in an attempt to find evidence for the mode of fishing, but the results were inconclusive, as the smallest fish was about 300 grams and the most frequent sizes correspond to those caught in modern times by both methods. Likewise, the bimodal distribution curve of size group frequencies (Figure 1) is more likely to be a reflection of the structure of the living populations than of the selective effects of hooks. Finally, if net-fishing was the method employed at this site two things need to be explained. The first is the absence of the net sinkers and the second is the relatively small size of the community. For line-fishing is still today a much more individualistic activity than the more cooperative work required by netting. On the other hand these objections could be met if we suppose that the netting was a cooperative venture among the men of the separate families occupying the various adjoining bays of Ponui Island. In this light, the menfolk would be out on the water fishing from their canoes while the women remained in the

From "Prehistoric Diet and Economy on a Coastal Site at Galatea Bay, New Zealand" by Wilfred Shawcross, *Proceedings of the Prehistoric Society* 33, No. 7 (1967) 125–130. Reprinted by permission of the author and the Prehistoric Society. Footnotes and references are omitted, and figures renumbered.

Note: The articles reprinted in this chapter are not chosen to give accounts of the origins of food production but to summarize some theories relating to this radical change in human subsistence. See the note on page 130 for three references that provide narrative accounts.

* [Moa — a prehistoric flightless bird. — Ed.]

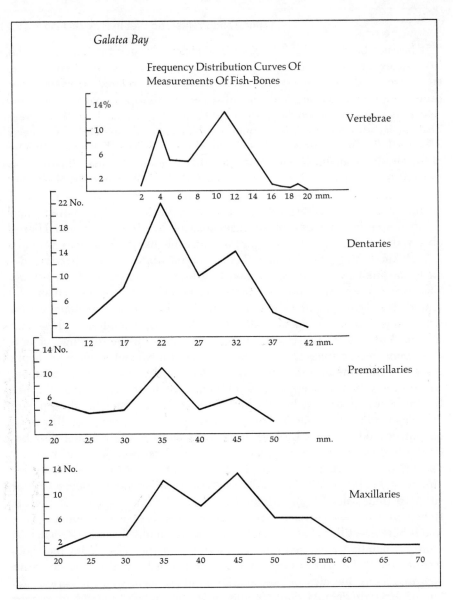

Figure 1 *Frequency distribution curves of the measurements of vertebrae, den-taries, premaxillaries, and maxillaries of the subfossil fish-bones from the Galatea Bay site.*

It will be observed that all the curves are bimodal and that both peaks closely coincide for each bone. The scales for the jawbones are all the same, as these bones are of approximately the same size, whereas the scale of the vertebrae, which are much smaller, has been increased.

family group ashore, gathering food, particularly shellfish. Augustus Hamilton gives an eyewitness account of this latter activity, carried out by three women. These would wade out into deep water, where they held one of their number upside down under the surface while she scraped the shellfish into a basket for as long as her breath lasted.

The reconstruction of the diet of the Galatea Bay (Figure 2) community has, up to this point, been based entirely upon the available, visible evidence. However, there are good grounds for supposing that this is incomplete. In the first place, documentary evidence copiously describes the use of such animal foods as crayfish, crabs, and sea-urchins, and, much more important, vegetable foods, including seaweeds and other wild products, particularly fern root (*aruhe*), the rhizome of *pteris aquilina,* and cultivated crops, of which the sweet-potato is generally considered to have been the one of greatest importance. However, because of the readily decomposible nature of these foods there is never any direct archaeological evidence for them. This is sharply at variance with other areas of the world, as for example, California, where R. Ascher, having calculated that nearly 2,000 kilograms of meat protein were represented by a particular midden, was then able to assume a much larger quantity of vegetable protein, on the basis of the relatively small number of animals other than shellfish and, more directly, because of the large numbers of milling stones. On the other hand, Grahame Clark was able to ignore for practical purposes the importance of vegetable foods at the large mammal-hunting camp of Star Carr [Clark, 1954]. In the case of New Zealand the importance of plant foods is well enough documented, but impossible to quantify alongside the sea animal foods, certainly until the results are available from considerably more research, which is at present under progress. Therefore, it is only possible to make a number of very generalized statements: first, it is unlikely that the forest and bush were capable of supporting other than very small numbers of people, in spite of the impression to the contrary which might be gained from such authorities as Elsdon Best. The plant foods of the forest which Best described, principally as the *hinau, karaka,* and *kahikatea* berries, are not distributed in such large and readily replenishible quantities throughout the bush as to be able to occupy more than a very subsidary role in the diet of a community; probably more important was their role as a minimal food supply for travellers. It is worth pointing out here that the economic importance of the New Zealand forest should not be thought of on equal terms with such areas, well known for their relative richness, as Southern California. On the other hand, the fern root, which grows in open areas, was . . . of fundamental importance in the economy, for which [Best] cites a great body of early documentary evidence. It would also seem that the fern root was far more generally important than *kumara* (sweet-potato), owing to the soil and climatic restrictions on the latter's cultivation. It is therefore not possible to arrive at more

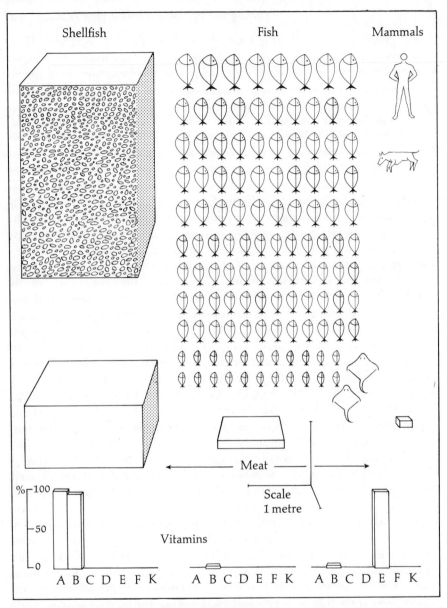

Figure 2 Graphic representation of the kinds and quantities of food represented in the excavated part of the Galatea Bay midden.

 The constituents and their products have been drawn approximately to scale and are in three vertical columns, showing the volume of shellfish on the top left, the number of fish in the center, and the mammals on the right. Below these quantities are representations of the approximate wet volumes of meat produced from these three sources. The lowermost line shows in a simplified manner the relative importance of each food source in terms of the total supply of vitamins, but it should however be noted that though the mammals would appear to supply the entire amount of vitamin E, this is in fact a relatively insignificant quantity.

than a very general estimate that the plant foods would supply an amount of energy probably equal to that derived from animal foods, though the range of variation could lie between nothing and double that quantity. A similar level of generalization must be approached in trying to estimate the total quantity of midden which formerly existed and of which only a part has been excavated. On two sides the midden has well-defined boundaries, abutting the steeply rising sides of the valley. On the third side it may be seen to be thinning out; on the fourth side an unknown amount has been eroded away by the sea. Once again, the most reasonable estimate will be that the excavated part represents about half the original site, though, because it is obvious that a certain amount is still unexcavated, the minus error cannot equal the estimated addition. These two further estimates will bring the total energy inferred for the occupation to 12,000,000 ± 9,000,000 calories, which represents either 4,444 ± 3,155 man/days or 692 ± 699 days for the family group.

SEASONALITY

... Earlier ... evidence was brought forward that this site had been occupied during the summer only, and must have been abandoned for part of the year: the dentition of the snapper demonstrated the season and the absence of their body parts suggested that these had been dried and taken elsewhere. This raises two questions. The first is how far we should modify the values in length of occupation or size of population so far obtained to take account of this discontinuous occupation and the storage of food for another season. The second is why there should be such a seasonal movement and where the winter quarters might be.

Clearly seasonal occupations, during which a food surplus was being created for the lean season by storage methods, complicates any estimate of the length of occupation or community size on quantities of food represented on the site, for the food debris represents a surplus of unknown quantity beyond the immediate needs of the community. In the analysis made above of the relative frequencies of the different parts of the snapper bodies, it was concluded that about three-quarters of the number had their dried bodies taken elsewhere. But this is in fact no guide, because it is impossible to tell either whether the surplus would represent the total needed by the community during the seasons in which it was absent from the site or if it was augmented by other food gathering activities during the lean season, or, again, for how great a proportion of the year the community spent its time at Galatea Bay gathering its surplus. These variables allow a wide range of interpretations, but they may conveniently be reduced to five broad possibilities:

> (1) The Galatea Bay site represents the virtually continuous occupation by a community throughout the year. But this is unlikely on several grounds, chiefly those proposed in previous sections, that the

fish appear to have been caught at a particular season, while their selective representation of body parts, indicating a technique of food preservation, both of which correspond to ethnographic accounts of seasonal movements of the Maori.

(2) The possibility of an occupation over nine months, with an absence of perhaps three months during the lean season, can also be ruled out on the grounds that the dentition of the fish appears to last for only a much shorter period in the state of exfoliation. And it would seem even more unlikely that fishing would only go on for a strictly limited period during an extended occupation of a coastal site.

(3) The seasonality could consist of approximately half the year spent on the coast, accumulating a sufficient surplus to support the population for the other half of the year elsewhere. But the argument against this must be that there would be no point in abandoning this locality where, after all, fish may be caught throughout the whole year, for another locality where, it must be assumed, there are no food supplies at all. This is a strong argument against the supposition that the amount of food prepared at seasonal sites, like Galatea Bay, for storage was sufficiently large to tide the community over a long, otherwise foodless period.

(4) Judging by the observations made above the choice is reduced to about three months of the year, which might be interpreted in one way if a relatively insignificant surplus was produced at the time, leaving the remaining nine months of the year to be spent elsewhere, at one or more different locations, during which food consumption and supply remained about equal. This could well have been the case, reflecting a purely hand-to-mouth economy, dangerously susceptible to any unforeseen failure of supply, but it would also indicate a state which is not associated with Maori culture. Under these conditions communities would have been small and thinly dispersed and incapable of developing the economic surpluses which must have been necessary for the practice of warfare, building of fortifications, and for the existence of such vigorous forms of Maori art as wood-carving, which is certainly prehistoric. Therefore, while there were, no doubt, instances when this would have been the correct interpretation, another must be sought.

(5) It is reasonable to assume that the stimulus for seasonal movement was an economic one, though it must be admitted that possibly some of the reasons why the modern New Zealander migrates to the coast in the summer may have worked in the past. However, if an economic reason is looked for, it has already been pointed out that life on the coast would be capable of providing at least a continuous supply of food, in which case there must have been some more powerful reason for drawing the population away from this source for a good part of the year, yet not for the whole year. The reason must be that adequate food-producing activity could only be carried out elsewhere. This leads to the final interpretation of the seasonality of the Galatea Bay site, which is thought to be the correct one, namely that the loca-

tion was occupied for perhaps three months of the year, during which a modest surplus was stored, and that for the remainder of the year the community lived elsewhere, for six or more months of which it was perhaps engaged in other food gathering and preparing activities, maybe adding further preserved foods, which when combined with those prepared at the fishing camp were sufficient to tide the community over the leanest season as well as providing a surplus for trade, warfare, or other activities.

If the argument for the site being occupied for only a short summer season of about three months, and that during this time only a relatively small proportion of the food was preserved (it being supposed that the drying of the fish was preferred to that of shellfish, though no doubt both were so preserved), and if the estimated size of the community based on Captain Cook's evidence is also accepted, then it may be readily calculated that the site could not have been occupied for more than six successive years. This would be the maximum, assuming that no significant surplus was preserved, but as it seems certain that preservation was being carried out, the probable answer would be a year or two less. This short period of reoccupations would find confirmation in the analysis of the size group frequencies of the snapper (Figure 1); because, if the site had been regularly reoccupied over many years the frequency curves would reasonably be expected to conform to a normal curve, instead of which they are distinctly bimodal, which can only be understood to represent a few fish populations.

Turning to the final question, posed earlier in the paper, on why there was seasonal movement and where the occupation for the rest of the year might be, the first part will already have been seen to have been answered. The economic reason, and it would be fruitless to speculate on any other kind of reason, must be that other, presumably inland localities were important sources of food. It may be added that "inland" need not be taken to mean far inland. A cursory examination of the most thorough field surveys of sites which have so far been published, notably that by Dr. A. G. Buist, of North Taranaki, indicates that about 90 percent of sites are within three miles of the coast, while the majority of the remainder are close to large rivers or lakes. It is probable that the inland sites would be close to patches of land suitable for cultivation, or open, fern-covered land. On the Auckland isthmus, at a distance of about thirty kilometers from Galatea Bay, there were extensive areas of good volcanic soil, represented by market gardens today, though fast disappearing under building developments. But these soils are missing, closer to the site, and they are probably too far distant for the island community to have exploited them. Otherwise, the mainland closer to the site, or the large island of Waiheke, or Ponui itself, appear to present rather similar conditions of quite high, broken ground, probably mainly covered by forest and with occasional, rather small patches of alluvial soil. Certainly the coastlines of the mainland, Waiheke and Ponui itself were extensively, if not necessarily densely, settled as is shown by the number of beach, stream sites, and fortified *pa* still visible.

V. Gordon Childe

16 THE NEOLITHIC REVOLUTION

V. Gordon Childe was the doyen of Old World archaeologists during the thirties and forties, a scholar whose books and articles were, and still are, widely read by laymen and experts. Childe, who became an authority on the prehistoric archaeology of Europe and the Near East, was an Australian; he started his archaeological career by studying the prehistory of the Danube Valley. Widening his scope, he wrote a series of major syntheses of Old World archaeology in which he recounted his theories of economic and cultural development. To Childe, the Near East was a source of great inventions and ideas, which flowed westward into Europe following two major "revolutions." A "Neolithic Revolution" saw the beginnings of agriculture; this was followed by an "Urban Revolution," when mankind first began to live in cities. In the passage that follows, Childe recounts his hypothesis of a "Neolithic Revolution," emphasizing the ways in which it occurred and relying heavily on a theory of climate change as part of his explanation. Childe's "Neolithic Revolution" is no longer accepted by many scholars, although it still appears in the literature, but it was an important pioneer hypothesis of which everyone should be aware.

The period when the food-producing economy became established was one of climatic crises adversely affecting precisely that zone of arid subtropical countries where the earliest farmers appear, and where the wild ancestors of cultivated cereals and domestic animals actually lived. The melting of the European ice sheets and the contraction of the high pressures or anticyclones over them involved a northward shift in the normal path of the rain-bearing depressions from the Atlantic. The showers that had watered North Africa and Arabia were deflected over Europe. Desiccation set in. Of course the process was not sudden or catastrophic. At first and for long, the sole harbinger would be the greater severity and longer

From *Man Makes Himself* by V. Gordon Childe, C. A. Watts Ltd., London (1951), pp. 67–72. Reprinted with permission of the publishers.

duration of periodical droughts. But quite a small reduction in the rainfall would work a devastating change in countries that were always relatively dry. It would mean the difference between continuous grasslands and sandy deserts interrupted by occasional oases.

A number of animals that could live comfortably with a twelve-inch annual rainfall would become a surplus population if the precipitation diminished by a couple of inches for two or three years on end. To get food and water, the grasseaters would have to congregate round a diminishing number of springs and streams — in oases. There they would be more exposed than ever to the attacks of beasts of prey — lions, leopards, and wolves — that would also gravitate to the oases for water. And they would be brought up against man too; for the same causes would force even hunters to frequent the springs and valleys. The huntsman and his prey thus find themselves united in an effort to circumvent the dreadful power of drought. But if the hunter is also a cultivator, he will have something to offer the famished beasts: the stubble of his freshly reaped fields will afford the best grazing in the oasis. Once the grains are garnered, the cultivator can tolerate half-starved mouflons or wild oxen trespassing upon his garden plots. Such will be too weak to run away, too thin to be worth killing for food. Instead, man can study their habits, drive off the lions and wolves that would prey upon them, and perhaps even offer them some surplus grain from his stores. The beasts, for their part, will grow tame and accustomed to man's proximity.

Hunters today, and doubtless in prehistoric times, have been accustomed to make pets of young wild animals for ritual ends or just for fun. Man has allowed the dog to frequent his camp in return for the offal of his prey and refuse from his feasts. Under the conditions of incipient desiccation the cultivator has the chance of attaching to his ménage not only isolated young beasts, but the remnants of complete flocks of herds, comprising animals of both sexes and all ages. If he just realizes the advantage of having a group of such half-tamed beasts hanging round the fringes of his settlement as a reserve of game easily caught, he will be on the way to domestication.

Next he must exercise restraint and discrimination in using this reserve of meat. He must refrain from frightening the beasts unnecessarily or killing the youngest and tamest. Once he begins to kill only the shyest and least amenable bulls or rams, he will have started selective breeding, eliminating untractable brutes, and consequently favoring the more docile. But he must also use his new opportunities of studying the life of the beasts at close range. He will thus learn about the processes of reproduction, the animals' needs of food and water. He must act upon his knowledge. Instead of merely driving the herd away when the time comes round for sowing his plots again, he must follow the beasts, guide them to suitable pastures and water, and continue to ward off predatory carnivora. It can thus be imagined how with lapse of time a flock or a herd should have been bred that was not only tame, but actually dependent upon man.

That result could happen only provided the peculiar climatic conditions continued long enough, and suitable animals were haunting human settlements. No doubt experiments were tried with various species; herds of antelopes and gazelles were kept by the Egyptians about 3000 B.C. These and other unknown experiments were fruitless. Luckily, cattle, sheep, goats, and pigs were included in the wild fauna of the desiccated regions in Asia. These did become firmly attached to man and ready to follow him.

At first the tame or domesticated beast would presumably be regarded only as a potential source of meat, an easily accessible sort of game. Other uses would be discovered later. It might be noticed that crops flourished best on plots that had been grazed over. Ultimately the value of dung as a fertilizer would be realized. The process of milking can only have been discovered when men had had ample opportunity of studying at close quarters the suckling of calves and lambs and kids. But once the trick was grasped, milk would become a second staple. It could be obtained without killing the beast, without touching your capital. Selection would again be applied. The best milkers would be spared, and their young reared in preference to other calves, lambs, or kids. Still later the hair of sheep or goats would win appreciation. It could be treated by processes, perhaps originally applied to plant fibers, and woven into cloth or else beaten into felt. Wool is entirely the artificial product of selective breeding. On wild sheep it is merely a down between the hairs. It was still unknown to the Egyptians even after 3000 B.C. But in Mesopotamia sheep were being bred for their wool before that date. The harnessing of animals to bear burdens or draw plows and vehicles is a late adaptation, and will be considered among the steps leading up to the second revolution in human economy.

The minimal characteristics of simple cultivation have already been considered. But these must now be pictured as combined with stock-breeding if we are to understand the basic economy revealed in neolithic settlements in North Africa, Hither Asia, and Europe. If the number of animals kept remains quite small, the account already given will hold good: the animals will be put to graze on the stubble after the harvest and at other seasons on natural pastures round the settlement. Beyond telling off a few youths to look after the herd, the communal economy can be left as already described. But as soon as the flocks exceed a low limit, special provision may have to be made for them. Trees and scrub may be burned off to make room for grass. In a river valley it may be thought worth-while to clear or irrigate special meadows to serve as pasture for cattle. Crops may be deliberately grown, harvested, and conserved to serve exclusively as fodder. Or the animals may be driven far afield to find pastures in the dry season. In Mediterranean lands, Persia, and Asia Minor there is good summer grazing on the hills which in winter are snow-clad. And so sheep and cattle are driven up to hill pastures in the spring. And now a regular company of the village's inhabitants must accompany the herds to ward off wild beasts, to milk the cows and ewes. The herders must generally take with them supplies of grain and other equipment. In some cases the fraction of the community that migrate with their gear to the summer pastures is quite small. But in hot and dry countries, like Persia, parts of the Eastern Sudan, and in the northwestern Himalayas, the bulk of the community abandons its village in the stifling valley and accompanies the herds to the cooler hills. Only a few stay behind to look after the fields and dwellings.

From this it is no far cry to a purely pastoral economy in which cultivation plays a negligible role. Pure pastoral nomadism is familiar, and is illustrated by several peoples in the Old World; the Bedouin of Arabia and Mongolian tribes of Central Asia are the best-known examples. How old such a mode of life may be is uncertain. Pastoralists are not likely to leave many vestiges by which the archaeologist could recognize their presence. They tend to use vessels of leather and basketry instead of pots, to live in tents instead of in excavated shelters or huts supported by stout timber posts or walls of stone or brick. Leather vessels and baskets have as a rule no chance of surviving; tents need not even leave deep post holes to mark where they once stood. (Though wood decays, modern archaeology can recognize the hole made by a post five thousand years ago.)

The failure to recognize prehistoric settlement sites or groups of relics belonging to pure pastoralists is not in itself any proof that such did not exist. To that extent the postulate of the "historical school," that pure pastoralism and pure hoe-culture were originally practiced independently by separate peoples and that mixed farming resulted from their subsequent fusion, is irrefutable. Yet [anthropologist Daryl] Forde has recently emphasized the instability of pure pastoralism. Many typical pastoral tribes today, like the patriarchs in Genesis, actually cultivate grain, though in an incidental and rather casual manner. If they grow no grain themselves, pastoral nomads are almost always economically dependent upon settled peasant villages. The cultivators may be tributaries or serfs to the pastoralists, but they are essential to their subsistence.

Whatever its origin, stock-breeding gave man control over his own food supply in the same way as cultivation did. In mixed farming it becomes an equal partner in the food-producing economy. But just as the term "cultivation" covers many distinct modes of gaining a livelihood, so the single phrase "mixed farming" marks an equal disparity and diversity. The several different modes of cultivation may be combined in varying degrees with distinct attitudes to the livestock. The diversity of the permutations and combinations has just been suggested. The multiplicity of concrete applications of the food-producing economy must never be forgotten.

It must be remembered, too, that food-production does not at once super-sede food-gathering. If today hunting is only a ritual sport and game is a luxury for the rich, fishing is still a great industry, contributing directly to everybody's diet. At first hunting, fowling, fishing, the collection of fruits, snails, and grubs continued to be essential activities in the food-quest of any food-producing group. Grain and milk began as mere supplements to a diet of game, fish, berries, nuts, and ants' eggs. Probably at first cul-tivation was an incidental activity of the women while their lords were engaged in the really serious business of the chase. Only slowly did it win the status of an independent and ultimately predominant industry. When the archaeological record first reveals neolithic communities in Egypt and Iran, survivals from the food-gathering régime clearly stand on an equal footing with grain-growing and stock-breeding. Only subsequently does their economic importance decline. After the second revolution, hunting and fowling have become, as with us, ritual sports, or else, like fishing, specialized industries practiced by groups within the community or by independent societies, economically dependent upon an agricultural civi-lization.

Two other aspects of the simple food-producing economy deserve atten-tion. In the first place, food-production, even in its simplest form, provides an opportunity and a motive for the accumulation of a surplus. A crop must not be consumed as soon as it is reaped. The grains must be con-served and eked out so as to last till the next harvest, for a whole year. And a proportion of every crop must be set aside for seed. The conserva-tion is easy. But it means on the one hand forethought and thrift, on the other receptacles for storage. These are quite as essential as, and may actually be more elaborate than, dwellings. In the neolithic villages of the Fayum, perhaps the oldest of their kind, excavated silos, lined with straw basketry or matting, are the most substantial constructions that have sur-vived.

Again, livestock that has been laboriously carried over the dry season must not be indiscriminately slaughtered and devoured. The young cows and ewes at least must be spared and reared to provide milk and to aug-ment the herd or flock. Once these ideas have been driven home, the production and accumulation of a surplus are much easier for food-pro-ducers than for food gatherers. The yield of crops and of herds soon out-strips the immediate needs of the community. The storage of grain, the conservation of live meat "on the hoof" is much simpler, especially in a warm climate, than the preservation of stocks of slaughtered game. The surplus thus gathered will help to tide the community over bad seasons; it will form a reserve against droughts and crop failures. It will serve to support a growing population. Ultimately it may constitute a basis for rudimentary trade, and so pave the way to a second revolution.

Secondly, the economy is entirely self-sufficing. The simple food-producing community is not dependent for any necessity of life on imports obtained by barter or exchange from another group. It produces and collects all the food it needs. It relies on raw materials available in its immediate vicinity for the simple equipment it demands. Its constituent members or households manufacture the requisite implements, utensils, and weapons.

This economic self-sufficiency does not necessarily spell isolation. The variations in the simple food-producing economy already indicated, the simultaneous pursuit of several methods of obtaining nourishment by different groups, are liable to bring the several communities concerned into mutual contact. Driving their flocks to summer pastures, the herdsmen from one village are likely to meet their counterparts from another. On hunting expeditions across the desert, huntsmen from one oasis may cross parties from another. In such ways the isolation of each community is liable to be broken down. Far from being a scattering of discrete units, the neolithic world should be viewed as a continuous chain of communities. Each would be linked to its neighbors on either side by recurrent, if infrequent and irregular, contacts.

The simple food-producing economy just described is an abstraction. Our picture is based on a selection of supposedly distinctive traits from materials afforded by ethnographers' observations on modern "savages" and inferences from particular archaeological sites. The precise stage of economic development here adumbrated may never have been fully realized in precisely this concrete form. Archaeology alone could justify the presentation of a "neolithic" economy as a universal historical stage in the progress toward modern civilization. But all archaeology can do at present is to isolate temporary phases in what was really a continuous process. We have tacitly assumed that similar phases were realized nearly simultaneously in several areas. But in prehistoric times such simultaneity cannot be proved, even in the cases of regions so close together as Tasa in Middle Egypt, the Fayum, and the Delta. Strict parallelism in time between Egypt and, say, North Syria would be hard to establish. To claim it as between Egypt and North Europe would be almost certainly false; our best examples of a simple food-producing economy in Britain or Belgium are to be dated in terms of solar years perhaps thirty centuries later than their counterparts in Egypt. And we have deliberately cited contemporary savage groups as illustrating the same economic stage.

Kent V. Flannery

17 ORIGINS AND ECOLOGICAL EFFECTS OF EARLY DOMESTICATION

Kent V. Flannery is one of those archaeologists who have recently proposed a theory regarding the origins of food production somewhat different than that espoused by Childe. In contrast to earlier colleagues, Flannery argues that the stage for domestication was set by an important shift in subsistence patterns. Sometime after twenty thousand years ago, the inhabitants of the Near East shifted their economic strategies toward exploiting a wide range of game and vegetable resources. Cultivation may have begun in marginal areas where natural stands of wild grasses did not grow in abundance. People began to plant the cereal grasses there because growing populations in optimum zones forced settlement of marginal areas. Soon favorable mutations in the cereals occurred, mutations that encouraged harvesting and storage of grain. Unfortunately, Flannery's article cannot be reprinted in its entirety here. It and a collection of other articles on prehistoric agriculture can be found in Stuart Struever's admirable reader *Prehistoric Agriculture* (Garden City, N.J.: Natural History Press, 1971).

INTRODUCTION

Late in the Pliocene there began a series of movements of the earth's crust, which caused the central plateau of Iran to be drawn closer to the stable massif of Arabia. The land between, caught in the grip of these two far-heavier formations, was compressed and folded into a series of parallel mountain ridges or anticlines. Gradually the center of this compressed zone collapsed and subsided, so that the parallel ridges, trending from north-west to south-east, appear to rise out of it like the successive tiers of a grandstand, eventually reaching the Arabian and Iranian plateaus to either side. The sunk land in between, still settling and filling with the erosion products of the mountains, became the rolling and irregular plain known as Mesopotamia; the parallel ridges to the east of it are the Zagros Mountains (Lees, Falcon 1952:24–39).

The result was an area in which altitudinal differences produce a great

Reprinted from "Origins and Ecological Effects of Early Domestication in Iran and the Near East" by Kent V. Flannery, in Peter J. Ucko and G. W. Dimbleby (eds.), *The Domestication and Exploitation of Plants and Animals,* by permission of the author and the publishers Gerald Duckworth & Co. Ltd. © 1969 Peter J. Ucko and G. W. Dimbleby.

number of contrasting environments in a relatively limited geographic area — a mosaic of valleys at different elevations, with different rainfall, temperature, and vegetational patterns. Like some of the other areas where early civilizations arose — Mesoamerica and the Central Andes, for example — the Near East is a region of "vertical economy," where exchanges of products between altitude zones are made feasible and desirable by the close juxtaposition of four main environmental types: high plateau (c. 5,000 ft.), intermontane valleys (1,500–4,000 ft.), piedmont-steppe (600–1,000 ft.), and alluvial desert (100–500 ft.). A similar pattern arose in the Levant, where the same late Pliocene tectonic movements produced the great Jordan Rift Valley, flanked by the wooded Lebanon-Judean mountains and the arid Syrian Plateau. It was in this kind of setting that the first steps toward plant and animal domestication were made.

Stages in Near Eastern prehistory. In a recent article, Frank Hole and I have divided the prehistory of Western Iran into three main adaptive eras (Hole, Flannery 1967). The first was a period of semi-nomadic hunting and gathering, which lasted until roughly 10,000–8000 B.C. The second era we have called the period of early dry-farming and Caprine domestication, and it seems to have involved predominantly emmer wheat (*Triticum dicoccum*), two-row hulled barley (*Hordeum distichum*), goats (*Capra hircus*), and sheep (*Ovis aries*). This period lasted until about 5500 B.C., and its hallmarks are already familiar to members of this symposium: permanent villages, early hornless sheep, goats with medially-flattened and/or helically-twisted horn cores, and cereal grain samples which show a mixture of wild (tough-glumed, brittle rachis) and domestic (brittle-glumed, tough-rachis) characteristics. The third adaptive era was one which involved the previously-mentioned cultivars plus bread wheat (*Triticum aestivum*); six-row barley which might be either hulled or naked (*Hordeum vulgare*); lentils; grass peas; linseed; domestic cattle (*Bos taurus*); pigs (*Sus scrofa*); and domestic dogs (*Canis familiaris*), and featured irrigation in those zones where its use was feasible without elaborate technology. This era culminated, in the lowlands at least, in the rise of walled towns, about 3000 B.C. (Adams 1962).

There is no reason to believe that the entire Near East went through these eras synchronously; in addition, evidence suggests that each of the cultivars may have appeared earlier in some areas than in others. Nevertheless, with these caveats in mind, I find this framework useful enough so that I will follow it in this paper, and apologize in advance for viewing the rest of South-western Asia through Iranian eyes. The stages are, it should be emphasized, ones of farming adaptation: they imply nothing about level of social and political development. They allow, in other words, for the simultaneous existence of tiny four-acre villages in Kurdistan and immense, 32-acre sites like Çatal Hüyük in Anatolia.

The basic argument of the paper is as follows. An important change in subsistence pattern, midway through the Upper Paleolithic in the Near East, set the stage for domestication of plants. This shift, which represented a trend toward "broad spectrum" wild resource utilization, continued long after cultivation had begun. In this sense, our Western view of early cultivation as a drastic change or "improvement" in man's diet is erroneous, as is the frequently-cited notion that early agriculture gave man a "more stable" food supply. Given the erratic nature of rainfall in South-west Asia, the era of early dry-farming was still one of unpredictable surpluses and lean years, with considerable reliance on local wild products. I suggest that early caprine domestication, apart from its food aspects, represented a way of "banking" these unpredictable surpluses in live storage, analogous to the use of pigs by Melanesian peoples (Lees 1967) or the exchange of imperishable, exotic raw materials which characterized early village farmers in Mesoamerica (Flannery 1968b). Early irrigation modified this pattern, and also aggravated environmental destruction to the point where the return to a wild resource economy would have been nearly impossible. It also set the stage for both dramatic population increases in the lowlands and "ranked" or stratified societies in which a hereditary elite controlled the small percentage of the landscape on which the bulk of the food was produced. A bit of indulgence on the reader's part will be required by the fact that in a paper of this length only the meagerest documentation can be offered for these points of view.

Prime movers and subsistence change. A basic problem in human ecology is why cultures change their modes of subsistence at all. This paper, while not relying on the facile explanation of prehistoric environmental change, is hardly destined to settle that problem. The fact is, however, that for much of South-west Asia we have no evidence to suggest that late Pleistocene or post-Pleistocene environmental changes forced any of the significant subsistence shifts seen in the archaeological record. I will therefore use, as one possible mechanism, a model of population pressure and disequilibrium relative to environmental carrying capacity, drawn from recent ethnographic data on hunting and gathering groups.

A growing body of data supports the conclusion, stated with increasing frequency in recent years, that starvation is not the principal factor regulating mammal populations (Wynne-Edwards 1962). Instead, evidence suggests that other mechanisms, including their own social behavior, homeostatically maintain mammal populations at a level *below* the point at which they would begin to deplete their own food supply. The recent conference on "Man the Hunter," held at Chicago in 1966, made it clear that this is probably also true of human populations on the hunting-gathering level (Birdsell 1968). In addition, a number of current ethnographic studies indicate that, far from being on a starvation level, hunting-gathering groups may get all the calories they need without even working very hard (McCarthy 1957; Bose 1964; Lee 1965). Even the Bushmen of the relatively desolate Kalahari region, when subjected to an input-output analysis (Lee 1969), appeared to get 2,100 calories a day with less than three days' worth of foraging per week. Presumably, hunter-gatherers in lusher environments in prehistoric times did even better. This is not to say that paleolithic populations were not limited by their food supply; obviously, they were. But *in addition*, they engaged in behavior patterns designed to maintain their density below the starvation level.

What, then, would persuade a hunter-gatherer to modify his subsistence pattern significantly — for example, to adopt agriculture? In the course of this paper I would like to apply the equilibrium model recently proposed by Binford (1968b) as a means of explaining post-Pleistocene changes in the archaeological record. This model will be used to offer tentative explanations for subsistence changes which took place in the Near East at the three critical points mentioned in the start of this paper: the Upper Paleolithic, the beginning of domestication, and the beginnings of irrigation.

Binford, drawing on both Birdsell and Wynne-Edwards, postulates that prehistoric hunting populations, once reasonably well-adapted to a particular environment, tended to remain stable at a density below the point of resource exhaustion. He argues that their adaptation would change only in the face of some disturbance of the equilibrium between population and environment. Two kinds of disturbances might take place: either (1) a change in the physical environment which would bring about a reduction in the density of chosen plant and animal foods, or (2) a change in demography which would raise local human populations too close to the carrying capacity of the immediate area. The first kind of disturbance might be reflected in the palynological record; the second might be reflected in a shift in site density and settlement pattern in the archaeological record. Disturbances of both kinds occurred in the prehistoric Near East, but it is perhaps the second kind which is most useful theoretically, because it does not rely on the *deus ex machina* of climatic change, an event which does not seem to have taken place with sufficient frequency to explain all (or even most) prehistoric cultural changes (Binford 1968b).

Binford points out that, even in the hunting-gathering era, certain areas supported higher populations than others because of their high level of edible resources. Butzer (1964) makes the same point, singling out the "grassy, tropical deciduous woodlands and savannas; the mid-latitude grasslands; (and) the lower latitude Pleistocene tundras" as having the optimal carrying capacity for hunting-gathering populations. In the case of the Near East, for example, it would appear that the mixed oak woodland of the Levant Coast supported higher upper paleolithic populations than some of the treeless inland steppe areas, at least where survey has been comparably extensive. One sees, therefore, a mosaic of "optimal" habitats, with a somewhat higher carrying capacity and population density, separated by "less favorable" habitats with a somewhat lower carrying capacity and population density. Binford argues that one source of stimulus for culture change is the cyclical demographic pressure exerted on these marginal habitats by their optimal neighbors. It is the optimal habitats which are regional growth centers; it is in them that populations rise, followed by buddings-off and emigrations of daughter groups before the carrying capacity has been strained (Birdsell 1957). They are the "donor systems"; the marginal habitats are the "recipient systems." And it is in the marginal habitats that the density equilibrium would most likely be periodically disturbed by immigrations of daughter groups, raising populations too near the limited carrying capacity. Thus Binford argues that pressures for the exploitation of new food sources would be felt most strongly *around the margins* of population growth centers, not in the centers themselves.

The first change I would like to deal with took place in the upper paleolithic period, before 20,000 B.C., and amounted to a considerable broadening of the subsistence base to include progressively greater amounts of fish, crabs, water turtles, molluscs, land snails, partridges, migratory water fowl (and possibly wild cereal grains in some areas?).

The Upper Paleolithic of the Near East has a number of chronological phases and regional variants, from the "Antelian" and "Kebaran" of the Mediterranean Coast (Howell 1959) to the "Baradostian" and "Zarzian" of the Zagros Mountains (Solecki 1964a). Its environmental context in the coastal Levant may have been an open Mediterranean woodland not unlike today's (Rossignol 1962; 1963), while the Zagros Mountains seem at that time to have been treeless *Artemisia* steppe (Van Zeist, Wright 1963; Van Zeist 1967). In both areas, hunting of hoofed mammals accounted for 90% of the archaeological bones, and when weights of meat represented are calculated, it appears that ungulates contributed 99% (Flannery 1965). In the Zagros, archaeological settlement patterns suggest that the basic residential unit was a "base camp" composed of several families, which shifted seasonally; from this base, hunting parties made periodic forays to "transitory stations," vantage points from which they stalked and eventually killed game, which was then cut up into portable sections at temporary "butchering stations" (Hole, Flannery 1967). There are indications that a similar pattern may have characterized the Levant. On the basis of multivariant factor analysis of flint tools, Binford and Binford (1966b) have described the various living floors of Rockshelter I at Yabrud as brief "work camps" made at varying distances from a base camp, sometimes for hunting, sometimes for processing plant material. Near the Wadi Antelias, where Ksar Akil was presumably the "base camp," Ewing (1949) describes "hunting sites on the surface higher up in the mountains," some of which may be analogous to the transitory stations or butchering stations of the southern Zagros.

Midway through the "Antelian" or "Baradostian" phases, one can see the aforementioned trend toward increasing use of small game, fish, turtles, seasonal water fowl, partridges, and invertebrates — the latter including terrestrial and marine snails, freshwater mussels, and river crabs. It would be oversimplified to view this as a "shift from large to small game," for even at late paleolithic sites, ungulates contributed 90% of the meat supply. The trend is rather from exploiting a more "narrow spectrum" of environmental resources to a more "broad spectrum" of edible wild products. This "broad spectrum" collecting pattern characterized all subsequent cultures up to about 6000 b.c., and I would argue that it is only in such a context that the first domestication could take place. It is a pattern in which everything from land snails (*Helix* sp.) to very small crabs (*Potamon* sp.), and perhaps even cereal grasses, was viewed as potential food. It was also accompanied by a number of "pre-adaptations" for early cultivation.

One of these was the development of ground stone technology. At sites like Ksar Akil in Lebanon (Ewing 1951) and Yafteh Cave in Iran (Hole, Flannery 1967), small coarse grinding stones occasionally appear; abraders are increasingly common in later Zarzian sites in the Zagros, where they come to include grooved rubbing stones (Hole, Flannery 1967; Garrod 1930). Evidence suggests that these implements were at first used mainly (but not necessarily solely) for milling ochre. However, the ground stone technology was there, and when man eventually turned to the cereal grasses, he had only to adapt and expand a pre-existing technology in order to deal with grain processing.

Still another "pre-adaptation" for what was to follow can be detected in the later stages of the Paleolithic in the Near East: the development of storage facilities, which are not at all well-represented in earlier phases. In the Zarzian level at Shanidar Cave, for example, "several pits . . . which may have been storage pits" are reported by Solecki (1964a; 1964b). These features increase with time; many sites of the period 9000–7000 b.c. are reported to have subterranean pits, e.g. Zawi Chemi Shanidar (Solecki 1964a; 1964b), Karim Shahir (Braidwood, Howe 1960), and Mureybat (van Loon 1966). Some were plastered, evidently for storage, e.g. at Aïn Mallaha (Perrot 1966), while others may have been used for roasting grain over heated pebbles, e.g. at Mureybat (Braidwood, Howe 1960). In any event, these subterranean pits seem to be a feature of the broad-spectrum collecting era, and would presumably have been more effective for storing or processing invertebrate or vegetal foods (snails, acorns, pistachios, etc.) than for any activity connected with ungulate hunting.

It seems unlikely that the shift to a broad-spectrum pattern was a direct result of environmental change. It is true that the earlier Pleistocene "big game" of the Near East — elephant, rhinoceros, hippopotamus, and so on — had vanished, but as pointed out by Howell (1959), these species disappeared midway in the Mousterian period, that is, many thousands of years before we can see any substantial increase in the use of fish, invertebrates, and (possibly) vegetal foods. Moreover, use of these latter foods is more striking in some areas than others. For example, in the Levant area none of the Mount Carmel caves shows much in the way of invertebrate foods (Garrod, Bate 1937), while "thousands" of *Helix* snails are reported from Ksar Akil in the Wadi Antelias. In the Zagros, certain caves like Palegawra have more abundant remains of snails, mussels, and crabs than do those in other areas (Ewing 1949; Reed, Braidwood 1960); we recovered virtually no land snails from our Khorramabad Valley caves (Hole, Flannery 1967).

Regional variations like those mentioned above suggest that Binford's model of disturbed density equilibrium may not be far wrong: pressure for the use of invertebrates, fish, water fowl, and previously-ignored plant resources would have been felt most strongly in the more marginal areas which would have received overflow from the expanding populations of the prime hunting zones, raising their densities to the limit of the land's carrying capacity. At this point they would tend to turn, I suggest, not to small *mammals* — which do not appear to be a very secure resource anywhere in the Near East — but to those smaller resources which are readily and predictably available in some quantity at certain seasons of the year. These are water fowl, fish, mussels, snails, and plants. Many of these resources are storable, and though small, are not to be scoffed at. Land snails, for example, although less rich in protein than ungulate meat, are actually much richer in calcium (Platt 1962), especially in limestone mountain regions, since they use lime to synthesize their protective mucous (Hesse et al. 1951). Mussels supply vitamin A and acorns and pistachios are very high calorie foods, much more so than wild game (Platt 1962). Present data tentatively suggest that the "broad spectrum revolution" was real, that it was nutritionally sound, and that it originally constituted a move which counteracted disequilibria in population in the less favorable hunting areas of the Near East. Once established, however, it spread to and was eventually taken up even by the favorable areas. And one other aspect of it might be noted: the invertebrate (and vegetal?) foods involved are ones which could easily have been collected by women and children, while the men continued ungulate hunting. The broad-spectrum collecting pattern may therefore have contributed to the development of division of labor in the late Pleistocene and early post-Pleistocene era.

EARLY DRY FARMING

The environmental context of early domestication. The "broad-spectrum" revolution set the cultural stage for domestication, and with the close of the Pleistocene the oak woodland belt expanded over the upland Near East, even into areas of the Zagros which had formerly been treeless steppe (Van Zeist, Wright 1963). This "optimum" wild resource zone, which includes the densest stands of edible nuts, fruits, and wild cereal grasses had apparently been present in the Levant throughout the last glaciation (Rossignol 1962; 1963), but was now available over a much wider area.

A number of environmental characteristics of this zone today (which presumably have characterized it since the Pleistocene drew to a close) should be mentioned here, for they are variables which affected man's use of the region and set the environmental stage for domestication. Low average precipitation inhibits dense forest growth, but cool, moist air from the Mediterranean in winter results in enough rain (or snow) to guarantee some spring growth of edible grasses and legumes. Hot, dry air circulating out of Eurasia in the summer (plus even hotter local winds off Arabia) produces a prolonged rainless period which inhibits the growth of perennials; most of the vegetation thus consists of annuals which have a peak growing season in March or April, after which they must be harvested in a three-week period. This set the seasonal collecting pattern. Further, like most arid or semi-arid regions, the zone has a low vegetation diversity index (Odum, Odum 1959), which means that certain species (like wild cereal grasses) may form nearly pure stands. This is true of the fauna as well; while the number of mammalian species is low (relative to wetter areas), many of these are species which tend to form herds, e.g. sheep, goat, gazelle, and onager. Harlan and Zohary (1966) have discussed the implications of the nearly-pure cereal stands, and Reed (1959; 1960) has considered the pre-adaptive role of "herd behavior" in the ungulates which were first domesticated.

The origins of cultivation. The beginning of cultivation is a second shift which may have taken place in the less favorable valleys and wadis around the periphery of the zone of maximum carrying capacity.

For many years it was assumed, quite logically, that domestication must have begun in the zone where the wild ancestors of the domesticates are most at home. Then, in an eye-opening paper, Harlan and Zohary (1966) revealed that "over many thousands of hectares" within this zone "it would be possible to harvest wild wheat today from natural stands almost as dense as a cultivated wheat field." Harlan (1967) then proceeded to do just that: armed with a flint-bladed sickle, he harvested enough wild wheat in an hour to produce one kilo of clean grain — and the wild grain, after chemical analysis, proved to be almost twice as rich in protein as domestic wheat. Harlan and Zohary (1966) therefore closed with a warning: "Domestication may not have taken place where the wild cereals were most abundant. Why should anyone cultivate a cereal where natural stands are as dense as a cultivated field? . . . farming itself may have originated in areas adjacent to, rather than in, the regions of greatest abundance of wild cereals."

Harlan's wild wheat harvest also suggested that a family of experienced plant-collectors, working over the three-week period when wild wheat comes ripe, "without even working very hard, could gather more grain than the family could possibly consume in a year" (Harlan 1967). Such a harvest would almost necessitate some degree of sedentism — after all, where could they go with an estimated metric ton of clean wheat?

This was, of course, what archaeologist Jean Perrot (1966) had been saying for years about the Natufian culture in Palestine — that they had been semi-sedentary, based on intensive wild cereal collection. A further suggestion of this nature has since come from Tell Mureybat, a site on the terrace of the Euphrates River in inland Syria, dating to c. 8000 B.C. Preliminary analyses of carbonized barley and einkorn wheat from pre-pottery levels at the site — which have clay-walled houses, grinding stones, and roasting pits presumably used to render the cereal glumes brittle for threshing — suggest that the grain may be all wild (van Loon 1966). Such data indicate that sedentary life based on wild cereal collecting and hunting may be possible, and that consequently pressures for domestication may not be as strong in the heart of the wild cereal habitat as elsewhere.

This impression is reinforced by the fact that some of our most ancient samples of morphologically domesticated grain (e.g. emmer wheat) come from "marginal" habitats well outside the present wild range of that plant; for example, in the Wadi Araba region (Kirkbride 1966) and the Khuzistan steppe (Helbaek 1969), in areas where dense stands could only be produced by deliberate cultivation. It is possible, therefore, that cultivation began as an attempt to produce artificially, around the *margins* of the "optimum" zone, stands of cereal as dense as those in the *heart* of the "optimum" zone. Binford had already suggested that this might have taken place in response to population pressure exerted on the marginal habitats by expansion of sedentary food-collectors from the heart of the wild cereal zone. It appears that efforts at early cultivation were probably soon reinforced by favorable mutations in the cereals themselves, such as toughening of the rachis, polyploidy, and loss of tough glumes.

The spread of the early dry-farming complex across the Near East is striking; where surveys are adequate, it appears that very few environmental zones were without farming communities at this time, although population densities were higher in some areas than others. In the Zagros Mountains, densities of sites are highest in intermontane plains with a high sub-surface water table and frequent marshy areas (Hole, Flannery 1967), suggesting that a critical resource sought by early farmers were lands of high water-retention, where soil moisture helped the planted cereals to survive annual fluctuations in rainfall. At Ali Kosh on the lowland steppe of Southwest Iran, early farmers planted their cereals so near swamp margins that seeds of club-rush (*Scirpus*) were mixed in with the carbonized grain samples (Helbaek 1969). This is analogous to the practices of early farmers in parts of arid highland Mesoamerica, who also utilized permanently-humid bottomlands and high-water table zones (Flannery et al. 1967). Such types of farming may also have facilitated the spread of agriculture out of the Near East and into Europe, which took place sometime during this time period.

More complicated techniques accompanied the extension of early dry-farming to its limits in very marginal habitats to the north-east (e.g. the Turkoman steppe), and the south-west (e.g. the Wadi Araba region). At Beidha, in the south Jordan desert, it is possible that farming sites were located in such a way as to take advantage of rainfall run-off concentrated by steep nearby cliffs (Kirkbride 1966). On the Turkoman steppe, early cultivators used small "oasis" situations where streams from the Kopet Dagh formed humid deltas along the base of the mountain range (Masson 1965). In all such cases, where rainfall agriculture must have been pushed to its absolute limit, barley seems to have been the main crop (Helbaek 1966a; 1966b; Masson 1965); otherwise, wheat was preferred.

Richard S. MacNeish

18 TEHUACÁN

More about the origins of food production in the New World is known than about those in the Near East or Asia, largely because the arid conditions of the American Southwest, parts of Mesoamerica, and Peru are more conducive to the survival of grains in the archaeological record. Maize has long been a staple of American agriculture, and the search for the ancestry of this important crop has occupied archaeologists and botanists for many years. The name of Richard S. MacNeish is synonymous with the search for maize, for this well-known archaeologist was responsible for the discovery of early corn in the Tehuacán Valley in Mexico. Tehuacán has become a yardstick for studies of the origins of New World agriculture, for the cultural sequence in the valley is studied by almost all American archaeologists. In the paper that follows, MacNeish describes the cultural sequence in the valley and states that the events traced in such detail at Tehuacán were almost certainly duplicated at other localities, in the Old World as well as in the Americas, even if the crops were different.

The main purpose of the Robert S. Peabody Foundation's archaeological endeavors in the Tehuacán Valley of central Mexico was to try to understand the beginnings of food production (mainly corn agriculture) and the

Reprinted from "Speculation about How and Why Food Production and Village Life Developed in the Tehuacán Valley, Mexico" by Richard Stockton MacNeish, *Archaeology*, Vol. 24, No. 4, with permission of the author and the Editor of *Archaeology*. Copyright 1971, Archaeological Institute of America. Some illustrations are omitted.

rise of village life. To accomplish this, archaeological reconnaissance was undertaken in this small ecological zone with its four micro-environs, and thus 454 sites were found. Later, twelve stratified sites with 138 superimposed floors were excavated. Study of the 10,000 artifacts, 500,000 sherds, and 50,000 ecofacts (remnants of the environment) from these floors, plus 120 radiocarbon determinations, together with many interdisciplinary studies, resulted in our defining a long cultural sequence from about 10,000 B.C. to A.D. 1520. The first six of our nine culture phases, roughly from 10,000 to 850 B.C., have given us considerable new information in understanding how and why agriculture and village life began in this small region. In the following pages, I shall summarize these earlier culture phases and attempt to explain why the major culture changes occurred.

The earliest components from 10,000 to 6700 B.C. have been classified into the Ajuereado phase [Figure 1], so called from the site. The sustenance of these earliest peoples seems to have been mainly meat (perhaps over 70%) with a lesser amount gained from vegetal foods. In terms of subsistence activities, hunting was of prime importance: drives, ambushing with lance and dart-stalking were techniques utilized in all seasons. In the winter, hunting was probably the only means of subsistence. In other periods of the year, meat was supplemented by collecting pods in the spring, seeds in the spring and summer, fruits in the fall, and by cutting opuntia and agave leaves in all of these seasons.

Stone tools give evidence of industrial activity. These were usually hard stone percussion chipped flakes derived from blocky cores, usually without prepared striking platforms. Some of these flakes were finished by pressure retouching. Diagnostic tool types include Lerma and Abasolo points, flake and slab choppers, crude blades, well-made end scrapers, gravers and side scraper knives. These latter tools hint that there probably was a hideworking industry. Chipped spokeshaves possibly indicate a woodworking industry.

All components uncovered came from site areas of less than one hundred square meters, and most excavated components had only one or two fireplaces. In this way, I consider all components to have been occupied by less than three families, and I have classified all such sites as microband camps. When looking at the site distribution over the valley, no clustering can be discerned, so there is no evidence of territoriality, nor is there any correlation between seasonal occupations and any particular micro-environment. On the basis of this data I have classified the community pattern of Ajuereado as *Nomadic Microbands*, that is, groups of families who hunted game in all seasons without regard to any well-regulated subsistence scheduling or well-defined territories.

In my opinion the change from *Nomadic Microbands* to *Seasonal Macro-Microbands* (the community type characteristic of our next two phases) was

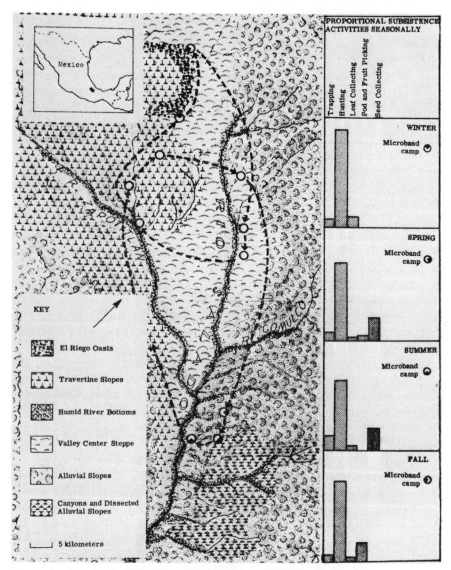

Figure 1 Ajuereado Phase (10,000 to 7000 B.C.) *with estimates of proportions of subsistence activities by season* (right column) *and the distribution of seasonal microband camps with their hypothetical wanderings that form Nomadic microband communities in the micro-environments of the Tehuacán Valley, Mexico* (left column).

a slow process which began about a thousand years before the transition actually took place — roughly during the late Ajuereado phase, say, about 9600 B.C. Previous to this time our evidence reveals that the Valley people had specialized in various kinds of hunting activities, but in the long period of the development of these techniques, they also acquired, as a by-product, a tremendous knowledge of the other food potential of their micro-environment at various seasons. As a supplement to their meat diet they had experimented with seed collection, pod and fruit picking, and leaf cutting. This gradual accumulation of subsistence and ecological knowledge coincided with the waning of the Pleistocene with its changes in weather and rainfall which resulted in a greater diversity in seasons, a drier and warmer climate, a diminution of grassland steppes and water holes, as well as an expansion of the thorn forests on the alluvial slopes, and an expansion of the cactus forests on to the travertine slopes. In part, these changes brought about the extinction of the various "herd" animals, such as horse and antelope, as well as the disappearance of other Pleistocene fauna ranging from the jack rabbit to the mammoth and mastodon. In this way, changes in the ecosystem became interconnected with changes in subsistence; with changes in subsistence patterns, there were alterations to the ecosystem. An interstimulating feedback cycle was in process. Although climatic changes and changes in the ecosystem had probably occurred previously in the Tehuacán Valley, apparently never before had they coincided at a time when men were ready with exactly the right variety of eco-subsistence knowledge crucial to cause a major culture change.

We may speculate, in terms of seasonal cycles, that in the spring, the Ajuereado people, as was their wont, hunted for herd animals on the grasslands in most of the center of the valley, but as the waning Pleistocene caused this grassland to shrink in size, causing some herd animals to die off, other animals disappeared because man could more easily kill off the remainder in this more limited area. This meant that through time, in the spring, groups began to subsist more and more on the seed and pod foods from the steppe rather than from the meat. They collected these seeds and pods from spots they already knew and by techniques they had already developed.

The summer wet season that formerly had always been the time when the food was plentiful now saw man move out of the grasslands since seeds had already been picked and game had already been hunted out. The people turned to exploit any of the other available micro-environs. But, again, game was disappearing, so more and more of man's summer food also came from leaves, fruits and seeds, again from places they knew well and by techniques they had earlier developed but previously used little.

Fall, which formerly would have yielded game in any ecological niche, now had little game. Pod, seed, and leaf foods had also been collected from most areas, so man moved on into the few areas he knew about where there were still fruits and plants to pick.

The winter season which, even in Pleistocene times, had never been productive as far as plant food was concerned had allowed for hunting in a number of areas. Winter hunting now became even worse because of the increased dryness and smaller grassland area. Both man and animal were forced instead to cluster around the few well-watered areas, which again meant man further diminished the supply of game. Thus, the Tehuacanos shifted gradually from hunting over a wide area, in all seasons, to a system of well-scheduled subsistence activities in terms of particular seasons and micro-environments.

Life style changes such as these may have later led to new developments in technology, for instance, perhaps paintstones developed into mortar and milling stones to grind the increasing quantity of plant-derived foods. Certainly, by the end of Ajuereado times, Valley people were moving about in well-regulated regional cycles so that bands became tied to territories and, gradually, as they found abundant foodstuffs at particular places in the wet seasons, small groups coalesced into larger groups (macrobands) for brief periods. Changes in the social system may also have taken place in response to the new way of life and the slightly greater population. These changes in technology, territoriality, settlement patterns, population growth, and social structure, however, came after the changes in environment, and after the necessary accumulation of ecological and subsistence knowledge. I am, therefore, suggesting that environmental and subsistence changes are the causative factors, resulting in changed settlement patterns, technology, etc.

What I am leading up to is this. Is the above described process not similar to that which occurred in the Zagros Mountains of the Near East between the cultural phases of Baradostian and Zarzi, after the climatic change of 14,000 B.C. as indicated in the pollen profile? And, aren't these two instances of cultural change similar to what happened in the Andes of Peru in the change from the cultural phase of Huanta to Puente, just after the final extinction of the Pleistocene fauna at about 7400 B.C.? I am suggesting these three illustrations are comparable.

But to return to the Tehuacán Valley. The El Riego phase [Figure 2], 6700–5000 B.C., brought certain new changes in subsistence patterns although at this time period 54% of their food was still from meat, 40% came from vegetal stuffs and 0–6% was from agricultural produce. The major difference as formerly, however, was in the particular scheduling of their subsistence activities. The picture for the El Riego phase, as I see it, seemed to be as follows: in the winter, these people obtained most of their food by hunting (mostly by lance-ambushing or dart-stalking) and they supplemented this activity with leaf cutting and trapping. In the spring, their predominant activity was seed collecting and pod picking which was also supplemented by hunting and leaf cutting. The summer season continued these spring practices, except that activities were now augmented by barranca horticulture of mixta squash, amaranth and chile.

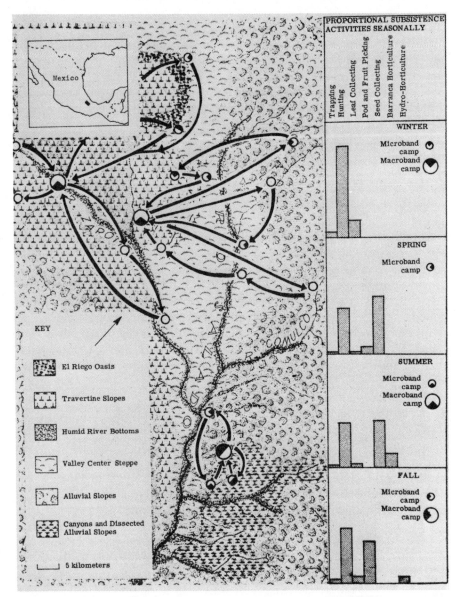

Figure 2   El Riego Phase (7000 to 5000 B.C.*) with estimates of proportions of seasonally scheduled subsistence activities* (right column) *and the distribution of seasonal microband-macroband camps with their possible cyclical movements that form communities of Seasonal micro-macrobands in territories within the microenvironments of the Tehuacán Valley* (left column).

Fall saw fruit picking becoming the predominant activity which in turn was supplemented by hunting, leaf cutting, and avocado cultivation which required a system of hydro-horticulture.

Industrial activities had also changed although our most substantial evidence still comes from chipped stone tools. Flakes and crude blades are now struck from cores usually with prepared platforms by hard and soft (antler) hammers, and then retouched. Tools so made include such point types as Flacco, El Riego, Trinidad, and Hidalgo. There were gouges and crude blades, too. Many tools, however, are at this time made from the cores themselves, such as, bifacial choppers and scraper planes turned out by percussion chipping with soft hammers. A new ground stone industry occurs, and we now find mortar, pestle, milling stones, and mullers. We also find wooden tools, the weaving of non-interlocking stitch baskets and knotted and knotless nets. There is mat twining, string making, and bone awl and antler hammer manufacturing as well as bead making.

We also found a few group burials and there is some evidence of cremation, and possibly of human sacrifice and infanticide. These latter ritual activities which became so prevalent in later Mesoamerica evidently were developing at these earlier times.

A study of the twenty-four microband and eleven macroband occupations of the El Riego phase is the basis for the belief that the community pattern here represented might be classified as *Seasonal Micro-Macrobands* having territoriality and a scheduled subsistence system. Here, a number of family groups or microbands staying within their own designated territory would usually gather together into macrobands in various places in the river bottoms, or at lusher niches on the alluvial slopes in the summer when food was plentiful. Then, with the coming of fall they would break up into microbands to hunt and collect fruits on the alluvial slopes, or in the dissected canyons, or on the steppes of the various parts of their band territory. In the drier winter months, the microband would move again to hunt in the oasis area, the travertine canyons, the humid river bottoms, the alluvial slopes or the dissected canyons, or anywhere else where they could find game. As spring came on and as pods and seeds became available, the small family groups would move into any of the various zones of their territories where these foods were available, and then the cycle would start over again with the coming of the wet summer.

The Coxcatlan phase [Figure 3], from 5000 to 3400 B.C., sees some changes from El Riego times in the proportion of foodstuffs consumed, with wild plants composing 52% of their diet, meat 34%, and agricultural produce 14%, but the subsistence activities and their scheduling is much the same. The fall and winter activities were also similar to the El Riego phase and in the spring seed collection is still predominant, but it is now supplemented by leaf cutting, pod picking, hunting, root digging and barranca horticulture involving the growth of amaranth. The summer season during Coxcatlan times is different with the emphasis being on seed collection and barranca horticulture of a wide variety of plants, such as corn, beans, zapotes, gourds, etc. with only minor supplemental hunting subsistence activities.

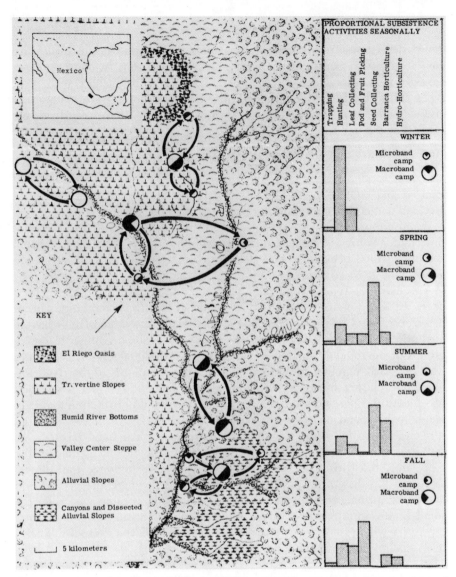

Figure 3 Coxcatlan Phase (7000 to 3400 B.C.) with estimates of proportions of seasonally scheduled subsistence activities (right column) *and the distribution of seasonal macroband and microband camps with their possible cyclical movements that form communities of seasonal macro-microbands in territories within the micro-environments of the Tehuacán Valley, Mexico* (left column).

Techniques of chipping flint are little different from previously but there is more fine pressure retouching and some blades are struck from cylindrical cores by indirect percussion. There are, however, a host of new chipped stone types such as Tilapa, Coxcatlan, Almagre, and Garyito points, fine blades, end of blade scrapers, etc. The ground stone industry continues with manos, metates and anvil stones being new types. More wooden tools include digging sticks and atlatl (a throwing stick) dart parts. Bone needles are added to the bone tool complex. The weaving and string making industry is little changed but interlocking and split stitch baskets appeared for the first time. Complex burials continue to occur. Our study of sites and occupational floors indicated that the Coxcatlan phase had a settlement and community pattern like that of El Riego, Seasonal Macro-Microbands, with territoriality and with a scheduled subsistence including horticulture.

Now to speculate about the change from Seasonal *Macro-Microbands* to *Central-Based Bands,* our next community pattern type: it would appear that the use of a scheduled subsistence system in the ecosystem of the Tehuacán Valley led at first to the development of more and more specialization in various kinds of collection techniques, such as, seed collection and fruit picking.

One might guess that at an early stage it was merely a matter of returning to the same seed or fruit area each year. This in turn led to some clearing (weeding), some enrichment and general improvement of the area which then provided a new artificial environment for the seeds or fruits. This in turn would have led to various genetic changes in the seed or fruit population. Eventually, this may have led to actual cultivation (perhaps at first merely taking seeds or leaves from one environs and dropping them in another), then to purposeful planting, and finally to seed selection and horticulture. This process coupled with the introduction of other domesticates from other regions must have led to longer residence at the halting places and to rescheduling of macroband activities. Perhaps, macrobands came to collect some seeds in the spring along the barrancas, as well as planting some seeds and fruits. These latter plants reached fruition in the summer rainy seasons, thereby allowing the bands to be in the same spot for two seasons, and this then became a base for hunting and collecting camps in other regions in the leaner seasons. This process again would gradually result in some technological advances, greater populations, and new changes in their social system. In this way, the basic causative factors were again changes in subsistence techniques, for the Coxcatlan phase, the two principal factors were an intensified scheduled subsistence system and the diffusion of many domesticated plants into this region. Obviously, there are environmental limitations to these changes.

In the Ayacucho region of highland Peru, there is a similar life zone with great micro-environmental diversity and with some wild plants (and animals) susceptible to domestication, and a similar development seems to have occurred during Jaywa and Piki times from 6700 to 9300 B.C. Did such a process occur during Zarzi times, 15,000 to 9000 B.C. in the Zagros Mountains in the Near East?

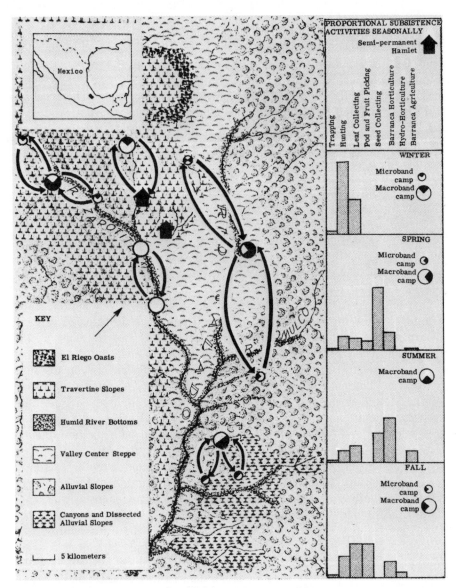

Figure 4   Abejas Phase (3400 to 2300 B.C.) with estimates of proportions of seasonally scheduled subsistence activities (right column) *and the distribution of their hamlets and macroband camps that were the bases for the seasonal microband and macroband camps, forming communities of Central based bands within the micro-environments* (left column).

But back to Mexico, and the following Abejas phase [Figure 4] from 3400 to 2300 B.C. which sees the rise of agricultural produce (at least 25%) at the expense of both meat (25%) and wild plant foods (50%). The scheduling of the subsistence activities is like that of Coxcatlan, but again in the summer and spring the barranca horticulture increases. These increased activities may have at this time produced surpluses that could be stored and then eaten in the leaner fall and winter months.

Chipping techniques are much the same as those of Coxcatlan, although more fine blades and cores appear. Again, of course, new types of chipped stone artifacts turn up such as Catan and Pelona points, fine rectangular blades and bifacial disks. More new types of ground stone tools also appear such as discoidal beads, ovoid plano-convex metates, rubbed pebbles, paint palettes, cuboid pestles, polishing pebbles, spherical manos, and stone bowls. Bone and wood tools and types of cordage are about the same, as was the weaving industry. Burial practices are little known.

Although the settlement pattern information has similarities to both El Riego and Coxcatlan, the presence of linear waterway hamlets along with an increased number of camp sites tend to make me believe that a new type of community pattern was emerging which I have termed *Central Based Bands*. Here, I believe, most bands had a permanent base at a hamlet or macroband camp, and that groups banded together as macrobands in the spring and stayed together through summer and/or fall. Probably, they collected and planted in the spring and then later in the summer and/or fall ate their limited agricultural produce as well as wild stuffs. Their agricultural production in the main was still not sufficient, however, for all macrobands to live all year round either in their macroband camps or in the hamlets. So, with the coming of the leaner months, in the fall and winter some of them had to move and to exploit (mainly by collecting and hunting) other zones.

Nevertheless, with the coming of spring they returned once again to their hamlets or macroband base camps. Obviously, this type of community pattern is transitional from the earlier seasonal macro-microband type and the next type called *Semi-permanent Hamlets* which existed in Ajalpan times but may have commenced in Purron.

The development from Central-Based Bands to Semi-permanent Hamlet communities was in large part due to three factors. One was a change in the mode of food production, that is, a shift from horticulture with a wide variety of domesticated or cultivated plants, to intensively growing a few plants (corn, chile, beans, and squash) in/or just before the rainy seasons in the barrancas, i.e., barranca agriculture. This subsistence activity, plus the fact that a number of the plants they grew were now vigorous hybrids, a second factor, produced sufficient food to allow them to live in hamlets all year round. Further, this relatively stable subsistence allowed them to make improvements in technology, and as well to borrow a number of cultural improvements, such as, pottery-making, wattle-and-daub house making, the figurine cult, etc. It follows that a stimulating interaction with other slightly different cultural developments in other environs became a third crucial factor in cultural change. Needless to say, the population increased and new mechanisms of social control developed which again changed their social system.

Isn't the process of change in the Zagros of Iraq from the time of Zawi Chemi or Karim Shahir to Jarmo, so succinctly described by Braidwood, similar to what I have just speculated for Tehuacán? There are also hints that in periods from Piki to Chihua and/or Cachi in highland Peru a simi- lar process may have evolved.

The next phase in Tehuacán, Purron, 2300 to 1500 B.C., is extremely poorly known, but barranca agriculture probably increased in the summer and spring to give surpluses that could be eaten in the fall and winter. The only discernible new aspect of their technology was the introduction of pottery. Only two cave floors were uncovered so there is little we can say about settlement patterns.

The next cultural phase, Ajalpan [Figure 5], 1500 to 850 B.C., is better known. Foodstuffs from excavation reveal that about 40% of their diet came from agricultural produce, 31% from wild plants, and 29% from meat. In terms of subsistence activities the year was now divided into two parts — the "wet" spring-summer season when they still did hunting and col- lecting but with the hamlets as their base camps. In other words, they were growing sufficient food in one season to last all year and for this reason I refer to this system as *Subsistence Agricultural* production rather than effective food production.

Their technology also saw a shift with the ceramic industry now of major importance with ten monochrome pottery types and six or seven fig- urine types being manufactured. The weaving industry also changed with cotton string now being made by use of a spindle whorl and cloth woven on a loom, while baskets and mats were twilled. As well, various kinds of beads and pendants were made. New utilitarian types of ground stone tools come to the fore. The chipped stone, woodworking, leather, and bone working industries changed but little, even though new types occurred.

Burials now were placed in deep bell-shaped pits and there is evidence of "cult" object ceremonies.

Settlement pattern studies of Ajalpan reveal that there were now twelve hamlets, a single macroband spring-summer occupation and a single micro- band summer occupation in caves. And this pattern made up three or four separate communities aligned along the edge of waterways. Thanks to intensive agriculture in the spring and summer wet seasons in the bar- rancas or river bottoms which gave a whole year's supply of food, the resi- dents were now sedentary, although occasional trips were still made out from their homes for planting, harvesting, plant collection, and hunting. This community pattern which I have classified as the Semi-permanent Hamlet type represents the time when village life based on subsistence food production began in the Tehuacán Valley. It also represents the first

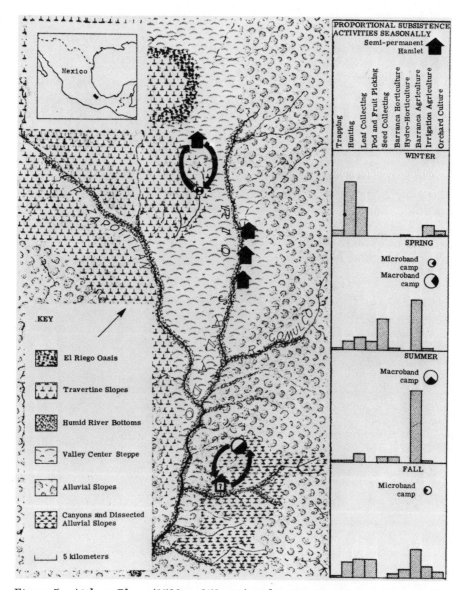

Figure 5   Ajalpan Phase (1500 to 850 B.C.) with estimates of proportions of subsistence activities that were basically food producing at all seasons (right column) and distribution of semi-permanent sedentary hamlets or villages and their seasonal microband and macroband camps for planting and harvesting in the microenvironments of the Tehuacán Valley, Mexico (left column).

time that population increased markedly, a major causative factor for cultural change in later periods.

The next phase, Santa Maria, 850 to 150 B.C., sees the rise of templed villages, a figurine cult, the beginning of irrigation agriculture, truly effective food production, and many other cultural innovations, but this is outside our present realm of discourse, and after the period under discussion. Also later is the later Palo Blanco phase, 150 B.C. to A.D. 700, with its great population increases, hilltop towns, and classic Monte Alban-like features, and in addition our final Venta Salada phase, A.D. 700 to 1500, with its city-states and Mixteca-Puebla type of culture is beyond the scope of this essay.

Therefore, as far as the Tehuacán Valley is concerned, the Ajalpan phase sees the first establishment of village life, and sees the end of the story about the beginnings of food production. This whole picture is, of course, far from complete, but I believe we now have at least some inklings about how and why it happened, at least in one valley, in one culture area, in one world — the New World. Was not the process analogous to processes in other similar areas where pristine civilization occurred?

CHAPTER SIX

Farmers

Stuart Struever

19 WOODLAND SUBSISTENCE-SETTLEMENT SYSTEMS

In recent years an archaeological program in the Illinois Valley has
resulted in the discovery of many new farming sites on the banks
of a sluggish stream that flows through central Illinois. Northwestern
University archaeologist Stuart Struever has spent several seasons
working on the changing settlement patterns and subsistence
activities of the so-called Hopewell culture. During the last few
centuries before Christ, major culture changes occurred in the
Illinois Valley. They were reflected in a rapidly growing population,
the development of ceremonial burial practices, and a greater
intensity of trade among different communities throughout the
eastern United States. One major population group was centered
in the Illinois Valley. Struever wrote a long essay on these cultural
changes, which assumed that economic change initiated cultural
development. What model of systematic change, he asked, could
best explain the available evidence for the cultural developments
in the Illinois Valley? The closing pages of this essay appear below
because Struever's approach is an example of the sophisticated
studies of prehistoric subsistence that are characteristic of
New World archaeology.

MIDDLE WOODLAND SUBSISTENCE-SETTLEMENT SYSTEM

Middle Woodland sites in the lower Illinois Valley, then, have three characteristic locations: (1) at the base of the talus slope along the valley margins; (2) on river shorelines in the Illinois Valley floodplain; and (3) immediately proximal to the Hopewellian burial site.... Furthermore, it has been seen that in structural terms the floodplain sites can be separated into two types, with Mound House a unique example of one type.

The totality of evidence supports the interpretation that the bluff-base Middle Woodland site represents a community occupied continuously or intermittently over a long time span. It reflects an adaptation characterized by a high level of residential stability.

Differentiation in soil color alone suggests that the bluff-base site is the remains of a discrete, bounded settlement. The internal structure of the community, as seen at Apple Creek, supports the idea of long-term residence. High frequencies of storage pits and a house with heavy supporting framework are seen as evidence for permanent constructions. The artifactual evidence indicates that tool manufacturing was important at this site, and that recreational activity was part of the daily life of the local inhabitants. The occurrence of artifacts associated with manufacturing and recreational activities itself suggests sustained occupation of the site. Ethnographically in the eastern Woodlands it was during the long winter occupations that the bulk of tool manufacturing and repair, as well as games and other entertainment took place.

In sum, bluff-base sites like Apple Creek provide evidence of sustained occupation of a specific site locus. The site may have been occupied year-round, or for a span of several months each year.

The analyses of the food remains from Apple Creek indicate heavy dependence on white-tail deer, wild turkey, migratory waterfowl, and fish. Large quantities of hickory nut and acorn shell indicate these were collected in quantity, while smaller numbers of charred smartweed, lamb's-quarter, and marsh-elder seeds suggest they *may have been* exploited at the time the site was occupied. Noteworthy here is the apparent selectivity in natural foods exploited. From the various Apple Creek data it is inferred that the bluff-base settlement was occupied during all or part of the fall, winter, and spring.

Because none have been excavated, the Middle Woodland sites located on the sand ridges in the flood plain — sometimes three or more miles from the nearest bluff-base site — remain a mystery.

It may be noteworthy that these sites are located in the microenvironment where the backwater lakes occur with their shorelines of rich alluvial silt.

The Mound House site, from the surface evidence alone, is distinguishable from all other known Middle Woodland sites in the lower Illinois. Its size is several times that of the next largest Middle Woodland site. Its surface yields an unequaled density and diversity of debris; and the materials collected there include a high proportion of imported raw materials used exclusively in making Hopewellian sociotechnic items.

The Peisker Middle Woodland component is different from Apple Creek and any of the aforementioned sites. High densities of animal bone are lacking. Occupations of the site may have been of short duration, since storage pits and other features interpreted as permanent constructions are lacking. Tools of exploitative and maintenance technology relating to subsistence are scarce, while manufacturing tools and recreational paraphernalia are absent. That food was prepared and cooked on the site is indicated by bone fragments, apparent roasting pits, and char-covered sherds from culinary vessels.

Noteworthy in this Middle Woodland occupation site at Peisker was direct evidence for ceremonial-mortuary activity. This was reflected in the high proportion of sociotechnic artifacts, the occurrence of two ritual features and a possible ceremonial precinct (inferred from the localization of sociotechnic artifacts on the site), and the immediate proximity of the occupation area to five log mausoleums covered by earth mounds. Each tomb contained a few adult burials with associated Hopewellian goods.

MIDDLE WOODLAND CULTURE CHANGE: AN EXPLANATORY MODEL

What model most economically explains the observed structural changes between the Early and Middle Woodland archaeological complexes described here?

The following hypothesis suggests that a shift in subsistence-settlement system occurred between Early and Middle Woodland times. Changes also occurred in social organization, reflecting different integrative requirements created by higher population densities, larger local aggregates, and changes in the manner of segmenting and partitioning the population required for performing the new subsistence tasks.

It is inferred that a marked change in ecological adaptation occurred in the lower Illinois Valley about the time of Christ. Caldwell (1958:31) has noted that following the establishment of primary forest efficiency in the eastern Woodlands by Late Archaic times (ca. 2500 to 1000 B.C.), the hunting-gathering pattern continued, and in favored areas it was characterized by more "specific adjustments to regional resources." The lower Illinois Valley is seen as one such "favored area" and here collecting of natural foods reached a new high level of efficiency by at least the Hopewell phase of the Pike tradition (Middle Woodland period, ca. A.D. 100 to 400).

This new subsistence base can be termed *Intensive Harvest Collecting*. Intensive Harvest Collecting denotes an adaptation centering on exploitation of *selected, high-yielding* natural food resources characteristic of certain biomes that have a sharply restricted geographic distribution within the woodlands of northeastern United States.

Two factors are seen as essential to the biomes in which Intensive Harvest Collecting is feasible: (1) natural food products must occur in large, concentrated populations and lend themselves to harvesting (that is, they can be collected in quantity with relatively small labor output); and (2) the plant and animal populations from which these food products are derived must be regularly renewed.

At least five resources available to Woodland groups in the lower Illinois Valley meet these criteria: (1) nuts and acorns; (2) the seeds of commensal plants such as *Iva* (marsh-elder), *Polygonum* (smartweed), and *Chenopodium* (lamb's-quarter); (3) white-tail deer; (4) migratory waterfowl; and (5) certain species of fish. All five resources can be efficiently exploited by means of a simple harvest technology. Annual fall nut crops, with hickory nuts and acorns especially important, have their highest productive potential in the Hillside-Talus Slope and Upland Forest zones occupying the steep slopes and dissected uplands along the margins of the Illinois and secondary stream valleys (Allison 1966). *Chenopodium* and the other seed-bearing plants mentioned above colonize natural scars in the mantle of vegetation. In the valley bottomlands, spring floods are constantly opening new areas of soil, the most extensive of which are the mud-flats bordering permanent floodplain lakes and the silt deposits remaining after temporary catch-basins of floodwater have entirely evaporated. It may be that here, naturally or through man's intervention, grew stands of lamb's-quarter and other plants whose carbonized seeds at Apple Creek, Newbridge, and other sites attest to their economic importance. Indeed, Allison's (1966) botanical study highlights the localization of these species on the floodplain lake shorelines.

During the winter deer tend to move out of the Illinois Valley floodplain and into the valleys of feeder streams and into the forested areas of the talus slope and adjacent uplands where browse is more plentiful. Here, by various ambush and drive techniques, large numbers might be killed. The Illinois Valley is an important waterfowl migration route, part of the Mississippi flyway. Ducks and geese move along this narrow corridor twice annually. The migrating birds stay largely within the confines of the river valley, feeding and resting on the floodplain lakes. On these lakes, by means of cast nets or other trapping devices, it was feasible for Middle Woodland hunters to harvest these birds. In the early twentieth century, market hunters using different techniques have demonstrated this all too successfully. Paloumpis (1966) demonstrates that on the basis of both

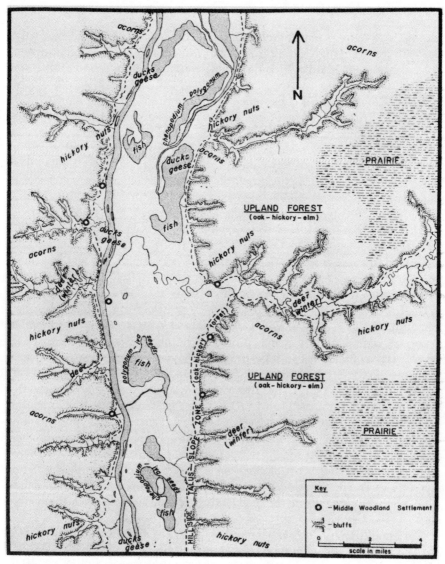

Figure 1   *Middle Woodland Settlements and the distribution of harvestable natural foods.*

species composition and size range within species determined on fish remains from the Apple Creek site, entire fish populations characteristic of riverbottom lakes were apparently collected by the Middle and/or early Late Woodland residents. Possible techniques for harvesting fish in this situation would include use of natural poisons, draining the lake, and stunning the fish by stirring up the muddy bottom and thus reducing the oxygen level of the water.

In short, the food remains from Apple Creek suggest selective exploitation of those natural plants and animals that could be harvested efficiently and with resulting high yields. This change in subsistence practices appears to have begun in Middle Woodland and continued into White Hall times (at least to A.D. 700).

With these changes in subsistence there occurred a concomitant shift in settlement. From the survey and excavation data, four settlement types can be tentatively recognized constituting a Middle Woodland settlement system. The *Base Settlement* is represented by Apple Creek and all those sites located at the talus slope along the sides of the Illinois Valley. The valley-edge lies midway between *all* the microenvironments in which occur one or more of the aforementioned harvestable natural foods. Inhabitants of the Base Settlement had immediate access to all five resources. It is guessed that these resources were exploited in season from this site, and also that processing and storage of these foods constituted major tasks performed in these communities. These foods are available at various times from fall through early spring, and it is hypothesized that valley-edge settlements were occupied continuously during this period.

The few Middle Woodland sites on the sand ridges in the floodplain may represent *Summer Agricultural Camps.* These sites are located proximal to former lake shorelines which provided the only extensive soil areas on which plant cultivation could be practiced, given a simple hoe technology. Until one of these floodplain sites is excavated, little more can be said to support the thesis that these sites were occupied primarily during the summer to perform agricultural tasks. There is some suggestion from the pollen evidence that Apple Creek was abandoned during the summer (Schoenwetter, 1964). During this period the occupants may have moved into the floodplain, setting up temporary camps on the sand-ridge shorelines of the river and lakes to carry on agricultural activities nearby. Summer and early fall were seasons in which inhabitants of the bottomlands were relatively safe from the floods that regularly inundated the valley floor.

The Mound House site is a unique example of the third tentative Middle Woodland settlement type: the *Regional Exchange Center.* Here, finished goods and raw materials characteristic of the Hopewell Interaction Sphere (Caldwell, 1964; Struever, 1964) may have entered the lower Illinois Valley and been exchanged for local products (pearls?). At Mound House, members of the local Middle Woodland groups throughout the lower Illinois Valley area may have congregated periodically to trade and carry on ritual activities by means of which these foreign imports — copper, mica, marine shells, obsidian, etc. — were distributed over the region, eventually to become burial goods in status graves covered by earth mounds that occur in small groups scattered along the valley margins.

The fourth Middle Woodland settlement type here is the *Mortuary Camp.* These small habitation sites proximal to Hopewell mound cemeteries appear to represent short-lived, specialized occupations undertaken to perform mortuary tasks. The archaeological evidence from Peisker, the only excavated example of this settlement type, reflects activities relating both to mortuary tasks themselves and to maintenance of the participants engaged in this work.

CONCLUSIONS

This paper attempts to demonstrate a major change in subsistence-settlement systems from Early to Middle Woodland periods in the lower Illinois Valley. The new subsistence pattern involves the intensive "harvest" exploitation of select natural food resources, with possible cultivation of local seed-bearing plants along the shorelines of riverbottom lakes. The resulting higher levels of economic productivity were accompanied by population expansion (documented by the marked increase in total number and size of habitation sites). Population expansion, combined with new patterns of segmenting and partitioning the population necessitated by the harvest-collecting technology, created new integrative requirements. Now perhaps larger numbers of people were organized into a single sociopolitical system. Differential access to goods and services, so apparent in Hopewell burial sites in the lower Illinois Valley, reflects increased status differentiation. Imported raw materials and craft items fashioned from them occur with relatively few burials interred in tombs or mausoleums. These constructions involved major outlays of labor; one Hopewellian mound in the lower Illinois is built from more than an estimated one million cubic feet of soil. Associated with these inferred changes in social structure is the extension and intensification of long-distance trade which, for the first time on any scale, brought exotic raw materials and finished goods into the region. Again, for the most part these imported goods appear archaeologically as burial associations with selected individuals.

How can this episode of culture change — at this time and place — be explained? David Aberle (personal communication) reminds us that cultures do not *necessarily* maximize the exploitative potential of their environment. It is only in certain, still-to-be-defined coping situations involving particular relationships of culture to other cultures and culture to biophysical environment that "maximizing adaptations" occur. It remains to be determined what changing selective pressures provided the impetus for maximization of productivity based on collecting, as documented here for Middle and early Late Woodland in the lower Illinois Valley. It is important only to reaffirm that it is in the nature of the shifting coping situations during Early Woodland and initial phases of Middle Woodland that we must seek an explanation for the culture changes described here.

Whatever the shifting selective pressures from Early to Middle Woodland times in the lower Illinois Valley, they were not present equally — or at least did not produce the same results — throughout the entire western

Great Lakes-Riverine area. Judging from the distribution of Hopewellian goods and mortuary sites, the shift in adaptation described here — involving changes in the structure of subsistence and settlement, an increase in population density, increased social complexity, and participation in long-distance trade — appears to have been a localized phenomenon confined largely to the central and lower Illinois Valley, sections of the central Mississippi Valley, and a few other localities.

Increased economic productivity is regarded as prerequisite to the other manifestations of change noted here. To the extent that increased productivity was dependent on an intensification of collecting like that inferred here for the lower Illinois Valley, it is not surprising that major culture change during Middle and early Late Woodland was *geographically restricted* in the western Great Lakes area. The complex of potentially harvestable natural resources described here for the lower Illinois have a very *limited* distribution. Paloumpis (1966) demonstrates that fish in river-bottom lakes of the central Mississippi drainage have an exceedingly high biomass; furthermore, he points out how restricted within the Great Lakes area are broad floodplain situations with extensive backwater lakes. Waterfowl routes within the Mississippi flyway are narrow corridors along which great flights of ducks and geese move seasonally. Outside these routes, which follow certain major river valleys, waterfowl numbers diminish sharply. Cleland (1965) points out that deer prefer deciduous forest "edges," that is, places where forest borders on scrub and grassland, and Taylor (1956, p. 137) notes that white-tail deer have always produced their largest populations where edges are most extensive. One such edge situation is the forest-grassland ecotone, an example of which is the strip of forested uplands bordering the Illinois and other river valleys that dissect the long-grass prairie south of the western Great Lakes. It can be expected that this forest-grassland zone supported a dense deer population in prehistoric times.

The northern boundary of the temperate deciduous forest lies in southern Illinois and Indiana. North of it, and extending into southern Wisconsin and Michigan, lies the prairie peninsula. Within the prairie peninsula nut crops were restricted to the narrow strips of forest bordering stream courses. The dissected terrain adjacent to the Illinois Valley and feeder streams leading to it supported a heavy oak-hickory forest with excellent potential for nut production. And, finally, large stands of *Chenopodium* and similar seed-bearing plants occur only where stable plant associations are prohibited from forming over extensive areas. The most extensive areas of this kind in the eastern Woodlands occur in the broad river floodplains.

Intensive Harvest Collecting, then, is a subsistence type that, given certain selective pressures, may develop in an ecological context supporting a number of particularly high-yielding natural food resources. In the western Great Lakes area these conditions are found in certain broad river valleys only. These valleys have extensive floodplains with a shallow river channel, low gradient, and poorly developed natural levees. Flooding is an annual occurrence. These valleys have a high productive potential in fish, a fact traced to the great expanse of backwater lakes with their high biomass and fish populations that are renewed through regular flooding (Paloumpis, 1966). These same conditions create extensive areas of raw soil on which seed-bearing chenopods, marsh elder, and other plants flourish. During the spring and fall, waterfowl migrate along certain of these valleys. Heavy forests along the valley margins produce nut crops and provide maximal conditions for support of a dense white-tailed deer population (Cleland, 1965).

It is interesting that culture change during the Middle Woodland period in the western Great Lakes area appears most marked in localities where this convergence of high-yielding populations of several plant and animal species seems to have existed. Hopewell burial sites have their greatest density in areas characterized by such an environment. It can be hypothesized that, were the evidence available, these same areas would also disclose significant population expansion and extensive participation in the Hopewell "interaction sphere," or trade system, during the Middle Woodland period.

This is not to imply that *all* culture change during Middle Woodland in eastern United States was based on this *particular* shift in subsistence practices. Rather, it might be expected that marked regional variability in both ecological conditions and selective pressures gave rise to a complex mosaic of regional developments. Each was characterized by greater or lesser rates and varying types of change and influenced in varying ways by occurrences in contiguous and non-contiguous regions. David Aberle (personal communication) cautions that developments in any one region must be understood in terms of changes in the total environmental context of a culture, and this context includes the whole sphere of between-culture interaction in which the group under investigation resides. Therefore, the eventual explanation of the accelerated culture change in Middle Woodland groups of the lower Illinois Valley may lie more in a response to significant culture change occurring in southern Ohio, the Gulf Coastal Plain, or elsewhere, than in the changing availability of fish, chenopods, hickory nuts, deer, and ducks in the lower Illinois Valley, or in a new realization that these resources could be collected on a large-scale by means of new techniques.

In short, it may well be to changes in the *social* environment of these Illinois Valley Middle Woodland groups that we will eventually ascribe the changes in subsistence, settlement, population density, and social structure that are only now beginning to emerge from the archaeological record.

B. A. L. Cranstone

20 THE TIFALMIN

How did early farmers make their living? What technological
limitations were imposed on them by lack of metals or of simple
agricultural techniques? One approach to such problems has been
collaborative work between ethnographers and archaeologists. Many
archaeologists are concerned about the limited archaeological
evidence for reconstructing prehistoric agriculture, because much
agricultural activity leaves little tangible trace in the archaeological
record. B. A. L. Cranstone has written a fascinating essay on the
Tifalmin, a small tribal group living in the central New Guinea
mountains, which addresses this problem by examining a simple
farming culture. The Tifalmin cultivate taro, the sweet potato, and
bananas; they keep domestic pigs; hunting and collecting are also
important. They depend on trade for certain essentials. Cranstone
discusses Tifalmin culture in the context of potential archaeological
investigation and shows that the surviving evidence would be both
incomplete and misleading.

Both the Sepik and the Fly Rivers have their main sources in the mountains east of the West Irian border, flowing respectively north and south.
The watershed is formed by the Hindenburg and other ranges, which rise
over 11,000 ft. Much of this area falls within the limestone belt which extends along the central mountain spine of New Guinea. The ranges are
very steep and heavily eroded, with deep fissures, pot-holes and jagged
outcrops. They are covered by dense forest, with much oak and beech,
merging into mist forest at the cloud line, and a dense tangled heathy
vegetation with rhododendrons on the exposed tops. Although rain falls on
most days surface water is difficult to find. Even in the valleys there are
few subsidiary streams. The limestone belt formed a formidable barrier
to European explorers with large numbers of carriers and native police
(Champion 1966), but is much less of an obstacle to native movement.
A small party or an individual, travelling light, can cross the Hindenburgs
and reach a hamlet on the other side in two or three days.

The Tifalmin inhabit part of the valley of the Ilam, a minor tributary
of the Sepik, in the Telefomin Sub-district [Figure 1]. The floor of the

From "The Tifalmin: A 'Neolithic' People in New Guinea," World Archaeology, vol.
3, no. 2, 1972, 132–142, by permission of B. A. L. Cranstone, Deputy Keeper, Museum
of Mankind, London. Photographs reproduced by permission of the author and the British
Museum; some illustrations are omitted.

valley, at about 4,500 ft., seems to be an old lake bed, in which the Ilam has cut itself a deep trench. The Tifalmin number between 500 and 600 people, and are divided into four groups, all of which fought the others though they formed temporary alliances. All were enemies of the Urapmin, who live in the lower part of the valley. The two upper groups have friendly relations with the Wopkeimin, on the southern slopes of the Hindenburg Range where the streams drain to the Fly, and say they never fought them; the two lower groups have similar relations with the Fegolmin, to the east of the Wopkeimin. All the Tifalmin trade with the Atbalmin, a semi-nomadic people in the wild mountains to the north, but they also fought. All these tribes were cannibals but not head-hunters.

When studying the material culture of the Tifalmin and making a collection for the British Museum in 1964 I was struck by the paucity of evidence for their technology and way of life which would, I thought, survive to be found by an archaeologist working after a lapse of a few hundred, let alone a few thousand, years. It is this aspect that I wish to emphasize in the following account.

MATERIAL CULTURE AND SUBSISTENCE

The Tifalmin have a "neolithic" technology and economy. When used in such a context the word always requires qualification; any close comparison with the neolithic of Europe and the Near East could be deceptive. Steel

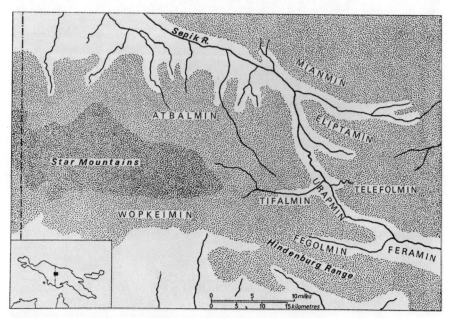

Figure 1   The tribes of the Western Sepik–Fly watershed.

axes became generally available after 1944 when they were introduced to the Telefomin valley with the establishment of an emergency landing strip. The traditional tool was a ground stone adze fitted to an elbow haft. By 1964 the introduction of the steel axe and the bush-knife had not significantly affected the general technology. Any middle-aged man was familiar with the use of the stone adze [Figure 2]. One cut down a tree of 3 ft. 4 in. circumference, with a stone adze, in 24 minutes of steady work. He later cut down another of the same species and of 3 ft. 10 in. circumference, with a steel axe, in eight minutes. This efficiency ratio for steel to stone, of about 4:1 or 3:1, is confirmed by other observations in New Guinea (e.g. Salisbury 1962:219–220; Townsend 1969). Stone would show less favorably over a longer working period because of the need for more frequent resharpening.

Apart from the stone adze the traditional kit of wood-working tools re-

Figure 2

mained in use. Only a few knives had been obtained. Relief carving on wood was carried out with small chert flakes (obtained from the Fegolmin) or with a small stone adze blade, quite different in shape from the hafted adzes, held in the hand. Only one of these was seen, and its origin could not be discovered. A round-ended gouge of cassowary femur is used to lower the level in relief carving. Half of the mandible of a small marsupial with an incisor tooth in place is used to sharpen bamboo arrowheads or to incise patterns on bamboo cigarette-holders. The serrated lower mandible of a species of lizard provides a miniature saw to make a nick in small-diameter bamboos so that they can be broken cleanly.

Bamboo knives serve for skinning and cutting meat and preparing vegetables. Unlike those of some other parts of New Guinea, they are not carefully prepared. A sliver of bamboo of suitable length is used; when it becomes blunt a strip is peeled back to give a new sharp edge, and after use the knife is discarded. A pig was quickly and efficiently butchered with only bamboo knives and an unworked stone which was used to break the ribs and the pubic bone.

Like many other peoples of highland New Guinea, the Tifalmin believe that contact with women diminishes the essentially male qualities necessary for success in societies in which power is in the hands of self-made "big-men." They therefore have two sorts of houses. At night the family houses are occupied by women, girls, and males too young or too old to count as men in a social sense. Men and older boys sleep in the men's house, which is the center of male affairs. Women may never enter it. Hamlets vary in size from two to about ten houses: they can never have less than two because even a single family must have its separate men's house.

Men's houses and family houses are identical in construction. They are about twelve feet square with rounded corners. The floor, which is constructed first, is raised about a foot above ground level, supported by a number of short posts. In the center is a square opening for the hearth. This is made by placing short split timbers with their lower ends on the ground and their upper ends against the floor poles. Some large stones are placed in the bottom; then clay is piled in and is trodden and smoothed by hand or with a round stone to make a shallow bowl-shaped hearth. Four poles at the corners support a rack for drying wood. The walls are of light poles driven into the ground and lashed with strips of bark. The pitched roof is supported rather haphazardly by the wall poles, and is thatched with grass. Finally the floor and the walls are lined with sheets of bark of the mountain pandanus. Occasionally, a family house may have inside it a pen for an ailing pig. The houses are placed round a dancing ground of bare earth.

At a short distance from each hamlet there is a house to which women retire periodically and at childbirth. This is usually a low hut with an earth floor.

Hamlets were sited, for defensive reasons, on promontories jutting out into the river trench, on low hillocks, or on steep-sided spurs in the bush of the valley sides. They moved frequently, though often only short distances, moves being dictated, apparently, by the fact that until the Administration persuaded the Tifalmin to dig latrines they had no sanitary arrangements. They told me that when people and pigs started to be unhealthy it was time to move. Exhaustion of garden land was not a main reason.

Houses are also built in the gardens. Often these are simple sheds to give shelter from rain and sun, but in the more distant gardens there are houses, like those in the hamlets, in which families live for several weeks.

The only other considerable structures made by the Tifalmin are bridges and garden fences. There are two bridges in their territory. Both span the Ilam where it runs through gorges. They consist of rigid pole footways, with handrails, lashed with creeper or strips of bark. The span of each is about 23 ft. and the height above water over 50 ft. [Figure 3].

Figure 3

For their subsistence the Tifalmin depend mainly on their gardens. They practice long-fallow cultivation, clearing a patch of forest and abandoning it after two or three years, probably for fifteen years or more. They do not cultivate the valley floor because much of it is badly drained and, by native methods, the grass is uncontrollable. The gardens are therefore on the sides of the valley or of the river trench. The trees are killed by ring-barking or by building bonfires against them (but many are left standing), and undergrowth and scrub are cut and burnt. The main crops are taro and sweet potato. Taro, the most valued, is really unsuited to the altitude and takes up to two years to mature. Sweet potato is the stand-by in times of scarcity, but the Tifalmin say that it is fit only for white men (who usually prefer it) and pigs. Unlike taro it has no part in ritual. They also grow bananas, sugar-cane, beans, cucumbers, gourds, tobacco, a very few yams, and some greens. The only cultivating tool is the digging stick, a pointed stake about four feet long, which is used both for planting and for digging up the root vegetables. It is a very practical tool, for the ground is a mass of roots and a spade or hoe would be of little use.

The gardens are strongly fenced against wild pig, which are common. Building fences and the heavy clearing are men's work; burning, clearing lighter growth, planting, and weeding are shared by both sexes. The Tifalmin are continually clearing, planting, and harvesting. Though rainfall varies somewhat from month to month there are no marked seasons.

There are separate gardens at about 6,000 ft. in which the mountain pandanus is cultivated. Usually nothing else is grown in these gardens.

The only domestic animals are the pig and the dog, both of which are eaten. Pigs forage for themselves by day but come home to be fed at night.

Hunting and gathering occupy a good deal of time and provide an important though minor proportion of the food consumed. Game is more plentiful than in the densely-populated Highlands districts to the east. If a wild pig is seen every man in earshot grabs his bow and goes after it. Whenever possible the hunt is carefully organized, beaters driving the pig on to a line of bowmen. Cassowary are relatively common. The several species of lesser marsupials are hunted, and no bird is considered too small to be eaten. The only hunting weapon is the bow, made from black-palm wood strung with rattan. Arrow-heads are of carved wood or bamboo, the latter being preferred for shooting pig or cassowary. Special arrows with blunt heads are used for shooting birds-of-paradise, to avoid drawing blood and spoiling the plumage; and arrows with several points splayed outward (the type often used elsewhere for shooting fish) are used against small birds, which if not pierced are often held between the points.

Pit traps are dug for pig. They are not armed with spikes as are those of some neighboring tribes — fortunately, for one was said to have caught three pigs, one of the owner's sons, and a man from the next valley. Traps consisting of nooses tightened by a bent wood spring with a toggle release are made to catch game of all sizes.

Women and boys collect eggs, wild fruits, fungi, insects, grubs, small lizards, frogs, and tadpoles (there are no fish in the streams). Men will not eat these latter, though they may help to collect them. Tadpoling expeditions have the air of a family outing. Certain male foods are taboo to women and children.

In war too the only weapon was the bow. War arrows usually had barbed wood heads. In formal fighting a large carved wood shield was carried by one man and one or two others used their bows from its cover, but for raiding or ambushing shields were left behind (Cranstone 1968). Bone daggers, used elsewhere in New Guinea, were not known. The only other artifact associated with warfare was the cuirass, or corselet, of plaited rattan, which gave some protection to the thorax and abdomen.

The bow is not an accurate weapon. The arrows are not feathered, the wood or bamboo heads are often unsymmetrical, and the shafts are frequently not straight. But the bow is very powerful and the rate of fire high. Many middle-aged men bore the scars of arrow wounds.

For internecine quarrels, in which the use of the bow was not permitted, formidable-looking wooden clubs were employed; but these were not normally used in warfare.

The traditional male dress is the penis gourd: a piece of the stem end of the gourd, varying in length from about three to more than twelve inches, into which the penis is inserted, leaving the scrotum exposed. It is fastened by a cord to a waist-string or girdle. Female dress consists of very short skirts back and front, leaving the flanks bare, made by doubling lengths of sedge over a waist-cord and securing them with a running string. The sedge is cultivated in swamp pools.

Both sexes, but especially the men, have a variety of ornaments: necklaces of pigs' teeth, fresh-water mussel pendants, pigs' tusks, string bands to which cowrie or nassa shells are attached, seeds of *Coix lachryma*. Men wear a variety of fur and feather head ornaments when dancing. They also have girdles of dogs' canines on a string base, and chest pendants of cone shell.

Male nose ornaments are especially elaborate. The septum and the *alae* are pierced and two holes are made in the tip. The septum takes a stone, bamboo, or bird-bone pin, or a pig's tusk. Through the nostrils cassowary quills are passed vertically, sometimes decorated with feathers, and either held back by a forehead band or curving forward like antennae; into the holes in the tip are inserted a pair of horns of a rhinoceros beetle or the ends of a grass stem holding a small pearl-shell plate.

The peoples of New Guinea do not weave. In the Telefomin area they do not make bark cloth by felting bark fibers, as do some other mountain peoples. They have no knowledge of pottery, and they do not make baskets or mats (though the cuirasses are made by a basketry technique).

For holding liquids they use gourds or lengths of bamboo. For storing and carrying solids string bags meet most requirements. The bags are made with continuous interlocking figure-of-eight loops, the only implement used being a fine needle of "flying-fox" wing-bone. The string is made from bark fibers rolled on the thigh. As there are no knots the bag stretches in any direction. They range in size from not much more than an inch (to contain a charm) to those large enough for a heavy load of vegetables or firewood. Babies sleep happily in them, slung on the mother's back or from a branch while she works in her garden. Women wear the sling across the forehead, and the bag is almost an article of female clothing. Some men's bags, decorated with feathers, are worn on the back as dance ornaments.

Daily meals consist mainly of taro or sweet potato roasted in the fire, with raw or cooked banana. Any small game is often roasted on the spot. Some foods, such as tadpoles or certain leaves, are boiled in lengths of bamboo, the food being cooked before the bamboo chars through. Tadpoles, beetles, and grubs are often eaten raw and alive. For more important occasions, such as when a pig is killed, a variant of the Oceanic earth oven is employed. Stones, heated on a fire, are fairly closely spaced on flat ground, and banana leaves are spread over them. The meat, in leaf packets, and vegetables are laid on top and covered with more leaves. Unburnt logs from the fire are often put on top to hold the leaves in place. Some foods are served on rather crudely carved wood platters, and spoons are made from pigs' scapulae; one collected was made from a hornbill's beak (the hornbill is not found at this altitude). A few dishes made from sago-spathe were seen. These are obtained from the Wopkeimin, in the lower parts of whose territory wild sago grows.

Fire is made by the flexible thong method. A stick is split, the split is held open with a wedge, and the split end is laid on tinder: dry leaves or old grass thatch pulled from a roof. A length of rattan is passed under the split, the stick is held down with one foot, and the rattan is sawed rapidly to and fro. Smoke appears in five seconds or upward and a flame is obtained in forty seconds or less. Some of their neighbors make fire by striking two pieces of iron pyrites together (Craig 1967), but this is not a traditional Tifalmin method.

Tobacco, grown in the gardens, is smoked as cigarettes rolled in leaves of certain bushes and usually held in cigarette holders of creeper or small-diameter bamboo. The latter often bear incised patterns.

Musical instruments are few and simple. Waisted wood drums, with a lizard-skin membrane at one end, are beaten by men as an accompaniment to dancing. The lower ends are carved in relief and colored. Men play bamboo jews' harps, and girls have a simple one-string musical bow. There are two forms of cane flute, one of which at least may be a recent introduction.

It is impossible to make a clear distinction between religion, magic, and medicine. The traditional cult is one of ancestral spirits, and its center, for the Tifalmin, is the cult-house in Brolemavip hamlet. This is in construction exactly similar to the family and men's houses; but it is unique in the valley in having its façade covered with about twenty carved boards set vertically. These are merely attached and have no structural function (Cranstone 1967). The house is not inhabited, and only senior men may enter it. Inside are a number of string bags containing ancestral relics (bones, wisps of beard, and the like); a crocodile's skull (the crocodile does not penetrate into the Ilam); and two stone-headed clubs. The walls are lined with pigs' lower jaws. The clubs, of the type associated with the southern lowlands, are ritual objects, not weapons. A number of the stone heads, painted with red ocher, were piled outside the cult-house at Telefolip in the Telefomin valley, the main cult center for the whole district, and these as far as I know were never hafted or removed. Boys and men were progressively admitted to the secrets of the cult by a series of initiation rites, after which certain food taboos were lifted and others imposed.

Many other spirits, living on the mountain tops or in the bush, are feared; but the sanctions which uphold social life come from the ancestors, whose influence is naturally conservative. Their power can be utilized in a direct way: for instance the jawbone of a notable gardener, buried in a garden (to be recovered later), brings a good taro crop.

All men possess a number of charms, and some of these include human relics. Two pieces of human skull were said to be powerful hunting charms; but they had been bought from the Atbalmin, and their power therefore can be regarded as purely magical, not connected with the ancestor cult. The Atbalmin are the great providers of charms, though some come from the peoples to the south. Most are objects foreign to the Tifalmin valley or of unusual size or form. Fossils, obtained from the Atbalmin, are among the most common; but bones, claws, or other relics of animals from the foothills, naturally-pierced stones, unusually large seeds, are also often found. Most charms are connected with a specific activity, such as hunting or war. One conferred invisibility when stealing from a garden.

Charms are also effective in healing. A fossil shark's tooth was said to have been used for cutting arrow-heads from wounds, for which purpose its magical qualities would no doubt have reinforced its functional ones. Bones and fossils are used for massaging painful places. Massaging by hand is also a common practice, always with the accompaniment of a spoken spell. Some methods seem to be practical rather than magical, such as the treatment of headache by thrusting grass stems up the nostrils to make the nose bleed.

The Administration has now persuaded the Tifalmin to bury their dead near the hamlets. Traditionally corpses were left in caves or overhangs of the limestone outcrops on the sides of the valley, or exposed on platforms in trees, or placed in hollow trees. All such sites are accessible to birds or other animals, and bones are usually disturbed and mixed. Remains of personal belongings, such as string bags, can occasionally be seen. The mass of bones in one cave included sixteen skulls. After a period of exposure certain bones of particularly notable men would be recovered and kept in the cult house or the men's house.

TRADE

Simple though their technology is, the Tifalmin could not have existed without trading. Owing to the altitude and other factors the environment does not provide certain essentials, two in particular. In the limestone belt there is no suitable stone for making adze blades, and without adzes not only could houses, bridges, shields, and other items not be made, but forest could not be cleared for gardening. Adze blades were obtained from the Atbalmin or the Wopkeimin. The other essential item is the bow stave, made from black palm, which is not obtainable — not, at least, of the right quality — at this altitude. The bow is effectively the only weapon, and life would have been impossible without it. It is still of great importance for hunting, and no man moves far without one. The staves are mostly acquired from the Wopkeimin. Many other items are obtained by trade: drums (which for some reason are not made by the Tifalmin) and charms from the Atbalmin; rattan for bow strings, dogs' teeth, string bags, sago-spathe dishes, stone nose-pins, stone club-heads, from the Wopkeimin. Chert flakes come from south of the Hindenburg Range. Trade axes and bush knives seem to have first reached the Tifalmin from Dutch New Guinea through the Wopkeimin. Sea-shells of several types were seen by the first Europeans to arrive, though the people knew nothing of the sea.

In return for these imports the Tifalmin's main export was tobacco, which grows well in their valley. Pigs and large string bags are both exported and imported, and other items too, such as plumes of the various species of bird-of-paradise, move in both directions. Arrows are exchanged freely, a common practice in New Guinea. Nowadays the Tifalmin obtain trade goods when the missionary visits them and pass them on to their neighbors; but tobacco is still their most valuable product.

THE TIFALMIN AND THE ARCHAEOLOGIST

Tifalmin culture is a very simple and small-scale one: simple even by the standards of other "neolithic" cultures in New Guinea, where many single villages contain more people than the whole Tifalmin population. But in spite of its simplicity it strikes one as an efficient and stable adaptation to environmental circumstances. There is at present plenty of land. The continual warfare seems to have caused a steady drain of casualties but not catastrophic losses, though tribal groups were undoubtedly broken and driven from their territories over a period of time (see Cranstone 1968 for a discussion of this point). Food shortages seem rarely to have been serious, and are caused mainly by inefficient planning, for extended drought is rare. High winds or destructive storms are very unusual.

The whole limestone belt along the Fly-Sepik watershed is in some respects unstable. Major earthquakes, such as occur in north-coastal areas, are not common, but minor shocks are fairly frequent. The very steep forested slopes are liable to landslides, the scars of which can be seen everywhere from the air (and see Champion 1966 passim). Tifalmin hamlets are usually built on the lower slopes or floor of the valley and so are generally not in danger from the type of movement which occurs on the steep ranges, where a thin layer of soil slides off the underlying rock. However, on some grassy slopes one can see cracks where the hillside is beginning to slip. A greater danger arises from the fact that some hamlets are placed below, or at the crest of, the steep slopes of the river trench, which being cut in sedimentary deposits are very unstable. In March 1971 a slide about 400 ft. high and a third of a mile wide totally obliterated a hamlet beside the river Ilam (I am indebted to the Rev. Brian Beaver of the Australian Baptist Mission for this information). Even if they escape such catastrophe the situation of many hamlets makes them particularly liable to erosion, often accelerated by run-off from the bare dancing ground. Erosion can be very rapid: a side-gully near our camp was cut back more than a foot during one night of heavy rain. So it seems likely that in the course of a few centuries many sites would disappear completely.

As sites were not occupied for long the accumulation of débris from one occupation would be relatively slight; but because the sites were chosen not arbitrarily but for defensive reasons they would probably be reoccupied frequently. There are no man-made defensive works. What would one expect to find on a hamlet site?

First, the evidence for the houses. Poles are rarely set in the ground more deeply than about a foot, and no trench is dug: the poles are set by repeatedly thrusting them in, exactly as in using a digging-stick. When a house is moved any sound poles — together with the floor as one unit, and the halves of the roof as two — are taken to the new site. The most obvious remains are the stone and burnt clay of the hearth, which lie on the natural surface.

The Telefomin hamlet of Telefolip is an exception. Because of the sacredness of the site it has not moved and there is a considerable accumulation of debris under the houses. There is no comparable site in the Tifalmin valley.

In several instances it appeared that gardens had been made on old hamlet sites. These sites might be especially difficult to detect, because tree roots, during the fallow period, would tend to destroy such evidence as postholes; and, moreover, postholes are little deeper than the holes made by the digging-stick in planting taro or banana slips, so that any recognizable pattern would be obscured. The meticulous clearing of débris which follows burning would scatter the remains of hearths. The same considerations would apply to the garden houses which are sometimes inhabited for quite long periods.

The garden fences, strongly made with pairs of vertical posts and horizontal poles, would probably leave as much trace in the ground as housepoles; but the gardens are scattered over a very wide area, mostly in bush, and have an altitude range of about 2,000 ft., so the finding of fence-post holes would presumably be a matter of chance. Bridges would leave hardly any trace. Their main supports are often living trees.

Apart from the traces of houses, other cultural evidence would depend on what the lapse of time and local conditions allowed to survive. If all had perished except stone the evidence would consist mainly of adze blades, perhaps including the small aberrant type mentioned. There could also be a small number of unworked chert fragments. Stone club-heads might give a false impression that they were important weapons. There might be an occasional stone nose-pin, and there would certainly be fossils. All these articles could be proved to be imported. It would also be possible to find unworked river pebbles, used for such purposes as breaking bones and crushing pigments or pandanus nuts, which would not easily be recognized as implements; a flat stone which had been exposed to fire (used in straightening arrow shafts); and stones on which adze blades had been reground, bearing the marks of this use.

Shell could add nothing of technological importance; only ornaments of various kinds. It could be guessed that pierced fresh-water mussel shells, of local origin, must have been neck pendants or components of necklaces. Other shell ornaments — of conus shell, pearl-shell, cowrie, or nassa shells — are of marine origin.

If bone and teeth survived there would be a good deal more. Cassowary-bone gouges might present problems of function: they are in fact used for carving fairly soft wood and in preparing the fruit of the *marita* pandanus, but elsewhere in New Guinea similar tools are used for a variety of purposes. It might be suspected that a half marsupial jaw with an incisor tooth was a carving tool, but no special preparation would prove this. Pigs' scapulae adapted as spoons, bone needles and awls, a cassowary breast-bone used to hold red ocher — this completes the list of bone tools and utensils. There would also be ornaments: bird-bone or pig's tusk nose ornaments; vertebrae, claws, feet, tails of various creatures as part of necklaces. Numbers of pigs', dogs', and marsupials' teeth, perhaps found together, would suggest necklaces or girdles. There would also be bones of animals not now found in the higher valleys: river turtle, echidna, crocodile. Their magical significance might be deduced. Who would also suspect the use of some of them in massage? And who would suspect that fragments of human skull were imported for magical use? On the other hand, human and animal bones would no doubt be found mixed together in circumstances which would rightly suggest cannibalism.

Human bones would also be found in and near the caves and shelters in which bodies were deposited, but they would be much scattered and mixed. Some of the shelters may have been habitation sites in the past; but most are a long way from a water supply. At higher altitudes they would have traces of occasional overnight occupation by hunters or travellers.

If wood had not survived there would be no evidence of weapons, except the misleading presence of stone club-heads. These could suggest closer cultural links with the club-users of the southern lowlands than seem in fact to exist (though artistic and linguistic links have been suggested: Craig 1966). The Tifalmin use nothing except wood or bamboo for their arrowheads (the only exception seen was an unmodified vertebra stuck on a broken foreshaft for use as a bird-bolt). Nor would there be positive evidence for the presence of the essential string bags, except bone needles which could have other uses; moreover string bags can be made without them (Blackwood 1950:49).

It is difficult to see what evidence could be found for the reliance on root vegetables, still less for the presence of sweet potato and taro and the uneconomic preference for the latter, except that the sweet potato does flower and produce pollen. In view of the casual habits of the Tifalmin the finding of coprolites seems unlikely. Indeed, what firm evidence would there be for cultivation? The population is little above the level which could be supported by hunting and collecting. There are no store-houses. Gardens would be difficult to identify. Since domestic pigs forage freely and interbreed with wild pig it would hardly be possible to distinguish a domestic strain unless their remains showed evidence of castration, which is commonly practiced.

Finally, a point which I have discussed elsewhere in a wider context (Cranstone [1972]) but which is particularly relevant to the Tifalmin situation: the estimation of population on the basis of settlement and house sites. In some archaeological contexts it is justifiable and reasonably accurate to do this by estimating the average size of the basic social unit and multiplying by the number of houses. In other instances it can be highly unreliable; and the Tifalmin seem to provide a good example.

There is often difficulty in deciding whether individual houses or settlement sites were occupied simultaneously. This would certainly be true of the Tifalmin with their pattern of frequent movement. Further, at any time one or more houses in a hamlet are likely to be unoccupied. A family may have gone to visit their Wopkeimin friends, with whom they may stay for a month or more, working in the gardens in return for their food and taking the opportunity to do some trading; or they may be living in a distant garden which has come into production. On the other hand a Wopkeimin family may be present on a visit, doubling up in the family and men's house.

Brolemavip, the hamlet in which the ancestor-cult house is situated, had ten houses (not counting two earth-floored women's retirement houses a little distance away). Of these ten, one was the cult house; three were men's houses; six were family houses. An estimate based on equating the number of houses with the number of families would therefore be 40% in excess. Two of the family houses were removed to another hamlet within six weeks, as a result of quarrels. A similar calculation for the one-family hamlets, of which there are a number especially among the Dubalmin sub-group, would be 100% in error since each consists of two houses, a men's house and a family house.

It may be that I underestimate the resources of modern archaeology, and I am sure that archaeologists are alert to such difficulties as I have described. My purpose has been to demonstrate, with a concrete example, that it may be impossible to draw the right conclusions because of the nature of the surviving evidence.

Part Three

MAN ACHIEVES CIVILIZATION

*"God made the country and man made the
town."*

William Cowper (1731–1800)

INTRODUCTION

*Man achieves civilization, which comes to mean urban life,
crowding in cities, epidemics, literacy, class distinctions,
pollution, and overexploitation of the environment. How did city
life begin? What were the causes for this new direction in
human life that today dominates much of the world's life styles?*

*V. Gordon Childe, who proposed a "Neolithic Revolution,"
thought in terms of an "Urban Revolution" as well. To Childe,
the techniques of metallurgy and smelting were far more
exacting than the normal tasks of the peasant farmer. "The
first step towards escape from the rigid limits of . . . barbarism
was the establishment of a metallurgical industry . . . that not
only provided farmers with superior weapons but . . . overturned
the barbarian social order, based on kinship, and evoked a new
population of full-time specialists. The latter is my excuse for
calling it the Urban Revolution," he wrote (Childe 1958:78).*

*Full-time craftsmen were essential to this revolution, and had
to be supported by the food surpluses of the peasants. The
products of the craftsmen needed distributing, and raw
materials had to be obtained from outside sources. Irrigation
increased food productivity, leading to centralized control of*

food supplies to feed the huge numbers of laborers who maintained large-scale canal systems. Writing became essential for record-keeping. Unifying religious forces soon dominated urban life, and priests and kings rose to power. Monumental architecture testified to their activities.

Gordon Childe thought of the Urban Revolution as a critical point in the gradual process of human cultural, economic, and social change. His notion of an Urban Revolution has dominated archaeological and historical thinking for years. But the revolution hypothesis has serious defects as an all-embracing definition of civilization and its causes. Childe's criteria are far from universal. Some highly effective and long-lasting civilizations like those of the Maya and the Mycenaeans never had cities. While some craft specialization and religious organization are typical of most civilizations, it cannot be said that these developments form a basis for an overall definition.

American archaeologist Robert McC. Adams has emphasized the importance of the development of social organization and craft specialization during the Urban Revolution. Adams has oriented his work toward changes in social organization and has described early Mesoamerica and central Mexico as following "a fundamental course of development in which corporate kin groups, originally preponderating in the control of land, were gradually supplanted by the growth of private estates in the hands of urban elites" (Adams 1966: 119). The result was a stratified form of social organization rigidly divided along class lines.

Most scholars agree that three main elements in Childe's list seem to have been of great importance to the growth of all civilizations. The first was the creation of food surpluses, used to support economic classes whose members were not directly engaged in food production. Second, the diversification of agricultural economies gave city people greater protection against the dangers of famine and stimulated the growth of trade networks and exchange mechanisms for food and other products. The third common factor was intensive land use, which probably increased the total agricultural output.

Intensive agriculture is normally taken to imply irrigation, often hailed as one fundamental reason for the emergence of civilization. In the case of Mesopotamia with its long, harsh summers, the floodplain's rich soils could only be cultivated by irrigation canals that had to be deep enough to carry water even when the Tigris and Euphrates rivers were at their lowest levels. Enormous expenditures of man-hours were needed to keep the canals in working order. From the earliest period of settlement in the Mesopotamian delta, some centralized organization of canal digging and maintenance work was needed. The large-scale irrigation works in both Mesopotamia and Egypt culminated a long process of evolution of intensive agriculture.

But social and economic changes brought about by irrigation were not in themselves sufficient to cause civilization, for the various developments mentioned here were interconnected. For example, the growth of population depended on increased food supplies and on higher productivity by farmers, a development linked in turn with the radical alteration of social organization. Urban life apparently began earliest in the Near East, but relatively soon afterward, literate civilization emerged in various forms in the Aegean, the Nile and the Indus valleys, the Far East, Mesoamerica, and Peru.

The consequences of urban life, however, were more lasting in terms of man's relationship with man than they were in terms of man's relationship with the environment. Man's dependence on his environment was lessened even further by new political and cultural institutions as well as by new social structures. More balanced economies were based on diversified resources in addition to trade in foodstuffs, allowing organizational initiatives to counter famines or the effects of extreme weather. The planning of food supplies reduced the city dweller's dependence on the day-to-day whims of his environment. But the ultimate consequence of urbanization was a greatly increased human capacity to alter and exploit the environment, which has brought us to today's environmental crisis.

John Pfeiffer's short essay on cities highlights some points made here, whereas Lionel Casson deals with diffusionist views of the origins of American civilizations, a pervasive and long-standing issue in New World archaeology. The discussion of cities closes with a short piece by Franklin Russell on Mesopotamian civilizations in which he spells out some consequences of urban civilization in the delta. In this evocative article, he recounts some impressions that can cross one's mind when visiting a famous archaeological site.

The selections in Chapter 8 reflect a new trend in archaeology, the study of towns and other settlements whose dates and confines are established from historical documentation — perhaps places whose kings and political leaders are known by name, whose landlords and tenants' quarrels are documented throughout successive centuries of city life.

In many cases archaeology can be used to illuminate details

of the day-to-day life of city people whose business transactions are recorded in historical archives. Andrew and Wendy Selkirk describe the detail obtained from a combination of archaeological evidence and historical documents, giving an account of a medieval street in the Brooks area of Winchester, England. Archaeologists have been studying Winchester's medieval archaeology for years, recording the grand plan and daily life of the ancient city before modern redevelopment destroys the evidence of early occupation. In North America, scholars like James Deetz and Ivor Noël Hume have studied the archaeology of colonial America and shown how useful historically checked records of stylistic evolution on such objects as gravestones can be for general studies of cultural change in archaeology.

Bernard L. Fontana's delightful essay on the unrespectable in archaeology brings us to the study of modern artifacts and their.ancestors in earlier centuries. It is possible to learn much about development and evolution of artifacts from a systematic study of modern objects. Studies of beer cans, crown bottle tops, shoes, nails, and other common items in use today have yielded valuable and also deliciously trivial information for archaeologist and layman alike. Indeed, archaeology does encompass a vast period of time and a multitude of artifacts, sites, and human cultures!

CHAPTER SEVEN

The Origin of Cities

John Pfeiffer

21 HOW MAN STARTED TO LIVE IN CITIES

John Pfeiffer, whose "Man the Hunter" appears in Chapter 4, has
recently been researching the origins of agriculture and of cities.
His essay below on the origins of cities follows some directions of
his earlier inquiry. As the caption on the story which was published
in *Horizon* says: "The wonder is not that man could live without
civilization but that he could begin to tolerate it." Pfeiffer's article
serves as a useful introduction to this complex subject.

The most striking mark of man's genius as a species, as the most adaptable
of animals, has been his ability to live in cities. From the perspective of all
we know about human evolution, nothing could be more unnatural. For
over fifteen million years, from the period when members of the family of
man first appeared on earth until relatively recent times, our ancestors
were nomadic, small-group, wide-open-spaces creatures. They lived on
the move among other moving animals in isolated little bands of a few
families, roaming across wildernesses that extended like oceans to the horizon and beyond.

Considering that heritage, the wonder is not that man has trouble
getting along in cities but that he can do it at all — that he can learn to
live in the same place year round, enclosed in sharp-cornered and brightly-

From John Pfeiffer, "How Man Invented Cities," © 1972 American Heritage Publishing Co., Inc. Reprinted by permission of the author and the publisher from *Horizon*,
Autumn 1972.

lit rectangular spaces, among noises, most of which are made by machines, within shouting distance of hundreds of other people, most of them strangers. Furthermore, such conditions arose so swiftly, practically overnight on the evolutionary time scale, that he has hardly had a chance to get used to them. The transition from a world without cities to our present situation took a mere five or six millenniums.

It is precisely because we are so close to our origins that what happened in prehistory bears directly on current problems. In fact, the expectation is that new studies of pre-cities and early cities will contribute as significantly to an understanding of today's urban complexes as studies of infancy and early childhood have to an understanding of adolescence. Cities are signs, symptoms if you will, of an accelerating and intensive phase of human evolution, a process that we are only beginning to investigate scientifically.

The first stages of the process may be traced back some fifteen thousand years to a rather less hectic era. Homo sapiens, that new breed of restless and intelligent primate, had reached a high point in his career as a hunter-gatherer subsisting predominantly on wild plants and animals. He had developed special tools, special tactics, and strategies for dealing with a wide variety of environments, from savannas and semideserts to tundras and tropical rain forests and mountain regions. Having learned to exploit practically every type of environment, he seemed at last to have found his natural place in the scheme of things — as a hunter living in balance with other species, and with all the world as his hunting ground.

But forces were already at work that would bring an end to this state of equilibrium and ultimately give rise to cities and the state of continuing instability that we are trying to cope with today. New theories, a harder look at the old theories, and an even harder look at our own tendencies to think small have radically changed our ideas about what happened and why.

We used to believe, in effect, that people abandoned hunting and gathering as soon as a reasonable alternative became available to them. It was hardly a safe or reliable way of life. Our ancestors faced sudden death and injury from predators and from prey that fought back, disease from exposure to the elements and from always being on the move, and hunger because the chances were excellent of coming back empty-handed from the hunt. Survival was a full-time struggle. Leisure came only after the invention of agriculture, which brought food surpluses, rising populations, and cities. Such was the accepted picture.

The fact of the matter, supported by studies of living hunter-gatherers as well as by the archaeological record, is that the traditional view is largely melodrama and science fiction. Our preagricultural ancestors were quite healthy, quite safe, and regularly obtained all the food they needed.

And they did it with time to burn. As a rule, the job of collecting food, animal and vegetable, required no more than a three-hour day, or a twenty-one-hour week. During that time, collectors brought in enough food for the entire group, which included an appreciable proportion (perhaps 30 per cent or more) of dependents, old persons and children who did little or no work. Leisure is basically a phenomenon of hunting-gathering times, and people have been trying to recover it ever since.

Another assumption ripe for discarding is that civilization first arose in the valleys of the Tigris, Euphrates, and Nile rivers and spread from there to the rest of the world. Accumulating evidence fails to support this notion that civilization is an exclusive product of these regions. To be sure, agriculture and cities may have appeared first in the Near East, but there are powerful arguments for completely independent origins in at least two other widely separated regions, Mesoamerica and Southeast Asia.

In all cases, circumstances forced hunter-gatherers to evolve new ways of surviving. With the decline of the ancient life style, nomadism, problems began piling up. If only people had kept on moving about like sane and respectable primates, life would be a great deal simpler. Instead, they settled down in increasing numbers over wider areas, and society started changing with a vengeance. Although the causes of this settling down remain a mystery, the fact of independent origins calls for an explanation based on worldwide developments.

An important factor, emphasized recently by Lewis Binford of the University of New Mexico, may have been the melting of mile-high glaciers, which was well under way fifteen thousand years ago, and which released enough water to raise the world's oceans 250 to 500 feet, to flood previously exposed coastal plains, and to create shallow bays and estuaries and marshlands. Vast numbers of fish and wild fowl made use of the new environments, and the extra resources permitted people to obtain food without migrating seasonally. In other words, people expended less energy, and life became that much easier, in the beginning anyway.

Yet this sensible and seemingly innocent change was to get mankind into all sorts of difficulties. According to a recent theory, it triggered a chain of events that made cities possible if not inevitable. Apparently, keeping on the move had always served as a natural birth-control mechanism, in part, perhaps, by causing a relatively high incidence of miscarriages. But the population brakes were off as soon as people began settling down.

One clue to what may have happened is provided by contemporary studies of a number of primitive tribes, such as the Bushmen of Africa's Kalahari Desert. Women living in nomadic bands, bands that pick up and move half a dozen or more times a year, have an average of one baby every four years or so, as compared with one baby every two and a half years for Bushman women living in settled communities — an increase of five to eight babies per mother during a twenty-year reproductive period.

The archaeological record suggests that in some places at least, a comparable phenomenon accompanied the melting of glaciers during the last ice age. People settled down and multiplied in the Les Eyzies region of southern France, one of the richest and most-studied centers of prehistory. Great limestone cliffs dominate the countryside, and at the foot of the cliffs are natural shelters, caves and rocky overhangs where people built fires, made tools out of flint and bone and ivory, and planned the next day's hunt. On special occasions artists equipped with torches went deep into certain caves like Lascaux and covered the walls with magnificent images of the animals they hunted.

In some places the cliffs and the shelters extend for hundreds of yards; in other places there are good living sites close to one another on the opposite slopes of river valleys. People in the Les Eyzies region were living not in isolated bands but in full-fledged communities, and populations seem to have been on the rise. During the period from seven thousand to twelve thousand years ago, the total number of sites doubled, and an appreciable proportion of them probably represent year-round settlements located in small river valleys. An analysis of excavated animal remains reveals an increasing dietary reliance on migratory birds and fish (chiefly salmon).

People were also settling down at about the same time in the Near East — for example, not far from the Mediterranean shoreline of Israel and on the border between the coastal plain and the hills to the east. Ofer Bar-Yosef, of the Institute of Archaeology of Hebrew University in Jerusalem, points out that since they were able to exploit both these areas, they did not have to wander widely in search of food. There were herds of deer and gazelle, wild boar, fish and wild fowl, wild cereals and other plants, and limestone caves and shelters like those in the Les Eyzies region. Somewhat later, however, a new land-use pattern emerged. Coastal villages continued to flourish, but in addition to them, new sites began appearing further inland — and in areas that were drier and less abundant.

Only under special pressure will men abandon a good thing, and in this case it was very likely the pressure of rising populations. The evidence suggests that the best coastal lands were supporting about all the hunter-gatherers they could support; and as living space decreased there was a "budding off," an overflow of surplus population into the second-best back country where game was scarcer. These people depended more and more on plants, particularly on wild cereals, as indicated by the larger numbers of flint sickle blades, mortars and pestles, and storage pits found at their sites (and also by an increased wear and pitting of teeth, presumably caused by chewing more coarse and gritty plant foods).

Another sign of the times was the appearance of stone buildings, often with impressively high and massive walls. The structures served a number of purposes. For one thing, they included storage bins where surplus grain could be kept in reserve for bad times, when there was a shortage of game and wild plants. They also imply danger abroad in the countryside, new kinds of violence, and a mounting need for defenses to protect stored goods from the raids of people who had not settled down.

Above all, the walls convey a feeling of increasing permanence, an increasing commitment to places. Although man was still mainly a hunter-gatherer living on wild species, some of the old options no longer existed for him. In the beginning, settling down may have involved a measure of choice, but now man was no longer quite so free to change locales when the land became less fruitful. Even in those days frontiers were vanishing. Man's problem was to develop new options, new ways of working the land more intensively so that it would provide the food that migration had always provided in more mobile times.

The all-important transition to agriculture came in small steps, establishing itself almost before anyone realized what was going on. Settlers in marginal lands took early measures to get more food out of less abundant environments — roughing up the soil a bit with scraping or digging sticks, sowing wheat and barley seeds, weeding, and generally doing their best to promote growth. To start with at least, it was simply a matter of supplementing regular diets of wild foods with some domesticated species, animals as well as plants, and people probably regarded themselves as hunter-gatherers working hard to maintain their way of life rather than as the revolutionaries they were. They were trying to preserve the old self-sufficiency, but it was a losing effort.

The wilderness way of life became more and more remote, more and more nearly irretrievable. Practically every advance in the technology of agriculture committed people to an increasing dependence on domesticated species and on the activities of other people living nearby. Kent Flannery of the University of Michigan emphasizes this point in a study of one part of Greater Mesopotamia, prehistoric Iran, during the period between twelve thousand and six thousand years ago. For the hunter-gatherer, an estimated one-third of the country's total land area was good territory, consisting of grassy plains and high mountain valleys where wild species were abundant; the rest of the land was desert and semidesert.

The coming of agriculture meant that people used a smaller proportion of the countryside. Early farming took advantage of naturally distributed water; the best terrain for that, namely terrain with a high water table and marshy areas, amounted to about a tenth of the land area. But only a tenth of that tenth was suitable for the next major development, irrigation. Meanwhile, food yields were soaring spectacularly, and so was the population of Iran, which increased more than fiftyfold; in other words, fifty times the original population was being supplied by food produced on one-hundredth of the land.

A detailed picture of the steps involved in this massing of people is coming from studies of one part of southwest Iran, an 880-square-mile region between the Zagros Mountains and the Iraqi border. The Susiana

Plain is mostly flat, sandy semidesert, the only notable features being man-made mounds that loom on the horizon like islands, places where people built in successively high levels on the ruins of their ancestors. During the past decade or so, hundreds of mounds have been mapped and dated (mainly through pottery styles) by Robert Adams of the University of Chicago, Jean Perrot of the French Archaeological Mission in Iran, and Henry Wright and Gregory Johnson of the University of Michigan. Their work provides a general idea of when the mounds were occupied, how they varied in size at different periods — and how a city may be born.

Imagine a time-lapse motion picture of the early settling of the Susiana Plain, starting about 6500 B.C., each minute of film representing a century. At first the plain is empty, as it has been since the beginning of time. Then the pioneers arrive; half a dozen families move in and build a cluster of mud-brick homes near a river. Soon another cluster appears and another, until, after about five minutes (it is now 6000 B.C.), there are ten settlements, each covering an area of 1 to 3 hectares (1 hectare = 2.47 acres). Five minutes more (5500 B.C.) and we see the start of irrigation, on a small scale, as people dig little ditches to carry water from rivers and tributaries to lands along the banks. Crop yields increase and so do populations, and there are now thirty settlements, all about the same size as the original ten.

This is but a prelude to the main event. Things become really complicated during the next fifteen minutes or so (5500 to 4000 B.C.). Irrigation systems, constructed and maintained by family groups of varying sizes, become more complex. The number of settlements shows a modest increase, from thirty to forty, but a more significant change takes place — the appearance of a hierarchy. Instead of settlements all about the same size, there are now levels of settlements and a kind of ranking: one town (7 hectares), ten large villages (3 to 4 hectares), and twenty-nine smaller villages of less than 3 hectares. During this period large residential and ceremonial structures appear at Susa, a town on the western edge of the Susiana Plain.

Strange happenings can be observed not long after the middle of this period (about 4600 B.C.). For reasons unknown, the number of settlements decreases rapidly. It is not known whether the population of the area decreased simultaneously. Time passes, and the number of settlements increases to about the same level as before, but great changes have occurred. Three cities have appeared with monumental public buildings, elaborate residential architecture, large workshops, major storage and market facilities, and certainly with administrators and bureaucrats. The settlement hierarchy is more complex, and settlements are no longer located to take advantage solely of good agricultural opportunities. Their location is also influenced by the cities and the services and opportunities available there.

By the end of our hypothetical time-lapse film, by the early part of the third millennium B.C., the largest settlement of all is the city of Susa, which covers some thirty hectares and will cover up to a square kilometer (100 hectares) of territory before it collapses in historical times.

All Mesopotamia underwent major transformations during this period. Another city was taking shape 150 miles northwest of Susa in the heartland of Sumer. Within a millennium the site of Uruk near the Euphrates River grew from village dimensions to a city enclosing within its defense walls more than thirty thousand people, four hundred hectares, and at the center a temple built on top of a huge brick platform. Archaeological surveys reveal that this period also saw a massive immigration into the region from places and for reasons as yet undetermined, resulting in a tenfold increase in settlements and in the formation of several new cities.

Similar surveys, requiring months and thousands of miles of walking, are completed or under way in many parts of the world. Little more than a millennium after the establishment of Uruk and Susa, cities began making an independent appearance in northern China not far from the conflux of the Wei and Yellow rivers, in an area that also saw the beginnings of agriculture. Still later, and also independently as far as we can tell, intensive settlement and land use developed in the New World.

The valley of Oaxaca in Mexico, where Flannery and his associates are working currently, provides another example of a city in the process of being formed. Around 500 B.C., or perhaps a bit earlier, buildings were erected for the first time on the tops of hills. Some of the hills were small, no more than twenty-five or thirty feet high, and the buildings were correspondingly small; they overlooked a few terraces and a river and probably a hamlet or two. Larger structures appeared on higher hills overlooking many villages. About 400 B.C. the most elaborate settlement began to appear on the highest land, 1,500-foot Monte Albán, with a panoramic view of the valley's three arms; and within two centuries it had developed into an urban center including hundreds of terraces, an irrigation system, a great plaza, ceremonial buildings and residences, and an astronomical observatory.

At about the same time, the New World's largest city, Teotihuacán, was evolving some 225 miles to the northwest in the central highlands of Mexico. Starting as a scattering of villages and hamlets, it covered nearly eight square miles at its height (around A.D. 100 to 200) and probably contained some 125,000 people. Archaeologists are now reconstructing the life and times of this great urban center. William Sanders of Pennsylvania State University is concentrating on an analysis of settlement patterns in the area, while Rene Millon of the University of Rochester and his associates have prepared detailed section-by-section maps of the city as a step toward further extensive excavations. Set in a narrow valley among mountains and with its own man-made mountains, the Pyramid of the Sun and the Pyramid of the Moon, the city flourished on a grand scale. It housed local dignitaries and priests, delegations from other parts of Mesoamerica, and workshop neighborhoods where specialists in the manufacture of textiles, pottery, obsidian blades, and other products lived together in early-style apartments.

The biggest center in what is now the United States probably reached its peak about a millennium after Teotihuacán. But it has not been reconstructed, and archaeologists are just beginning to appreciate the scale of what happened there. Known as Cahokia and located east of the Mississippi near St. Louis, it consists of a cluster of some 125 mounds (including a central mound 100 feet high and covering 15 acres) as well as a line of mounds extending six miles to the west.

So surveys and excavations continue, furnishing the sort of data needed to disprove or prove our theories. Emerging patterns — patterns involving the specific locations of different kinds of communities and of buildings and other artifacts within communities — can yield information about the forces that shaped and are still shaping cities and the behavior of people in cities. But one trend stands out above all others: the world was becoming more and more stratified. Every development seemed to favor social distinctions, social classes and elites, and to work against the old hunter-gatherer ways.

Among hunter-gatherers all people are equal. Individuals are recognized as exceptional hunters, healers, or storytellers, and they all have the chance to shine upon appropriate occasions. But it would be unthinkable for one of them, for any one man, to take over as full-time leader. That ethic passed when the nomadic life passed. In fact, a literal explosion of differences accompanied the coming of communities where people lived close together in permanent dwellings and under conditions where moving away was not easy.

The change is reflected clearly in observed changes of settlement patterns. Hierarchies of settlements imply hierarchies of people. Emerging social levels are indicated by the appearance of villages and towns and cities where only villages had existed before, by different levels of complexity culminating in such centers as Susa and Monte Albán and Cahokia. Circumstances practically drove people to establish class societies. In Mesopotamia, for instance, increasingly sophisticated agricultural systems and intensive concentrations of populations brought about enormous and irreversible changes within a short period. People were clamped in a demographic vise, more and more of them living and depending on less and less land — an ideal setting for the rapid rise of status differences.

Large-scale irrigation was a highly effective centralizing force, calling for new duties and new regularities and new levels of discipline. People still depended on the seasons; but in addition, canals had to be dug and maintained, and periodic cleaning was required to prevent the artificial waterways from filling up with silt and assorted litter. Workers had to be brought together, assigned tasks, and fed, which meant schedules and storehouses and rationing stations and mass-produced pottery to serve as food containers. It took time to organize such activities efficiently. There were undoubtedly many false starts, many attempts by local people to work things out among themselves and their neighbors at a community or village level. Many small centers, budding institutions, were undoubtedly formed and many collapsed, and we may yet detect traces of them in future excavations and analyses of settlement patterns.

The ultimate outcome was inevitable. Survival demanded organization on a regional rather than a local basis. It also demanded high-level administrators and managers, and most of them had to be educated people, mainly because of the need to prepare detailed records of supplies and transactions. Record-keeping has a long prehistory, perhaps dating back to certain abstract designs engraved on cave walls and bone twenty-five thousand or more years ago. But in Mesopotamia after 4000 B.C. there was a spurt in the art of inventing and utilizing special marks and symbols.

The trend is shown in the stamp and cylinder seals used by officials to place their "signatures" on clay tags and tablets, man's first documents. At first the designs on the stamp seals were uncomplicated, consisting for the most part of single animals or simple geometric motifs. Later, however, there were bigger stamp seals with more elaborate scenes depicting several objects or people or animals. Finally the cylinder seals appeared, which could be rolled to repeat a complex design. These seals indicate the existence of more and more different signatures — and more and more officials and record keepers. Similar trends are evident in potters' marks and other symbols. All these developments precede pictographic writing, which appears around 3200 B.C.

Wherever record keepers and populations were on the rise, in the Near East or Mexico or China, we can be reasonably sure that the need for a police force or the prehistoric equivalent thereof was on the increase, too. Conflict, including everything from fisticuffs to homicide, increases sharply with group size, and people have known this for a long time. The Bushmen have a strong feeling about avoiding crowds: "We like to get together, but we fear fights." They are most comfortable in bands of about twenty-five persons and when they have to assemble in larger groups — which happens for a total of only a few months a year, mainly to conduct initiations, arrange marriages, and be near the few permanent water holes during dry seasons — they form separate small groups of about twenty-five, as if they were still living on their own.

Incidentally, twenty-five has been called a "magic number," because it hints at what may be a universal law of group behavior. There have been many counts of hunter-gatherer bands, not only in the Kalahari Desert, but also in such diverse places as the forests of Thailand, the Canadian Northwest, and northern India. Although individual bands may vary from fifteen to seventy-five members, the tendency is to cluster around twenty-five, and in all cases a major reason for keeping groups small is the desire to avoid violence. In other words, the association between large groups and conflict has deep roots and very likely presented law-and-order problems during the early days of cities and pre-cities, as it has ever since.

Along with managers and record keepers and keepers of the peace, there were also specialists in trade. A number of factors besides population growth and intensive land use were involved in the origin of cities, and local and long-distance trade was among the most important. Prehistoric centers in the process of becoming urban were almost always trade centers. They typically occupied favored places, strategic points in developing trade networks, along major waterways and caravan routes or close to supplies of critical raw materials.

Archaeologists are making a renewed attempt to learn more about such developments. [Gary] Wright's current work in southwest Iran, for example, includes preliminary studies to detect and measure changes in the flow of trade. One site about sixty-five miles from Susa lies close to tar pits, which in prehistoric times served as a source of natural asphalt for fastening stone blades to handles and waterproofing baskets and roofs. By saving all the waste bits of this important raw material preserved in different excavated levels, Wright was able to estimate fluctuations in its production over a period of time. In one level, for example, he found that the amounts of asphalt produced increased far beyond local requirements; in fact, a quantitative analysis indicates that asphalt exports doubled at this time. The material was probably being traded for such things as high-quality flint obtained from quarries more than one hundred miles away, since counts of material recovered at the site indicate that imports of the flint doubled during the same period.

In other words, the site was taking its place in an expanding trade network, and similar evidence from other sites can be used to indicate the extent and structure of that network. Then the problem will be to find out what other things were happening at the same time, such as significant changes in cylinder-seal designs and in agricultural and religious practices. This is the sort of evidence that may be expected to spell out just how the evolution of trade was related to the evolution of cities.

Another central problem is gaining a fresh understanding of the role of religion. Something connected with enormous concentrations of people, with population pressures and tensions of many kinds that started building up five thousand or more years ago, transformed religion from a matter of simple rituals carried out at village shrines to the great systems of temples and priesthoods invariably associated with early cities. Sacred as well as profane institutions arose to keep society from splitting apart.

Strong divisive tendencies had to be counteracted, and the reason may involve yet another magic number, another intriguing regularity that has been observed in hunter-gatherer societies in different parts of the world. The average size of a tribe, defined as a group of bands all speaking the same dialect, turns out to be about five hundred persons, a figure that depends to some extent on the limits of human memory. A tribe is a community of people who can identify closely with one another and engage in repeated face-to-face encounters and recognitions; and it happens that five hundred may represent about the number of persons a hunter-gatherer can remember well enough to approach on what would amount to a first-name basis in our society. Beyond that number the level of familiarity declines, and there is an increasing tendency to regard individuals as "they" rather than "we," which is when trouble usually starts. (Architects recommend that an elementary school should not exceed five hundred pupils if the principal is to maintain personal contact with all of them, and the headmaster of one prominent prep school recently used this argument to keep his student body at or below the five-hundred mark.)

Religion of the sort that evolved with the first cities may have helped to "beat" the magic number five hundred. Certainly there was an urgent need to establish feelings of solidarity among many thousands of persons rather than a few hundred. Creating allegiances wider than those provided by direct kinship and person-to-person ties became a most important problem, a task for full-time professionals. In this connection Paul Wheatley of the University of Chicago suggests that "specialized priests were among the first persons to be released from the daily round of subsistence labor." Their role was partly to exhort other workers concerned with the building of monuments and temples, workers who probably exerted greater efforts in the belief that they were doing it not for mere men but for the glory of individuals highborn and close to the gods.

The city evolved to meet the needs of societies under pressure. People were being swept up in a process that had been set in motion by their own activities and that they could never have predicted, for the simple reason that they had no insight into what they were doing in the first place. For example, they did not know, and had no way of knowing, that settling down could lead to population explosions.

There is nothing strange about this state of affairs, to be sure. It is the essence of the human condition and involves us just as intensely today. Then as now, people responded by the sheer instinct of survival to forces that they understood vaguely at best — and worked together as well as they could to organize themselves, to preserve order in the face of accelerating change and complexity and the threat of chaos. They could never know that they were creating what we, its beneficiaries and its victims, call civilization.

Lionel Casson

22 THE EARLY SETTLEMENT OF AMERICA: WHO GOT HERE FIRST?

The New World was not settled by hunter-gatherers until sometime during the last glaciation and then, to judge from over two centuries of research, only by *Homo sapiens*. The gradual cultural development of the early Americans has been ably chronicled by many authors, who have shown how the great states of Mesoamerica and Peru arose through indigenous developments within the New World. No subject has fostered more debate in both academic and non-academic circles than the origins of New World civilization. Basically, the issue is whether or not there was any contact between the Old World and the New before Columbus landed in the Caribbean in 1492. Lionel Casson has recently described the theories of pre-Columbian contact in the following entertaining article, which gives useful background data for further reading on New World civilizations.

In 1641 a Portuguese Jew named Antonio Montezinos, while journeying near Quito in Ecuador, met up with a native who, he was flabbergasted to discover, was Jewish. What is more, the man took him on an arduous week-long trip through the hinterland to a remote spot where an entire community of Jews was living; Antonio actually heard them recite in Hebrew the traditional prayer, "Hear, O Israel."

Returning to Europe, he reported this spectacular news to Manasseh ben Israel, the most eminent Jewish scholar of the day. Manasseh published it in a slim volume called *The Hope of Israel*, which was swiftly translated from Spanish into Latin, Hebrew, and English; the English version went into three editions within two years. Manasseh was not the first to claim that the Lost Tribes of Israel had crossed the ocean to America, but he was the one who really launched the notion on its long-lived career.

The theory that wandering Israelites were among the founders of New World civilization reached its heyday in the last century. Lord Kingsborough of England, for example, went through the family fortune and landed in debtors' prison no less than three times in order to publish deluxe volumes proving that the Mexican Indians were descendants of the Lost Tribes. And the Mormon sacred writings speak of two waves of Israelite migrants, an

From Lionel Casson, "Who Got Here First," © 1972 American Heritage Publishing Co., Inc. Reprinted by permission from *Horizon*, Spring 1972. Illustrations and footnotes are omitted.

early wave of Jaredites, who found their way across the Atlantic during the confused times after the toppling of the Tower of Babel and a later one made up of the followers of a certain Lehi, who left Jerusalem about 600 B.C., shortly before the rest of the city was led off into the Babylonian captivity.

How the émigrés negotiated the thousands of miles of open water bothered no one, since the Bible had a built-in explanation. The Lost Tribes had presumably gotten themselves lost sometime after 721 B.C., the year that Sargon II of Assyria conquered the northern part of Palestine and resettled its inhabitants in the upper reaches of the Tigris and Euphrates. At least two centuries before this, Solomon had "made a navy of ships in Ezion-geber . . . on the shore of the Red Sea," which he manned with Phoenician "shipmen that had knowledge of the sea" and which "came to Ophir, and fetched from thence gold . . . and silver, ivory, and apes, and peacocks." If the ships of the day could make it to Ophir and back — a three years' journey, we are told — obviously they could take an Atlantic crossing in stride.

The Bible pointedly mentions that Solomon used Phoenician crews. The Phoenicians were for a long while the mariners par excellence of the ancient world. They even boasted considerable oceanic expertise: not only did they sail to Ophir but, according to a tale reported by Herodotus, around 600 B.C. a fleet of Phoenician galleys successfully circumnavigated the continent of Africa.

With such impeccable nautical references, it was inevitable that the Phoenicians sooner or later would qualify as early transatlantic voyagers. One of their champions, writing in 1822, claimed that he knew of a manuscript — no longer available for consultation, of course — drawn up by a Phoenician named Votan who had seen the Tower of Babel being built and had come to the New World when forced out of his homeland by the Israelites. A few decades later, someone else "proved" that the Mayas were descended from the inhabitants of Tyre.

And, just four years ago, Cyrus Gordon, a well-known professor of Semitic languages who has a penchant for breathless arrival at controversial conclusions, announced in *The New York Times* his discovery of proof positive that a group of Phoenicians had landed in Brazil. He came on it by the sort of miraculous luck usually reserved for the nonacademics in the field. The chance purchase of a scrapbook for a few pennies at a benefit sale led to the discovery of a letter, written by a nineteenth-century savant, that contained a transcription of a stone inscribed in Phoenician characters; the stone had been found by a slave on a Brazilian plantation in 1872 and had been copied off by the owner's son. The inscription conveniently supplied all the desired details: the identity of the party that had erected the stone (businessmen from Sidon), the date (nineteenth year of Hiram), the point of departure (Ezion-geber, just like Solomon's expeditions to Ophir).

The original stone, naturally, had long ago gone the way of Votan's manuscript.

Around the beginning of the nineteenth century the drums started to beat loud and strong for the ancient Egyptians as ocean voyagers. Napoleon's Nile campaign had opened up the country to savants and scholars. The Western world, awed at the sudden revelation of what had been achieved there in the days of the Pharaohs, was ready and eager to accept ancient Egypt as the fountainhead of all civilization. So, when European visitors to Mexico returned with glowing tales of the spectacular monuments reared by the people who had lived there long ago, monuments that were sometimes pyramidal in shape or decorated with hieroglyphic carving, everything seemed to fall into place: migrants from the Nile must somehow have had a hand in shaping what happened in the New World.

But the claim for the Egyptians raised a nautical problem, and a difficult one. They were a river and valley people, presumably with limited maritime skill; how did they get from the banks of the Nile to the shores of Mexico? An answer was found in Plato's tale about an imaginary continent called Atlantis.

The countless words that have been written about the "lost Atlantis" all go back to a handful of pages in the dialogues the *Timaeus* and the *Critias*, particularly the latter. Plato, who was as much a poet as he was a philosopher, relates that Solon, the legendary lawgiver, had journeyed to Egypt at some early date in Greek history. There he met certain priests who told him that nine thousand years earlier, when Athens was the strongest and best-governed state of all, an island called Atlantis, larger than North Africa and Asia combined, lay beyond the Strait of Gibraltar. The king of Atlantis had tried to enslave Greece and Egypt, but Athens led the defense, fighting on alone after all others had deserted, until one day earthquakes and floods swallowed up Atlantis and the Athenian army with it.

Plato's ancient readers apparently never thought of trying to locate Atlantis. The search began some two millenniums after he wrote — and it has never stopped. Savants like Montaigne and Voltaire seriously debated the island's existence, a learned Swede of the seventeenth century wrote no less than three volumes to demonstrate that it had been in Scandinavia, and a stream of books that prove to each author's utter satisfaction precisely where it must have been still burbles cheerfully along. The latest, at this writing, was published in the spring of 1969. Atlantis, it tells us, was a volcanic island in the Aegean Sea that blew up about 1450 B.C. Plato, of course, talks not of a pocket-sized island but of an enormous land mass, located not in the Aegean but in the Atlantic, and destroyed not nine hundred years ago but a dim nine thousand years ago — but all this leaves the author undaunted. Undauntability, however, is the strong point of most writers on Atlantis.

Atlantis solved everything. With its vast bulk filling in most of the ocean, ancient voyagers no longer had to traverse thousands of miles of open water to go from the Old World to the New; all they had to do was get over a negligible stretch on either side, and thereafter they did most of their traveling on foot. Atlantis proved so convenient that it opened up other heady possibilities besides an Egyptian migration to America. One school of thought reversed the traffic and sent Mayas scuttling eastward across this paradise to bring pyramids to the valley of the Nile.

The most dazzling idea, and the one that probably came to command the greatest number of adherents, was that Atlantis itself deserved the credit for being the fountainhead of civilization. The lost continent, it was asserted, had supported a superlatively gifted people who, long before the disastrous total drowning, thought up things like pyramids and hierogly-phics and, migrating eastward and westward, were the common source for both Egyptian and Mayan civilization.

So far we have talked only about candidates for early crossings of the Atlantic. As far back as the sixteenth century, there were those who argued that pre-Columbian voyagers had come to the New World via the Pacific. They and their successors suggested the Chinese or Indians or Malaysians or Polynesians, and some even sent the Lost Tribes to America by way of the Far East. Others, eying the vast stretch of the Pacific, took a leaf from the book of Atlantis and conjured up a lost continent in the Pacific — Lemuria, or Mu. It once stretched, we are told, from Easter Island to the Ladrones, and its inhabitants, whose record for creativity was right up to the mark set by the Atlanteans, triumphantly carried Mu's gifts to civiliza-tion westward to India and eastward to America.

Still others offered candidates only a shade less fanciful than the inhabi-tants of a lost continent: Buddhist monks who had sailed off toward the east in the fifth century A.D.; Koreans escaping from Chinese tyranny; sur-vivors of a fleet that Kublai Khan had sent out against Japan and that was almost totally destroyed in a storm; and survivors from an expedition dis-patched to the Persian Gulf by Alexander the Great.

Fortunately, alongside the amateur theorizers, sober professionals — an-thropologists and archaeologists — were pondering the problem of New World origins. Today, after more than a century of patient digging and collecting and observing and study, they have been able to formulate some more or less convincing conclusions. The American Indians are physically proto-Mongoloid; they must, therefore, have come from Asia. They arrived in a series of waves almost certainly by way of Alaska; the migrations took place some ten thousand to twenty thousand years ago (new evidence may very well set the date farther back) when there was a bridge of land between Asia and America at what is now Bering Strait. Over the centuries they filtered south, gradually climbing the standard rungs in the ladder of civilization: they learned pottery-making, farming, metallurgy, building on a large scale, writing.

As the experts amassed more and more data and sifted it, curious apparent coincidences began to crop up: certain Mayan art motifs strangely resembled certain Chinese motifs; certain pots found in Mexico looked strangely like some found in China; certain architectural elements found in Yucatán looked strangely like some found in Cambodia, and so on.

Inevitably, then, a theory arose that, long before Columbus, there was trans-Pacific contact between the Old World and the New — not a mass migration of Chinese or Israelites who subsequently turned into Mayas or Incas but traders or other visitors who brought the know-how that sparked the upward march of civilization in America. The advocates of this theory are poles apart from the devotees of a Mu or the like; they are men with a lifetime of training in the technique of gathering and evaluating evidence.

They point to motifs on Chinese bronzes of the late Chou period and similar motifs in the so-called Tajin style of Mexico; to Chinese pottery of the Han period and similar pottery found in Guatemala; to the lotus motif as treated in Buddhist art and its very similar treatment in sculptures of Yucatán; to the way figures are represented seated or "diving" in Hindu-Buddhist art and the very similar way they appear on sculpture from Palenque or Chichén Itzá. They argue that these likenesses must reflect some early impact of the Old World upon the New. A number go even further and claim that artistic influence is just the icing on the cultural cake the Old World fed to the New.

Robert Heine-Geldern, a noted Austrian anthropologist who is the most radical advocate of trans-Pacific influence, has written that "future research will probably indicate that Asiatic influences of nonmaterial character were far more important than those in art and architecture. It must have been they which changed the whole structure of native society and transformed the ancient tribal cultures into civilizations more or less comparable to those of the Old World."

And so Heine-Geldern conceives of a "vast maritime expansion" of the peoples of coastal China toward the east. He has hardy Chinese mariners traveling to our shores as early as 700 B.C. By 200 B.C. he brings sailors from India into the picture, has the Chinese drop out about A.D. 200, and has Indians along with others from neighboring lands carry on so that trans-Pacific voyaging "was never really interrupted until the 9th or, perhaps, the 10th century A.D. Why it finally ended, we do not know." By the time it did, Heine-Geldern concludes, the New World had learned from Far Eastern visitors how to work metal, reckon time, write, and build monumental cities.

It is a grand theory. The trouble is that it has little more hard evidence to support it than the theories of the free-wheeling amateurs. The stylistic parallels are striking — but the dates just cannot be made to coincide. A Chinese bronze of the Shang period, which ended around 1000 B.C., has an amazing resemblance to a pot found near the mouth of the Amazon —

but the pot dates from A.D. 1200 at the very earliest. Motifs found in China during the Chou period do indeed resemble some of the monuments in Tajin style uncovered near Veracruz, but the Chou period ended about 200 B.C. and the Tajin monuments were built in A.D. 300 or 400. Some very ancient pottery found in Ecuador, which has been dated to 3000 B.C. and compared with Japanese pottery of the same period, seemed for a while to make a chronological fit, but recently doubts have been raised about the age of the material from Ecuador; a date of 1000 B.C., it has been suggested, would be more reasonable.

Moreover, no Chinese or Indian object — or any object at all from the Old World — has been found in the New World in archaeological levels that date to pre-Columbian times. If Chinese or Indian traders did come regularly, they somehow left no tangible trace of their presence. Nor did they pass on to the people with whom they traded any of their useful discoveries such as the wheel, the use of iron, the domestication of cows or pigs or dogs or horses, or the planting of wheat (the New World fed on corn). Finally, there is the matter of Chinese seamanship. For a very long while the Chinese preferred to let others do their ocean hauling. As a matter of fact, the first securely dated Chinese ocean voyage did not take place until as late as the fifteenth century A.D.

Yet the puzzling parallels are there, too many and too close to be explained away as mere coincidences. Surely occasional visitors must have come. The winds and currents of the North Pacific trend eastward. Any craft caught helpless in their embrace can easily be carried across the ocean; records show, for example, that between 1775 and 1875 about twenty Japanese junks were blown to the west coast of America.

If Japanese junks in the last century, why not Chinese or Indian or Malaysian ones in preceding centuries? No question about it, a certain number must have ended a storm-tossed journey on this side of the Pacific. Perhaps a few of the bolder spirits among their crews risked the long sail back home, but most must have chosen to settle down where they landed. Eventually they either died out or were wholly absorbed, leaving behind only tantalizing hints of their presence.

What about the South Pacific? If the North Pacific had the winds and currents to bring people willy-nilly across to America, the South Pacific had the mariners to make the trip of their own free will. The South Pacific is a world of multitudinous far-flung fragments of land; the name "Polynesia" derives from Greek elements that mean "many islands." Thanks to the maritime enterprise of the Polynesians, most of them were already populated by the time Europeans arrived on the scene, including those separated by great stretches of water.

The standard craft of these seamen was a canoe balanced by an outrigger and driven by a rig enabling it to travel to a certain extent against the wind. For transporting large groups they used double canoes made up of two hulls yoked by booms and with a platform spanning the space in between, an embryonic version of the catamarans that are the latest wrinkle in yacht design today. These ran large enough to accommodate as many as two hundred and fifty persons. Piloting such unsophisticated vessels fearlessly and with consummate ability, the Polynesians managed to reach almost every bit of land in the South Pacific. Their original home seems to have been southeastern Asia. From there they filtered through Micronesia or Melanesia and, at no very remote age, perhaps the fifth century A.D., made their debut in western Polynesia. The period of their most active colonization was probably as late as the twelfth to the fourteenth centuries.

These voyages were recalled in many a Polynesian legend, and anthropologists soon concluded that the Polynesian skipper, by using every primitive means of navigation available — observation not only of the stars but of wind and wave direction, of the flight of migratory birds, and of the distinctive clouds that hang above islands — could sail for weeks over trackless ocean to make a landfall on a tiny target. They credited him in effect with being able to set and hold a course as accurately as Europeans equipped with compass, log, and a knowledge of celestial navigation. Accordingly, they claimed that the Polynesians were the first people to have intentionally made their way over, if not all of the Pacific, at least a good part of it.

The Polynesians were as fine a race of seamen as the world has ever known. But they were not miracle workers. Some years ago, Andrew Sharp in his *Ancient Voyagers in Polynesia* took a close look at all the available evidence and demonstrated that they conducted regular two-way traffic over three hundred miles of open water at the most and usually only one to two hundred — in other words, voyages of but a day or two. Their fast-stepping canoes covered one hundred miles in twenty-four hours in good weather, and this in itself is achievement enough to place the Polynesians high on the honor roll of maritime races. But no regular traffic between points farther apart is recorded, for it was utterly beyond their powers. Stars offer scant help on north-south courses and no help at all during the day or on cloudy nights; wind and wave direction can change in an instant; and no skipper dares to count on steady sightings of distinctive birds or cloud formations.

Polynesians certainly did reach and populate the shores of Hawaii and Easter Island and other remote spots, but the founding fathers did not navigate their way there — they were brought by chance, with ladies luckily present to be pressed into service as founding mothers. Polynesian legend is full of stories of canoes blown by storm to far places, and many instances were noted by the Europeans who lived among the islanders before traditional ways had changed.

An even more significant contributor to haphazard long-distance colonization was war. War among Polynesians was usually fought to the death, and the losing side, faced with certain extinction, understandably preferred to load themselves, their goods, and some essential food plants aboard their canoes and take their chances that Heaven would direct them to an empty piece of land.

Did any Polynesians ever get blown clear across the Pacific? Since they were carried as far as Easter Island, a good thousand miles to the east of their nearest brethren, might they not have been swept on for another two thousand miles, right to the coast of South America? Those who think so point to the squashes and gourds, native to America, that are found in Polynesia — but the seeds could just as well have been carried by birds through the air as by Polynesians returning in boats. For a while it was believed that the New World's staple food, corn, might itself have been brought from Asia by Polynesians, but the discovery of corn pollen in America in levels that go back at least sixty thousand years put an end to that.

Only one agricultural product has so far weathered all the storms of scholarly controversy, the sweet potato. It is native to America and is called in Peruvian tongues *kumar;* it is found in Polynesia, and the general Polynesian word for it is *kumara.* An obvious conclusion is that Polynesians not only reached South America but made it safely back, taking with them one of the most useful items the New World had to offer, name and all.

But a few saw it just the other way around. They held that it was South Americans who brought the sweet potato to Polynesia. This was for years just another theory, more or less buried in the obscurity of professional books and journals. Then Thor Heyerdahl moved the argument to the public stage and stepped into the spotlight.

The Polynesians, Heyerdahl reminded everyone, were not the only gifted sailors in the area. The inhabitants of the west coast of South America were no slouches; they were able to cover great distances with their favored type of craft, a seagoing raft made of light balsa logs. Moreover, the winds and currents between South America and Polynesia in the warmer latitudes are prevailingly easterly: a Polynesian would have to buck both to get to South America, whereas a Peruvian needed merely to raise sail and coast. To clinch the argument, Heyerdahl made his celebrated grand gesture: he built a balsa sailing raft, the famed *Kon-Tiki,* shoved off from Callao in Peru, and 101 days and 4,300 miles later fetched up on one of the islands in the Tuamotu group. Having launched the *Kon-Tiki* so successfully, Heyerdahl then launched his pet theory, that the Polynesian islands were settled by South Americans who had been carried there by wind and current as he had.

As things turned out, it was easier to keep the *Kon-Tiki* afloat than the theory. Heyerdahl marshaled what seemed to be an impressive list of proofs. By the time his opponents had finished taking pot shots at them, hardly a one was left standing. Moreover, one of his many challengers, Eric de Bisschop, who was even wiser than Heyerdahl in the ways of seagoing rafts, took it upon himself to demonstrate that a raft could just as well make the voyage in the opposite direction.

To cross vast expanses of open water in little boats seems to have been De Bisschop's greatest joy in life. In 1937 he sailed a thirty-seven-foot double canoe from Hawaii across the Pacific to Australia, through the Torres Strait, across the Indian Ocean, around the Cape of Good Hope, up the Atlantic to the Strait of Gibraltar, and into the Mediterranean. In 1956, exasperated by all the publicity the *Kon-Tiki* and her skipper were getting, he decided, at the age of sixty-five, to demonstrate that, despite Heyerdahl's talk of winds and currents permitting a raft to voyage only from east to west, one could also do it from west to east.

De Bisschop's answer to the *Kon-Tiki* was the *Tahiti Nui*, a raft of bamboo logs. In November of 1956 he left from Tahiti, holding a course due south into lower latitudes, where he knew he had a chance to pick up westerlies. By May he was near the Juan Fernández Islands, no more than five hundred miles from Valparaiso, his intended destination. Here he ran into a series of vicious storms; the raft became too battered to be trusted, and he and his crew reluctantly abandoned it and allowed a Chilean cruiser to carry them to safety.

A year later he had readied the *Tahiti Nui II*, and on April 13, 1958, he sailed from Callao to repeat Heyerdahl's feat. But the sea is a dangerous gaming partner, and De Bisschop had gambled once too often: four months after their departure he and his crew ended up on a reef off Rakahanga in the Northern Cooks. His companions did their best to save him, but he was dead by the time they got him on the beach. Nevertheless, he had made his point: with ordinary luck a seagoing raft could get from Polynesia to South America and back.

But that was all he or Heyerdahl had proved: that a raft *could* make it. And whatever rafts — or canoes — ever did, did so by accident. So far as we know to this day, the first man to have laid and followed a course from one side of the Pacific to the other was Ferdinand Magellan in 1519. As for the Atlantic, it, too, *could* have been crossed by primitive craft. But so far as we know, no one intentionally sailed across it before Columbus.

As it happens, the first planned ocean crossing on record took place in the Indian Ocean in the second century B.C., but the voyage involved no great feat of seamanship. It was, in fact, almost humdrum.

Perhaps as early as the third millennium B.C., sailors were plying the waters of the Indian Ocean between the western shores of India and the Persian Gulf. By at least the first millennium B.C. they were making their way to the east coast of Africa and the mouth of the Red Sea, carrying precious cargoes of Chinese silks, Far Eastern spices, and other luxury goods. The traffic, extremely lucrative, was largely in the hands of Indian and Arab seamen, and they had no intention of letting anyone else in on it. And so for centuries they kept to themselves a priceless trade secret, the behavior of the monsoon winds. These, with splendid convenience, blow from the northeast during the winter and then shift to precisely the opposite quarter for the summer; sailing vessels were thus ensured a fair wind for both legs of the journey.

But about 120 B.C. the secret finally leaked out. One day a half-drowned sailor was brought to the court of Ptolemy VII at Alexandria. After being nursed back to health and taught Greek, he gave out the story that he was an Indian, the sole survivor of his crew, and he offered to prove it by showing anyone the king picked out the way back to his home. Eudoxus of Cyzicus, a well-known explorer was in town at the time and the choice fell on him; under government auspices, he twice sailed to India and back.

There was nothing to it. The route had been traveled by generations of anonymous skippers before him, he knew what he would find at the other end, and he was guaranteed a fair wind each way. During the homeward leg of the second voyage a bit of excitement developed when he was carried farther south than he expected and ended up on the coast of Africa below Cape Guardafui. But he made friends with the natives in the best explorer tradition by giving them strange delicacies (bread, wine, and dried figs did the trick), and even picked up a few words of their tongue.

Eudoxus's troubles began only after he got back. Both times he had landed with an invaluable cargo of spices and perfumes and gems, only to see Ptolemy's customs agents confiscate all of it. In a way they posed for him the same problem that the closing of the Suez Canal does for Mediterranean shippers today. His solution anticipated theirs: he readied an expedition to sail all around Africa from west to east and thereby bypass Egypt. He fitted it out to the nines, even taking aboard a number of dancing girls; whether for the harems of Indian rajahs or to help while away the long hours at sea, we cannot know. He sailed from Cadiz, but when he got as far as the Atlantic coast of Morocco, a mutiny sent him back. Undaunted, he equipped a second expedition just as carefully, set sail, and vanished without a trace.

So in compiling the list of recorded transatlantic voyages, we start with Eudoxus. Then, skipping over the legendary voyage of the sixth-century Irish Saint Brendan, we make a leap of more than a thousand years to the Vikings. In the tenth century Eric the Red led a group of colonists to Greenland, and thereafter Viking craft shuttled regularly between Norway and Iceland and Greenland. To be sure, the Atlantic crossing at this point is narrow, involving only some two hundred miles of open water, but it requires courage and seamanship beyond the call of crossings in lower latitudes. Eric's son Leif pushed on from Greenland to "Vinland," generally thought to be in Labrador or Newfoundland or Nova Scotia, but he very likely followed the coasts as much as he could rather than a course straight over the sea. From the Vikings we jump half a millennium to Columbus and Magellan.

The list is short and is not likely to grow any longer. But of course the list of nonauthenticated voyages grows annually. With the successful voyage of the *Ra II*, Heyerdahl has now added to it the ancient Egyptians who used to sail papyrus boats on the Nile — though never, so far as anyone knows, on the open sea. Not long ago, in a dispatch datelined Warsaw, *The New York Times* reported that "Polish scientists are planning to sail a primitive 82-foot boat from Casablanca to Mexico to prove that North Africans could have settled the new world 4,000 years ago." And, who knows? Maybe next year the Russians will launch an expedition to find Atlantis.

Michael D. Coe

23 THE SHADOW OF THE OLMECS

> The Olmec people were the first Americans "to achieve a level of social, cultural, and artistic complexity enough for them to be called civilized," writes Yale archaeologist Michael D. Coe of these remarkable Mesoamerican artists. In the following article he describes his excavations at the important Olmec site at San Lorenzo. He found traces of occupation going back to about 1500 B.C., although Olmec occupation did not reach its height until between 1150 and 900 B.C. Coe describes some of the magnificent Olmec art from the site and looks for Mayan origins in Olmec culture. This article gives a general introduction to Olmec archaeology, which has more technical literature. No one can study the ancient civilizations of Mesoamerica without first taking the Olmec and their contributions to American civilization into account.

More than one hundred years ago, in 1862, a Mexican scholar named José Maria Melgar set out from a sugar-cane hacienda on the lower slopes of the Tuxtla Mountains, in southern Veracruz, Mexico, to look into a report of a gigantic inverted "kettle" the natives had discovered buried in the soil. Instead of the "kettle," he found a ten-ton basalt head, the "Ethiopic" features of which led him to believe that African Negroes had settled

From Michael Coe, "The Shadow of the Olmecs," © 1971 American Heritage Publishing Co., Inc. Reprinted by permission of the author and the publisher from *Horizon*, Autumn 1971. Illustrations are omitted.

here in remote antiquity. His subsequent article describing this stone, one of a dozen such "Colossal Heads" now known, was the first published account of an object typical of what is called the Olmec civilization.

Just who were the Olmecs?

They were the first American Indians to achieve a level of social, cultural, and artistic complexity high enough for them to be called civilized. As such, they were precursors of the later Mexican and Central American cultures, whose great achievements could not have been realized without them.

Though we are familiar with the Aztec empire, and know something of the Mayas, the name "Olmec" probably means little to most of us. Yet today Olmec archaeology is laying bare one of the most exciting chapters in the history of our continent. Imagine a people capable of carving human heads on a gigantic scale and exquisite figurines from blue-green, translucent jade. Imagine an art style based on the combined features of a snarling jaguar and a human infant. Then transport these people back beyond all known Indian civilizations, to a distance in time of more than three thousand years, and put them down in the inhospitable, swampy jungles of Mexico's Gulf Coast.

The extraordinary discovery Melgar made in these jungles went largely unnoticed until the first decade of this century, when the stone was visited by the German scholar Eduard Seler. Then it was again forgotten by the archaeological world. Forgotten, that is, until the 1920's, when the pioneer archaeologists Frans Blom and Oliver La Farge discovered the great, swamp-bound site of La Venta. There they found another Colossal Head, along with a number of other great stone sculptures in a style they mistakenly ascribed to the Mayas.

La Venta intrigued several other scholars, who quickly noted that this style, while highly sophisticated, was very different from that of the Classic Mayas, who flourished in the Yucatán Peninsula and farther south from about A.D. 300 to 900. They also noticed that some figurines and ceremonial axes of jade and other fine stones that had been turning up in museums and private collections were stylistically similar to the objects found at La Venta. They christened the unknown, non-Mayan civilization that had produced them "Olmec," after the mysterious tribe (whose name meant "Rubber People" in the Aztec tongue) that dominated the southern Gulf Coast of Mexico on the eve of the Spanish Conquest. But who were the *archaeological* Olmecs? How old was their civilization, and what was its relationship to the other civilizations of Mexico and Central America, for example, the Mayan or Toltec? Only in recent years has enough attention been paid to these questions to provide at least partial answers.

The foundations of scientific archaeology in the Olmec area were laid by Matthew W. Stirling of the Smithsonian Institution during his expeditions between 1938 and 1946. The first task Stirling set for himself was that of excavating Tres Zapotes, the site of Melgar's Ethiopic head. There he came upon an Olmec-type carved stone, the now-famous Stela C, which bore a date in the Mayan system that seemed to match a day in the year 31 B.C. — over three centuries earlier than the most ancient date then known for the Mayas. This and other leads suggested to Stirling, as it did to leading Mexican archaeologists, that the Olmec civilization was probably the most ancient high culture yet known for the New World. After 1940 Stirling moved to La Venta, in neighboring Tabasco, and continued to make spectacular Olmec discoveries, particularly tombs of extraordinary richness.

One group, however, remained skeptical: the Mayan specialists. It seemed heresy to these American and British archaeologists to believe that the up-start Olmec civilization could have predated — and according to Stirling and his Mexican colleagues, even foreshadowed — Classic Mayan culture, which in many respects represented the highest achievement of the American Indian. Since 1840 the world had known and appreciated the splendid achievements of the ancient Mayas in writing, astronomy, calendrical science, art, and architecture. It was inconceivable that the Olmecs could have flourished before A.D. 300. Few Mayán buffs were ready to admit that Stela C at Tres Zapotes was a date to be read in the Mayan system.

The controversy over the Olmecs could not be settled until the advent of radiocarbon dating. In 1955 a University of California team under Dr. Robert F. Heizer opened a series of trenches at La Venta and secured a large number of charcoal samples. Most of the radiocarbon dates turned out to be far older than anyone would then have thought possible: 800–400 B.C. Incredibly, Olmec culture seems to have been at its height *seven to eleven* centuries before that of the Classic Mayas. La Venta — with its gigantic basalt monuments, mosaic pavements of serpentine blocks, a hundred-foot-high earthen pyramid, caches of carved jade and serpentine, and other wonders — was not a town or city in the usual sense but a mysteriously remote center for ceremonies and politics, isolated on its swamp-bound island. Why did it exist at all? And where did its builders come from?

There was no easy answer to the second question. Olmec sculptures had been found along the Gulf Coast as far north as the city of Veracruz, Olmec reliefs carved on a cliff had been located in the state of Morelos, and Olmec jades had turned up in puzzling profusion in the western state of Guerrero. The frequency of such finds prompted Miguel Covarrubias, the talented artist-archaeologist and long-time proponent of Olmec antiquity, to suggest Guerrero as the Olmec homeland, on the theory that they must have learned to carve small figures before moving to Veracruz and Tabasco, where their gigantic monuments are concentrated.

But many archaeologists, including myself, were convinced that Olmec origins would some day be found in the Olmec "heartland," the crescent-shaped, low-lying region along the Gulf Coast. Since the highest development of the culture was surely there, then why couldn't its beginnings, perhaps as far back in the pre-Classic period as 1500 B.C., also be there?

My own quest for Olmec origins — and for the conditions, ecological or otherwise, that may have stimulated the rise of native American civilization — led me, in December, 1964, on a trip of exploration up the sluggish, meandering Coatzacoalcos River, which drains the northern part of the Isthmus of Tehuantepec, to a riverside village called Tenochtitlán. A few miles south of the village lies a jungle-covered mesa known as San Lorenzo. In 1945 Matthew Stirling had been taken there by local Indians who had seen a great stone eye staring up from the dirt of a trail crossing the mesa. The eye turned out to belong to a new Colossal Head, one of a number of basalt monuments that Stirling found and excavated that season and the next. Some of these multi-ton heads, with their "football" helmets, flat faces, and staring eyes, have traveled as far afield as Leningrad and are the best-known examples of Olmec achievement in sculpture.

Two mysteries had immediately presented themselves to Stirling at San Lorenzo. First, the basalt from which the heads and other stones were carved did not occur anywhere around the site, the nearest source lying some fifty miles to the northwest.

The second mystery concerned the final disposition of the sculptures. Almost all of them were found either lying on the bottoms or the slopes of the deep, jungle-filled ravines that cut into the San Lorenzo mesa. Stirling guessed that some non-Olmec invaders had smashed or otherwise mutilated the monuments and then pushed them into the ravines. If so, there would be little chance of dating the Olmec occupation of San Lorenzo by associating the sculptures with archaeological layers.

The idea of mounting a major archaeological effort at San Lorenzo came to me during my trip in 1964. By the end of the next year I found myself, aluminum camera case in perspiring hand, standing in the grass-covered "street" of Tenochtitlán looking in vain for a sympathetic face. The natives were decidedly *not* friendly. Those Colossal Heads that had gone around the world had been removed by Veracruz archaeologists without the villagers' approval, and they were angry. Even so, I felt sure that a little diplomacy would make it possible to work there, and my optimism proved to be justified. We eventually claimed the majority of the local villagers as our friends and colleagues.

In 1966 Yale University, with financial backing from the National Science Foundation, began three years' work at the site. Our first step was to build a camp. In southern Mexico there are supposed to be two climatic seasons: a winter dry season, when it almost never rains, and the very wet summer. But in southern Veracruz some kind of moisture — drizzle, rain, or torrential downpour — is almost always falling. Shivering in our leaky tents, we found that fierce northers sweep down the Gulf Coast in winter, bringing cold drizzle and rain for days at a time. Until we put up houses with thatched roofs, we were a very soggy camp.

Our next job was to get San Lorenzo mapped. The picture that emerged after two seasons of surveying was very different from the one we had first imagined: San Lorenzo turned out to be one of the world's strangest archaeological sites.

The mesa, rising some 150 feet above the surrounding grass- and swamp-covered plains, was originally considered to be a naturally formed plateau, the ravines being the result of erosion. Indeed, it must in large part be the result of geologic uplift by tectonic forces, most likely one of the deeply buried salt domes that are common in the northern half of the Isthmus of Tehuantepec. But San Lorenzo as we see it today has clearly been altered by the hand of ancient man. Reaching out like fingers on its north, west, and south sides are long, narrow ridges divided by the ravines. A pair of ridges on the western side exhibit bilateral symmetry, that is, every feature on one ridge is matched mirror-fashion by its counterpart; another such pair, divided by an asymmetric ridge, can be seen on the south side. This is hardly consistent with a natural origin.

Our excavations over three years demonstrated that the ridges are artificial, consisting of fill and cultural debris to a depth of at least twenty-five feet. Presumably, the first inhabitants — the Olmecs or their predecessors — took advantage of an already existing sand- and gravel-covered hill to carry out their plans. What could they have had in mind? As our map began to take shape, my first thought was that they might have been trying to construct a running or reclining animal on a titanic scale, three-quarters of a mile long, with its legs stretching north and south. But a subsequent mapping of the entire zone by aerial photography revealed much more of the total plan of San Lorenzo than our field map did. It showed a gigantic bird flying eastward, its extended wing feathers forming the ridges on the north and south, with its tail trailing to the west.

This may sound like poppycock, since such a grandiose plan could only have been appreciated from the air. Yet similar effigy mounds were erected by the early Adena and Hopewell cultures of our own midwestern states, and the tremendous hilltop markings above the Peruvian deserts cannot be fully grasped from ground level either. My own guess is that some ancient Olmec ruler or priest (or both), inspired by cosmological ideas, ordered this construction on such a scale to impress the gods and men but that the plan was never completed.

There are several hundred earth mounds on the flat surface of San Lorenzo, but the site is not very impressive compared with such Mesoamerican giants as Teotihuacán or Tikal. At the center stands a very modest pyramid, probably once the substructure for a thatched-roof temple. Extending north and south of it are pairs of long mounds with narrow plazas between them. Presumably this was the focal point of San Lorenzo.

But was it an "empty" site, as we guess La Venta to have been, inhabited only by priestly bureaucrats and their entourages? Apparently not, for most of the two hundred structures are what we call house mounds: low, rectangular or ovoid platforms of earth designed to raise the pole and thatch houses of the commoners above the discomforts caused by summer (and winter) rains. A reasonable estimate of the ancient population might be a thousand persons, thus making Olmec San Lorenzo far from "empty."

When we arrived, there was no archaeological chronology for San Lorenzo, and we had to work one out for ourselves. This meant digging at least a dozen stratigraphic trenches and pits, peeling off layer by layer as we descended and segregating all broken pottery, stone tools, and other artifacts from each stratum. Having done this before at pre-Classic sites in coastal Guatemala, I was familiar with very early Mesoamerican pottery, but I was appalled by the number of potsherds — several hundred thousand in all — that accumulated in our three seasons at San Lorenzo. This material has now been analyzed, and I have worked out a pre-Classic sequence consisting of seven distinct phases, or cultures, followed by a long period of abandonment (from around the time of Christ to about A.D. 900), and finally, a very late reoccupation by another, Toltec-like people.

But it is the pre-Classic period that concerns us here, for in that time span lies the story of the Olmecs at San Lorenzo. This is a story with dates, too, for we were fortunate enough to find well-preserved hearths or cooking fires with ample charcoal for radiocarbon analysis. It now seems that the first people to inhabit the San Lorenzo plateau arrived about 1500 B.C. They were not Olmecs, since their finely made pottery showed no signs of Olmec influence, but they may have been their ancestors. Two and a half centuries later, around 1250 B.C., there are signs that the people at San Lorenzo were beginning to take on Olmec characteristics: beautiful figurines of white clay show the unmistakable baby faces of the Olmecs, and there is much of the white-rimmed black pottery distinctive of the culture. Most important, we found a stone fragment that must have been part of a monumental carving of basalt.

The height of civilization in the area was reached in what we call the San Lorenzo phase, reliably dated to 1150–900 B.C. Here we are faced with remains that are undeniably Olmec, and it is also apparent that the site itself had reached its present form by that time. Olmec figurines of all sorts are found, some showing ball players wearing the heavy, padded belts and gloves typically used in that sacred game. Neither we nor Stirling found jade at San Lorenzo, which is curious since the Olmecs of La Venta were master jade carvers.

We are confident that the bulk of the fifty-eight known monuments at

San Lorenzo were carved during the San Lorenzo phase. How do we know this? Remember that Stirling found most of his stones lying in or near the ravines, obviously not in their original positions. One morning in March, 1967, I spotted a rough stone slab, or stela, sticking out of the ground in one of the western ridges and ordered that it be dug up. It was this modest excavation that enabled us to date the Olmec sculptures of San Lorenzo and to solve the riddle of their final disposition.

The stela in question appeared to be in its original position, and I wanted to establish its relationship to whatever strata might exist in the ridge. It soon became clear, however, that the workman I had set at this task could not do his job within the limited excavation square I had measured off. Slightly to the north on the east-west ridge we started a new square, with the idea of enlarging the total work area. To my astonishment and delight we hit upon another sculpture, totally buried.

This turned out to be Monument 34, a magnificent, larger than life-size statue of a half-kneeling man in pure Olmec style. Like almost all other known Olmec monuments, this one had been mutilated before burial, in this case by having its head knocked off. At each shoulder was a disk, perforated in the center, to which movable arms could be attached; whether they were of wood or stone we had no way of knowing.

Here, then, were two monuments, one just north of the other. If we continued to excavate along the ridge in the same direction, mightn't we find a whole line of buried monuments? My guess was right. For weeks we dug on, uncovering one mutilated sculpture after another. And while following the same kind of lead west along another ridge, a second line of stones appeared, this time oriented east-west. Both "collections" produced a great variety of representations, ranging from a gigantic column embellished with a relief of a horrific werejaguar-god to a tiny carving of a fantastic spider. We now had strong evidence that a single monumental act of destruction had been inflicted on the Olmec sculptures of San Lorenzo. The iconoclasts had begun by smashing some monuments and pitting the features of others, sometimes by grinding axes on them. They had then dragged the objects of their fury onto specially prepared floors running along the ridges of the site, placed them carefully in long lines, and covered them with a special fill. Clearly, the stones found by Stirling in the ravines had *not* been pushed there by ancient hands but had slipped down, as the slope eroded, from their original positions in the ridges. This opened up the possibility that there might be a great many more stones still to be discovered.

Once we could associate the sculptures with archaeological strata, we were able to date them — or rather, date their final placement. From our study of the pottery and other artifacts lying on the floors and in the covering fill we learned that the great act of destruction took place no later than 900 B.C. But here again, we had settled one problem only to raise another: until now no archaeologist would have believed the Olmec sculptural style to be any older than 800 B.C. In the period 1150–900 B.C., when we are positive our monuments were carved, the rest of Mesoamerica had not yet shown the first glimmerings of civilized life. Only at San Lorenzo did civilization burn brightly, with no antecedents yet discovered. Where did these people come from, with their culture already in full development?

The mysteries of San Lorenzo were tied up with more than the monuments. In one of the ridges we uncovered a troughlike stone, U-shaped in cross section. In his 1946 explorations Stirling had found a number of these lying jumbled at the bottom of one of the ravines, along with a like number of flat, rectangular stones, also of basalt. He surmised that the latter were covers for the troughs, which had once been fitted end to end to form a drain. He was right. On the edge of that same ravine, on the southwestern border of the San Lorenzo plateau, one of my laborers pointed out to me the end of just such a drain, still in place and deeply buried.

We excavated the drain completely during the final season, no simple task as it was covered with twelve to sixteen feet of overburden. A very remarkable system it was: a "main line" sloping down in an east-west direction and measuring 558 feet in length, with three subsidiary lines, totaling 98 feet, meeting the main line at a steep angle. From loose stones lying on the surface elsewhere, we are reasonably sure that another system, the mirror image to this one, lies on the southeast edge of the site.

What was the purpose of this drain, which represents no less than thirty tons of hard basalt? At its upper end there are openings for water to enter. Nearby, on the surface of the site, are several artificial ponds constructed by the Olmecs. We have good reason to believe that during the San Lorenzo phase, when the drain system was put down, its starting point lay beneath the center of a large pond that was later covered up. Thus, it appears that the drain had no other function than to draw off water from the pond.

Since irrigation is unnecessary in the wet local climate, the ultimate function of this strange water-control system must have been purely ceremonial, perhaps connected with ritual bathing by the ancient Olmec leaders. Near the head of the drain we uncovered a remarkable statue of the Olmec rain god, complete with snarling, werejaguar face, while near its other end was a curious stone receptacle in the shape of a duck. The latter, discovered by Stirling, has an opening into which a trough-stone would fit perfectly.

What kind of a world did the Olmec leaders of San Lorenzo look out upon from their lofty plateau? Who owed them allegiance? Was theirs a tribal polity, ruled by chiefs, or a pristine state, dominated by kings? Since the Olmecs of those times left no writing, we must rely on other lines of inquiry to answer these questions. But first let us consider the magnitude of the Olmec achievement at San Lorenzo three thousand years ago.

The site itself represents hundreds of thousands of tons of material — gravel, soil, sand, and rock — carried in by basketloads on men's backs. Similarly, the monuments must have required an army of laborers. Geological analysis has shown that the source of the basalt used in almost all the San Lorenzo monuments is the Cerro Cintepec, an extinct volcano some fifty miles north-northwest of San Lorenzo. The Colossal Heads average about eighteen tons, and one of the so-called altars weighs even more than that.

The Olmecs must have selected boulders of a suitable shape from the slopes of the volcano, somehow transporting them to the nearest navigable stream (no small distance) and then floating them to the mouth of the Coatzacoalcos River on balsa rafts. From there they would have been poled and pulled up the river to a point near San Lorenzo. Finally, each boulder would have been hauled up 150 feet, probably with ropes and simple rollers, to their final destination. We ourselves had some experience using simple materials and methods to move the monuments, and I can attest to the enormous effort required to move a ten-ton stone just one foot! It took fifty men with ropes and poles to set one Colossal Head upright. Thus, moving the larger monuments must have involved using more than a thousand workmen at a time.

Then there is the testimony of the persons represented by the stones. Scholars seem to agree that the Colossal Heads are portraits of Olmec rulers. Likewise, the seated figures in the niches of the "altars," shown either with ropes holding captives or carrying the characteristic werejaguar infants, seem to depict real men. Great leaders, or their descendants, must have ordered the carving and setting up of these monuments — at what cost can only be imagined. Surely, then, we can postulate the existence of a polity that was more powerful than a mere tribal state.

But there is more. The existence of a political state implies a government with territorial jurisdiction not over a single tribe but over many. Whether an Olmec state can be postulated under this definition can never be fully determined, any more than it can be for *any* of the later civilizations of Mexico, other than the documented civilization of the Aztecs. Nevertheless, there is good reason to believe that the San Lorenzo Olmecs exerted an influence, political or otherwise, upon regions as distant as the highlands of central and western Mexico, where Olmec pottery and even Olmec rock paintings have been discovered during the past few years.

But the most compelling evidence for San Lorenzo's high cultural and political status under the Olmecs comes from what at first glance might be thought an unlikely line of inquiry: ecology. Working within a sample area of about thirty square miles, centering on San Lorenzo, we are now trying to arrive at some idea of what the upper limit of human population may

have been three thousand years ago. The extent of the sample area is probably that which would have been controlled by an agricultural tribe. If
our population figure turns out to be much lower than the number of
persons presumably involved in the construction and maintenance of the
Olmec center, then San Lorenzo would have to have drawn labor and
tribute from an area far greater than that of our sample.

Our calculation is based on the number of mouths that native systems
of cultivation could have fed. It is not an easy one to make. Our preliminary studies strongly suggest, however, that the local population could
never have constructed the artificial plateau and set up the monuments
unaided. We may assume, then, that the Olmec rulers held sway over more
than one tribe, and that they may, indeed, have exercised authority over
much of southern Mexico.

One significant outgrowth of our study has been the work of Dr. Elizabeth S. Wing of the Florida State Museum, who has managed to identify
scraps of bone contained in our Olmec rubbish heaps. The Olmecs were
more finicky in their culinary habits than the present-day natives, who eat
almost any kind of fish or game they can get their hands on. Olmec preferences, however, are curious, since the most common animals represented
are snook (a large and good-tasting fish), man, marine toad, and turtle!
We are not particularly bothered by the human remains, since cannibalism
is well attested for the rest of Mesoamerica, but the toads are a puzzle,
as they cannot be skinned without an extremely dangerous poison getting
into the meat. We are now looking into the possibility that the Olmecs
used them for a hallucinogenic substance called bufotenine, which is one
of the active ingredients of the poison.

Far more significant, however, has been our research into local farming
practices. The Olmecs, like all Mexican Indians, were basically corn eaters.
Here we think that we may have hit upon the secret of the very early rise
of native civilization in the San Lorenzo area. As in most of the world's
tropical lands, the basic system of agriculture is of the shifting, or slash-
and-burn, type, which means that a farmer will fell the trees or bush on
a plot of land, burn them when dry, and continue to plant and harvest on
the plot until declining yields or other factors force him to abandon it
and search for another patch of forest.

One must also remember that there is a dry season and a rainy one.
Most Mesoamerican farmers have only one major crop, planted with the
first rains and harvested in the fall. On the gently rolling upland soils of
the San Lorenzo area, however, there are *two* major crops, thanks to the
winter northers, which keep the soil moist. Furthermore, in summer, when
the rainstorms sweep daily across southwest Mexico, the winding, sluggish
Coatzacoalcos River rises rapidly and covers all of the low-lying land with
great sheets of water. San Lorenzo becomes a world afloat. As the rains
taper off and the floods recede, the gift of the river is revealed: fresh mud
and silt, deposited along the broad natural levees that flank the river.

These levees are classed by the natives as "prime land." While the upland areas tend to be communally owned, the levees are pretty much in private hands. Even though it is possible to cultivate only one crop on them, during the dry season, their production is incredibly high for indigenous corn farming. As might be expected, those who bid for economic — and political — power in the village must gain effective control of the levee lands.

Was this, then, how the Olmecs rose to power and civilization more than three millenniums ago? We are reminded of ancient Egypt, so obviously tied to the rise and fall of its one great river. It is hardly a coincidence that most of the world's early civilizations have arisen in major river basins, and our Olmecs of San Lorenzo seem to have been no exception.

Every story has an end, or at least an epilogue. Olmec civilization did not come to a close after the massive destruction of San Lorenzo around 900 B.C. Curiously enough, La Venta seems to have reached the summit of its achievement immediately *after* this brutal event, and it may be that the overthrow of San Lorenzo's rulers was instigated by the leaders of that island citadel. Thereafter, the Olmec character of San Lorenzo was lost, for the pre-Classic reoccupations that continued until the beginning of the Christian Era lack the art style that is the Olmec hallmark.

Eventually, even La Venta was destroyed, and perhaps its successor, Tres Zapotes. But Olmec civilization became transformed into some of the other brilliant civilizations of Mesoamerica's Classic period. The farther back we trace the Classic cultures of Mexico and Central America, the more characteristic of the Olmecs they seem to become.

The most clear-cut case for an Olmec heritage is presented by the famous Mayan civilization of the Classic period. It may seem a far cry from the earth or adobe constructions of the Olmecs to the towering pyramid-temples of the Mayas, but a closer look at Mayan art and learning reveals much in common. Take the day-to-day calendar system called the Long Count. Although for many decades scientists considered this a Mayan invention, Stirling and others have shown that it had far earlier roots in Olmec country. There is now good reason to believe that the well-known writing system of the Mayas may be of Olmec origin as well. Based on what we know of the earliest Classic Mayan art and culture, the Mayas themselves may, indeed, once have been Olmec, moving in the centuries before the Christian Era eastward into the jungles of Yucatán and Guatemala.

Strong Olmec influence may also be detected in the Oaxaca highlands of Mexico, where the Zapotec people held sway. Kent Flannery of the University of Michigan has recently identified a local Oaxaca culture that was either importing Olmec products or making very good imitations of them, and Olmec artistic traits are to be found in the well-known Danzante reliefs, the strange stone carvings of slain men erected at the great Zapotec site of Monte Albán.

The list could be expanded to encompass most early civilizations of Mexico and Central America. The Olmecs seem to be behind all of them —an ancient, shadowy, "mother culture" whose own origins remain shrouded in mystery even to this day.

Franklin Russell

24 THE ROAD TO UR

Franklin Russell's article on the Sumerians is an evocative piece which needs little introduction. He writes of the Sumerian civilization, of the harsh Mesopotamian delta where man first invented "democracy, crude but recognizable, and the concept of empire, brutal and familiar." Russell looks at the Sumerians through their sites; their prosperity depended on the soils that supported the teeming urban populations of the delta. But it is the reality of the city that has dominated history's view of the earliest human literate civilization. Russell gives insight into the thought processes that a visit to an archaeological site can invoke in an interested onlooker of the past.

The sun spills across the Euphrates at dawn and hits the great ziggurat, a brick mountain rising from an ocean of dust. Approaching it from the east, I feel the sun's heat burning my back at the same instant that the ziggurat flames red in the sunlight. The moment is eerie, unearthly, and it confounds any attempt I might make to describe it.

This is the ziggurat of Ur-Nammu, one of the last of the Sumerian kings who ruled in southern Mesopotamia, now modern Iraq. Standing on top of the ziggurat, a kind of stepped tower, or pyramid, which was the distinctive Sumerian contribution to architecture, it is possible to look down on the ruins of Ur, a five-thousand-year-old city tumbled into a disorder of sun-dried bricks.

The place has always had a special fascination for me because here is compressed the essence of man as he refined the most sublime invention on earth, civilization itself. Here, where the sun at six thirty this morning is hot enough to scorch the skin on my forearms, the Sumerians transformed man's image of himself and started the whole machinery of urban civilization forward on its endlessly enigmatic journey.

From Franklin Russell, "The Road to Ur," © 1972 American Heritage Publishing Co., Inc. Reprinted by permission from *Horizon*, Summer 1972. Illustrations are omitted.

Here, men first challenged nature with a boldness and success matched in human history only by the Americans some five millenniums later. Here was born the idea of creating a completely new geography in which man was indisputably the master of his environment, bending it to his will. Like our own, the Sumerians' need for material things was prodigious, and they made much more sophisticated use of techniques and tools invented several millenniums before.

Here, the wheel first rolled upon a gridwork of city streets and cuneiform writing was first inscribed on clay. The Sumerians were not merely master architects and superb hydraulic engineers, they were also the inventors of the military phalanx, the B-52 of its day, a devastating and seemingly omnipotent weapon. From out of their imaginations came deep-sea merchantmen, formalized schools, epic poetry, the arch, the city, traffic jams, pollution, and the world's first great crisis in ecology. It was here, not in Egypt, or Babylon, or Greece, or Rome, that men first codified rational laws to govern human behavior. They invented democracy, crude but recognizable, and the concept of empire, brutal and familiar.

Now, all around me there is a silence you find only in deserts and high mountains. The sun bakes the skin and the air shakes. The sky is clear and pale blue, dropping to a distant horizon that shows the mounds of other dead cities. At the foot of Ur-Nammu's monument, my Bedouin guide points to cuneiform marks on a crumpled brick wall. "Ibrahim," he says. "His house here."

Perhaps Abraham *did* live here thirty-seven hundred years ago, and perhaps Ur *was* a bustling port with ships moored not a hundred feet from where I stand. Perhaps this same sun *did* shine on the city's roofs and on the majestic march of irrigation canals. But this kind of imagining is easier in a library or a lecture hall, where the dreadful reality of the place does not intrude. The journey men made to reach this place cannot be rendered sensible merely by looking at it as an expression of a civilization's rise and fall. One must look to the earth itself, which supported man here, and then, groaning, let him drop.

To reach Ur by a road that has meaning for us today, it is necessary to leave the ruined city and move north and east along an uncertain path nearly fifty thousand years old. We are following the route of civilization back to its source. Instead of measuring monuments and chronicling the deeds of warriors, princes, gods, and kings, it makes more sense to look for those quiet events of natural history that took place unnoticed by most historians: how the grass grew, how the crops flourished, how the water flowed and the silt settled.

The facts are unreliable, the dates dubious, the order of events uncertain; but as I move eastward the landscape becomes more stimulating than the featureless plains of the Euphrates and the Tigris. I move along the banks of the Diyala, a tributary of the Tigris. For more than five thousand years life-giving water has been taken from this river for crops, first by the shadowy men of prehistory, then by Sumerians, Babylonians, Assyrians, Persians, Parthians, Mongols, Neo-Persians, Turks, and Arabs.

The river is a roadway leading to the Zagros Mountains, passing through scattered fields of rice, barley, and wheat, citrus orchards, and rows of date palms, then rising into treeless, rolling hills of grass. Flocks of sheep and cattle and goats graze on all sides. Nearchus, Alexander's lieutenant, traveled here more than twenty-two hundred years ago, and it impressed him as a place of "clear rivers and lakes, abundant rain, and forests full of wild animals."

The forests and wild animals are harder to find today, but the grasses are the same and so are the abounding wild grains and fruits. This is a natural landscape for the nomadic hunter, the shepherd, the grain-and-fruit gatherer, the simple farmer. The hills roll on for miles as the altitude increases toward its eventual peak of more than fourteen thousand feet in the still-distant Zagros Mountains. Deep, narrow valleys run into the Diyala, and defiles and precipices increase as the air chills with height. In these valleys, I know, early hunters found protection from winter weather, and it is not hard to visualize their environment.

The ancient landscape is African in its sweep and scope, and its lions and leopards, cheetahs and hunting dogs, hyenas and jackals, make the resemblance more than superficial. But the true significance is that there are so many domesticable animals here — wild sheep, goats, pigs, asses — grazing among so many plants that yield edible grains — barley, wheat, oats. The steppes, foothills, uplands, and mountains are a kind of geographic tinderbox inviting the nomadic hunter to strike a spark.

From November to March the mountains gleam with snow and the steppe country provides good grazing. As the heat and drought of summer grow unbearable on the plains and begin to steal into the hills, the animals and hunters move higher, toward the cooler mountain country where the grazing remains good. It does not need a lifetime of living here to understand the principles of rotational grazing, or to guess at the benefits to be gained from taming the wild animals.

But needed first are men who can change themselves, and a leisurely thirty thousand years or so pass while they take their first hesitant steps toward the plains. They barter natural asphalt mined in the tar pits of the northeastern steppes with men who live in the mountains of Turkey and use the asphalt to fit handles to their flint tools and weapons. In return, the traders get obsidian, from which they fashion their own tools and weapons. Trading increases the flow of ideas among men and helps power the movement toward a domesticated man.

Thirty-odd thousand years is long enough to change all previous agreements the men have made with their world. They tame the sheep, goats, and pigs. They develop and refine techniques of grazing. They breed selectively to improve their animals. They change the wild sheep's fur into wool and transform the pig from a lean, fast runner into a slow, fat waddler. They harvest wild fruits and grains, barter them for meat or tool materials, and watch for mutations in the wild plants that will give them more and bigger seeds.

When these barley seeds develop, domesticated to produce six rows of seed instead of the two that the wild grain produces, they eventually reach the hot plains flanking the Diyala and are watered by bucket. The dusty earth reveals itself as incredibly fertile. From a single seed, the harvester gets a two-hundredfold increase.

But hill farmers, shepherds, nomads, and traders are scarcely the kind to build awesome monuments to gods in hellish deserts. It is easy to water a garden plot, another thing to irrigate a farm. The amount of land that can be irrigated is limited both by muscle and by ambition. Men settle along the Diyala and the Tigris, and along the Euphrates, where the riverbanks are low. They suffer in the heat of the plains while the other men roam or work in the cooler uplands.

Sometime after 6000 B.C. the plainsmen consolidate themselves into larger, better organized communities, with some of their kind finding a haven at the southern end of the plains, in the hottest of all country, near and among the fever-ridden marshes of the Tigris-Euphrates delta. The fertility of the river-borne silt is phenomenal, and man intensifies his farming. He co-operates with scores, then hundreds, perhaps even thousands, of his fellows and begins to build irrigation systems with channels quite far from the water source and reservoirs to hold flood waters until they are released into the fields weeks later.

Little is known about these earliest farmers of the Tigris-Euphrates delta. At first they lack metal, and a system of writing, and most of the equipment necessary to build a great civilization. They find that their irrigation is no open-ended contract for success. The farther the water is moved from its source, the more difficult it becomes to maintain the dikes, ditches, and channels needed to carry it. There are proliferating problems of riparian rights, of land law and other social controls. Added to these are the dangers of flooding, which can wreck everything, the attacks of marauding nomads, who can seize the harvest, and pestilence, which can make maintenance of the system impossible.

The irrigation people hold a golden key to the future of man, but it is hard to bring them truly to life, impossible to measure their success. They leave the broken shards of their distinctive pottery in the silty earth, along with the remains of thousands of sickles made of sun-baked clay. But their power grows continuously, and they have a sense of the monumental long before they can speak to us in writing. A thousand of them can work together for five years to build a massive temple, yet they seem to find no special need for a king unless there is a war emergency or some other danger, and they govern themselves through councils of free men.

By 3500 B.C. the southern plains are dominated by the Sumerians, a short, stocky, black-headed race of people whose origins are obscure ("We come from where the sun rises"). If they are not the product of the environment, they are immigrants who understand how to increase its exploitation to the maximum. They grow wheat and barley in equal proportions. They extend irrigation systems, survive crippling floods, and laboriously build civilization in a loosely connected comity of city-states.

The genius of Sumer is in its cities, but its powerhouse remains an ecological one, that extraordinary link to the mutated grain, to the dormant fertile soil, to the road begun in the foothill country of the Zagros Mountains. The farmer is the silent hero of the great civilization growing above him. He cultivates his fields with meticulous care, using mallets to break up its clods, leveling it as flat as a table, coaxing bumper crops with three, four, or five floodings of irrigation water.

As the centuries roll on, the farmer learns that fertility is diminished when land is cropped without fertilizer. He rests his fields and grazes them, but even this does not restore the fertility completely. He knows, however, that when the river floods, his irrigation canals carry silt as well as water, and the silt is spread across the depleted fields. "Behold," the farmer says, "the inundation has come and the land is restored."

As a former farmer myself, I can watch his work with admiration and with some compassion. When he floods his flat fields, evaporation begins immediately, causing the calcium and magnesium in the water to precipitate as salts. The soil contains particles of clay, torn loose from mountain origins along with topsoil silt. These particles attract sodium ions, causing them to break down into even smaller particles. The farmer understands that when he overfloods, he sours his fields. But he does not understand the grand process, continuing over hundreds of years, in which the gradual erection of a near-to-impervious barrier prevents the soil from absorbing water, and so increases the rate of evaporation and the deposition of more salts. The road to Ur-Nammu's ziggurat, therefore, is a journey through the earth itself. The edifice of civilization, in these terms, is less subject to the king's will than it is to the health of the earthworm.

By this time, I have moved out of the foothills of the Zagros and am again heading south across the alluvial plains toward Ur. To reach this point of understanding, I have moved four hundred miles in distance and some forty-three thousand years in time from the hill country where the road to the ziggurat begins.

Now, I pause at the site of Telloh, one of the cities in the ancient Sumerian state of Lagash, about fifty miles north of Ur. Here, it is possible to take a closer look at the kind of urban miracle erected on this foundation of the soil. Here, again, is the same deadliness of landscape, seen now from the ruins of the great temple of Ningirsu, the god of Telloh. Although his temple is now nothing more than a fifty-foot mound of rubble, it is a symbolic point from which to view the Sumerian state at its zenith. When the temple was built in the third millennium B.C., the people of Lagash had been farming their land for a thousand years. Their city of Telloh sprawls for more than two miles along the banks of a great waterway that is visible now as an empty declivity in the dust.

The idea of the state, founded on phenomenal soil fertility and abundant water supplies, is fought to a resolution in Lagash. It is a bastion against hill barbarians, an incubator of high culture, imperialism, and exploitation. It covers about eighteen hundred square miles and holds about two hundred and fifty thousand people. The soil is indeed fertile. Lagash has a population density equivalent to about five billion people in the United States.

Every changeless facet of civilized society is expressed here. The center city of Telloh covers about four square miles, and trudging through the dust and sand, I imagine its ancient appearance. Outside the walls there is a hodgepodge of tumble-down buildings, reed hovels, even burrows in the ground. "The poor are always with us," the Sumerians are fond of saying. Blind beggars importune on all sides as the city's walls loom up. Inside the gates, the city is chaotic, unplanned, cramped — a mixture of narrow streets and walkways hardly wide enough for a donkey. The houses are tiny and the press and noise of people is daunting.

It is the reality of the city that dominates the view of the Sumerian civilization. The eighteen hundred square miles of cropland do not figure in the history books. Instead, there appears a disciplined, structured society dominated by the god, the king, the priests, and the patricians. But it is an oddly appealing society. Slaves buy their freedom, fight court cases, marry. Children argue with teachers. Ombudsmen cut down on the clutter of trivial civil court cases.

These people admire wealth, possessions, good food, yet their proverbs scorn this crass appreciation of the good life. Possessions, they say, are sparrows in flight with no place to land. Money guarantees nothing. Gold and food may give happiness, but a man with neither is more likely to have peace of mind. They are contemptuous of men who build like lords but then are forced to live like slaves. Abstinence, even poverty, they insist, can create contentment. They enjoin you to keep your mouth shut when in doubt. Don't cross your bridges until you come to them. Don't fantasize. Remember that love builds and hate destroys. And don't forget that a sweet word is everybody's friend.

The contradictions between the adages glorifying the simple life and the realities of abundant living are richly evident here. Through the narrow window of a one-story streetside house a wealthy family can be seen drinking from silver goblets shaped by an artist with an exquisite sense of line. A palace musician plays his lyre, an ornate, multistringed instrument as big as a cello and inlaid with carnelian and lapis lazuli. Regal-looking women walk through shaded courtyards wearing headdresses made of meticulously delicate beaten-gold leaves, their jewelry tinkling on their necks and wrists and ankles.

This is the surface veneer dominating the history. But already, by this time, there are warnings of ecological trouble. As a result of about a thousand years of irrigation, of millions of tons of water seeping down into the subterranean water table, the salt content of the underground waters has increased steadily. Wells that had once sustained entire villages are now undrinkable. Occasionally, when irrigation is especially intensive, or when there are long rains and floods, the water table rises until it reaches the roots of the crops and kills them.

Yet the civilization flourishes. It thrives despite the fact that in the previous thousand years the wheat crop has gradually diminished to only about a sixth of its former abundance. Wheat is intolerant of saline soil, and barley, which is less intolerant, replaces it wherever possible. But by 2500 B.C. yields of many crops are declining. Drainage ditches become clogged with rotting vegetation and provide a shelter for breeding mosquitoes, which multiply in great numbers and spread malaria among the farmers, weakening them so that they are less able to maintain the ditches. The water tables rise ominously, salinity becomes stronger, and the supply of food dwindles even further. In the crowded cities, bacteria thrive on the mix of human debris.

The civilization can survive only if the land remains rich, or if its productivity can be increased, or if the territory under cultivation can be extended. A king of Lagash, Eannatum, finds himself caught between the twin priorities of trying to conserve his irrigation supplies, partially under the control of a northern city-state, Umma, and of fighting expansionist wars. He brings the city-state of Uruk, a near-western neighbor, under his rule. He marches south on Ur and conquers it. He moves east and subjugates the Elamites, a foothill people with pretensions to civilization.

But he needs more cultivated land, with his crop yields declining and his demands rising. He turns his mass of workers to the construction of a great canal. In the middle of this project, the Elamites come down from the hills and attack him. He drives them off and returns to canal work, but before long he must fight two northern city-states, Kish and Akshak, which combine to invade his country. He beats them off, too, only to be hit by the Elamites once more. He smashes them, but is then forced to turn and fight the northerners again. He wins this last battle, but he cannot now finish his canal before his death. His son Entemena completes it and links it up with the Tigris. Because his canal network now joins the Tigris and the Euphrates, he acquires the awesome ability to swell or diminish the flow of either river at will.

The productivity of the soil has provided wealth, but it is an ambiguous blessing to any people lucky enough to possess it. The people of Lagash find themselves forced to pay for both expensive wars and massive public-works programs. There are taxes on divorce, on trade, on production, on income, on death. The penalties for late payment of taxes become more savage, and this is only a step from the outright seizure of livestock, of produce, even of a man's personal belongings. At the same time, war, or its threat, provides an excuse for authoritarian controls, including the draft, travel restrictions, and the erosion of civil liberties.

This repression leads logically to corruption, to periods of reform, to corruption again, and thence to what seems a rational solution of the problem: a coalition, an empire of city-states. A king of Uruk, Lugalzaggisi, subjugates all of Sumer. He says he will bring peace. He will stop the endless boundary disputes, the feuds over irrigation rights. His chroniclers note that all Sumer rejoices under his rule.

But Lugalzaggisi is merely an inspiration to a man with a better idea. Sargon, a Semite, not only seizes united Sumer, but extends his empire from the Persian Gulf to the Mediterranean, and his ships reach India and Africa. He builds the most glittering city on earth, Agade, in the Akkad region, and 5,400 other human beings sit down to eat with him each day. Yet beneath his feet the salt builds up in the soil and there is a melancholy decline in crop yields.

In Entemena's time, about 2400 B.C., the fields were yielding 2,600 liters of barley per hectare. But the power of the soil is declining so rapidly that barbarian conquest, and the rise of Ur-Nammu and his creation of a one-hundred-year renaissance, are anti-climactic. Ur-Nammu builds his marvelous ziggurat, but now, in 2100 B.C., his fields are yielding only 1,460 liters of barley per hectare. By 1750 B.C. Sumer is finished. Babylon, exploiting northern land, becomes pre-eminent.

It would be heartening to record that the Babylonians learn something from Sumer, but they do not. Their power becomes prodigious. Herodotus is astonished by the hundredfold yields of their vast farmlands and by the immensity of their public works, but the salt moves in just the same, and the decline of the farmlands is a mammoth disaster from 1300 to 900 B.C. The locus of the civilization moves even farther north, to Assyria. Amazingly, the term of the good earth's fertility is not over. From about 150 B.C. the Parthians are at work along the Diyala again, and they create a prosperous civilization that continues under the Persians until A.D. 600.

In this period, the mighty Nahrawan Canal is built, an artificial river nearly two hundred miles long, dug in a great semicircle to flank the course of the Tigris, to cross the desert, to bridge other rivers, until it finally rejoins the Tigris one hundred miles south of Baghdad. This fantastic engineering project contributes to the success of the Persian empire, but its life is even shorter than that of the salted southern lands. In five hundred years of cultivation of the Diyala region, the deposit of irrigation silt raises the level of farmlands more than three feet, and the irrigation engineers find it harder and harder to get the grade necessary to keep the water flowing.

By 1100 the water can only reach fields through branch canals flanking the main canal, and gradually towns and cities shrink and disappear. By the time the Abbasside caliphate is nearing its end, the silting of the system is a disaster. When a new Mongol invasion under Hulagu Khan, grandson of Genghis, captures Baghdad in 1258 and kills the last Abbasside caliph, much of the great farmland of the Diyala is again desert.

And this is the way the land is left — silted, salted, desolate. In the south, the average Iraqi gardener, working his vegetable plot on the banks of the Euphrates, raises a meager yield, not one-twentieth of that of his Sumerian predecessors. The modern farmer tilling a field near the ruins of Babylon brings forth a crop that would make Herodotus laugh. The Diyala might yield again, but while ancient Persians could build a two-hundred-mile-long canal, a similar effort would bankrupt Iraq, a country depleted by more than five thousand years of exploitation.

But land *can* be desalinated, and the Food and Agriculture Organization of the United Nations has brought back into production some ancient, salinated farmland in parts of Pakistan's Indus valley, home of another long-dead civilization. FAO experts, working for some years in the Mesopotamian plain, have found about 90 per cent of the arable land to be affected by salt or waterlogging. They have discovered the modern Iraqi farmers to be so far removed from the irrigation techniques of the past that they will have to be trained to work any reclaimed land. And reclamation is a tedious, expensive, and lengthy business of developing pilot areas, of leveling great sections of the plain, of perfecting drainage systems, and of continuing research. The work is under way, but the Iraqi farmer remains a miserable heir to the defeated land.

It is now late afternoon in the desert, and the mounds of old ruins cast squat, ugly shadows. There is just time for me to reach Ur before evening. Ur-Nammu's ziggurat looks even more unlikely, set in its empty landscape with a reddening sky behind it. At the top of the ziggurat again, I watch the sun dropping into the clean red line of the Arabian desert. A jackal appears out of a pool of shadow below.

Lugalzaggisi uttered a prayer when he saw his great empire knit together and working, and the words come to me now: "May the lands lie peacefully in the meadows; may all mankind thrive like plants and herbs; may the sheepfolds . . . increase; the good fortune which has been decreed

for me, may it never alter; unto eternity may I be the foremost shepherd. . . ."

The dream of eternity is itself eternal and does not change from generation to generation. It is seen most clearly among those who strive hardest
for power, for perfection, for improvement. Ur-Nammu earns eternal fame
with his mighty monument, but the landscape is reproachful. I leave the
ziggurat; the sun disappears. Fine phantoms of dust scamper through the
broken bricks of Ur.

CHAPTER EIGHT

Historical Archaeology

Andrew Selkirk
Wendy Selkirk

25 WINCHESTER: THE BROOKS

Historical archaeology is by implication the study of sites where
historical documentation is available to amplify the archaeological
record. The field covers both medieval towns in Europe and abandoned factories of the Industrial Revolution; frontier forts and
colonial settlements are also part of historical archaeology. This
exciting aspect of archaeology has attracted many scholars in recent
years, and some of their activities are reflected in this chapter.
Medieval Winchester has been systematically investigated by a team
of archaeologists under Martin Biddle for several years. Their work
has resulted in the recovery of many lost details of historic
Winchester, a lovely cathedral city in southern England. Andrew and
Wendy Selkirk wrote this general account of a part of medieval
Winchester where historians and archaeologists were able to work
together to produce a detailed interpretation of a series of houses
in a single area of the town. The narrative that follows recounts a
piece of historical archaeology at its best.

What was it like living in a Medieval town? The excavations carried out
in the Brook Street area of Winchester over the past eight years have tried
to find out. This small part of the Medieval town consists of eleven houses,
a row of cottages, and two churches. But since this is a historical period,

From "Winchester: The Brooks," by Andrew Selkirk and Wendy Selkirk, *Current
Archaeology* 20 (1970), 250–255. Reprinted by permission of the authors and Editors of
Current Archaeology, 9 Nassington Road, London. Photographs © copyright Winchester
Excavations Committee and reproduced by courtesy of the Committee.

excavation is not the only source of information and so, side by side with the excavations, extensive research has been carried out by Derek Keene among the Medieval documents with which Winchester is so plentifully endowed. Thus this is a story not only of an excavation, but also of actual people who lived on the site. It is a story not only of Lower Brook Street, but also of Richard Bosynton and his wife Cecilia.

The Brook Street area [Figure 1] has been preserved for the archaeologist by a series of happy accidents. In the first place, the area is very low lying; this means that in the Medieval period when there was a rising water table, there was no temptation to remove floors to level the site and, in fact, the floors may have been laid one on top of another to try to combat the damp. Secondly, the economic slump of the late Medieval period, which caused so many towns to decline, hit Winchester particularly hard. Thus this area was largely abandoned by the 16th century and became gardens and remained as such throughout the Medieval period. It was not until the 19th century that rows of cottages were laid out across the site, but as these had no cellars, they caused little disturbance. However, they have now been demolished, as the area is being redeveloped by the City Corporation which, being one of the most enlightened of our local councils, has agreed to make the space available for long term excavations, supervised by Don Mackreth.

MEDIEVAL INDUSTRY

In the Medieval period the Brook Street site was an industrial part of the town. It was in fact mainly given over to the most typical of the industries of Medieval England, that of cloth working, and in particular cloth finishing by dyeing and fulling. Clean water played a vital part, which is perhaps why the industry centered on this low lying part of the town, for in the Medieval period three brooks ran through the locality, down each of the streets, and special water channels were constructed to lead the water into the houses and the workshops were placed next to them, so that literally running water was laid on. These channels formed one of the most obvious features of the site today. In the post-Medieval period these streets were given the names of: Upper Brook Street, Middle Brook Street, and Lower Brook Street, but in the Medieval period, Lower Brook Street, where the excavations are being carried out, was known as Tanner Street. The name goes back to Saxon origins and when the Medieval cloth finishing industry was at its height the rather dirty process of tanning was carried out further downstream.

The crucial features of the actual block that is now being excavated are the church of St. Mary in Tanner Street, St. Pancras Lane, and Tanner Street, for these allow the topography to be tied up exactly with the documents [Figure 2]. For even though St. Mary's, like the rest of the site, was abandoned by the middle of the 16th century, yet knowledge of its

Figure 1 *The Brooks area was devoted to cloth working, and a series of water-channels brought running water from the streams that ran down the streets into the workrooms at the front of the houses. The street, and the front walls, are to the right of the photo: water entered from the top and ran down through the channels.*

Figure 2 General view of the Brook Street site, at fourteenth century level, seen from the top of a fire-engine ladder. In the center is the little church of St. Mary, with the circular stone base for the font clearly visible at the far end. To the left is Richard Bosynton's house, House IX/X. (The round pit in the middle with a channel leading off it is the remains of a nineteenth century steeping vat.) To the right of the church is first the little lane that led down to the church (with another nineteenth century pit in the middle of it), and then the row of four cottages. Beyond them is St. Pancras Lane, and to the extreme right is House 12. Along the bottom the chalk-lined water channels can be seen.

position still remained, and was recorded in the early 19th century. The church lies conveniently right in the middle of the site. The three houses that lie to the south of the church, Houses I, IX, and X, can to some extent be regarded as a single block together with the church. Indeed until 1407, houses IX and X were united. House I suffers, from the archaeological point of view, in that it was the first house in the area to be excavated — in 1962 as a rescue dig — and it now lies under the new road called Friarsgate. The house is particularly important as it had a substantial stone built hall of the 12th century to the rear. This, after the church, was the earliest stone building within the excavations. Indeed it is possible that originally in Saxon times these three houses and the church formed a single block consisting of a hall, private chapel, and work places. By the time of the survey of 1148, however, there were as many individual houses along Tanner Street as at any time later in the Middle Ages, so this must remain purely an hypothesis to be tested in the coming years as the Anglo-Saxon levels are reached [Figure 3].

The basic form of all these houses was similar. Fronting the street were the workrooms and shops, with water channels coming in through the front walls. The domestic quarters or storerooms lay behind, or on the floor above. In the 12th century, House I was the prosperous house, with a stone hall behind and a large workroom at right angles to the hall lying along the street frontage. However, as the Middle Ages progressed, House I declined in status while that of House IX appears to have risen. Unfortunately the boundary between Houses I and IX lies underneath the modern pavement and so the actual line remains uncertain. But by the Late Middle Ages, the stone hall of House I had been rebuilt in a much flimsier fashion while the workrooms had been reduced in size. Meanwhile House IX was expanding and was rebuilt across the site of House X (Rooms IX, 5 and X, 5) [Figure 4]. In the earlier period this seems to have been an open courtyard where bronze working took place right up against the wall of the church. In 1407 House IX/X was divided into two houses. The deed which still survives not only gives us valuable dating evidence and the details of the layout of the ground level rooms and upper floor, but also a valuable insight into the typical Winchester citizen who was living on the site.

Richard Bosynton, who divided House IX/X was in his way quite an important person, being one of the leading members of the fulling community in Winchester, and we can build up quite a picture of his activities from the documents. The first reference to him occurs in 1366 by which time he had already acquired his house in Tanner Street. In 1374/5 he held a minor civic post, being a bailiff of the 24, and by 1380/81 he had risen to being City Cofferer, that is City Treasurer. In 1390, he was fined six pence for throwing *wodgor* or dyers refuse in the stream which gives us vital evidence that he was engaged in dyeing as well as fulling. Indeed such fines for polluting the streams are an important indicator of who was involved in the dyeing industry in Medieval Winchester. But his best known exploit came in the summer of 1377. This was the year of the great French scare, when invasion was thought to be imminent, and Richard, being a forceful character, led a direct action group of his fellow fullers and other inhabitants of the Brooks area, and they went down to Durngate, broke down the bridge over the river, and blocked up the gate. This was all very well and patriotic, but when the scare subsided the people who lived just outside the gate and who depended on it for access to the city, objected. Richard was hauled off to court and the gate was unblocked.

By 1407 he was an old man, and it appears that he decided to retire from business and to split the property, keeping House X for himself and selling off House IX. The deed, which fortunately survives, gives an exact description of what House X looked like. In the front there was a rather

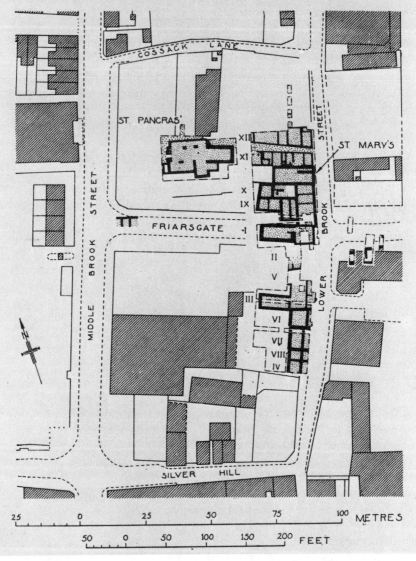

WINCHESTER
THE BROOKS SITES
1962-69

Figure 3

narrow shop (Room X, 5) with a chalk lined channel in front (F86) coming in under the front wall. Above it was a solar, that is the living quarters — a salutary warning to archaeologists that living quarters may well be on the first floor. Behind the shop was the kitchen (X, 4) and behind that, in line with the kitchen under one roof was another building (Room 3). Behind this was a small curtilage or courtyard. It was probably in this courtyard that the rack (tentorium) was situated on which cloths were stretched out to dry in the fulling process.

Having divided the house, Richard Bosynton did not live there for long, for in 1409 he entered the hospital of St. John where he was paid a pension of eight pence a week from the hospital funds. When he died we do not know, but thanks to the documents and the excavations, he and his wife Cecilia have become two of the best known inhabitants of Medieval Winchester.

To modern eyes the little church of St. Mary in Tanner Street presents something of a mystery. Just what was it there for? There were nearly 50 parish churches in Medieval Winchester, yet the Cathedral alone could accommodate most of the population. But a well organized church can be a highly profitable affair, as some of the more extreme modern sects have shown, and certainly from this point of view the church in Medieval England was very well organized and highly profitable. Thus a church like St. Mary's, established perhaps as a private chapel in the Late Saxon

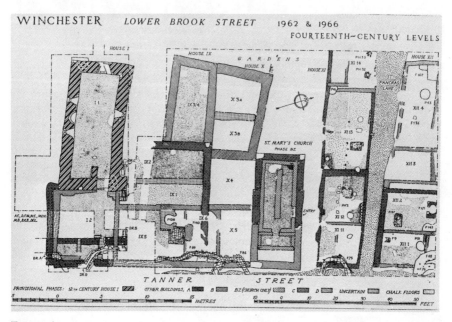

Figure 4

period, could become fully viable in the Medieval period, supported merely by the inhabitants of the immediate area. It is interesting to note that at one stage the church had two doors, and although the main one on the north side led out into a small lane, the other — and possibly the earlier — led directly into the area of House X. It may in fact have dated from before the construction of House X when the area was just an open yard; it was later blocked, but it does suggest that in the earlier stages the church may have been closely connected with the stone built hall of House I [Figure 5].

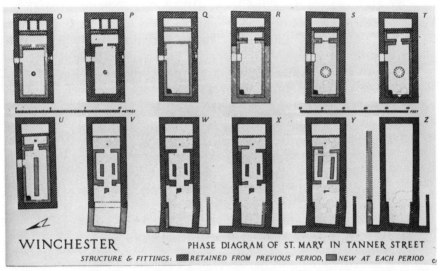

WINCHESTER   PHASE DIAGRAM OF ST. MARY IN TANNER STREET

STRUCTURE & FITTINGS: ▨ RETAINED FROM PREVIOUS PERIOD, ▨ NEW AT EACH PERIOD

Figure 5   The little rectangular church had its altar at the top (the east end), separated from the chancel by a screen. In the early phases there were two steps leading up to the altar, and benches round the walls of the church. In phase S a circular sump for the font appears. In phase U there is a central bench, replaced in phase V by elaborate choir stalls. In the later phases the church begins to encroach on the derelict properties, on either side, but by 1528 it too was abandoned.

Two factors make the church exceptionally suitable for the archaeologist. Firstly, since there was only one burial in the church the stratification is remarkably intact; the church went out of use before burials became common in Winchester parish churches. Secondly, perhaps because the area was low lying and swampy, the floor was often made up so that the archaeologists have already gone down over a meter in the 300 years they have explored so far.

The church seems to have been built in the Late Saxon period, with an apsidal east end — which is already peeping through the lowest layers so far reached. However, by the 12th century, it had a square end. The altar at the east end, nearest to the stream, was raised by two steps above the level of the rest of the church, and the altar base of the 12th century church still survives. The main feature of the earliest churches were benches around the walls on which the weak and elderly could sit — hence the phrase "the weakest go to the wall." At first these benches were flimsy affairs held in position by stakes, but in a later phase proper stone benches were built. The position of the font in the middle of the church can be seen in some of these 13th century stages only as a circular sump; in later phases a stepped chalk base appears.

During the 14th century, first a central bench was built and the font moved to the wall. When the church was extended to the west, elaborate choir stalls were built in the eastern half of the church. In the latest phases the church was enlarged and encroached onto the derelict properties on either side.

The economic decline of Winchester and particularly the Brooks area in the 15th century is surprisingly contrasted by the expansion of the remaining parish churches and a new vigor in parochial life. But the slump continued and the church was abandoned in the early 16th century. In 1528 the parish was united with that of St. Maurice, so the church must have gone out of use by this time.

North of the church lay a row of four cottages which opened onto St. Pancras Lane to their north. The cottages were owned by the Frary and Kalendar, a religious fraternity. The cottages appear to have been built in the middle of the 13th century, perhaps as a speculative development to house lower class workers. The cottage at the east end was probably a workshop for it had a channel entering it from the stream. But the other three cottages were simple dwelling houses. At first they were virtually identical, but during the succeeding centuries they went through a complex series of developments, becoming amalgamated at one time into a pair of houses, but by the middle of the 16th century they too had been deserted.

The cottages opened onto St. Pancras Lane, a narrow lane that led down to the church of St. Pancras [Figure 6]. This was a large church in the middle of the block, lying only 50 yds. away from St. Mary's. Last summer the Winchester team began excavating there too in order to compare it with St. Mary's. The differences are already obvious; it is bigger but with less depth of stratification than St. Mary's, for being in the middle of the block it was able to expand laterally.

North of St. Pancras Lane we come to House XII, and the sad story of John Shovelar, who lived there from about 1370 until he was evicted by William Bolt in 1402, as part of a long and complex legal tangle. It is hard to avoid the impression that John Shovelar was something of a feckless character, for our main information comes from the fines imposed upon him: encroaching on St. Pancras Lane; thatching an outhouse with straw (a serious offence in fire prone Medieval cities); or for erecting a public urinal on his property — urine being a vital ingredient in the fulling process, for it acted as a kind of soap. William Bolt, on the other hand,

Figure 6   This row of cottages faced out on St. Pancras Lane, which runs diagonally from the ... right. The cottages were built to a common design: the main door led out onto St. Pancras Lane, while a back door directly opposite led out onto St. Mary's Lane. In the corner opposite each front door is a small compartment which may have been the bedroom. Part of St. Mary's church can be seen in the top left.

was a thrusting and successful businessman; he had a thriving cloth finishing business, and was twice elected mayor. The lawsuit was a complex one, but it seems to turn on whether a transaction way back in 1339 was an outright sale or a lease.

The 14th century was a period of change in the tenure of property in Winchester, and the distinction between outright sale and lease was often obscure. At any event, in 1402, John Shovelar was ejected from his home; in 1404 Bolt strengthened his title by selling the house to trustees and then buying it back again; and finally, as the matter was still not settled, in 1408 he went up to Westminster where the case was finally and definitely settled in his favor. What became of the miserable John Shovelar we do not know; he passes from history, defeated.

Only a small portion of House XII is in the excavation area, so we cannot tell how far the whole property was subdivided. But the portion available seems similar to those to the south, with a workshop in front and living rooms behind. The workroom forms a very interesting example of a dyeing works. At one stage an area of cobbling led from the water channel which came in through the front wall of the house to a dyeing vat and a large open hearth in the workroom. It was clear that water was taken from the stream, boiled up in cauldrons over the open hearths, and then poured into dyeing vats kept boiling by a small fire underneath.

With the help of the documentary sources we can even build up a picture of what these houses looked like. The majority were built of timber throughout the whole period, but there was a considerable advance in sophistication. Before the 14th century, the timbers were set in a trench cut into the damp earth where it soon rotted. But by the 14th century, the practice grew up of building a low wall on which the timber frame could be set high and dry above the ground. The best example for the introduction of these "ground walls" can be seen in the accounts for the hospital of St. John, where throughout the 14th century, the expenditure on the repair and maintenance of these ground walls becomes more and more frequent. In this way, documents and excavation linked closely together can combine to build up a remarkably full picture of life in a Medieval town.

Bernard L. Fontana

26   THE UNRESPECTABLE IN AMERICAN ARCHAEOLOGY

Bernard L. Fontana has for many years studied the Indian cultures of the American Southwest and has taken an active interest in historical archaeology and all kinds of artifacts. His article "Bottles, Buckets, and Horseshoes" deserves a wide readership because it is a plea for serious study of artifacts of recent antiquity, which lie in profusion in the cultural landscape. Artifacts of non-Indian origin abound in rubbish dumps, junkyards, and antique stores. Many of these artifacts are regarded with mild tolerance or even with contempt by some archaeologists, who study older sites and artifacts of different types and traditions. Yet, as Fontana points out, the information that can be obtained from an apparently miscellaneous pile of junk is often of critical historical value. The abandoned junk of a century ago can be an admirable training ground for archaeologists interested in the development of artifacts and technological innovations. To quote the author: "Is there really anything to be learnt from a crown bottle cap?" This paper contains many useful references for those interested in studying non-Indian artifacts.

When I was a boy growing up in northern California, one of my favorite things to do was to take my dog and wander down to the town dump that lay between the levee and the Feather River. While my dog chased the huge rats whose baronial manor this was, I poked about in whatever piles of junk I could find that had been left by people the week before. The caretaker of the place, an old man who subsisted largely by selling a few salvageable goods, used to laugh at me. I never brought anything home. I never found anything. But now I know it was because I didn't know what I was looking for. It was simply the looking that mattered.

And just a few weeks ago I found myself contemplating a pile of rusty iron scraps, horseshoes, broken bottles, rotted tin cans, and other such mundane remnants of an Arizona military post occupied from 1861 to 1873. Outloud I wondered why more scholarly attention had not been paid to this kind of cultural hardware, and a colleague was quick to say, "Because people would laugh at you, that's why."

There was the keeper of the town dump, laughing. Here are the historians of culture doing likewise. There arises a suspicion that it is a kind of self-conscious, almost nervous laughter. It is one thing to have someone poke around in an Indian's junk pile; it is quite another to have someone poking around in our own back yard. It is almost as if we don't want our tee-totalling neighbors to discover those empty wine bottles we threw out last week. Are we embarrassed by our immediate past? Are we concerned that someone will remind us that this past, ignobly represented by decaying tin and purpling glass, had no future but our present?

There is, as Thoreau reminds us, something melancholy in antiquity. There is something melancholy about the village dump; about the falling adobe walls where men of the U.S. Seventh Cavalry swore and labored and loved before Taps was sounded on that final evening; about the low mounds of earth which mark the remains of a late-19th century ranch house; about the slowly desiccating wooden shell where a 20-stamp mill once crushed silver and gold from its matrix of rock.

We cannot dissolve this melancholy with laughter. It is useless to pretend that these exuviae with which our culture covered itself belonged to someone else. Indeed, Thoreau tells us that, "Nothing so restores and humanizes antiquity and makes it blithe as the discovery of some natural sympathy between it and the present" (Thoreau 1960:8)....

From "Bottles, Buckets, and Horseshoes: The Unrespectable in American Archaeology" by Bernard L. Fontana, *Keystone Folklore Quarterly*, 13, 3 (1968), 171–184. Reprinted by permission of the author and The Pennsylvania Folklore Society.

Most archaeologists I know concern themselves with prehistoric sites archaeology. When they see me examining an old harness buckle or a square cut nail and ask what I'm doing, I enjoy telling them I am doing the same thing they are doing, only with considerably more data at hand to support whatever conclusions might be reached.

Elsewhere I have proposed a fivefold classification of historic sites, those called protohistoric, contact, postcontact, frontier, and nonaboriginal historic locations; the latter two are types of nonaboriginal historic settlements (Fontana 1965a). This classification, however, has not been accepted, either because it appeared in print only a short time ago or, more likely, because it simply is not going to be accepted. There has instead grown up a kind of folk classification of historic sites, and we hear of colonial ruins versus what has been called "tin-can archaeology." The former in the United States refers to nonaboriginal places occupied during the colonial period of our history, whether these sites be English, Dutch, French, Spanish, Russian, or Swedish in origin. The latter, tin-can archaeology, has its referent in sites occupied during the 19th century, especially those occupied in the last half of the 1800's. Our antipathy toward such archaeology is in part betrayed in the label commonly applied to many abandoned 19th century villages: "ghost town."

Rather than dividing ourselves into "colonial-period archaeologists" and "ghost town archaeologists," it is perhaps more useful to think in terms of the manufacture of the artifacts we find on our respective sides of the time line. In this way we become "pre-interchangeable parts archaeologists" or "post-interchangeable parts archaeologists." The pre-interchangeable parts man is concerned with free-blown glass and hand-wrought iron. His is a world of individual creativity. Each product, while related to others, had its own unique quality and appearance. Goods were hand-crafted, sometimes with the aid of machines and of molds, but essentially hand-crafted nonetheless. There was a kind of personal relationship between an object and its maker. What we find in the pre-interchangeable parts era is a continuum of gradual development leading from simple, hand-held, primary stone tools to such sophisticated artifacts as exquisite glasswork and intricately-designed firearms of the 17th and 18th centuries. It may seem bold to compare a simple Olduvai stone chopping tool with a 16th century German petronel, but both are alike in that each had a single maker who relied on his manual dexterity.

In the 1720's one Christopher Polhem of Sweden began to make gears for clocks by using machinery and precision measurement to insure interchangeability. From this modest beginning there eventually grew one of the most underrated revolutions in the history of man's technology: the era of assembly line production and of interchangeable parts. In the United States it is usually Eli Whitney who is credited with the successful innovation of assembly line production. Whitney contracted with the United States government in June, 1798, to deliver an unprecedented 20,000 arms by December, 1801. He failed, however, to complete his contract until 1809. What came to be known in the 1850's as the "American system of manufacturing" can more properly be attributed to a Maine gunsmith named John Hancock Hall. Hall not only devised a breech loading firearm that is named for him, but he engineered the machinery to produce it on an assembly line. His equipment was installed at the Harpers Ferry Armory in 1817 (Woodbury, 1960). According to Harold Petersen (1962:169): "Hall's were the first completely interchangeable arms in America and quite possibly the first in the world. His contribution to arms manufacturing technique far exceeded his breech design and his work became a milestone in all industrial history."

It is to be hoped that the archaeologists who are eventually to excavate the armory at Harpers Ferry will be made duly aware of the measure of their responsibility. They will, after all, be digging up the cradle of the American industrial revolution. It is here that man's stride quickened its pace — whether forward or backward only time can tell. But what cannot be gainsaid is that at Harpers Ferry there was an enormous increase in the amount of energy put under control for utilization by men.

Viewed in this way it becomes difficult to sympathize with the bemused disdain with which literary historians and most archaeologists regard bottles, buckets, and horseshoes of the last half of the 19th century. These are the products of increasing division and specialization of labor. These are the bits of glass and steel and iron worked in such inventions as Frederick von Siemens' regenerative gas furnace. These are the signals marking the slow death of hand crafts, the symbols of mechanization and the impersonalizing of the relationship between creator and created. If in the sixth decade of the 20th century the phrase "Man the Tool Maker" has been replaced by "Tools, the Man Maker," it is to the same decade a hundred years ago that we need turn if we are to understand how this has come to pass. The secret is there among the tin cans, among the square cut and wire nails.

Because so little attention has been paid the study of non-Indian American-made artifacts of the last half of the 19th century, anyone proposing to teach the subject must chart his own course. And an unusual course it is sure to be.

Students must first of all be made to realize that we are talking about tools. Students who are willing to measure 10,000 stone projectile points become less skeptical about examining a rusted shovel blade when they learn that in 1879 one American manufacturer offered more than 50 distinct types for sale, each with a different shape and intended for a different use (Oliver Ames & Sons, 1879). They begin to see a kind of kinship between their prehistoric classification schemes and the classifications of tools promulgated by more modern American producers. And if they stay with it long enough, they discover that ketchup bottles, like yucca-fiber sandals, were made, distributed, and ultimately used by man. The rules of innovation, discovery, diffusion, acceptance, rejection, integration, adaptation, and of reinterpretation — whatever these rules may be — are not arbitrarily subject to change. Hand-crafted or machine-made, there is a level of analysis at which a tool is still a tool. Even assembly-line machine-made goods are subject to stylistic changes, as witness the evolution of the 20th century automobile. Somebody, some human being has to design the machines. It may do well, therefore, to inquire what important qualitative differences there are between pottery styles and the styles of the late 19th century suspender clasps.

Another part of the student's training involves the now-difficult process of acquainting him with the material culture of the late 19th century in something like an original context. It is the historic archaeologist who may at last heed the dictum of Diderot (1959:1:ix):

> Let us at last give the artisans their due. The liberal arts have adequately sung their own praises; they must now use their remembering voice to celebrate the mechanical arts. It is for the liberal arts to lift the mechanical arts from the contempt in which prejudice has for so long held them. . . . We need a man to rise up in the academies and go down to the workshop and gather material about the arts to be set out in a book which will persuade artisans to read, philosophers to think on useful lines, and the great to make at least some worthwhile use of their authority and their wealth.

Students need to be taken to the blacksmith's shop and, if a coal-fueled open forge can any longer be found, shown how wrought iron is worked into shapes. They should see the casting of metals; the blowing of glass. They should learn from a farrier about the intricacies of types of horseshoes; from a cabinet maker about nails; from a bricklayer about the ways in which walls can be adjoined on their corners. They should, if possible, visit an old farm and see old tools, buckles, straps, and bits of harnesses lying about — and learn from the farmer what they were used for. Rare is the archaeologist who knows traces from hip straps, bellybands from hames.

In Tucson, Arizona, we probably have one of the finest single collections of wagons and carriages in the world in our Rodeo Parade Equipment Museum. Here students can see the difference between a closed top physician's stanhope and an end spring buggy — not to mention literally dozens of other varieties of horse-drawn vehicles. They can examine the parts in detail and can imagine what might be left of these conveyances in an archaeological context. The metal parts are mainly what survive, and the only way to learn their use is to see them in place on an intact carriage.

Just as prehistorians should insist their students try their hands at chipping stone tools or making some earthenware pottery, so should we insist that students have some kind of first hand exposure to methods of manufacture and to whole and complete products of America's industrial revolution.

Once students have recovered from the shock of realization that they can dig up and analyze our own material culture as well as that of some Indian, they are ready to go to work to identify the hardware.

The identification of historic artifacts need not, like the identification of prehistoric artifacts, rest on analogy. The best and most reliable sources of identification of late 19th century goods are trade catalogues. These invaluable books offer a pictorial history of our own technology (see, for example, Kimbark 1876; Hibbard and others 1891; Pharmaceutical Era 1900). Unlike the cumbersome, if indispensable, records of the U.S. Patent Office, trade catalogues show us those things which were actually made and distributed. Too many Patent Office drawings are of things that might have been, but never were.

Unfortunately, trade catalogues are difficult to find. Most were discarded when the year in which they were issued passed by, and few, if any major libraries in the United States have had the foresight to collect these prime sources of technological history. As a matter of fact, I know of one head librarian of a major university who shares the view of his acquisitions librarian that trade catalogues somehow are not books. He does not want to buy trade catalogues; he does not want to house them. The academic taint placed on tin cans and nails spreads to catalogues which describe them. Parochialism strikes in unlikely places.

Catalogues, of course, can be found. A perusal of Lawrence Romaine's (1960) *A Guide to American Trade Catalogues* acquaints us with the scope of possibilities. The Smithsonian Institution probably has the largest trade catalogue collection in the world. And in Arizona we are particularly fortunate in that we have with us one of the great pioneers in historic archaeology, Arthur Woodward, and his incomparably fine private library filled with catalogues and other identification resources.

Not that catalogues are the only place to look up that buggy part or snaffle bit. Illustrated advertisements in magazines, newspapers, and trade journals are a help in research. Encyclopedias, dozens of journals and books concern themselves with antiques, and specialty items like bottle collectors' guide and books on the history of firearms or of metallic cartridges cannot be dispensed with. For identification of objects found in military posts there are hundreds of government publications and almost as many written by military history buffs that enable one to chase down everything from the date of issue of a snap from the head of a picket post to the inclusive dates of an enlisted man's coat button.

My impression is that most books about antiques are not what they should be for our purposes. Antique collectors prefer either the fine, the elegant, the expensive, or the cute, the unusual, the unique. The tin-can archaeologist usually is trying to identify the ordinary, the everyday, the commonplace. The average citizen did not eat from Wedgwood's finest; keep his flowers in a Tiffany vase; or surround himself with Empire furniture. He instead ordered his goods from a trade catalogue, those very catalogues now in such short supply.

Finally, most cities have a range of experts in various fields who are ready to help archaeologists with their knottier identification problems, and most cities have museums of history where fragmentary objects can be compared with whole specimens.

Once we have identified our tin-can treasures we are confronted with the problem of historical analysis. The histories of everything from horseshoes to thimbles can be uncovered if a student is willing to look long enough and to use his imagination in looking. There are virtually no guide lines to follow. Important data have a way of turning up in the least suspected places. The best source concerning the pottery manufacturing history for Ohio, for example, is bulletin number 26 of the Geological Survey of Ohio, a report entitled *Coal Formation Clays*. Here are listed all of Ohio's pottery manufacturers, their locations, their inclusive dates, and lists of their various products, whether marbles, tablewear, or sewer pipe (Stout 1923).

One of the most complete descriptions of turn-of-this-century bottle factories I have seen is in a book by John Spargo, one of the founders of the American Socialist Party. His book, *The Bitter Cry of the Children*, is an exposé of child labor abuses in early 20th century America. It seems that small manufacturers of bottles were among the most abusive employers in this respect, and in documenting his case, Spargo tells us a great deal about how bottles were made at the time (Anonymous 1906).

The proper place to begin a search, of course, is in the voluminous collection of bibliographic aids to be found in most large libraries. There are the various Library of Congress catalogues; the *Cumulative Book Index;* the *Reader's Guide;* the *Industrial Arts Index;* the *British Museum General Catalogue of Printed Books;* the *International Index;* and others too numerous to mention. There are also specialized bibliographies to consider, such as Eugene Ferguson's, "Contributions to Bibliography in the History of Technology," which has appeared in several issues of *Technology and Culture* (Ferguson, 1962–1965), and the "Check List of Recently Published Articles and Books on Glass," which has appeared in each volume of the *Journal of Glass Studies* since its inception (Buechner, Perrot, and Saldern, 1959, 1960; Perrot and Saldern, 1961, 1962; Perrot, 1963, 1964, 1965). If the latter is used in conjunction with George S. Duncan's (1960) *Bibliography of Glass*, a student can compile a useful list of references to such things as bottles and beads in a very short time.

Further obvious sources of material culture history are innumerable histories of technology and of manufacturing (Beckmann, 1797; Bishop, 1864;

Bolles, 1881; Butterworth, 1892; Chambers, 1728; Derry and Williams, 1961; Diderot, 1959; Diderot and Alembert, 1758; Dunsheath, 1951; Forbes, 1958; Greeley, 1872; Habakkuk, 1962; Knight, 1882; Lilley, 1948; Oliver, 1956; Singer and others, 1954–1958; Swank, 1884; Usher, 1929; Wilson, 1963); encyclopedia articles; specialized histories such as Warren C. Scoville's (1948) *Revolution in Glassmaking* or Henry D. and Frances T. McCallum's (1965) treatise on barbed wire, *The Wire That Fenced the West;* and government documents. The latter are catalogued in *A Descriptive Catalogue of the Government Publications,* a resource which has undergone name changes since publication of the 1774-to-1881 volume in 1885. *The American State Papers* afford another historic tool, in that much of the data on American tariffs is contained in them for the period 1789 through 1838. Tariff laws, fluctuation in tariff rates, and congressional testimony regarding tariffs afford a kind of index to the production of American-made goods.

Thus far one of the least fruitful sources for the identification and history of American-made and used goods of the last half of the 19th century has been the archaeological site report. Notable exceptions are a few of the River Basin Survey reports published by the Smithsónian Institution and in other series (see, for example, Mattes, 1960; Miller, 1960; Osborne, 1957; G. H. Smith, 1954, 1960a, 1960b; C. S. Smith, 1954); occasional articles in the *Florida Anthropologist;* and the Arizona Archaeological and Historical Society's study of *Johnny Ward's Ranch* (Fontana and others, 1962; Fontana, 1965b). A quick look at any extensive historic sites archaeology bibliography indicates that pre-interchangeable parts sites have been dug and reported on in a ratio of at least 10 to 1 to tin-can archaeological ruins.

Some archaeologists have argued conversationally that since we have abundant written documentation for 19th century history there is nothing to be gained from analyzing the artifacts. And in a somewhat different context, psychologist Jerome Bruner recently noted:

> A further speculation about preparation for change is that we are bound to move toward instruction in the sciences of behavior and away from the study of history. Recorded history is only about 5,000 years old. . . . Most of what we teach is within the last few centuries, for the records before that are minimal while the records after are relatively rich. But just suppose that the richness of records increases as a function of our ability to develop systems for storing and retrieving information. A thousand years from now we may be swamped. One would surely not dwell then with such loving care over the details of Brumaire or the Long Parliament or the Louisiana Purchase. These are the furbelows of documentary short supply . . . (Bruner, 1966: 103).

I think that Bruner, if we can accept the narrow definition of history implied in his remarks, is correct. I also think that archaeologists who believe we have adequate documentation for late 19th century technological history are themselves thinking of history in a narrow way. One would hope that prehistoric studies should culminate eventually in more than a mere literary chronicle of man's past. We cannot re-create the past; but we can pluck from history those timeless and transcendental elements that help us to know who we are.

In closing, I would like to mention one or two concrete ways in which our study of bottles, buckets, and horseshoes can be meaningful.

In the past few years there has been a fair amount of discussion among archaeologists concerning the nature and limitations of archaeological inference (see, for example, Thompson, 1956, 1958:1–8). M. A. Smith has challenged Sir Mortimer Wheeler's dictum that ". . . the archaeological excavator is not digging up things, he is digging up people." She has asserted that ". . . it follows that since historical events and the essential social divisions of prehistoric people don't find an adequate expression in material remains, it cannot be right to try to arrive at a knowledge of them in archaeological interpretation" (M. A. Smith, 1955).

Many of the arguments pro and contra the limits of inference and analogy could be tested in historic sites. In southern Arizona, for example, there is an abandoned mining camp, a veritable ghost town, called Austerlitz. It was begun in 1869 by two French brothers who gave the place its name. The site has been carefully mapped and the history of nearly every structure has been accounted for. It is known who constructed which buildings when; who owned the mine at various times; who lived in which houses; what the national and ethnic origins of most of the town's inhabitants were; who was rich and who was poor; and, in short, what the detailed history of this place was.

It would now be possible to excavate the remains of the town, to plot the footings of the old buildings, and to save every artifact with its archaeological provenience. Here, then, is an opportunity to make an archaeological reconstruction of Austerlitz — without consulting the detailed documented history — and to compare the two products at the project's end. The archaeologists, in other words, should not be told what is known of the site's past; they should be left to interpret it for themselves on the basis of material culture remains. In this way we could get a closer look at questions of inference and analogy; we could see what archaeologists are doing correctly, and why; we could see where archaeologists might be going astray. Historic sites, well-documented ones, are the only such sites which afford these kinds of possibilities. We shall never be able to answer questions about the limits of inference and analogy so long as we dig only sites whose analyses depend on inference and analogy.

Speaking in more general terms, a proper study of tin cans and nails goes far beyond their mere identification and dating. Physical anthropologists have spilled a lot of printer's ink over the matter of the relationship among the opposable thumb, brain convolutions, erect gait, and tools. As interesting as the problem of the biological emergence of man may be, how much more interesting — and complex — is the relationship between man and his tools in this era of interchangeable parts. This is to say nothing of the physical environment, and questions of what we are taking from and doing to this environment, and questions of what we are taking from and doing to this environment with our tools. Air and water pollution; the depletion of natural resources; contamination of the earth's upper atmosphere — what are these if not matters involving man and his material culture? It is strange that anthropologists whose intellectual province has long included man, social relationships, tools, and environment have not become more involved in some of these modern concerns.

What is so-called automation if not an age of tools, too many tools, perhaps? International Business Machines Corporation has given Harvard University a $5,000,000 grant to undertake a 10-year study of the effects of rapid technological change on the economy, on public policies, and on the character of society (Mesthene, 1965). Should not there be historians of 19th century technology with an interest in such matters? Who better might be able to discern the general nature of the connection between man and his tools in the present era?

It will strike the common man that we are asking too much from the study of piles of junk. Is there really anything to be learned from a crown bottle cap? From a piece of Homer Laughlin's "Hotel China"?

I agree with Alfred Kidder that "... archaeological knowledge will be broader, and many problems not now even suspected are sure to arise" (Kidder, 1925:223). New ideas and deeper insights are where we find them. No horseshoe, no bit of ironstone should be left scornfully unturned. For these reasons, and more, there should be no unrespectable in American archaeology.

Part Four

ARCHAEOLOGY–ITS FUTURE

"Without a sense of history, and of historical problem, archaeology can revert again to mere collection; and there is always a danger of a new antiquarianism."

Glyn Daniel, A Hundred Years of Archaeology.

"Is There a Future for the Past?"

Hester Davis, Archaeology.

INTRODUCTION

Two major crises exist in mid-twentieth-century archaeology, and the articles in Part Four touch on these. Both are urgent in different ways: one is a matter of professional orientation, the other a major public scandal.

In the flurry of digging up the past at an unprecedented rate, archaeologists have tended to give little thought to the future academic direction of their discipline. The past twenty years have seen a proliferation of new dating methods, quantitative techniques, and a pervasive concern with explaining the past, using systems models and more sophisticated theoretical models for interpretation and analysis than ever before. Long-term objectives have often been buried under the excitement of discovery and analysis.

Nineteenth-century archaeologists had no doubts where archaeology lay. For some it was a search for artistic treasures

313

and interesting artifacts that could be set in museum cases and classified with increasing precision. Others regarded archaeology as a descriptive science, which could write the history of prehistoric man.

From the latter school a strong humanistic feeling developed within archaeology, and this was reflected in major attempts at cultural-historical reconstructions of world prehistory. V. Gordon Childe's work on Near Eastern and European prehistory is a classic example, as is Grahame Clark's pioneer World Prehistory. In the New World, the research of Gordon Willey, Michael Coe, and others is closely tied to anthropological research, but it is also concerned with the reconstruction of culture history on a large scale in North America.

But the technically oriented studies of recent decades have concentrated on explanation and processes of culture change at the local level, sometimes to the exclusion of broader issues in archaeology, the major historical issues of world prehistory. Archaeology is regarded as part of anthropology. Many of its methods are related to those of the natural sciences. Some experienced archaeologists, like Jacquetta Hawkes, are deeply worried by this trend. Her recent essay on the subject, which is both provocative and controversial, is the first selection in this part. Glynn Isaac, a well-known authority on the archaeology of early man, challenges many of her statements in a thought-provoking response, which follows. Both articles are symptomatic of the academic crisis in archaeology today.

The public crisis in archaeology stems in part from agricultural and industrial development and in part from the continuation of the collecting traditions of nineteenth-century archaeology. For centuries, mankind has had an uncontrollable urge to own and collect antiquities of all descriptions. Early Chinese emperors acquired bronzes from the tombs of earlier rulers. European scholars and landowners went on the Mediterranean Grand Tour and brought back all manner of art objects from Greece and Italy. Lord Elgin's acquisition of the so-called Elgin marbles from the Parthenon is a case in point. Nineteenth-century looters like Giovanni Belzoni raped Egypt of her antiquities, which they sold to wealthy museums and collectors in Europe. Such looting and grave robbing has continued in Turkey, Cyprus, Italy, and Mesoamerica at an unprecedented rate in this century, with incalculable damage to serious archaeological inquiry.

The control of this despicable looting is extremely difficult, for even stringent antiquities laws cannot cure mankind's inherent greed for personal possessions and financial gain. Regrettably, the United States is not one of those nations with rigorous antiquities regulations. As a result, pothunters and treasure seekers have done irreparable harm to many of the most important archaeological sites in North America, and their nefarious activities continue unchecked.

As serious, however, is the destruction of archaeological sites during agricultural work, dam building, road construction, and industrial development. Patrick McGimsey, an archaeologist residing in Arkansas, has estimated that at least 25 percent of the sites in that state have been destroyed by agricultural and other activity, to say nothing of looters, within the past ten years. As he points out (1972:7), "This nation's past is contained in the soil. That soil is being disturbed and redistributed at an ever increasing rate. Those of us alive today will be the last ever to see any significant portion of it in an undisturbed state." McGimsey goes so far as to take the position that no one may "act in such a manner such that the public right to knowledge of the past is unduly endangered or destroyed" (1972:10).

He is right, for unless we act more responsibly there will soon be no archaeological sites left. To quote McGimsey again: "Archaeology presents the public with a problem which, unlike so many, will disappear completely, if they continue to ignore it." The public crisis in archaeology is simple: we cannot allow the past to have no future. All of us are constantly faced with the temptation to own or to destroy a critical part of our national heritage for personal gain or gratification. Not only is federal and state legislation needed, but we have to live responsibly in archaeological terms.

CHAPTER NINE

Archaeology ... Where Next?

Jacquetta Hawkes

27 THE PROPER STUDY OF MANKIND

The last twenty years have seen a massive injection of new scientific
aids into archaeological research. These include new dating methods,
statistical techniques, computers, electronic detection techniques,
and a whole new body of theoretical information. Archaeological
literature has become increasingly complex and jargon-filled. The
amount of detail resulting from more rigorous excavations and
new quantitative approaches is such that the broader issues of
archaeology are often submerged in trivia. British archaeologist
Jacquetta Hawkes, a veteran archaeological writer with a historical
approach to prehistory, has written an eloquent paper on what to
her were dangerous trends in archaeology toward a marriage with
the natural sciences and away from the humanities. She strongly
pleads that archaeological technology be prevented from overwhelming the subject, so that young scholars of "strong historical
imagination" may be attracted to archaeology.

In that highly successful Pinter film, *The Servant,* a rich and dashing
master is undermined and then dominated and destroyed by a young man
who in the opening scenes was his humble and hard-working servant. The
betrayal is gradual, insidious, and inevitable.

Many people, and they are not reactionaries or even conservatives, feel
that mankind is threatening itself with a similar fate. We have taken technology into our service to save us from labor and provide every comfort,

From "The Proper Study of Mankind" by Jacquetta Hawkes, *Antiquity* 42 (1968),
255–262. Reprinted with permission of the author and the Editor of *Antiquity*.

and now are in danger of surrendering to its power. Only a conscious effort to change direction can save us from denying our best values, all that is most distinctively human, to "please" the megamachine.

I have recently found myself wondering whether archaeology may not be moving toward such a surrender. Are not very strong forces enticing the subject from its allegiance to the humanities and trying to make it look as much as possible like one of the natural sciences? (Note that from this point I shall use science as meaning natural science.) This it can never properly be, since, however scientific the methods employed, the final purposes are historical: the reconstruction of individual events in time. In this division between means and purposes it is unique among academic subjects — which is why, of course, it is esteemed as a go-between for the Two Cultures.

We could probably all agree on a simple ideal for our subject: the employment of exact methods and devices, whether lent by other scientists or devised by archaeologists for themselves, to help us to reconstruct the human past, its historical events and ways of life, as accurately as possible. The nature of the imaginative insight required for this work of interpretation might provoke argument, but we could surely agree to differ. The more real difficulty comes, as I have already suggested, in keeping a right balance, in preventing the scientific and technological servant from usurping the throne of history.

To avoid this is in fact far more difficult than it appears to many scientific optimists. This is as true, I believe, for archaeology as for human affairs in general. The optimists give too little thought to the element of enforced choice in most of our undertakings — the crude fact that you can't have it all ways. This is most certainly true of archaeology in this country with its limited resources of men and money. As between its scientific and its humanistic values, one will go down if the other shoots up almost as certainly as with two children on a seesaw.

The scientific development of archaeology involves both scientific and technical aids and, far more profoundly, methods and aims. It might be thought that the aids make no threat at all, that they can easily be kept in their place as servants. Surely such devices as the proton magnetometer and other ingenious equipment advertised in the pages of *Archaeometry* can save time on excavations without causing harm, while all those techniques of mounting complexity that are intended to provide us with reliable dates and provenances need have no ill side-effects but simply contribute to the more accurate, less speculative writing of history?

Yet that is not how it turns out. Once again there is the tyranny of choice. It is not only that the expensive equipment and laboratory departments absorb money that might have gone in other directions, but far more that they attract to themselves a great part of the available energy, attention, intellectual love. Above all there is the selection they must impose on the kind of people attracted to the subject. Those of humanist imagination may not be attracted to studies increasingly dominated by proton magnetometers, neutron activation analysis, thermoremanent magnetism, thermoluminescence, graphs, statistics, and seemingly endless discussion concerning the effectiveness and reliability of all these things.

Note that already Ian Blake has written that archaeologists over thirty are unfit to carry on as they lack the ability to understand the new hardware and techniques. Yet it is the oldsters who do still labor to distil history from the welter of disparate facts that fill the journals and excavation reports. If there is anybody under the age of thirty or so producing historical writing of the quality and humanity of the work of the young Gordon Childe, Mortimer Wheeler, Christopher Hawkes, Stuart Piggott, or even, in his more austere way, Grahame Clark, I have failed to see it. It does not seem likely that many will begin to produce it in middle age.

If technical aids are not quite so innocent as they appear at first sight they are relatively harmless and are often to be seen working exactly as they should as the servants of history. I would quote as an example the study of the making-places of Minoan, Mycenaean, and Cypriote pottery published in *Archaeometry*. We should not be enslaved to the technical aids providing we keep our fundamental aims and values right. It is here that the issues are at once more difficult and far more important.

My apprehensions concerning these issues have often been aroused in recent years — most regularly by reading that in many ways valuable journal, *Current Anthropology*. Some of the discussions that fill its pages have seemed to me so esoteric, so overburdened with unhelpful jargon, so grossly inflated in relation to the significance of the matters involved, that they might emanate from a secret society, an introverted group of specialists enjoying their often rather squalid intellectual spells and rituals at the expense of an outside world to which they will contribute nothing that is enjoyable, generally interesting, or of historical importance. I remember Richard Crossman saying that when he first joined the Ministry of Psychological Warfare there were hundreds of able people employed in circulating thousands of documents from tray to tray, but that nothing had ever emerged from the building to contribute to the war effort. At my most pessimistic I feel that the lifeless and inconclusive labors of our specialists are hardly more fruitful.

My alarm was sharpened, however, after I had been invited to review Charles McBurney's monumental publication of his Cyrenaican excavations, *Haua Fteah*. This report, which describes the results of sinking a pit into a very small part of the wide and deep deposits of the cave, has been generously subsidized and yet still costs [$30]. In addition to the usual plans, sections, drawings, and poor-quality photographs of an excavation report, it contains some 250 graphs and statistical tables giving an exhaustive analysis of artifacts, fauna, and soils. At the end are three enormous folding inventories covering tens of thousands of artifacts. This immense analytical labor occupied Dr. McBurney for ten years and also absorbed heaven knows how many man-hours contributed by his students at Cambridge. In his Foreword Professor Grahame Clark praises this total, non-selective handling and suggests that the unique thoroughness of Dr. McBurney's methods might shorten the work of other excavators and so "check the inevitable trend toward posthumous publication."

I do not for a moment question the importance of the Haua Fteah excavations, nor that the careful analysis of their results has helped to strengthen the cultural and climatic framework on which a history of the Upper Paleolithic Age is being built. What I do question is whether the statistical apparatus is not extravagantly overdone; whether much of it really contributes enough to our present understanding or future study of the period to justify the time and money lavished upon it. Is it really true that by conning these graphs and tables, and in no simpler way, excavators in other lands will be able to say "there undoubtedly is the counterpart to the industry I am finding, or there plainly is the climatic equivalent to this horizon of mine"? If so then Dr. McBurney, his colleagues, students, and the patient technicians of the Cambridge University Press are indeed great benefactors who can feel that they have given so many irrecoverable hours to a good cause.

I very much doubt whether it is true. There is no question here of providing a Petrie-style corpus of tool types: Dr. McBurney says that he is very much against such attempts at standardization. It is slight modal fluctuations that he finds significant. Are not the local factors that could explain these fluctuations too considerable to allow of any certainty? Moreover Dr. McBurney himself admits that it is still necessary to examine the other man's actual material in the old-fashioned way.

It is the same with the greater part of the faunal analysis. Purely local conditions, as the report insists, often play a dominating part in the variation of species. Only the simplest indicators of fluctuations in temperature are of general value.

In short I am doubting Professor Clark's suggestion that "it is reasonable to hope" that the Herculean labors at Cambridge will save much time elsewhere, and I am therefore left with his amazing admission that there is "an inevitable trend toward posthumous publication." This seems to me a proof of wrong values leading to disastrously wrong choices. The idea that statistical elaboration is of such importance that it justifies an expectation for the author-excavator to die before he can publish — or publish in senility, which could be worse — would be funny if it did not carry such serious implications.

First, of course, there is the time factor itself, other workers being deprived of information for a decade or more. Secondly there is the very grave loss that must result from the author-excavator's departure for the next world before his findings can be examined in this one. The third disadvantage is the cost in hard cash, if, as in the instance of Haua Fteah, exhaustive analyses and inventories are not only made but published. [Thirty dollars] for a report which has been subsidized both in cash and free labor appears to me altogether out of proportion to the value of the product. The archaeological purse, at least in this country, is not bottomless and extravagance in one direction must lead to deprivation in another.

It is difficult not to feel that the longing to participate in the prestige of the natural sciences has led archaeologists to put up a scientific façade far too grandiose for the modest historical building behind it. It makes me think of those little towns in the mid-west of the United States often to be seen in section from the height of the railway. Lofty, painted frontages impress the citizens on the high street; lowly shacks at the back contain the goods and services.

I would like to illustrate this pretentiousness by a single, easily explained example from another very recent excavation report. Professor Evans and Dr. Renfrew's *Excavations at Saliagos* costs no more than [$13] and has seen the light only three years after the end of the digging, yet it does in my judgment show too much influence from the statniks. The partial excavation of this little Neolithic settlement established the presence of three distinguishable strata. So far as the pottery was concerned, it proved that evolutionary change was negligible throughout the occupation. Yet because one of the methods used to prove this fact was to relate various traits to the total weight of pottery in each stratum within three selected squares, we are presented with a "histogram" showing these weights. It occupies most of a page, consumes much ink, is very ugly and entirely without significance. If the information were worth conveying at all, it could have been done in a single sentence.

I am not wishing to be particularly critical of the Saliagos report, for it does in general keep its statistical apparatus within bounds and is redeemed (for those who share my point of view) by a few pages of pleasant, humanistic writing. I have picked on it only because it provides this and one or two other examples of what I judge to be false scientific showiness.

A long time ago G. M. Trevelyan wrote: "The substitution of a pseudo-scientific for a literary atmosphere in historical circles has not only done much to divorce history from the outside public, but has diminished its humanizing power over its own devotees in school and university." To appreciate the meaning of this to the full, one has only to turn from the ultra-scientific analytical type of excavation report to Professor Mallowan's volumes on Nimrud. He was not afraid to make his account of his digging personal and human: he deliberately decided to recreate the "atmosphere" of Henry Layard. So his two volumes are alive and attractive to the outside world. I am not denying that it is easier to write in this way of Assyrian than of Paleolithic archaeology. Nevertheless I am certain that there are plenty of archaeologists today who would crush this ancient city and its people under the weight of their statistics and bar all individuality from their pages.

This is the place to look very carefully at the difference between the values of archaeological and other types of scientific fact — accepting as a premise that archaeology exists for the service of history. The main distinction must be that whereas most of the facts of biology, chemistry, physics are virtually universal and unchanging, the significance of archaeological facts is usually quite narrowly limited in time and space. Thus all scientific facts once they have been checked by the experimental method become part of a totally impersonal and unchanging body of knowledge that can be used again and again in the most various contexts. Archaeological facts on the other hand must nearly always carry at least a slight subjective element in their discovery as in their interpretation, they cannot be experimentally checked in the true sense (I notice the word "experiment" being rather loosely used in recent publications) and usually have meaning only for writing one particular fragment of history.

That is one of the reasons why it is the duty of archaeologists to be as economical as possible in their presentation of data. Otherwise the subject will be swamped by a vast accumulation of insignificant, disparate facts, like a terrible tide of mud, quite beyond the capacity of any man to contain and mold into historical form. From this it follows that it is the duty of every archaeologist presenting a mass of factual data, himself to extract the essential historical meaning and to set this out in clear, firm, and humane language. If the excavator or research worker fails to do this, no one can be expected to do it for him, and his findings will merely add to the advancing mud.

The provision of clear statements in humanistic terms might also serve to check a growing characteristic of much archaeological and related work which I find particularly distressing. This is a combination of extreme precision of detail with endless uncertainty of interpretation. It is experienced at its worst, like walking across coarse scree, in the pages of *Current Anthropology* — for the reason that this journal makes a practice of inviting large numbers of rival specialists to print their criticisms below every article, and for the authors to add a reply. The effect is always the same: all of these experts share the jargon, dispute only a few of the facts — but what different stories they make out of them.

It is said that the theories of yesterday become the facts of today, but I wonder whether most of these painful screes will ever be consolidated? For instance the attempts to establish and coordinate throughout the world the minor climatic phases of the Pleistocene Age? While preparing this article, I was very much interested to read a statement in the current number of *Current Anthropology* itself. (It occurs in a light-hearted little book review in which eight summaries by the editor and authors of a volume on linguistics are followed by thirty-four critiques and then again by the eight replies: fifty-four tight-packed, three-column pages in all.) In one of her several contributions Rebecca Posner of York tucks in this general comment: "The restlessness of modern linguistic scientists is revealed in their apparent desire to be always knocking down old-established constructions in order to rebuild on new theoretical foundations.... Swings in fashion have led to the abandonments of the methods of 19th century linguistics before they were adequately exploited...."

Perhaps the desire for the latest model in theories is not so keen here as in the United States, but we live in one world and no one can ignore any innovations by recognized experts. I suspect that many much-disputed problems are not finally soluble, while others must wait a long time for further discoveries to bring certainty. Meanwhile I believe it would be better not to put in the shop window this half-cooked, unleavened dough.

The natural sciences have triumphed through analysis, through breaking down larger into smaller and smaller parts. Scientific archaeologists try to emulate them, but it may well be that our admittedly different kind of facts cannot in the end usefully be handled in this way. For those of us who believe that history is an art and therefore concerned not with breaking down but with creating larger meanings, these methods need constant checking and to be kept firmly in their place. To quote G. M. Trevelyan again, "It is not man's evolution but his attainment" that is the greatly significant aspect of his past.

That extraordinarily successful book, *The Naked Ape,* contains a minute-by-minute analysis of human copulation, yet makes no mention of the exaltation that has come to inspire the act for highly conscious, deeply individualized, men and women. The spirit behind *The Naked Ape* determines that the higher experiences and achievements of *Homo sapiens* must be set aside in this way. I sympathize with Desmond Morris's judgment that it is most perilous for us to forget or disguise the primitive element in our make-up, but this is no reason for devaluing our humanity. Our forebears may have been naked apes, but we have clothed ourselves. The greatest danger in the narrow scientific outlook is the assumption that because analytical and statistical methods cannot properly be applied to values that most differentiate man from the other animals, those values must be ignored. Only that counts that can be counted. I already see signs of this kind of devaluation in archaeology.

So far as ages before the Upper Paleolithic are concerned it can fairly be claimed that human qualities had hardly emerged and in any case are inaccessible to archaeology. Yet even for these remote ages more might be done if the interests of investigators were tilted in that direction. Test pits provide statistics, but total excavation, as Louis Leakey has exceptionally shown at Olduvai, can give an idea of how even Australopithecines lived. Again, Leakey has suspected that these beings liked bright or unusual stones, and hints of such tastes were noticed also at Choukoutien; there are issues such as the aesthetic element in hand-axe forms. These things may never amount to much, but do they ever get any serious attention at all?

When we come to later ages the balance of interest must make an enormous difference to what is found and given loving attention and what is neglected. Not long ago I visited Professor Mazar's excavations along the east wall of Jerusalem. There had been some statements in the press about discrepancies between his findings and Kathleen Kenyon's, so I asked him to comment. Having mentioned a few particular points he said, "Miss Kenyon is a most skilful digger. There are few better. But she made test pits, she did not excavate Jerusalem."

I am not intending this as a criticism of Kathleen Kenyon's methods. Whether at Haua Fteah or Jerusalem the need to get the outline story right must be met before the richer aspects of history can properly be considered. Yet (perhaps because of the symbolic undertones of the name) I was much affected by this simple statement "she did not excavate Jerusalem." If the trend toward the purely scientific continues, shall we not more and more go after what can be analyzed and forget Jerusalem?

Many people would say that this is a false alarm, that there is no evidence that this dehumanization is in fact taking place. They could reasonably insist that "Camelot" is being explored in a spirit that allows quite as much human interest and popular appeal as was Camulodunum (or Verulamium or Maiden Castle) while no one could claim that Silbury Hill is being reopened in an excessively remote or austere spirit. This is true, and I admit I may be looking ahead of the facts, yet still I feel that my note of alarm may be justified.

I would say that the relative neglect of the higher human achievements is conspicuous. Art and religion receive very little of the serious attention that is available in our world of archaeology. Returning recently to Minoan studies, I was astonished to find how little had been done in the way of serious art criticism, either for its own sake or as a way of solving some of the famous Knossian controversies. Nor, to my knowledge, had any archaeologist in this country gone much beyond Evans in the interpretation of Minoan religion. Yet the whole value of life for the Cretans lay in their religious and aesthetic experience, and there is unquestionably a vast amount to be found out about them in the light of modern understanding.

As two people who have done most in that side of Minoan studies are both women — Rachel Levy for religion and Hilde Groenewegen-Frankfort for art — I would like to believe that my sex is the more devoted to humanistic values. (In the far less encouraging field of African prehistory this belief also finds support in Sonia Cole.) Yet it was also a woman who most startled me by her total flouting of them. I attended a lecture at Burlington House on the subject of Mother Goddess figurines. I did not expect that the young speaker would be mainly concerned with either the history or the psychological and religious implications of the worship of the Goddess, but I was astonished when she announced that she had no intention of saying anything at all about these matters. For her, the figurines were type fossils and nothing more: they might as well (indeed much better) have been ammonites or belemnites.

I can imagine this kind of treatment passing in some highly specialized paper, but not in an address to a varied audience in the premises of the Society of Antiquaries. Moreover such narrowness of vision can lead to error. Some of the things that archaeologists have said on the subject of Mother Goddess figurines reveal total ignorance of the psychological roots of religious imagery in general and of the Goddess in particular.

It was narrowness, too, coupled with a certain scientific arrogance, that led to the interpretation of Stonehenge I as a celestial computer. The lack of historical imagination, the ignoring of historical knowledge, made it possible to identify this ancient monument with an abstract diagram and analyze it from the point of view of wholly modern concepts. In this way, in my opinion, follies were committed quite as fantastic, because equally obsessional, as those of the British Israelites and their reading of the Great Pyramid.

The nature of the expert advice that we seek is an unconscious exposure of our values. We regularly turn to the chemists, physicists, botanists, zoologists. . . . Why seldom or never to the art historians, the depth psychologists, the authorities on religion, folklore, magic? How very little archaeological work has been done, for instance, on the symbolic meaning of designs or the magic of numbers. Could we not occasionally have appendices dealing with such matters, instead of being limited to those daunting and not always very significant pages devoted to soils, snails, and other tabulable aspects of the natural environment or of material artifacts?

I have suggested that scientific archaeologists sometimes behave like members of a secret society, cutting themselves off behind ramparts of jargon and other specialist defenses. When I come to the question of communications, I can see at once that this picture must look like a caricature. With Thames and Hudson and other publishers pouring out splendid histories of ancient arts and civilizations, with the extraordinary success of such generally accessible series as our Editor's *Ancient People and Places*, and with the range of information available in Pelicans and other paperbacks, how can there be any fear of the humanity of our subject being killed by scientific specialization?

The sumptuous art and civilization books, internationally commissioned and marketed, are so far from the main stream of British archaeology that I think they have to be left out of the present discussion. But with the paperbacks and other series that have become so much a part of the publishing scene it is otherwise.

The silver lining for my clouds of gloom is certainly provided by popularization. It is more and better done than in the days of my youth, and public interest, if past its peak, has been admirably stimulated. Several of our most respected pundits have consented to take part in it, even although its practitioners, unless they are very cautious, receive a slight stigma that may on occasion do them harm.

The only disturbing fact in this happy situation is that most of those who have proved able and willing to write well for a wide readership belong more or less to my generation and were educated in the humanities. I think it unlikely that those mechanically adept under-thirties recognized by Ian Blake as typical of the new generation will be either able or willing.

However this may prove to be, the work of popularization, though most valuable, and indeed a duty in our kind of society, cannot altogether answer my case. What does appear to me to be already in decline is the thinking and writing that synthesize archaeological findings into true history. With the spate of new factual material flowing in from every age and every quarter, there is a pressing need and a glorious opportunity for master works of historical synthesis. During the last two decades there has been a breaking-down of systems and theories rooted in the prewar period, but very much less reconstruction or new building on a grand scale.

Our learned journals and specialist reports are packed with material that will never be carried outside the specialists' compound.

As I have already said, most of the work of turning archaeological data into history still comes from the old guard — and this is most certainly not because they are holding back a rising generation of talent. In this context one thinks at once of Gordon Childe. His dogmatic materialism may (though I doubt it) have helped to push archaeology toward the natural sciences, but as Sir Mortimer Wheeler reminds us in the admirable last chapter of *Archaeology from the Earth,* where so many of the science versus the humanities issues are discussed, Childe himself was a classicist by training, the sort of man who liked to read Pindar after dinner. No one else in the last half-century has done quite so much as he did to draw the findings of archaeology into the intellectual life of Europe (to the Urals!). Perhaps the combination of the Marxist vigor of his day with the still pristine freshness of much archaeological discovery gave him ideal circumstances. Yet I remain convinced that there are today equally great opportunities for a new synthesis and a new vision.

In writing our histories of archaeology we have sometimes been too inclined to see its development as a teleological one heading always for our own ideal of scientific archaeology. Yet this is in part misleading. We have mocked the explorers of a century and more ago because they dug for "loot." Yet they were justified in that they drew their discovery of the past into their own culture; both classicists and romantics used their loot to enrich their art, their architecture, their domestic designs, and even their poetry. That was the kind of archaeology they wanted and that was right for their time. In the same spirit, we have criticized those great and dynamic men of pre-World War I vintages for imposing their personalities too strongly upon their work. Yet in doing so they caught the imagination of the public, made the periods and peoples they revealed appear real and important.

It has certainly been right for us in our turn to accept the scientific bias of our age and to concentrate upon laboriously established objective fact. That is being done with a devotion and ingenuity that are awe-inspiring. We do not, of course, want to turn back to older ideals, but we should appreciate them and perhaps learn something from them.

The need of the age that we are now entering is to protect our humanity, to keep our technological Frankenstein's monster in control. Archaeology with its revelations not only of our humble beginnings but still more of our marvellous variety of achievements, has, I believe, a considerable part to play in this defense. If we are not to fail in it, we must remember that all our ingenious devices, all our exact measurements and statistical analyses, are of no value in themselves. We must not allow them to absorb too much of our time, energy, and intellectual love. We must not allow them even to appear to be dominating our subject or they will repel those young men and women of strong historical imagination whom we should be recruiting.

I am sure that I am right in my archaeological values; I am not so confident that I am right in seeing them seriously threatened. It may be that I am suffering from the sense of universal decay that so often invades the passing generation. This is one of those rare occasions when I earnestly hope to be proved wrong.

Glynn Ll. Isaac

28   WHITHER ARCHAEOLOGY?

The reaction to Jacquetta Hawkes' "The Proper Study of Mankind" was so strong that the Editor of the journal *Antiquity*, which published her paper, decided to pursue the matter further. So he announced a competition for essays entitled "Whither Archaeology?" Glynn Ll. Isaac's paper, which follows, was a prize-winning entry. Isaac does not attempt a rebuttal of Hawkes but points out that archaeology is engaged in experimentation with a wide range of new methods and techniques. The subject has diversified vastly in the past half century. He argues that the goals of archaeology have been well defined during the past hundred years. The problem is rather how we can improve ways of doing it, which accounts for the concern with new approaches found among younger scholars. These two essays show up very clearly the basic tensions in archaeology today, a subject in which there is intense debate concerning the future direction of archaeology.

V. Gordon Childe made a characteristically clear statement about the position of prehistoric archaeology within the realms of knowledge. He wrote: "By the inclusion of prehistory the preview of history is extended ... history joins on to natural history" (Childe 1941: 4). Archaeological studies are at their most significant when they attempt to elucidate the development of relationships both amongst men, and between man and the material world. Indeed it becomes increasingly clear that is is not possible to understand either kind of development independently of the other. Prehistoric archaeology is thus in its total aims not a natural science, a social science, or a branch of the humanities; rather it is a distinctive pursuit in which all of these meet.

Archaeology can also be described as a worm's eye view of human behavior. The archaeologist derives his information from the traces of men's activities which linger in the ground long after the death of the men themselves. These relics are extremely varied: they may be ruins, refuse, tools, or works of art, or they may be soil erosion and modifications to living organisms and to plant and animal communities. However, most of the marks that man has left on the face of the earth during his two-million-year career as a litterbugging, meddlesome, and occasionally artistic animal have one aspect in common: they are things, they are not deeds, ideas, or words. Thus for better or for worse archaeologists are involved along with natural scientists in the study of objects and materials. When archaeology is at its best, the things are studied in order to make possible insight into the functioning of the economic, social, and ideological systems of prehistoric communities. However, the scope and penetration of our perception of extinct human orders is directly proportional to the extent and acuity of our primary observations of objects.

Given widespread appreciation of the need of archaeology to cast its net broadly, it is scarcely surprising that successive generations of archaeologists have sought help and inspiration amongst an ever expanding range of sciences and disciplines. In the first instance, as Jacquetta Hawkes recently pointed out, co-operation has been obtained from partially subservient specialists such as soil scientists, metallurgists, and paleontologists. Meanwhile the study of artifact design, the inner sanctum of archaeology, remained secure. More recently however, the notion that archaeologists can profit even in the study of artifacts from the help and experience of

From "Whither Archaeology?" by Glynn Ll. Isaac, *Antiquity*, 45, 178 (1971), 123–129. Reprinted with permission of the author and the Editor of *Antiquity*.

biometricians, statisticians, and experts in cybernetics has apparently caused widespread alarm.

This essay is a response to the editor's invitation to archaeologists under forty to offer alternatives to Jacquetta Hawkes's pessimistic survey of contemporary trends in archaeology. The opening paragraphs will have made it clear that I differ markedly in my view of what archaeology ought to encompass. I do not advocate that archaeology should sever its connections with history and the humanities, but I believe that it differs significantly from them in its character. Archaeology is used throughout this paper to mean prehistoric archaeology because the discipline is most distinctive when the process of reconstruction is unaided by writing or oral tradition. Since most aims and methods are held in common between studies of prehistoric and historic periods, I think that this simplifies discussion without invalidating the main arguments.

This essay is not written simply as a rebuttal since that would contribute little to discussion of the issues confronting archaeology. Moreover, although several of the whipping boys attacked by Jacquetta Hawkes were in my view singularly ill-chosen, there is no doubt that some of her general criticisms are fair ones. Her essay deserves careful reading even by those whom it annoys, because the onus of demonstrating the value of the new concepts and methods which alarm some traditionalists does lie with those who are developing them.

As a preliminary to any consideration of contemporary archaeology, it is essential to stress the point that the subject has diversified enormously since its nineteenth-century origins. It is safe to predict that branching and the establishment of liaisons with an ever widening range of disciplines will continue to be one of the most conspicuous trends. This diversity is one of the causes of excitement for those who work in the field and for spectators, but it requires tolerance. The phenomenon of man is sufficiently complex to demand examination from many standpoints. Uniformity of training or approach are not desirable and fortunately there is no sign that archaeologists are getting more alike. *Quot homines, tot sententiae: suo quoque mos.*

Given the need for archaeology to incorporate scholars with educational roots in the sciences, I would argue that it is an unjustifiable conceit to suppose that these colleagues will be less sensitive to certain values than scholars trained in the humanities. Such great biologists as Julian Huxley, J. B. S. Haldane, or Gaylord Simpson, by becoming concerned with man and nature have shown the deep humanistic significance that the scientific approach can acquire.

The extent and scale of modern archaeology is prodigious. Research now spans two million years of prehistory and successive phases of cultural diversification over the faces of five continents. Most of this activity naturally consists of the application of established methods to the task of filling in the details of prehistory. On a global scale, current investigations of two critical prehistoric developments are proving particularly interesting. First there is the study of the roots of human behavior patterns in the Lower Pleistocene. Secondly there is the elucidation of the processes by which human behavior was transformed through intensive use of farming techniques in both the Old and New Worlds. Despite their interest, these are advances in knowledge and understanding rather than in method and concept; and consequently have limited relevance as a basis for guesses about the future characteristics of archaeology as a discipline. However, some aspects of the best early man or early farming studies do appear to indicate the shape of things to come. In a number of cases the problem to be studied has been carefully formulated and a team of investigators has been assembled, amongst which a variety of scientists interested in anthropological problems take their place as partners rather than as technicians. The range of past human behaviors reconstructed by such teams has tended to be much broader than it usually was in days when conventionally trained archaeologists often restricted their interests to tool typology and art history.

Cutting across the present dispersal and diversity of archaeological studies are two movements which tend particularly to have appeal for the younger generation of workers. These movements involve the kinds of changes in attitude which alarm Jacquetta Hawkes. Neither of them was actually started by young archaeologists but they have been vigorously espoused by them and are often loosely characterized as the "new archaeology." A great deal of unnecessary sound and fury has accompanied numerous declarations by angry young men, but it would be quite wrong to conclude from this that the commotion signifies nothing.

One of the movements is in response to a growing self-consciousness of archaeology as a thoroughly distinctive pursuit which, despite borrowing, is methodologically independent of all others. The growth of this awareness has been accompanied by a clamor for systematization of archaeological inference and for the development of a more explicit conceptual framework. The other movement is distinguishable, but closely related. It consists of a tendency to increasing use of quantitative data of all kinds in the documentation of archaeological reports and arguments; this is often felt to be an obligation rather than an option.

ARCHAEOLOGICAL INFERENCE

For better or for worse, archaeology has hitherto undergone a century of development without becoming highly organized as a discipline. At an empirical level artifacts and field data have commonly been described and classified in diverse ways indicated by experience, intuition, and convenience. At an interpretative level, inferences concerning cultures, evolution, migration, and diffusion are treated as realities demonstrated by this material. In most archaeological writing the process of deriving the interpretational level from the empirical level is tacitly treated as though it were self-evident or a matter of common sense. This split-level arrangement served well during much of the development of archaeological knowledge; in particular it was serviceable when the number of professional archaeologists was quite small and it was possible to form a personal understanding of the nuances of each scholar's use of words and concepts.

Two cumulative changes have combined to create the present sense of crisis with regard to archaeological reasoning. First, there has been a steady increase in the number of professional archaeologists all over the world; and in the years since 1945 the increase might almost be described as explosive. The luxury of unstated personal assumptions, and unexplained systems of nomenclature and inference, has become increasingly a barrier to communication. Secondly, as archaeology has grown through the pioneer phases of establishing in outline major divisions of prehistoric culture, there has arisen the opportunity and the demand for ever finer exegesis of the evidence. While the concepts and entities involved in the bold outlines may have been in large measure self-evident, this is not true for finer constructs: hence the tumult. This is not simply a phenomenon dividing generations of archaeologists: important attempts to cope with these problems have a long history.

To single out but a few examples of writings which have sign posted developments in this movement one might mention V. G. Childe's essay "Changing methods and aims in prehistory" (1935), his book *Piecing Together the Past* (1956), and Willey and Phillips's *Method and Theory in American Archaeology* (1958). More recently the volume *Background to Evolution in Africa,* edited by Bishop and Clark (1967), reports the deliberations of older and younger scholars at an international symposium. Discussion centered on the need for clarification of concepts and stressed the importance of well-defined terms to convey these concepts.

The difference between the generations is partly marked by an actual sense of revolt amongst many younger scholars and by a tendency toward excessive use of jargon by the same group. However it would be unfortunate if distaste for a barrage of new terms, some necessary, some redundant, were to give rise to the delusion that the whole proceeding is contemptible. What is going on is a most lively process of exploration. Amongst the methodological forays in which the "new archaeologists" engage, some are vain and ill-conceived or merely iconoclastic, others are well-conceived but will prove unproductive, yet others will surely lead to clearer and more explicit insight into the nature of archaeological patterns. It can be anticipated that the combination of such attempts will enable archaeology to integrate the split levels of operation and become a more mature discipline with more widely understood interpretative principles.

Two recently published books deserve mention as particularly important representatives of this movement. One, a symposium entitled *New Perspectives in Archeology* edited by S. R. and L. R. Binford (1968) contains a broad spectrum of reformist views. The other, *Analytical Archaeology* by

D. L. Clarke (1968), makes valuable attempts at generalizations regarding order and pattern amongst artifacts and archaeological evidence. Amongst other things, Clarke has experimented with the application of concepts and methods derived from systems analysis and numerical taxonomy. The book shows extraordinarily broadly based scholarship, with material from archaeological, historical, and ethnographic sources being considered in original ways. It does not make very easy reading because, at the present stage of understanding, simple formulations are probably inadvisable. Evaluation of Clarke's work should be made in relation to the widespread sense of a need for exploration. Its importance probably lies not only in the wealth of apparently fruitful new lines of thought which are developed but in the stimulus his formulations should provide to constructive critics who view things differently.

QUANTITATIVE METHODS

There is wide agreement amongst younger archaeologists the world over that archaeology would be better off if certain kinds of *judgements and decisions* were made with due regard to *relevant* quantitative information. The phrase "judgements and decisions" is italicized because some contemporary writers tend to imply that the use of numerical data deprives the investigator of the opportunity to judge and interpret. "Relevant" is stressed because the usefulness of quantities in archaeology, or any other discipline, will always depend on the existence of a significant relationship between what is measured and the problem to be solved. It is true that precision with regard to quantities and frequency distribution patterns can sometimes spoil a good scholastic debate by settling it conclusively, but this can hardly be advanced as a serious argument for refusing to admit these as legitimate methods even in a humanistic discipline.

The use of some quantitative data is practically as old as archaeology, and during this century there has been an erratic tendency to increase in the systematic use of numbers. However the current situation is distinctive in that the preoccupation of many younger archaeologists with quantitative methods has become so intense that something akin to a cult of numbers has arisen in certain quarters. This flurry of interest is commonly associated with concern over the theoretical foundations of archaeology. Taking a long view it seems likely that quantitative methods will prove indispensable to aspects of archaeology, but present hyperconsciousness of numbers will probably subside when trial and error has resulted in the development of a more sound conceptual framework and when a stock of effective analytical methods has been established.

Meanwhile we have to put up with a partly tedious intermediate situation. Extensive and often dull explanations of method are at the present stage frequently necessary. Many authors understandably feel obliged to present their data both by orthodox verbal and illustrative exposition and by attempts at quantitative characterization. Further, many users of numbers are rightly or wrongly not sufficiently confident of the virtues of statistics to have the courage to replace hundreds of measurements by a few items of information such as the mean, median, standard deviation, and range. In addition there are reports where numbers ramble like sacred cows: their contribution to the author's argument is not explicit and the likelihood that anyone else can use them may also be slender. In other cases valuable numerical data may be compiled and then in effect abandoned by a reversion to conventional classificatory systems which ignore the continuous property of numerical scales. It is also apparent that numbers create an illusion of purity and have a fascination of their own. Archaeologists should heed the warning provided by the barren years which craniometry spent in the wilderness searching for formulae which would make numbers the universal key to understanding evolution and race (cf. Washburn 1969).

The deficiencies of the present situation cause as much concern amongst exponents of quantitative methods as they do amongst traditionalists. However, the difference lies in the fact that proponents advocate rendering the morass fertile by drainage, while traditionalists appear to be advocating mere retreat back into a forest where at least the mystique of half comprehension is familiar. This is not an appropriate place for a full parade of arguments in favor of the development and application of suitable quantitative methods. Suffice it to say that quantitative considerations have long played an essential but unspecified role in archaeological interpretations. Standard words such as "common," "rare," "typical," are all labels for inherently quantitative properties of the evidence.

Awareness of modes in artifact design is so much a part of our culture that mathematicians borrowed the word as their term for the phenomenon in general. We need hardly be shy of re-introducing the methods which they have devised for clarifying the concept.

There are some worthwhile perceptions of patterns in archaeological data which may only be possible through the use of quantitative analysis. Examples of this kind of pattern may prove to include really complex geographic or chronological seriation patterns, or the unravelling of complex interactions between stylistic and functional factors which determined the form of tools or the composition of tool kits. Some interesting studies have already demonstrated that subtle patterns with considerable sociological and humanistic significance can be detected in assemblages of archaeological materials by quantitative methods when normal inspection would have revealed little or nothing. An outstanding example of this is Richardson and Kroeber's (1940) study of cycles of European dress style and the apparent influence of social tension on degrees of variability. Deetz's work on relationships between aspects of the potter's craft and socio-economic changes amongst the proto-historic Arikara is another case holding out promise for this kind of approach (Deetz 1965).

The advent of electronic computers provides important opportunities for those interested in developing the necessary knowledge to take advantage of them. These devices are capable of many varied operations which can cross-reference intricate records and which can express aspects of patterning in very complex data. It is safe to predict extensive contributions to archaeological theory and knowledge by investigations which would not be possible without computers.

Many archaeologists share the anxiety expressed by Jacquetta Hawkes (1968, 258) concerning a "vast accumulation of insignificant, disparate facts, like a terrible tide of mud, quite beyond the capacity of man to contain and mold into historical form." However, brevity can be achieved in two ways: replacement of information by vaguely substantiated judgments or by the definition of patterns which can be demonstrated to be valid, significant orderings of the total complexity. In practice, of course, both processes are involved in preparing an archaeological report, but clearly pattern summary is less destructive of information than unspecified personal judgements, however sound. Statistical operations can often fairly be characterized as processes for making controlled generalizations from sets of otherwise disparate items of information. Clearly it is possible that statistics may prove to be one of the filters which can help to hold back the tide of mud while releasing a clear stream of water into the pool of knowledge.

If we are in a phase of trial and error searching for effective methods of quantitative analysis and pattern recognition then it is to be expected that parts of the work now being done will prove sterile, other parts will later appear as tentative gropings, while only a comparatively small proportion can be expected to provide the kind of elegant clarification of archaeological situations that we may fairly demand of quantitative methods if they are to become an established part of archaeological procedure.

THE ARCHAEOLOGY OF LIVING PEOPLE

Archaeology has become fairly adept at reconstructing from flimsy traces significant aspects of otherwise unknown extinct human behavior patterns. However, there is a growing conviction amongst many archaeologists that we could get some novel insights into our methods and perhaps added vitality for our reconstructions if we were to take the scarcely precedented step of observing closely, potential archaeological traces amongst peoples whose economy, sociology, and ideology is already known. I envisage observations of the relationships between refuse patterns, including chemical residues, and living habits; careful records of settlement size and form in relation to community size and social structuring. Also of crucial importance are observations of variation in artifact morphology amongst individual craftsmen, amongst communities and craft lineages, and amongst larger social units.

Observations of these kinds of material manifestations are made by ar-

chaeologists as a matter of course on sites, where exact behavioral significance is a matter for reconstruction, but the observations have no counterpart
in classic ethnography where the behavior and the material traces could
both be determined. This kind of study has been dubbed action archaeology
(Kleindienst and Watson, 1956) and there is now a small literature on the
subject (e.g. Ascher, 1962, Brain, 1967, Foster, 1960), but further work is
a matter of urgency since the expansion of mass-produced plastic and
canned food will displace behavioral arrangements of the kind that prevailed through prehistory. It is conceivable that such studies may help to
do for archaeology what genetics and primate behavior studies have done
for human paleontology.

CONCLUSION

From the foregoing discussion, the view emerges that archaeology is currently engaged in experimentation with a vast range of new techniques
and methods. Any attempt to hamper this process by deliberate reversion
to the situation which prevailed during the youth of established archaeological scholars would be stultifying and unsuccessful. The contributions of
many of the great names cited by Jacquetta Hawkes as exponents of balanced humanistic archaeology have been incorporated into the foundations
of modern archaeology. Their potential successors would hardly be worthy
of the training they have received at these hands if they were content to
devote their lives simply to more of the same.

There tends to be an inverse relationship between complexity of subject
matter and the degree of maturity of the discipline engaged in its study.
Physics has been characterized as the very complex study of comparatively
simple processes; biology as the comparatively simple study of enormously
complex processes. Anthropology is at the next remove up in complexity
of subject matter, and at several steps down in the degree of penetration
hitherto achieved by its methods. Because anthropology in its broadest
sense subsumes archaeology and history, it is no discredit to archaeology
that it has only now accumulated sufficient experience to organize an explicit conceptual framework for dealing with its particular complexity. It
should also not occasion surprise that the transformation is proving in part
to be traumatic and inelegant. However, if we follow Jacquetta Hawkes
in her belief that "it would be better not to put in the shop window this
half-cooked, unleavened dough" — then it is not clear how the body of
archaeologists is going to find out which recipes are more promising than
others.

It seems undeniable that the prime responsibility of any scholarly discipline must be to maintain its factual basis in good order. It is equally true
that the superstructure of insight and understanding is what really interests
most of the participant scholars and the rest of intellectual humanity. It

would be a distressing discovery if it proved true that the pursuit of significant information is incompatible with the achievement of insight. Also, if the goals and values of humanistic studies really are irreconcilable with those of scientific studies, then archaeology would be condemned eternally to the present schizophrenia so well depicted by Jacquetta Hawkes. However, it seems equally probable that when the new stock of ideas has been sorted and allowed to mature, archaeology will be greatly enriched. New levels of precision in presenting data and in interpreting them can surely lead to briefer and more interesting technical reports as well as providing the basis for more lively portrayals of what happened in prehistory.

The goals of archaeology have been well defined over the past century and will require little change. Archaeology ought to be what archaeology already is. The problem is how can we improve our ways of doing it? This is a challenge that every generation faces afresh.

Hester A. Davis

29   IS THERE A FUTURE FOR THE PAST?

This volume ends on a bleak note, with a frank and hard-hitting paper by Hester A. Davis on the destruction of archaeological sites. The future of archaeology is closely tied to the future of archaeological sites. Like so many of the earth's valuable resources, archaeological sites are being destroyed at a record rate, by the developer and the road engineer as well as by the treasure hunter and the amateur collector. So rapid is the destruction, that in parts of the United States few undisturbed archaeological sites remain. The issue is the permanent destruction of historical archives in the form of settlements and artifacts long abandoned by their inhabitants. From these archives alone can present and future archaeologists write the history of the American Indian and other prehistoric peoples whose descendants are found in other parts of the world. Convincing the archaeological community of its urgency is part of the problem. The public has to be educated, too, and legislation is urgently needed at the federal and the state levels. The subject is introduced here in the hope that you will become one of those who care about protecting the past. The interested reader is referred to Charles R. McGimsey, III, *Public Archeology* (New York: Seminar Press, 1972), for a detailed account of legislative programs.

It might seem a little ridiculous to be concerned about preservation of the record of prehistory. It has lasted in some cases thousands of years, so why might it not last another several thousand. But modern technology has accelerated many changes in the world today, and the rate of destruction of the evidence of the past is among these changes.

It is the task of the New World archaeologist to record the more than 20,000 years of human occupation. Almost all the evidence lies buried in the ground — sometimes several feet, more often no more than a few inches below the surface. Pueblo ruins and other structures are covered with debris and wind-blown sand; caves and sheltered bluffs have wind and water-carried materials covering evidence of occupation; natural soil growth and vegetal accumulation cover the tumbled down or burned structures, the fire hearths and other remains of open sites. All of this evidence is endangered, for anything which disturbs the earth to a depth of a foot or two is going to destroy the context of artifacts and features in an Indian site.

This has always been true, of course, but modern land alteration has increased at a tremendous rate in the last few years, and will continue to do so as the need increases for more farm acreage, more housing developments, more open coal mining, more roads, more reservoirs, more shopping centers. The very places which appeal to people to live today, are often the same spots which were attractive to the Indians. Any disturbance to the stratigraphy and the original context of materials left by the Indians, destroys the only evidence available to the archaeologist for interpreting the way of life in the past. Once destroyed it is gone forever, for archaeological resources are non-renewable.

Salvage archaeology in the large federally built reservoirs has been going on for twenty years or more. Surveys were made to locate the sites which would be inundated, and selected ones were excavated. The federal government in cooperation with numerous private and state agencies has funded this work, and a tremendous amount of information has been recovered before the areas were inundated. Obviously, however, only a small proportion of the sites in any one reservoir could be excavated, and it would not be an exaggeration to say that seventy-five per cent of the sites within any one reservoir area were flooded without more than a surface collection being made. As a current example, in the area of the huge Amistad International Reservoir on the Rio Grande River, between Mexico and the United States, approximately four hundred sites were located in the surveys, and no more than twenty-five were adequately tested. Federally sponsored work on reservoirs, river channels, levees, retarding dams, small

Reprinted from "Is There a Future for the Past?" by Hester A. Davis, *Archaeology*, Vol. 24, No. 4, pp. 300–306, with permission of the author and the publisher. Copyright 1971, Archaeological Institute of America. Photographs reproduced by permission of the author and the publisher; some illustrations are omitted.

water control ponds is increasing. The Corps of Engineers and the Soil Conservation Service both plan a tremendous amount of land alteration and/or flooding in the immediate future which will affect thousands of archaeological sites.

Farming, of course, has always disturbed archaeological sites to some extent, but a mule drawn plow doesn't do the damage of a chisel plow or a subsoiler, which can turn the earth to a depth of two or three feet. The drive for maximum production from the land means larger and heavier equipment which does greater and more complete damage to archaeological sites. Indian mounds are no longer an obstruction which must be left in trees — they can be leveled easily with large bulldozers. Need for increased farm land means that thousands of acres are being cleared for production for the first time — sites protected for centuries are being exposed and destroyed within one season.

The need for "new" land, and for level land everywhere in the country is destroying and will destroy sites daily. Farmers need this level land in order to use their large equipment efficiently; trailer parks need level land, shopping centers need level land. Almost nothing is an obstruction: sides of mountains are gouged out, trees torn up, mounds, terraces, levees flattened. All the action about which the conservationists are so voluble today, are just as destructive to the non-renewable archaeological resources as they are to the natural portions of the environment, except the destruction of archaeological resources is more permanent. You can't grow a new Indian site.

All parts of the country are faced with this problem although the agents of destruction may be different: in the Mississippi Alluvial Valley the need for increased crop production has meant that thousands of acres of land have been leveled and/or cleared in the past five years and within twenty years all levelable land will be leveled. In the area around the western Great Lakes a major problem in site destruction is vacation and resort development and the construction of man-made lakes for recreation; in the Southwest thousands of acres are cleared by "chaining," where two large pieces of machinery, with a heavy chain between them, drive across the land uprooting and dragging all growing things — and ancient pueblo ruins — with them; strip mining in the Midwest obliterates prehistoric remains; pothunters and history buffs with metal detectors dig through important prehistoric and historic sites in search of items for their collections; and, shamefully, many museums aid and abet this last source of destruction by buying or accepting artifacts collected without scientific data thus providing added incentive for further destruction.

After 15,000 years of occupation by man there are very few areas of the country which do not have *some* evidence of earlier prehistoric or important historic life-ways. An example of what concerned archaeologists are saying will give some indication of the situation: the largest Mississippian site in Minnesota is now the largest man-made hole next to the Hull-Rust iron mine; state highway and county gravel borrow pit operations have made the hole. Rezoning of rural lands and construction of massive housing tracts in Hawaii have turned thousands of acres over to the bulldozer — only occasionally are prominent individual sites saved.

In a deeply buried Archaic campsite in Kansas some thirty hearths were exposed and destroyed in a two acre tract in the borrow pit for a small federally sponsored watershed project. One of the mounds at the Great Mayersville site in Mississippi was hauled away recently to help improve the county roads. One of the largest and most important concentrations of historic sites in southeast Texas, consisting of a French trading post, a Spanish presidio and mission, and a large Orcoquizac Indian village has been heavily damaged in recent years by several large high-pressure pipe-lines, a huge borrow pit for an interstate highway, and partial inundation by a reservoir.

A conservative estimate is that there are over 5,000 persons engaged in pothunting and rock-hounding in Oregon, both of which activities destroy sites. A large site on Lake Champlain in Vermont, described in 1922 as being 500 meters in extent and covered with village debris, was bulldozed between 1960 and 1965 for a housing development. A large village midden in Arkansas was trucked fifteen miles by a housing contractor to spread on the lawn areas of the new houses — because the soil was so black and rich; it was a nuisance that it was also full of bones and chipped stone artifacts [Figure 1]. All accessible land in Maryland has been cultivated by Euro-Americans so that practically every site has been decapitated. A large early site on the Malibu coast of California was in the path of residential construction and was to be buried under fill; unauthorized bull-dozing opened up the site, exposing human burials, and swarms of souvenir hunters and vandals began to dig; local amateurs were able to salvage some, but the site was completely leveled by construction [Figure 2]. Destruction of a huge Adena site in Delaware, by construction of a highway, resulted in the loss of one of the most important sites on the east coast, and of over 1,000 artifacts. In Florida, coastal development and dredging activities — docks, commercial marinas, channels — are disturbing large numbers of sites from historic shipwrecks to submerged Paleo-Indian sites. This kind of documentation could go on for pages.

The federal government has indicated its concern for preservation of the past since the passage of the 1906 Antiquities Act. Other subsequent federal laws have continued to show basic federal responsibility for recognizing and taking into account historic and prehistoric sites affected by federal programs (e.g., the Historic Sites Act of 1935, the Reservoir Salvage Act of 1960, and the Historic Preservation Act of 1966). However, in those

Figure 1 In Arkansas, four land-leveling machines work while archaeologists try to salvage the bottoms of trash pits and crushed burials exposed by the machines.

Figure 2 In California, emergency salvage in the wake of huge machinery recovers only scattered remnants of occupation.

states where various federal agencies hold over seventy-five per cent of the land, destruction of sites on federal property goes on apace because of lack of means for protecting them or lack of concern by those in immediate charge. The National Park Service, of course, is the specific agency responsible for looking after the nation's prehistoric and historic past, and it attempts to do so with completely inadequate funding. It is encouraging to note that the Forest Service is now employing archaeologists, and a recent Presidential Order directs all federal agencies to make an inventory of all their properties in order to identify archaeological, historical, and architectural sites and objects of significance. The Bureau of Public Roads and the Department of Housing and Urban Development also sometimes fund archaeological work under special circumstances.

Despite these encouraging signs, the federal government and state governments have not demonstrated adequate active leadership in preserving the past; archaeologists have been wringing their hands, and the public has not been informed of what is happening. Action must be taken in all these areas, or there will be no future for the past. To be truly effective any action *must* actively involve the public, for they control the land and the legislatures [Figure 3].

A staggering amount of information is irretrievably gone — but all is not lost if action is taken soon. Many archaeologists are heartened by the good relationships with companies, contractors, and landowners which have resulted from efforts to acquaint these people with the archaeological situation. Private industry is beginning to fund salvage work on land where they will construct new facilities — in Texas, in Indiana, in Georgia cooperation like this is providing for much important archaeological excavation. The instance cited above in Delaware so disturbed everyone that the state provided more funds for the Delaware Archaeological Board. In Florida, the Marco Island Development Corporation is going to alter the entire island; the Bureau of Historic Sites and Properties has been able to carry out research there for four years, and will continue for another four years — with state, historical society, and the Development Corporation all providing funds. These examples will have to be multiplied many fold.

Based on the assumption (a reality in some parts of the country) that all sites will be adversely affected to one degree or another by land alteration, archaeologists must review their current knowledge of the prehistoric occupation of particular geographical — and cultural — regions, and on the basis of this over-view, choose sites for study. Before it will be possible to know which sites can provide this needed information, archaeologists must reorient their view of salvage archaeology. Rather than digging a site *because* it is to be destroyed, sites must be chosen for excavation because of the information they contain. Some sites are obviously more important than others, in terms of the amount and kinds of information they contain,

Figure 3   Both these groups consider archaeology to be a hobby and avocation: (top) *one group is destroying evidence of the past by its digging technique, the other* (bottom) *is preserving it.*

to fill in gaps of knowledge of local and regional developments. These should either be excavated or they should be set aside and not disturbed further until it is possible to do a proper and complete excavation. It won't be easy to watch some sites being destroyed without salvaging anything. But knowledgeable decisions will have been made which indicate that the site being destroyed does not contain as much scientific information as does another where efforts must be concentrated to save or to preserve it or several sites of an area, for the future.

We will never have enough professionally trained archaeologists to test, even partially, all the sites which potentially will be destroyed. There is a large, interested, and enthusiastic source of help in the amateur archaeologists; cooperation between amateur and professional is vital, if the goal of an adequately preserved past is to be attained.

What is needed with equal urgency is an alerted public, a concerned public. Interest in the past, both historic and prehistoric has increased as leisure time has increased. If America knows that its past, and the past which it inherited from the Indians is being completely, irrevocably destroyed — largély through ignorance and lack of concern — some, perhaps even enough of the past could be preserved for the future to understand it and to profit from its successes and failures.

Digging destroys archaeological information, whether it is done by a bulldozer or a professional archaeologist. If the professional archaeologist is given a chance to dig before the bulldozer, then a scientific and photographic record is made and interpretations are possible about the way of life of that particular segment of prehistory. The site is destroyed, but the information is saved.

The destruction of sites for economic reasons, by businesses and corporations completely unaware of the fact that a site exists is tragic enough. The destruction of sites by individuals wanting relics for a collection, or by individuals completely innocent of the damage they are doing, is inexcusable. The ones in these latter cases who are really to blame are the knowledgeable archaeologists, be they professional or amateur, who have made no effort to make others aware that archaeology is more than digging in the ground; that without the observations and written information about the relationships of artifacts to soil features, to structural features, and to each other, the artifacts themselves mean nothing.

A concerted effort must be made by archaeologists, by laymen, by archaeological societies, by state legislators, by the federal government, if the fragments from the past which are left to us are not to be completely destroyed. The ideal of a basic knowledge of cultural change and adaptation throughout the history of human occupation in the New World, and in all environmental regions, is still not impossible if we act NOW. By tomorrow yesterday will be gone.

BIBLIOGRAPHY

Aberle, David F.
    1968   "Comments by David F. Aberle, S. R. Binford, and L. R. Binford."
             In Binford and Binford 1968: 353–359.
Aberle, David F., and others
    1963   "The Incest Taboo and the Mating Patterns of Animals." *American Anthropologist* 65: 253–265.
Adams, R. E. W.
    1969   "Maya Archaeology, 1958–1968: A Review." *Latin American Research Review* 4, no. 2: 3–45.
Adams, Robert McC.
    1962   "Agriculture and Urban Life in Early Southwestern Iran." *Science* 136: 109–122.
    1965   *Land behind Baghdad.* Chicago: University of Chicago Press.
Adams, W. Y.
    1968   "Invasion, Diffusion, Evolution?" *Antiquity* 42: 194–215.
Allison, April L.
    1966   "Reconstruction of Pre-Modern Vegetation in the Lower Illinois Valley: A Study of Floral Communities and Their Distribution with Reference to Prehistoric Cultural-Ecological Adaptations." Unpublished manuscript.
Andrews, E. W.
    1965   "Archaeology and Prehistory in the Northern Maya Lowlands: An Introduction." In *Handbook of Middle American Indians,* Gordon R. Willey, editor, vol. 2, pp. 288–330. Austin: University of Texas Press.
Anonymous
    1906   "Tragic Significance of Cheap Bottles." *Current Literature* 41, no. 2: 218–220. New York: Current Literature Publishing Co.
Arkell, Anthony J.
    1957   "Khartoum's Part in the Development of the Neolithic." *Kush* 5: 8–12.
Ascher, Robert
    1959   "A Prehistoric Population Estimate Using Midden Analysis and Two Population Models." *Southwestern Journal of Anthropology* 15: 168–178.
    1961   "Function and Prehistoric Art." *Man* 61:73–75.
    1962   "Ethnography for Archaeology: A Case from the Seri Indians." *Ethnology* 1: 360–369.
Bayard, D. T.
    1969   "Science, Theory, and Reality in the 'New Archaeology.' " *American Antiquity* 34: 376–384.

343

Beckmann, John
  1797   *A History of Inventions and Discoveries.* Translated from the German by William Johnston. 3 vols. London: J. Bell.
Best, Elsdon
  1929   *Fishing Methods and Devices of the Maori,* Wellington: Dominion Museum.
Biek, L.
  1963   *Archaeology and the Microscope.* London: Lutterworth Press.
Binford, Lewis R.
  1962   "Archaeology as Anthropology." *American Antiquity* 28: 217–225.
  1963   " 'Red Ochre' Caches from the Michigan Area: A Possible Case of Cultural Drift." *Southwestern Journal of Anthropology* 19: 89–108.
  1965   "Archaeological Systematics and the Study of Cultural Processes." *American Antiquity* 31: 203–210.
  1967a   "Comment on K. C. Chang's "Major Aspects of the Interrelationship of Archaeology and Ethnology." *Current Anthropology* 8: 234–235.
  1967b   "An Ethnohistory of the Nottoway, Meherrin, and Weanock Indians of Southeastern Virginia." *Ethnohistory* 14: 104–218.
  1967c   "Smudge Pits and Hide Smoking: The Use of Analogy in Archaeological Reasoning." *American Antiquity* 32: 1–12.
  1968a   "Archaeological Perspectives." In Binford and Binford 1968, pp. 5–32.
  1968b   "Post Pleistocene Adaptations." In ibid.: 313–341.
  1968c   "Some Comments on Historical vs. Processual Archaeology." *Southwestern Journal of Anthropology* 24: 267–275.
Binford, Lewis R., and Sally R. Binford
  1966a   "The Predatory Revolution: A Consideration of the Evidence for a New Subsistence Level." *American Anthropologist* 68: 508–512.
  1966b   "A Preliminary Analysis of Functional Variability in the Mousterian of Levallois Facies." Ibid.: 238–295.
Binford, Lewis R., and Sally R. Binford, editors
  1968   *New Perspectives in Archeology.* Chicago: Aldine.
Binford, Sally R.
  1968   "A Structural Comparison of Disposal of Dead in the Mousterian and the Upper Palaeolithic." *Southwestern Journal of Anthropology* 24: 139–164.
Birdsell, Joseph B.
  1957   "Some Population Problems Involving Pleistocene Man." *Cold Spring Harbor Symposia on Quantitative Biology* 22: 47–69.
  1968   "Some Predictions for the Pleistocene Based on Equilibrium Systems among Recent Hunter-Gatherers." In Lee and De Vore, 1968: 229–240.
Bishop, J. Leander
  1864   *A History of American Manufactures from 1608 to 1860.* 2 vols. Philadelphia: Edward Young & Co.; London: Sampson Low & Son Co.
Bishop, W. W., and J. D. Clark, editors
  1967   *Background to Evolution in Africa.* Chicago: University of Chicago Press.
Blackwood, B.
  1950   *The Technology of a Modern Stone Age People in New Guinea.* Occasional Papers in Technology 3. Oxford: Pitt-Rivers Museum.
Bloch, M. R.
  1963   "The Social Influences of Salt." *Scientific American* 209: 88–98.

Blom, F.
1932   *Commerce, Trade, and Monetary Units of the Maya.* Tulane University Middle American Research Series, Publication 4.

Bolles, Albert S.
1831   *Industrial History of the United States.* Norwich: Henry Bill Publishing Co.

Bose, Saradindu
1964   "Economy of the Onge of Little Andaman." *Man in India* 44: 298–310.

Boulière, François
1963   "Observations on the Ecology of Some Large African Mammals." In *African Ecology and Human Evolution,* F. Clark Howell and François Boulière, editors, pp. 43–54. Chicago: Aldine.

Brace, C. Loring
1964   "The Fate of the Classic Neanderthals: A Consideration of Hominid Catastrophism." *Current Anthropology* 5: 3–43.

Braidwood, R. J., and Bruce Howe, editors
1960   *Prehistoric Investigations in Iraqi Kurdistan.* University of Chicago, Oriental Institute, Studies in Ancient Oriental Civilization, no. 31.

Brain, C. K.
1967   "Hottentot Food Remains and Their Bearing on the Interpretation of Fossil Bone Assemblages." *Scientific Papers of the Namib Research Station,* no. 32. Pretoria: Namib Desert Research Association.

British Museum
1931–   *British Museum General Catalogue of Printed Books.* 261 vols. London: Trustees of the British Museum.

Brothwell, D. R., and E. S. Higgs, editors.
1963   *Science in Archaeology.* London: Thames and Hudson.

Brues, Alice
1959   "The Spearman and the Archer: An Essay on Selection in Body Build." *American Anthropologist* 61: 457–469.

Bruner, Jerome S.
1966   "Education as Social Invention." *Saturday Review,* February 19, pp. 70–72, 102–104.

Buechner, Thomas S., Paul N. Perrot, and Alex von Saldern
1959–60 Check List of Recently Published Articles and Books on Glass. *Journal of Glass Studies* 1: 116–132 [for 1956–1958]; 2: 149–165 [for 1959]. Corning: Corning Museum of Glass.

Bullard, W. R., Jr.
1960   "Maya Settlement Pattern in Northeastern Petén, Guatemala." *American Antiquity* 25: 355–372.
1970   "The Status of Postclassic Archaeology in Petén, Guatemala." Paper read at the 35th Annual Meeting of the Society for American Archaeology, May 1970, Mexico City.

Butterworth, Benjamin
1892   *The Growth of Industrial Art.* Washington, D.C.: Government Printing Office.

Butzer, Karl W.
1964   *Environment and Archaeology: An Introduction to Pleistocene Geography.* Chicago: Aldine.

Caldwell, Joseph R.
1958   *Trend and Tradition in the Prehistory of the Eastern United States.* American Anthropological Association, Memoir no. 88.

1964   "Interaction Spheres in Prehistory." In *Hopewellian Studies: Scientific Papers no. 12, 6,* pp. 133–143. Springfield: Illinois State Museum.

Carr, E. H.
1962   *What Is History?* New York: Alfred A. Knopf.

Chambers, Ephraim
1728   *Cyclopedia, or Universal Dictionary of Arts and Sciences.* 2 vols. London: D. Midwinter.

Champion, I. F.
1966   *Across New Guinea from the Fly to the Sepik.* Melbourne: Lansdowne.

Chang, K. C.
1958   "Study of the Neolithic Social Grouping." *American Anthropologist* 60: 298–334.
1962   "A Typology of Settlement and Community Patterns in Some Circumpolar Societies." *Arctic Anthropology* 1: 28–41.
1967   *Rethinking Archaeology.* New York: Random House.

Chang, K. C., editor
1968   *Settlement Archaeology.* Palo Alto, Calif.: National Press.

Chapman, A. C.
1957   "Port of Trade Enclaves in Aztec and Maya Civilization." In *Trade and Market in the Early Empires,* K. Polyani, C. M. Arensberg, and H. W. Pearson, editors, pp. 114–153. New York: Free Press.

Childe, V. Gordon
1925   *The Dawn of European Civilization.* London: Routledge and Kegan Paul.
1935   "Changing Methods and Aims in Prehistory." *Proceedings of the Prehistorical Society,* n.s. 1: 1–15.
1936   *Man Makes Himself.* London: Watts.
1942   *What Happened in History.* Harmondsworth: Penguin Books.
1946   *Scotland before the Scots.* London: Routledge and Kegan Paul.
1951   *Social Evolution.* New York: Schuman.
1958   *The Prehistory of European Society.* Harmondsworth: Penguin Books.

Clark, J. Grahame D.
1951   "Folk-Culture and the Study of European Prehistory." In *Aspects of Archaeology in Great Britain and Beyond: Essays Presented to O. G. S. Crawford,* W. F. Grimes, editor, pp. 49–65. London: Methuen.
1952   *Prehistoric Europe: The Economic Basis.* London: Methuen.
1953a   "Archaeological Theories and Interpretations: Old World." In *Anthropology Today,* A. L. Kroeber, editor, pp. 343–360. Chicago: University of Chicago Press.
1953b   *The Economic Approach to Prehistory.* Albert Reckitt Archaeological Lecture. London: British Academy.
1954   *Star Carr.* Cambridge: Cambridge University Press.
1957   *Archaeology and Society.* 3rd ed. London: Methuen.
1968   *Analytical Archaeology.* London: Methuen.

Cleland, Charles E.
1965   "The Evolution of Subsistence Patterns in the Eastern United States." Unpublished manuscript.

Coe, M. D.
1961   "Social Topology and the Tropical Forest Civilizations." *Comparative Studies in Society and History* 4: 65–85.

1969   "Photogrammetry and the Ecology of the Olmec Civilization." Paper read at Working Conference on Aerial Photography and Anthropology, Cambridge, Mass., 10–12 May.

————, and Kent V. Flannery

1964   "Microenvironments and Mesoamerican Prehistory." *Science* 143: 650–654.

Coe, W. R.

1965   "Tikal, Guatemala, and the Emergent Maya Civilization." *Science* 147: 1401–1419.

Cook, S. F., and R. F. Heizer

1968   "Relationships among Houses, Settlement Areas, and Population in Aboriginal California." In Chang 1968: 79–116.

Coon, Carleton, S.

1957   *The Seven Caves.* New York: Alfred A. Knopf.

1965   *The Living Races of Man.* New York: Alfred A. Knopf.

Cornwall, I. W.

1958   *Soils for the Archaeologist.* London: Phoenix.

Craig, B.

1966   "Art of the Telefolmin Area, New Guinea." *Australian Natural History* 15: 218–223.

1967   "Making Fire by Percussion in the Telefolmin Area, New Guinea." *Mankind* 6: 434–435.

Cranstone, B. A. L.

1967   "Some Boards from a New Guinea *Haus Tambaran.*" *Man,* n.s. 2: 274–277.

1968   "War Shields of the Telefomin Sub-district, New Guinea." *Man,* n.s. 3: 609–624.

1972   "Environment and Choice in Dwelling and Settlement: An Ethnographical Survey." In *Man, Settlement, and Urbanism,* P. J. Ucko, R. Tringham, and G. W. Dimbleby, editors, pp. 487–504. London: Duckworth.

Crawford, O. G. S.

1921   *Man and His Past.* Oxford: Clarendon Press.

Culbert, T. P.

1970   "Sociocultural Integration and the Classic Maya." Paper read at the 35th Annual Meeting of the Society for American Archaeology, May 1970, Mexico City.

Cumulative Book Index

1898–   *Cumulative Book Index: World List of Books in the English Language.* New York: H. W. Wilson.

Dales, George P.

1964   "The Mythical Massacre at Mohenjodaro." *Expedition* 6.

Daniel, G. E.

1963   *The Idea of Prehistory.* Cleveland: World Publishing Company.

1968a   *The First Civilizations.* London: Thames and Hudson.

1968b   "One Hundred Years of Old World Prehistory." In *One Hundred Years of Anthropology,* J. O. Brew, editor, pp. 57–93. Cambridge, Mass.: Harvard University Press.

Dart, Raymond A.

1957   "The Makapansgat Australopithecine Osteodontokeratic Culture." In *Third Pan-African Congress on Prehistory,* J. Desmond Clark and Sonia Cole, editors, pp. 161–171. London: Chatto & Windus.

Deetz, James
    1965   *The Dynamics of Stylistic Change in Arikara Ceramics.* Urbana:
            University of Illinois Press.
    1968   *Invitation to Archaeology.* New York: Natural History Press.
Derry, T. K., and Trevor I. Williams
    1961   *A Short History of Technology.* New York and Oxford: Oxford Uni-
            versity Press.
Dethlefsen, E., and J. Deetz
    1966   "Death's Heads, Cherubs, and Willow Trees: Experimental Archae-
            ology in Colonial Cemeteries." *American Antiquity* 31: 502–510.
De Vore, Irven, and K. R. L. Hall
    1965   "Baboon Ecology." In *Primate Behavior,* Irven DeVore, editor, pp.
            127–163. New York: Holt, Rinehart and Winston.
De Vore, Irven, and Sherwood Washburn
    1963   "Baboon Ecology and Human Evolution." In *African Ecology and
            Human Evolution,* F. Howell Clark and François Boulière, editors,
            pp. 335–367. Chicago: Aldine.
Diderot, Denis
    1959   *A Diderot Pictorial Encyclopedia of Trades and Industry; Manufac-
            turing and the Technical Arts.* Edited with an introduction and notes
            by Charles E. Gillespie. 2 vols. New York: Dover Publishers.
Diderot, Denis, and Jean Le Rond d'Alembert, editors
    1751–65 *Encyclopédie, ou dictionnaire raisonné des sciences, des arts et des
            métiers.* 33 vols. Paris: D. Diderot.
Dimbleby, G. W.
    1967   *Plants and Archaeology.* London: John Baker.
Dirección General de Cartografía de Guatemala
    1964   *Atlas preliminar de Guatemala: segunda edición.*
Dixon, Roland B.
    1928   *The Building of Cultures.* New York: Charles Scribner's Sons.
Doran, J.
    1970   "Systems Theory, Computer Simulations, and Archaeology." *World
            Archaeology* 1: 289–298.
Duncan, George S.
    1960   *Bibliography of Glass from the Earliest Times to 1940.* Edited by
            Violet Dimbleby; foreword by W. E. S. Turner. London: Society of
            Glass Technology.
Dunsheath, Percy, editor
    1951   *A Century of Technology, 1851–1951.* New York: Roy Publishers.
Edmondson, Munro S.
    1961   "Neolithic Diffusion Rates." *Current Anthropology* 2: 71–102.
Ekholm, Gordon F.
    1964   "Transpacific Contacts." In *Prehistoric Man in the New World,*
            Jesse D. Jennings and Edward Norbeck, editors, pp. 459–510.
            Chicago: University of Chicago Press.
Elton, G. R.
    1969   *The Practice of History.* New York: Growell.
Erasmus, Charles J.
    1950   "Patolli and Pachisi, and the Limitation of Possibilities." *Southwest-
            ern Journal of Anthropology* 6: 369–387.
    1961   *Man Takes Control.* Minneapolis: University of Minnesota Press.
    1968   "Thoughts on Upward Collapse: An Essay on Explanation in Anthro-
            pology." *Southwestern Journal of Anthropology* 24: 170–194.

Erikson, E. H.
 1959   *Young Man Luther.* New York: Norton.
Ewing, J. Franklin
 1949   "The Treasures of Ksar 'Akil." Fordham University, *Thought* 24: 255–288.
 1951   "Comments on the Report of Dr. Herbert E. Wright, Jr., on His Study of Lebanese Marine Terraces." *Journal of Near Eastern Studies* 10: 119–122.
Ferguson, Eugene S.
 1962–65 "Contributions to Bibliography in the History of Technology." *Technology and Culture* 3, no. 1: 73–84; no. 2: 167–174; no. 3: 298–306; 4, no. 3: 318–330; 5, no. 3: 416–434; no. 4: 578–594; and 6, no. 1: 99–107. Detroit: Wayne State University Press; Chicago: University of Chicago Press.
Fischer, J. L.
 1961   "Art Styles as Cultural Cognitive Maps." *American Anthropologist* 63: 79–93.
Flannery, Kent V.
 1965   "The Ecology of Early Food Production in Mesopotamia." *Science* 147: 1247–1256.
 1968a   "Archaeological Systems Theory and Early Mesoamerica." In *Anthropological Archaeology in the Americas*, Betty J. Meggers, editor, pp. 67–88. Washington, D.C.: Anthropological Society of Washington.
 1968b   "The Olmec and the Valley of Oaxaca: A Model for Inter-Regional Interaction in Formative Times." In *Dumbarton Oaks Conference on the Olmec*, Elizabeth Benson, editor, pp. 79–110. Washington, D.C.: Dumbarton Oaks Research Library.
Fleure, H. J., and W. E. Whitehouse
 1916   "The Early Distribution and Valley-ward Movement of Population in South Britain." *Archaelogia Cambrensis* 16: 101–140.
Fontana, Bernard L.
 1965a   "On the Meaning of Historic Sites Archaeology." *American Antiquity* 31, no. 1: 61–65.
 1965b   "The Tale of a Nail: On the Ethnological Interpretation of Historic Artifacts." *The Florida Anthropologist* 18, no. 3; pt. 2: 85–101.
Fontana, Bernard L., Cameron Greenleaf, Charles W. Ferguson, Robert A. Wright, and Doris Frederick
 1962   "Johnny Ward's Ranch." *The Kiva* 28, nos. 1 and 2: 1–115.
Forbes, R. J.
 1958   *Man the Maker: A History of Technology and Engineering.* London and New York: Abelard-Schuman.
Foster, G. M.
 1960   "Life Expectancy of Utilitarian Pottery in Tzintzuntzan, Michoacán, Mexico." *American Antiquity* 25: 606–609.
Fox, Cyril
 1923   *The Archaeology of the Cambridge Region.* Cambridge: Cambridge University Press.
 1932   *The Personality of Britain.* Cardiff: National Museum of Wales.
 1959   *Life and Death in the Bronze Age.* London: Routledge & Kegan Paul.
Freeman, Derek
 1964   "Human Aggression in Anthropological Perspective." In *The Natural History of Aggression*, J. D. Carthy and F. J. Ebling, editors, pp. 216–241. New York: Seminar Press.

Fried, M. H.
  1967   *The Evolution of Political Society: An Essay in Political Anthropology.* New York: Random House.
Fry, R.
  1969   "Ceramics and Settlement in the Periphery of Tikal, Guatemala." Ph.D. dissertation, University of Arizona, Department of Anthropology.
Garrod, D. A. E.
  1930   "The Palaeolithic of Southern Kurdistan: Excavation in the Caves of Zarzi and Hazar Merd." *American School of Prehistoric Research Bulletin* 6: 9–43.
Garrod, D. A. E., and Dorothea Bate
  1937   *The Stone Age of Mt. Carmel.* Vol. 1. Oxford: Clarendon Press.
Goldenweiser, Alexander A.
  1913   "The Principle of Limited Possibilities." *Journal of American Folklore* 26: 259–292.
Goldschmidt, Walter R.
  1959   *Man's Way: A Preface to the Understanding of Human Society.* New York: Henry Holt.
  1966   *Comparative Functionalism: An Essay in Anthropological Theory.* Berkeley: University of California Press.
Graebner, Fritz
  1911   *Methode der Ethnologie.* Heidelberg: C. Winter.
Graham, I.
  1967   *Archaeological Explorations in El Petén, Guatemala.* Tulane University Middle American Research Series, Publication 33.
Greeley, Horace, and others
  1872   *The Great Industries of the United States.* Hartford: J. B. Burr and Hyde.
Greenberg, Joseph H.
  1957   *Essays in Linguistics.* Chicago: University of Chicago Press.
Habakkuk, H. J.
  1952   *American and British Technology in the Nineteenth Century: The Search for Labor-Saving Inventions.* Cambridge: Cambridge University Press.
Hamburg, David A.
  1963   "Emotions in the Perspective of Human Evolution." In *Expression of the Emotions in Man,* P. H. Knapp, editor, pp. 111–127. New York: International Universities Press.
Hamilton, Augustus
  1908   *Fishing and Sea Foods of the Ancient Maori.* Wellington: Dominion Museum.
Harlan, Jack R.
  1967   "A Wild Wheat Harvest in Turkey." *Archaeology* 20: 197–201.
Harlan, Jack, and Daniel Zohary
  1966   "Distribution of Wild Wheats and Barley." *Science* 153: 1074–1080.
Harris, M.
  1966   "The Cultural Ecology of India's Sacred Cattle." *Current Anthropology* 7: 51–66.
  1968   *The Rise of Anthropological Theory.* New York: Crowell.
Hawkes, C. F. C.
  1954   "Archaeological Theory and Method: Some Suggestions from the Old World." *American Anthropologist* 56: 155–168.

Hawkes, J.
1968   "The Proper Study of Mankind." *Antiquity* 42: 255–262.
Helbaek, Hans
1966a   "Commentary on the Phylogenesis of *Triticum* and *Hordeum*." *Economic Botany* 20: 350–360.
1966b   "Pre-Pottery Neolithic Farming at Beidha." In Diana Kirkbride, "Five Seasons at the Pre-Pottery Neolithic Village of Beidha in Jordan." *Palestine Exploration Quarterly* 98: 61–66.
1969   "Plant Collecting, Dry Farming, and Irrigation Agriculture in Prehistoric Deh Luran." In *Prehistory and Human Ecology of Deh Luran Plain*, Frank Hole, Kent V. Flannery, and James Neely, editors. University of Michigan, Museum of Anthropology, Memoirs, no. 1: 383–426.
Hesse, R., W. C. Allee, and K. P. Schmidt
1951   *Ecological Animal Geography.* New York: Macmillan.
Hibbard, Bartlett, Spencer, & Company
1891   (hardward trade catalogue) Chicago.
Hill, James N.
1966   "A Prehistoric Community in Eastern Arizona." *Southwestern Journal of Anthropology* 22: 9–30.
1968   "Broken K. Pueblo: Patterns of Form and Function." In Binford and Binford 1968: 103–142.
Hodgen, Margaret T.
1952   *Change and History.* Viking Fund Publications in Anthropology 18.
Hodges, H. W. M.
1964   *Artifacts: An Introduction to Early Materials and Technology.* London: John Baker.
Hole, Frank, and Kent V. Flannery
1967   "The Prehistory of Southwestern Iran: A Preliminary Report." *Proceedings of the Prehistoric Society* 33: 147–206.
Howell, F. Clark
1959   "Upper Pleistocene Stratigraphy and Early Man in the Levant." *Proceedings of the American Philosophical Society* 103: 1–65.
Industrial Arts Index
1913–   *Industrial Arts Index.* New York: H. W. Wilson C. [Title changed in
1957   1953 to *Applied Sciences and Technology Index*]
International Index
1907–   *International Index: A Quarterly Guide to Periodical Literature in the
present   Social Sciences and Humanities.* New York: H. W. Wilson Co.
Jones, Howard M.
1959   "Ideas, History, and Technology." *Technology and Culture* 1, no. 1: 20–37. Detroit: Wayne State University Press.
Kenyon, Kathleen
1960   *Archaeology in the Holy Land.* London: Ernest Benn.
Kidder, Alfred V.
1925   "Pecos Excavations in 1924." *El Palacio* 18, nos. 10–11: 217–223. Santa Fe: Museum of New Mexico and the School of American Research.
Kimbark, Daniel A. (compiler)
1875   S. D. Kimbark's Illustrated Catalogue. Chicago: Knight and Leonard.
Kirkbride, Diana
1966   "Five Seasons at the Pre-Pottery Neolithic Village of Beidha in Jordan." *Palestine Exploration Quarterly* 98: 3–72.

Kleindienst, Maxine R., and Patty Jo Watson
 1956   " 'Action Archaeology': The Archaeological Inventory of a Living Community." *Anthropology Tomorrow* 5: 75–78.

Knight, Edward H.
 1882   *Knight's American Mechanical Dictionary.* 3 vols. Boston: Houghton Mifflin.

Koford, Carl B.
 1966   "Population Changes in Rhesus Monkeys: Cayo Santiago, 1960–1964." *Tulane Studies in Zoology* 13: 1–7.

Kroeber, A. L.
 1925   *Handbook of the Indians of California. Bureau of American Ethnology,* Bulletin 78.
 1940   "Stimulus Diffusion." *American Anthropologist* 42: 1–20.
 1948   *Anthropology.* New ed. New York: Harcourt, Brace and World.
 1952   *The Nature of Culture.* Chicago: University of Chicago Press.

Lee, Richard B.
 1965   "Subsistence Ecology of the !Kung Bushmen." Ph.D. dissertation. University of California (Berkeley) microfilm.
 1969   "!Kung Bushmen Subsistence: An Input-Output Analysis." In *Environment and Cultural Behavior: An Anthropological Reader,* A. P. Vadya, editor. New York: Natural History Press.

Lee, Richard B., and Irven De Vore, editors
 1968   *Man the Hunter.* Chicago: Aldine.

Lees, S. H.
 1967   "Regional Integration of Pig Husbandry in the New Guinea Highlands." Paper presented at the Michigan Academy of Sciences, Annual Meeting for 1967.

Lees, S. H., and N. L. Falcon
 1952   "The Geographical History of the Mesopotamian Basin." *Geographical Journal* 118: 24–39.

Leone, M. P.
 1968   "Economic Autonomy and Social Distance: Archaeological Evidence." Ph.D. dissertation. University of Arizona, Department of Anthropology.

Lilley, Samuel
 1948   *Men, Machines, and History: A Short History of Tools and Machines in Relation to Social Progress.* London: Cobbett Press.

Longacre, William A.
 1966   "Changing Patterns of Social Integration: A Prehistoric Example from the American Southwest." *American Anthropologist* 48: 94–102.
 1968   "Some Aspects of Prehistoric Society in East-Central Arizona." In Binford and Binford 1968: 89–102.

Longyear, J. M., III
 1952   *Copan Ceramics: A Study of Southeastern Maya Pottery.* Carnegie Institution of Washington, Publication 597.

Lorenz, Konrad Z.
 1966   *On Aggression.* New York, Harcourt, Brace and World.

Lowie, Robert H.
 1937   *The History of Ethnological Theory.* New York: Holt, Rinehart and Winston.

McBryde, F. W.
 1945   *Cultural and Historical Geography of Southwest Guatemala.* Smithsonian Institution, Institute of Social Anthropology, Publication 4.

McCall, Daniel
 1964   *Africa in Time-Perspective: A Discussion of Historical Reconstruc-
         tion from Unwritten Sources.* Boston: Boston University Press.
McCallum, Henry D., and Frances T. McCallum
 1965   *The Wire That Fenced the West.* Norman: University of Oklahoma
         Press.
McCarthy, Frederick D.
 1957   "Habitat, Economy, and Equipment of the Australian Aborigines."
         Australian Journal of Science 19: 88–97.
McGimsey, Charles R., III
 1972   *Public Archeology.* New York: Seminar Press.
MacNutt, F. A., editor and translator
 1908   *Letters of Cortes: The Five Letters of Relation from Fernando Cortes
         to the Emperor Charles V.* New York: G. P. Putnam's Sons.
MacWhite, Eoin
 1956   "On the Interpretation of Archaeological Evidence in Historical or
         Sociological Terms." *American Anthropologist* 58: 3–25.
Mair, Lucy
 1965   *An Introduction to Social Anthropology.* Oxford: Clarendon Press.
Masson, V. M.
 1965   "The Neolithic Farmer of Central Asia." *Proceedings of the 6th In-
         ternational Congress of Pre- and Protohistoric Sciences* 2: 205–215.
Mattes, Merrill J.
 1950   "Historic Sites Archaeology on the Upper Missouri." *Bulletin of the
         Bureau of American Ethnology,* no. 176: 1–82. Washington, D.C.:
         Government Printing Office.
Mayr, Ernst
 1963   *Animal Species and Evolution.* Cambridge, Mass.: Harvard Uni-
         versity Press.
Means, P. A.
 1917   *History of the Spanish Conquest of Yucatan and the Itza.* Peabody
         Museum of American Archaeology and Ethnology Papers 7.
Meggers, Betty J.
 1954   "Environmental Limitations on the Development of Culture." *Amer-
         ican Anthropologist* 56: 801–824.
 1960   "The Law of Cultural Evolution as a Practical Research Tool." In
         Essays in the Science of Culture, G. E. Dole and R. L. Carneiro,
         editors, pp. 302–316. New York: Crowell.
 1964   "North and South American Cultural Connections and Conver-
         gences." In *Prehistoric Man in the New World,* Jesse D. Jennings
         and Edward Norbeck, editors, pp. 511–526. Chicago: University of
         Chicago Press.
Mesthene, Emmanuel G.
 1965   "On Understanding Change: The Harvard University Program on
         Technology and Society." *Technology and Culture* 6, no. 2: 222–
         235. Chicago: University of Chicago Press.
Miller, Carl F.
 1960   "The Excavation and Investigation at Fort Lookout Trading Post II
         (39LM57) in the Fort Randall Reservoir, South Dakota." *Bulletin of
         the Bureau of American Ethnology,* no. 176: 49–82. Washington,
         D.C.: Government Printing Office.
Montelius, O.
 1899   *Der Orient und Europa.* Stockholm.

Morgan, Lewis Henry
1871   "Systems of Consanguinity and Affinity of the Human Family."
        Smithsonian Institution Contributions to Knowledge 17, no. 218.
Morley, S. G.
1937–38 *The Inscriptions of Petén.* Carnegie Institution of Washington, Pub-
        lication 437.
Morley, S. G., and G. W. Brainard
1946   *The Ancient Maya.* Stanford: Stanford University Press.
Murdock, George Peter
1959a   *Africa: Its Peoples and Their Culture History.* New York: McGraw-
        Hill.
1959b   "Cross-language Parallels in Parental Kin Terms." *Anthropological
        Linguistics* 1, no. 9: 1–5.
Nagel, E.
1961   *The Structure of Science.* New York: Harcourt, Brace and World.
Napier, John R.
1962   "Monkeys and Their Habitats." *New Scientist* 15: 88–92.
Nash, M.
1967   "Indian Economies." In *Handbook of Middle American Indians,*
        Manning Nash, editor, pp. 87–102. Austin: University of Texas
        Press.
Nelson, Nels C.
1919   "The Archaeology of the South-West: A Preliminary Report." *Pro-
        ceedings of the National Academy of Sciences* 5: 114–210.
Odum, Eugene P., and H. T. Odum
1959   *Fundamentals of Ecology.* 2nd ed. Philadelphia: W. B. Saunders.
Oliver, John W.
1956   *History of American Technology.* New York: Ronald Press.
Oliver Ames & Sons Corporation
1879   *Price List of Shovels, Spades, Scoops, and Drainage Tools.* Boston:
        Rand, Avery.
Osborne, Douglas
1957   "Excavations in the McNary Reservoir Basin near Umatilla, Oregon."
        Bulletin of the Bureau of American Ethnology, no. 166. Washington,
        D.C.: Government Printing Office.
Palerm, A., and E. R. Wolf
1957   "Ecological Potential and Cultural Development." In *Pan American
        Union Social Science Monograph* 3: 39–69.
Palmer, Leonard R.
1965   *Mycenaeans and Minoans: Aegean Prehistory in the Light of Linear
        B Tablets.* 2nd ed. London: Faber and Faber.
Paloumpis, Andreas A.
1966   "Prehistoric Utilization of Fish Populations in the Lower Illinois
        Valley." Unpublished manuscript.
Perry, William
1923   *The Children of the Sun.* London: Methuen and Co. Ltd.
Perrot, Jean
1966   "Le Gisement Natufien de Mallaha (Eynan), Israël." *L'Anthropologie*
        70: 437–484.
Perrot, Paul N.
1960–65 "Check List of Recently Published Articles and Books on Glass."
        Journal of Glass Studies 5: 161–168 [for 1962]; 6: 172–202 [for
        1963]; 7: 141–164 [for 1964]. Corning: Corning Museum of
        Glass.

Perrot, Paul N., and Alex von Saldern
   1961–62 "Check List of Recently Published Articles and Books on Glass."
            Journal of Glass Studies 3: 154–172 [for 1960]; 4: 152–175 [for
            1961]. Corning: Corning Museum of Glass.
Petersen, Harold L.
   1962   The Treasury of the Gun. New York: Golden Press.
Petrie, William M. F.
   1939   The Making of Egypt. London: Sheldon Press.
Pfeiffer, John
   1970   The Emergence of Man. New York: Harper & Row.
Pharmaceutical Era
   1900   The Era Blue Book: A Universal Price List and Directory of Manu-
            facturers for Drug Trade Buyers. New York: D. O. Haynes & Co.
Platt, B. S.
   1962   Tables of Representative Values of Foods Commonly Used in Trop-
            ical Countries. Medical Research Council, Special Report Series, no.
            302. London: Her Majesty's Stationery Office.
Plog, F.
   1968   "A Study in Experimental Archaeology." Bulletin of the American
            Anthropological Association (Abstracts of the 67th A.G.M.) 1; no. 3:
            110.
Powell, T. G. E.
   1958   The Celts. London: Thames and Hudson.
Raglan, Fitz Roy
   1939   How Came Civilization? London: Methuen.
Rands, R. A., and R. E. Smith
   1965   "Pottery of the Guatemalan Highlands." In Handbook of Middle
            American Indians, vol. 2, Gordon R. Willey, editor, pp. 95–145.
            Austin: University of Texas Press.
Rands, Robert L.
   1961   "Elaboration and Invention in Ceramic Tradition." American An-
            tiquity 26: 247–257.
Rands, Robert L., and C. L. Riley
   1958   "Diffusion and Discontinuous Distribution." American Anthropolo-
            gist 60: 274–297.
Rappaport, R.
   1967   Pigs for the Ancestors: Ritual in the Ecology of a New Guinea People.
            New Haven: Yale University Press.
Rathje, William L.
   1972   "Praise the Gods and Pass the Metates: A Hypothesis of the De-
            velopment of Lowland Rainforest Civilizations in Mesoamerica." In
            Contemporary Archaeology, Mark P. Leone, editor, pp. 365–392.
            Carbondale: Southern Illinois University Press.
Redfield, R.
   1941   The Folk Culture of Yucatan. Chicago: University of Chicago Press.
Readers Guide
   1890–   Readers Guide to Periodical Literature. New York: H. W. Wilson Co.
   present
Reed, Charles A.
   1959   "Animal Domestication in the Prehistoric Near East." Science 130:
            1629–1639.
   1960   "A Review of the Archaeological Evidence on Animal Domestication
            in the Prehistoric Near East." In Prehistoric Investigations in Iraqi
            Kurdistan, Robert J. Braidwood and Bruce Howe, editors. Univer-

356   Bibliography

sity of Chicago, Oriental Institute, Studies in Oriental Civilization, no. 31, pp. 119–145.

Reed, Charles A., and Robert Braidwood
1960   "Toward the Reconstruction of the Environmental Sequence of North-eastern Iraq." In ibid., pp. 163–173.

Renfrew, A. C.
1969   "Trade and Culture Process in European Prehistory." *Current Anthropology* 10: 131–169.

Richardson, J., and A. L. Kroeber
1940   "Three Centuries of Women's Dress Fashions: A Quantitative Analysis." University of California Press, Anthropological Records 5, no. 2.

Riley, Carroll L.
1952   "The Blowgun in the New World." *Southwestern Journal of Anthropology* 8: 297–319.

Romaine, Lawrence B.
1960   *A Guide to American Trade Catalogues, 1744–1900.* New York: R. R. Bowker Co.

Rosenfeld, A.
1965   *The Inorganic Raw Materials of Antiquity.* New York: Praeger.

Rossignol, M.
1962   "Analyse pollinique de sédiments marins quaternaires en Israël, II—Sédiments Pleistocènes." *Pollen et Spores* 4: 121–148.
1963   "Analyse pollinique de sédiments quaternaires dans la Plaine de Haifa, Israël." *Israel Journal of Earth Sciences* 12: 207–214.

Rouse, Irving
1958   "The Inference of Migrations from Anthropological Evidence." In *Migrations in New World Culture History*, Raymond H. Thompson, editor. Tucson: University of Arizona, Social Science Bulletin no. 27, pp. 63–68.
1960   "The Classification of Artifacts in Archaeology." *American Antiquity* 25: 313–323.
1964a   "Archaeological Approaches to Cultural Evolution." In *Explorations in Cultural Anthropology*, W. H. Goodenough, editor, pp. 455–468. New York: McGraw-Hill.
1964b   "Prehistory of the West Indies." *Science* 144: 499–513.

Rowe, John H.
1966   "Diffusion and Archaeology." *American Antiquity* 25: 313–323.

Sabloff, J. A., and G. Tourtellot
1969   "Exchange Systems and the Ancient Maya." Paper read at the 68th Annual Meeting of the American Anthropological Association, November 1969, New Orleans.

Sabloff, J. A., and G. R. Willey
1968   "The Collapse of Maya Civilization in the Southern Lowlands: A Consideration of History and Process." *Southwestern Journal of Anthropology* 23: 311–336.

Sade, Donald S.
1965   "Some Aspects of Parent-Offspring and Sibling Relations in a Group of Rhesus Monkeys, with a Discussion of Grooming." *American Journal of Physical Anthropology* 23, no. 1: 1–17.
1966   "Ontogeny of Social Relations in a Group of Free Ranging Rhesus Monkeys (*Macaca mulatta* Zimmerman)." Ph.D. dissertation, University of California, Berkeley.

Sahlins, M. D.
  1958   *Social Stratification in Polynesia.* Seattle: The American Ethnological
            Society, University of Washington Press.
  1963   "Poor Man, Rich Man, Big-Man, Chief: Political Types in Melanesia
            and Polynesia." *Comparative Studies in Society and History* 5: 285–
            303.
Sahlins, M. D., and E. R. Service
  1960   *Evolution and Culture.* Ann Arbor: University of Michigan Press.
Salisbury, R. F.
  1962   *From Stone to Steel.* Melbourne: Melbourne University Press.
Sanders, W. T.
  1964   "Cultural Ecology of the Maya Lowlands." *Estudios de Cultura Maya*
            4: 203–241.
  1968   "Hydraulic Agriculture: Economic Symbiosis and the Evolution of
            States in Central Mexico." In *Anthropological Archaeology in the
            Americas,* Betty J. Meggers, editor, pp. 88–108. Washington, D.C.:
            Anthropological Society of Washington.
Sanders, W. T., and B. J. Price
  1968   *Mesoamerica: The Evolution of a Civilization.* New York: Random
            House.
Sapir, Edward
            Time Perspective in Aboriginal American Culture. Canada Depart-
            ment of Mines, Memoir no. 90.
Schaller, George B.
  1963   *The Mountain Gorilla: Ecology and Behavior.* Chicago: University of
            Chicago Press.
Schmidt, Wilhelm
  1939   *The Culture Historical Method of Ethnology.* Trans. S. A. Sieber.
            New York: Fortury's.
Schoenwetter, James
  1964   "Pollen Studies in Southern Illinois." Unpublished report.
Scholes, F. V., and R. L. Roys
  1968   *The Maya Chontal Indians of Acalan-Tixchel: A Contribution to the
            History and Ethnography of the Yucatan Peninsula.* 2nd ed. Nor-
            man: University of Oklahoma Press.
Scoville, Warren C.
  1948   *Revolution in Glassmaking: Entrepreneurship and Technological
            Changes in the American Industry, 1880–1920.* Cambridge, Mass.:
            Harvard University Press.
Sears, W. H.
  1961   "The Study of Social and Religious Systems in North American
            Archaeology." *Current Anthropology* 2: 223–246.
Semenov, S. A.
  1964   *Prehistoric Technology.* Trans. M. W. Thompson. London: Cory,
            Adam and Mackay.
Service, Elman R.
  1962   *Primitive Social Organization: An Evolutionary Perspective.* New
            York: Random House.
Sharp, Andrew
  1957   *Ancient Voyagers in the South Pacific.* Baltimore: Penguin.
Shwartz, D. W.
  1968   *Conceptions of Kentucky Prehistory: A Case Study in the History of
            Archaeology.* Lexington: University of Kentucky Press.

358   Bibliography

Singer, Charles, E. J. Holmyard, and A. R. Hall, editors
    1954   A History of Technology. Vol. 1. New York and London: Oxford
            University Press.
Singer, Charles, E. J. Holmyard, A. R. Hall, and Trevor I. Williams, editors
    1956–58 A History of Technology. Vols. 2–5. New York and London: Oxford
            University Press.
Slater, Miriam K.
    1959   "Ecological Factors in the Origin of Incest." American Anthropolo-
            gist 61: 1042–1059.
Smith, Carlyle S.
    1954   "Cartridges and Bullets from Fort Stevenson, North Dakota." Plains
            Anthropologist 1, no. 1: 25–29. Lincoln: University of Nebraska.
Smith, Grafton Elliot
    1915   The Migrations of Early Culture. Manchester: Manchester University
            Press.
    1924   Elephants and Ethnologists. New York: E. P. Dutton.
Smith, G. Hubert
    1954   "Excavations at Fort Stevensen, 1951." North Dakota History 21,
            no. 3: 127–135.
    1960a   "Archaeological Investigations at the Site of Fort Stevensen (32MLI),
            Garrison Reservoir, North Dakota." Bulletin of the Bureau of Amer-
            ican Ethnology, no. 176, pp. 159–238.
    1960b   "Fort Pierre II (39ST217): A Historic Trading Post in the Oahe Dam
            Area, South Dakota." Ibid., pp. 83–158.
Smith, M. A.
    1955   "The Limitations of Inference in Archaeology." Archaeological
            Newsletter 6: 1–7.
Sokal, R. R.
    1966   "Numerical Taxonomy." Scientific American 215, no. 6: 106–117.
Solecki, Ralph
    1964a   "Shanidar Cave: A Late Pleistocene Site in Northern Iraq." Pro-
            ceedings of the 6th International Congress on the Quaternary 4:
            413–423.
    1964b   "Zawi Chemi Shanidar: A Post Pleistocene Village Site in Northern
            Iraq." Ibid., pp. 405–412.
Sollas, W. J.
    1911   Ancient Hunters. London: Methuen.
Sonnenfeld, J.
    1962   "Interpreting the Function of Primitive Implements." American An-
            tiquity 28: 56–65.
Spaulding, A. C.
    1968   "Explanation in Archaeology." In Binford and Binford 1968: 33–39.
Stenberger, Marten
    1969   Sweden. London: Thames and Hudson.
Steward, Julian H.
    1929   "Diffusion and Independent Development: A Critique of Logic."
            American Anthropologist 31: 491–495.
    1942   "The Direct Historical Approach to Archaeology." American An-
            tiquity 7: 337–343.
    1955   Theory of Culture Change. Urbana: University of Illinois Press.
Steward, Julian H., and F. M. Setzler
    1938   "Function and Configuration in Archaeology." American Antiquity
            4: 4–10.

Stout, Wilbur
    1923   "History of the Clay Industry in Ohio." *Bulletin of the Geological Survey of Ohio.* 4th ser. no. 26, pp. 7–102.
Struever, Stuart
    1964   "The Hopewell Interaction Sphere in Riverine–Western Great Lakes Culture History." In *Hopewellian Studies: Scientific Papers no. 12, 3.* Joseph R. Caldwell and Robert L. Hall, editors. Springfield: Illinois State Museum, pp. 85–106.
    1968a   "Problems, Methods, and Organization: A Disparity in the Growth of Archaeology." In *Anthropological Archaeology in the Americas,* Betty J. Meggers, editor, pp. 131–151. Washington, D.C.: Anthropological Society of Washington.
    1968b   "Woodland Subsistence-Settlement Systems in the Lower Illinois Valley." In Binford and Binford 1968: 285–312.
Suggs, Robert C.
    1960   *The Island Civilizations of Polynesia.* New York: Mentor Books, New American Library.
Swank, James M.
    1884   *History of the Manufacture of Iron in All Ages, and Particularly in the United States for Three Hundred Years from 1585 to 1885.* Philadelphia: Published by the author.
Tax, Sol
    1937   "Some Problems of Social Organization." In *Social Anthropology of North American Tribes,* Fred Eggan, editor, pp. 37–49. Chicago: University of Chicago Press.
Tax, Sol, L. C. Liseley, I. Rouse, and C. F. Voegelin, editors
    1953   *An Appraisal of Anthropology Today.* Chicago: University of Chicago Press.
Tax, Sol, and R. Hinshaw
    1969   "The Maya of the Midwestern Highlands." In *Handbook of Middle American Indians,* vol. 7, Evon Z. Vogt, editor, pp. 69–100. Austin: University of Texas Press.
Taylor, Walter P.
    1956   *The Deer of North America.* Harris, Pennsylvania: Stackpole Press.
Taylor, Walter W.
    1948   *A Study of Archeology.* American Anthropological Association Memoirs, no. 69.
Thompson, Donald F.
    1939   "The Seasonal Factor in Human Culture." *Proceedings of the Prehistoric Society* 5: 209–221.
Thompson, J. E. S.
    1951   "The Itza of Tayasal, Petén." In *Homenaje Caso.* Mexico.
    1964   "Trade Relations between the Maya Highlands and Lowlands." *Estudios de Cultura Maya* 4: 13–49.
    1967   "The Maya Central Area at the Spanish Conquest and Later: A Problem in Demography." *Royal Anthropological Institute of Great Britain and Ireland, Proceedings,* pp. 23–37.
Thompson, Raymond H.
    1956   "The Subjective Element in Archaeological Inference." *Southwestern Journal of Anthropology* 12, no. 3: 327–332.
    1958   *Modern Yucatecan Maya Pottery Making.* Memoirs of the Society for American Archaeology, no. 15.

Thoreau, Henry D.
    1950   *A Writer's Journal.* Selected and edited with an introduction by Laurence Stapleton. New York: Dover Publications.
Tolstoy, Paul
    1969   "Review of W. T. Sanders and B. J. Price: Mesoamerica." *American Anthropologist* 71: 554–558.
Townsend, W. H.
    1969   "Stone and Steel Tool Use in a New Guinea Society." *Ethnology* 8: 199–205.
Trevelyan, G. M.
    1949   *Illustrated English Social History* 1. London: Longmans, Green.
Trigger, Bruce G.
    1965   *History and Settlement in Lower Nubia.* Yale University Publications in Anthropology, no. 69.
    1966   "The Languages of the Northern Sudan: An Historical Perspective." *Journal of African History* 7: 19–25.
    1967   "Settlement Archaeology — Its Goals and Promise." *American Antiquity* 32: 149–160.
    1968a   *Beyond History: The Methods of Prehistory.* New York: Holt, Rinehart and Winston.
    1968b   "Major Concepts of Archaeology in Historical Perspective." *Man* 3: 527–541.
    1970   "Aims in Prehistoric Archaeology." *Antiquity* 44: 26–37.
    1972   "The Cultural Ecology of Christian Nubia." In *Nubische Kunst in Christlicher Zeit,* E. Dinkler, editor. Hamburg.
Tylor, Edward B.
    1879   "On the Game of Patolli in Ancient Mexico and Its Probably Asiatic Origin." *Journal of the Royal Anthropological Institute* 8: 116–129.
Ucko, Peter J.
    1968   *Anthropomorphic Figurines of Predynastic Egypt and Neolithic Crete.* London: A. Szmilda.
    1969   "Ethnography and Archaeological Interpretation of Funerary Remains." *World Archaeology* 1: 262–280.
Ucko, Peter J., and A. Rosenfeld
    1967   *Palaeolithic Cave Art.* London: World University Press.
United States Congress
    1832–51 *American State Papers.* Washington, D.C.: Gales and Seaton.
    1885   *A Descriptive Catalogue of the Government Publications of the United States, September 5, 1774 to March 4, 1881.* Washington, D.C.: Government Printing Office.
    1905   *Comprehensive Index to the Publications of the United States Government, 1881–1893.* 2 vols. Washington, D.C.: Government Printing Office.
Usher, Abbott P.
    1920   *A History of Mechanical Inventions.* New York and London: McGraw-Hill.
Vallois, Henri V.
    1961   "The Social Life of Early Man: The Evidence of Skeletons." In *Social Life of Early Man,* S. L. Washburn, editor, pp. 214–235. Chicago: Aldine.
van Lawick-Goodall, Jane
    1965   "Chimpanzees on the Gombe Stream Reserve." In *Primate Behavior,*

Irven De Vore, editor, pp. 76–93. New York: Holt, Rinehart and Winston.

van Loon, Maurits
1966   "Mureybat: An Early Village in Inland Syria." *Archaeology* 19: 215–216.

Van Zeist, W.
1967   "Late Quaternary Vegetation History of Western Iran." *Review of Palaeobotany and Palynology* 2: 301–311.

Van Zeist, W., and H. E. Wright, Jr.
1963   "Preliminary Pollen Studies at Lake Zeribas, Zagros Mountains, Southwestern Iran." *Science* 140: 65–69.

Washburn, S. L.
1969   "One Hundred Years of Biological Anthropology." In *One Hundred Years of Anthropology,* J. O. Brew, editor. Cambridge, Mass.: Harvard University Press.

Wauchope, Robert
1949   "The Evolution and Persistence of Ceramic Motifs in Northern Georgia." *American Antiquity* 15: 16–22.

Webb, M. C.
1964   "The Post-Classic Decline of the Petén Maya: An Interpretation in the Light of a General Theory of State Society." Ph.D. dissertation, University of Michigan, Department of Anthropology.

White, Leslie A.
1945a   "History, Evolutionism, and Functionalism." *Southwestern Journal of Anthropology* 1: 221–248.
1945b   "Diffusion vs. Evolution: An Anti-Evolutionist Fallacy." *American Anthropologist* 47: 339–356.
1949   *The Science of Culture.* New York: Farrar, Straus.
1959   *The Evolution of Culture.* New York: McGraw-Hill.

Willey, Gordon R.
1953a   "A Pattern of Diffusion-Acculturation." *Southwestern Journal of Anthropology* 9: 369–384.
1953b   *Prehistoric Settlement Patterns in the Viru Valley, Peru.* Washington, D.C.: Smithsonian Institution.
1966   *An Introduction to American Archaeology.* Vol. 1: *North and Middle America.* Englewood Cliffs, N.J.: Prentice-Hall.
1968   "One Hundred Years of American Archaeology." In *One Hundred Years of Anthropology,* J. O. Brew, editor. Cambridge, Mass.: Harvard University Press.

Willey, G. R., W. R. Bullard, Jr., J. B. Glass, J. C. Gifford, and others
1955   *Prehistoric Maya Settlements in the Belize Valley.* Peabody Museum of American Archaeology and Ethnology Papers 54.

Willey, Gordon R., and Philip Phillips
1958   *Method and Theory in American Archaeology.* Chicago: University of Chicago Press.

Wilson, Everett B.
1963   *Early America at Work: A Pictorial Guide to Our Vanishing Occupations.* New York: A. S. Barnes.

Wissler, Clark
1926   *The Relation of Nature to Man in Aboriginal America.* London: Oxford University Press.

Wittfogel, K. A.
1957   *Oriental Despotism.* New Haven: Yale University Press.

Wolf, E. R.
  1967   "Levels of Communal Relations." In *Handbook of Middle American Indians.* Vol. 6, Evon Z. Vogt, editor, pp. 299–316. Austin: University of Texas Press.
Woodbury, Robert S.
  1960   "The Legend of Eli Whitney and Interchangeable Parts." *Technology and Culture* 1, no. 3: 235–253.
Wynne-Edwards, V. C.
  1962   *Animal Disposal in Relation to Social Behavior.* Edinburgh: Oliver and Boyd.
Yamada, Munemi
  1963   "A Study of Blood-Relationship in the Natural Society of the Japanese Macaque." *Primates (Journal of Primatology)* 4: 43–66.
Zeuner, Frederick E.
  1963   *A History of the Domesticated Animals.* New York: Harper & Row.